THREE ARCHAIC POETS

Three Archaic Poets

Archilochus, Alcaeus, Sappho

Anne Pippin Burnett

Harvard University Press

Cambridge, Massachusetts

1983

Library of Congress Cataloging in Publication Data

Burnett, Anne Pippin, 1925–
   Three archaic poets.

   Includes index.
   1. Greek poetry—History and criticism.
2. Archilochus—Criticism and interpretation.
3. Alcaeus—Criticism and interpretation. 4. Sappho—
Criticism and interpretation. I. Title.
PA3105.B87   1983   884'.01'09   83–157
ISBN 0–674–88820–0

Printed in Great Britain

MNHMEION
for
Gene Pippin

Contents

Acknowledgments

I am grateful to the Center for the Humanities at Wesleyan College, in Connecticut, for providing the genial atmosphere in which this book was begun, in the autumn of 1974. My thanks are due also to my friend Mary Lefkowitz for her patient, astringent encouragement in the years since, and to the editor of this series, Hugh Lloyd-Jones, for eradicating hundreds of errors. I must also thank my student, Stanley Szuba, for swift and accurate help with fugitive references.

I am deeply indebted to two recent editions, Martin West's *Iambi et Elegi Graeci* (Oxford 1971) and Eva-Maria Voigt's *Sappho et Alcaeus* (Amsterdam 1971), referred to with respectful familiarity as W and V. All of the Greek texts reproduced come from one or the other of these sources, with the exception of the Cologne fragment of Archilochus, which is cited from D. L. Page's *Supplementum Lyricis Graecis* (Oxford 1974). That no step is taken in Lesbian poetry without the aid of E. Lobel and D. L. Page, *Poetarum Lesbiorum Fragmenta* (Oxford, Clarendon Press, 1955), need hardly be said.

The translations here offered are purposely incautious in that they try to convey the most, not the least, that the texts suggest. Everyone will have his own quarrel with them, but perhaps two things may be said in further explanation: these versions are meant to contain a hint of their Greek metres, and they are meant to keep concepts (and, wherever possible, words) in their ordained positions, while yet producing English sense. Phrases that render restorations or guesses are placed in square brackets, and eccentric choices of meaning are discussed either in the essays or in the footnotes that follow.

Introduction

The poems and fragments discussed in this book have already been thoroughly studied as documents. Their testimony has been taken for surveys of dialect, for histories of the archaic period, for theoretical reconstructions of Aegean society, and for biographies of the three poets. The same poems have also been treated by students of literature who have measured their dependence upon the works that preceded them and their influence upon those that came after, as well as their part in a process known as the 'unfolding of the Greek spirit'. One result of so much careful consideration, however, has been that individual songs are often taken simply as members of a class – one is a demonstration of the 'abnormal' employment of a certain linguistic practice, another is (or is not) the location of the first 'ship of state' metaphor, and a third displays a peculiarly 'archaic' concept of knowledge. Another, more negative consequence is that critics, persuaded that the early Greek 'spirit' has been correctly measured, seek in the poems only what they believe they are licensed to find. For a time, the songs of this period were all expected to reveal a passionate consciousness of self, along with something called 'the archaic sense of helplessness', but then the emphasis changed and scholarly attention was directed to the question of the singer's place in his community and to the social function of song. In consequence, most critics of the present moment operate as if under a double license, by which either private confession or public utility may be pursued and taken as the informing element of archaic song.

The search for passionate individuality in archaic poetry is motivated by the conviction that all lyric is or should be the expression of vivid personal emotion, and it seems to be justified by the fact that the monodic songs of early Greece sometimes carry direct first-person assertions – 'I don't like', 'I am confounded', or 'I wish to die'. Certain scholars have recognised in these phrases a sudden exsurgence of ego that occurred in the early seventh century, endured for a brief time, and then sank away mysteriously, leaving the souls of a few poets eternally revealed in song. The archaic singer presumably spoke directly from his heart, and since the human heart is everywhere the same the modern critic has only to listen with his own, and he will be in full possession of a personal message from deepest antiquity.[1] Such is the theory, but in practice the critic of this persuasion is often baffled, since archaic lyric poets frequently stand as far from their material as any faceless story-teller could, and even in the first-person they refuse to be as spontaneously passionate as they are asked to be. The *ou phileō* of Archilochus (114W) introduces a conventional trope, the *asunnetēmmi* of Alcaeus begins an elaborate allegory (208V), and Sappho's *tethnakēn d' adolōs thelō* comes from an anecdote that the singer relates (94V). The *cri du coeur* critics do their best, classifying the faceless works as abnormal and inventing warm background episodes for songs that seem too cool, but sometimes, when they wholly fail to find what they want, they censure whatever it is that they discover instead. Any hint of conventional artistry is distasteful to a critic whose ideal lyric is the naif expression of a violent emotion, and all too often we hear that a certain song is 'too Homeric', another 'too Horatian', and that a third is 'lacking in sincerity'. The authors of such judgments expect early monody to be not only passionate but also free of any awareness of its generic difference from ordinary speech, and the perversity of this demand is plain when a great scholar chides Sappho for her ornamentation and her 'detachment'. With evident regret he notes that she is a conscious entertainer who, 'even at the height of her suffering', indulges her audience with 'a flight of fancy' and 'much detail irrelevant to her present theme'.[2]

The idea of the sudden outburst of ego does not find much support in the surviving work of the archaic lyricists, for this work is more artful and less passionate, more conventional and less individual than the advocates of this notion might have wished. What is worse, the theory necessarily creates certain questions that even its own followers are unable to answer. They are forced to ask themselves why this important psychic phenomenon should have appeared just when it did, and why the ego, having learned to sing, should have gagged itself and grown quiet again, and they grow confounded when they try to explain. The brusque emergence of 'personal' poetry is supposed to have resulted from a weakening of the bonds of the epic tradition, as if the making of dactylic tales were repressive of the personality, and as if the work of Archilochus, Alcaeus and Sappho were clearly counter-epic (or at least extra-epic) in impulse and form. In actuality,

---

[1] This way of reading is not exclusively post-Romantic; cf. Synesius of Cyrene (370–412 A.D.) who reported that 'Archilochus and Alcaeus used the sweetness of song to sing life itself, and so posterity has a record of what they rejoiced or suffered' (*de insomn.* 20 = 11.1 p.188 Terzaghi).

[2] Denys Page, *Sappho and Alcaeus* (Oxford 1955) 18, in his comment on the hymn to Aphrodite.

however, Sappho's dactyls about Hector and Andromache (44V) and Alcaeus' song of Ajax (298V) testify – along with the many Homeric phrases of Archilochus – to an epic tradition that had neither weakened nor become burdensome. Unless they are rejected as spurious,[3] these pieces must be treated either as anomalies or as evidence that the iconoclasts occasionally surrendered to conventionality, and so the initial false problem ('How did lyric individuality suddenly arise?') is replaced by another as critics strive to explain how their anti-epic poets sometimes came to write epic-like verse. And meanwhile the matching invented mystery continues to be impenetrable, for no one can say why – once the tyranny of epic had been ended and the ego enthroned – the ego did not continue to express itself in the lyrics that had been its own discovery.[4]

As well as the passionate ego, critics now hunt the immediate occasion when they study archaic poetry, and though the two activities are sometimes allowed to become one they express two very different sets of preconceptions. The first pursuit is aesthetic and intuitive and it is justified, presumably, by a sense of what all lyric ought to be, while the second is sociological and pragmatic and based, presumably, upon observations of what this particular kind of poetry really was. The formulators of the occasional theory remark the genuine similarities between early lyric and certain kinds of ritual song; then they note that a few monodies proclaim themselves as having a ritual application, and finally they conclude that every early song depended upon a concrete and simultaneous public occasion to give it its shape and its matter. Stated in the negative, this conclusion takes on a dangerous exclusivity, for we are told that no archaic song could come into being apart from a unique and formative communal ceremony. Naturally, early song is much less available when it is viewed in this way, for human institutions (unlike the human heart) are known to change continually. Instead of a universal and timeless emotion, an archaic poem is now expected to express a particular and time-bound cultural utility, and a modern admirer can therefore no longer listen alone, but must ask an anthropologist to monitor the message he receives.

The search for occasions has been pursued with most determination among the fragments of Sappho, for a certain number of her songs announce themselves as meant for wedding celebrations. Others that are not technically epithalamia have been accommodated by invented extensions of the ceremony – processions, salutations and the like –

---

[3] See, for example, Max Treu, who would deny the Sapphic authorship of 44V on the grounds that it lacks 'Selbstaussage' (*Sappho*, Munich 1968, 197).

[4] Note the puzzled remarks of Page, who wonders why 'personal loves and hates and experiences were never again expressed in lyric or iambic metre?' (*Fondation Hardt, Entretiens X, Archiloque*, Geneva 1964, 220).

and others still are attributed to even more fanciful nuptial rites which are supposed to have been celebrated within the Sapphic circle. Not all the members of the occasional school are pleased by these hypothetical 'Sapphic marriages', but an astonishing number of scholars will give it as known fact that the song about the symptoms of desire (16V) was sung, cabaret-style, among eating and drinking wedding guests who all are pleased when the hired singer pretends to have fallen violently in love with the bride.

Faced with the work of Alcaeus and Archilochus, the rigorous occasionalist has a harder time, though there have been random efforts to derive the scurrilous songs of the latter from 'traditional entertainment with some (perhaps forgotten) ritual basis'.[5] As far as I know, however, no one would take these pieces to be actual parts of actual rustic mummery, and consequently their contemporary occasion is still undetermined. Unable to point to a public festival, and unable to admit that the archaic singer could sing informally, simply because he wanted to, certain critics at this pass borrow from the alternate camp and propose the Passionate Occasion – a concrete event in the poet's life which, like a public ceremony, demands a simultaneous accompaniment of song. With this hybrid notion, however, the method that set out to be sociological is necessarily compromised, and the result is a criticism far more biographical than that of the advocates of the lyric ego. That group expected song to distil emotion and to find its universal aspects, but these expect it to be an immediate, recording response to a unique experience. A critic of overwhelming influence says of Alcaeus, 'If he raises his voice, an actual agony of the moment stands before him',[6] and others hasten to reconstruct the details of that 'agony', just as they reconstruct the details of curious wedding rites for the poetry of Sappho. In homage to the essential occasionalist principle of simultaneity, performance is assumed to have taken place on the spot, and consequently a song that mentions a temple is described as having been sung in that place, verses about a parting are supposed to have been given out, opera-fashion, to a retreating back, and Archilochus is expected to stand on board among his shipmates when he counsels them to drink, casting his verses into the teeth of a storm.[7]

These propositions are absurd in themselves, and in addition they create unavoidable difficulties for their advocates, who are unable to explain how songs that were thus organically joined each to its particular moment were able to survive. Such performances could never be repeated in a society that knew the law of occasionality ('Song may

---

[5] Martin West, *Studies in Elegy and Iambus* (Berlin, New York 1974) 27.

[6] Bruno Snell, writing of Alcaeus in *Poetry and Society* (Bloomington, 1961) 33.

[7] Compare Page (*S&A*, 185), who rejects the idea of recitation during a storm in the case of Alcaeus 208V only after giving it serious consideration.

not exist apart from formative occasion'), so how is it that texts of them ever appeared?[8] If Sappho actually stood under the moon, side by side with Atthis on one matchless night and sang to her about a girl in Lydia, how did anyone else ever hear of that song? In this particular case, the song seems to place itself in something like a ritual occasion, but the problem remains, for even if it were meant for a more public moment, how did it come to be repeated in a society that knew only situational song? Never again would Atthis be in the same relation to the girls around her and this means that never again could there be a fully occasional performance of these particular lines.

If he is to explain their preservation, the occasionalist has to admit that archaic songs were repeated, and this admission destroys his own theory by recognizing performances that were *not* determined by their immediate situation. If a singer could sing, in a new spot and on a later day, the same song that he or another had made for a different place and day, it follows that in this new spot, on this later day, songs were being sung for themselves and the law of the immediate occasion, if it ever existed, was now inoperative. Instead of reflecting the actual present moment, these repeated songs ignored it in a performance situation that did *not* dictate matter and form, and such license could not have been granted exclusively to those who sang old songs. The singer of a fresh piece would in such a situation follow his conserving colleagues and transcend the present moment with poetic immediacies of his own imagining, and this means that the most uncomfortable consequences of the occasionalist presumption may be left behind. Song did not always need to reduplicate the present, it did not even need to suit it, and so Alcaeus could stand at ease among banqueting companions while he sang of a self who skulked in exile, Archilochus could urge the breaking of casks without singing from a pitching deck, and Sappho could address an Atthis who may, for all we know, already have left her company. In each case there will of course have been an audience whose potential delight or displeasure contributed to the formation of the song, but their presence will not have commanded its particulars in the rigid way of a funeral when it commands a lament, a victory when it commands a victory cry, or a mission to Delos when it commands a hymn for Apollo.

The *cri du coeur* school has insisted upon the sense of self, the occasionalist upon the sense of community as the informing source of poetry for the early lyricists, and taken together (in their more moderate expressions) the two theses produce a fair description of archaic song, where most of the surviving examples depict poets and listeners

---

[8] Page admits this difficulty: 'Ich weiss nicht, z.B., wie ein Gedicht das für eine bestimmte Situation geeignet ist (wie Sappho's *phainetai moi*) jemals wieder recitiert werden könnte, wenn die dazu anregende Situation und die dazu gehörigen Personen längst vergessen waren' (*FH* X, 174).

who externalise and socialise what we would call inner experience. Within this song-created world (which may or may not reflect the real), sacred and secular mingle as the movements of the psyche are ritualised: hatred becomes a formal curse sent against an enemy, love becomes a prayer, and scorn a fable that turns away depravity with apotropaic laughter. This means, however, that while both the standard approaches are right, both are wrong as well, for the passionate critics are mistaken when they deny the conscious conventionality of these lyrics, while their occasional colleagues are equally mistaken when they refuse the archaic singers the freedom to create their own fictions.

The songs of Archilochus, Alcaeus and Sappho are obviously neither the sudden inventions of a freshly liberated 'archaic ego' nor the purely conventional projections of fixed communal gestures. Their metres and some elements of their language and matter mark them as deriving from the ancient popular chants that accompanied cult and work, but their exploitation of epic motifs and diction shows that their makers were conscious of artistic kinship with poets of another sort, and meanwhile touches of irony prove that the singers of these songs enjoyed the fact that their own vision was not always that of their society. It is true that time, by tearing their work to bits, has produced a few disjointed phrases that seem to be 'searingly personal', but nevertheless every extended passage displays an intense consciousness of form, while it profits from both court and folk conventions. And it is true on the other side that all three singers were public musical figures whose songs on occasion served their communities, but it is nevertheless impossible to find any one of them using an exclusively ritual voice, unless perhaps Sappho does so in certain of the wedding chants.[9] The rhythms of their 'hymns' prove that they were meant for pleasure, not for sacred business, just as the rhetoric and form of the songs of 'passion' show that these too were created, not as simple confessions, but as amusements for audiences that were both knowing and fastidious.

It is the contention of the present study that the archaic poets, like poets everywhere, invented both ego and occasion when they composed their songs. 'I' might mean 'I, a Singer', 'I, a Lover', 'I, a Citizen', and it might also mean 'I, a Young Girl' (even in a male singer's mouth)[10] or 'I, an Old Creature' (whatever the singer's actual age). And in the same way the temple hiding-place, the drunken watch, and the cele-

---

[9] Perhaps also the Archilochean songs for Dionysus that were once recorded on the Mnesiepes stone (251W); see the discussion of West, *Studies*, 24.

[10] Unable to understand the dramatic complexity of the poetic first person, some scholars have been forced to suppose that male poets were in the habit of bringing 'female colleagues' (?) with them into the banquet hall when their compositions employed a female persona; see Page, *FH* X, 214 and West, *Studies*, 17, note 26.

brations for Atthis might or might not be wholly invented – we cannot know the degree to which they reflected incidents from actual life and it does not matter, for these events are not offered as autobiography or as reportage. They are instead evocations, fresh poetic actualities open to all, 'fictions' now (whatever their relation to mere passing fact) in which the singer develops a truth that is permanent. In this fundamental sense the archaic monodist was like the lyric poets who stand nearer to us in time, but in the decisive question of audience his situation was peculiar to himself. Like his successors, the archaic composer had various listeners in mind – sometimes a special friend, always a larger group of acquaintances, beyond this a public of fellow-citizens, rivals, admirers and perhaps enemies, and finally a remembering posterity. His peculiarity, however, lay in the fact that as far as he knew the only way to reach any of these audiences was with his own or someone else's voice. Writing and reading were in his time the tools of business or religion, not pleasure's implements (unless you count the inscriptions on the *kalos* cups) and so his poem could only exist as physical sound. And this meant that it had to find and conform to an outward situation that would provide listeners ready to attend, if it was ever to come alive, while it had to continue to please in other such situations, if it was not to die. Such were the facts of performance that necessarily tempered, though they did not dictate, the inventions of the ancient monodists.

In its minimal definition, monody was simply song that came from a single throat, accompanied by the music of a lyre. In that it was sung, it was absolutely distinct from epic (though not from elegy, where music had a greater importance), and in that it used just one performer who did not dance,[11] it was totally different from the choral lyrics that enlivened so many secular and religious ceremonies. Being in no way costly, monody had no need of princely patronage, and unlike epic and choral, it did not demand an audience well-accommodated and willing to be quiet for a long period of time. It was made of familiar melodic phrases, repeated in short sequences that could easily grow tedious, and in its consequent brevity it tired neither the singer nor his hearers. Its conventions were strict, but the single-voice song lent itself to improvisation both actual and pretended, and its air of informality could charm common people as well as sophisticated listeners. It was, in other words, a performance that was easily consumed, and for this reason the singer of archaic monody had always a multiplicity of audiences ready to hear his compositions. Families

[11] Several scholars imagine a strong element of miming in the performance of monody (but how far can one go with lyre in hand?) and even the use of costume (did one dine disguised? could one, once costumed, sing only one song on a given evening? was *ex tempore* song thus impossible, or was there a props box?). See the remarks of K. J. Dover, *FH* X, 215, and West, *Studies*, 29ff.

gathered for weddings and funerals, and more indiscriminate groups came together for field rituals, dedications, soldiers' messes and ceremonies inaugurating war or peace, as well as for regular religious festivals, and in all these circumstances there was an extra-occasional, informal place for secular song. In some cities men were given to serenading (with intentions that could be abusive, laudatory, or amorous) and everywhere they met in groups of varying definition to dine together, while women met likewise in the more strictly familial household factory, and for both sexes music of some sort or other was the chief embellishment of such concourse.

The symposium and the women's circle were the most available and the most secular of these potential audiences and most of the archaic lyrics that we know seem to have been composed in this friendly ambience, among comrades, allies, or members of the singer's own house or sodality. There was ease within such gatherings, but there was a strong component of formality too, for even the riotous gang that chanted insults in the streets practised an art of vilification that derived from popular rites of abuse, and even the noble ladies of the shuttered gynaikeion amused one another with versions of the spells, work-chants, and nursery ditties that had always brought measure into female lives. A favoured singer thus knew the general nature and the specific mood of his hearers; he knew where he was free and where he must provide the expected; he knew too what the singers who had come before him (on this day and in the deeper past) had done. With all these things in his mind, he fitted his own poetic notions to the various indulgent but passively tyrannical groups that would listen to him, and in doing so he created the early lyric style.

(Here, incidentally, is the response to the false historical question raised by the heart's message men, for it was not a psychic consciousness of self that appeared in the archaic period and disappeared in early classical times, but instead only a vogue for a particular kind of poetry. The monodic style was created in small, aristocratically dominated communities where life's most important hours were spent in gatherings of peers, and where the perfect audience for the single voice could always be found. Being neither pretentious nor costly, this kind of song did not really appeal to the tyrants of the later sixth century; some monodists did go to court, but the great men wanted praise and they wanted poetry that expressed power – poetry that not everyone could have. They liked to hear the many voices of a chorus singing in unison, even when the sentiment expressed was of a 'personal' or 'individual' sort, and the same predilection for the colour and the scale of a danced spectacle continued when the tyrants were gone. Attic democracy, needing an art form that could be consumed by a crowd, turned all its best poets into tragedians – or perhaps one should say, chose to remember only their tragic poetry, for lyric monody did not totally disappear at the beginning of the fifth century any more than it appeared from nowhere with Archilochus. It continued to exist in the symposium, but the symposium was no longer at the heart of the city, and this meant that an ambitious singer no longer cast his best efforts in its antiquated and élitist forms. It may also have meant that these later lyrics were purposely not written down, because having them by heart was the badge of an elegant but outnumbered nobility.)

Monody made use of a variety of metres, according to its purpose and also according to the skill of the singer, the customary usages of his place, and in the case of improvisation doubtless also according to the choice of the performer who had just finished his song.[12] If the poet's wisdom was of a practical sort, he might choose elegy as being easy for an audience to absorb and also because the secure old distich could make the most pedestrian sentiment ring with a momentary profundity. If, on the other hand, the singer's intention was to work upon the values or the vision of his listeners, if he was musically knowing and sure of his wit, he might choose some local form that depended on shifting rhythmic phrases instead of dactylic lines. For attack and riposte, for teasing a friend, belittling a rival or defaming an enemy, for boasting and ironic self-deprecation, men of Paros and Thasos often used iambics or the epode (an alternation of single-short lines with lines that mixed single- and double-short elements) since these melodies already had a kind of banter in them. Iambics, however, could also be philosophical,[13] and on the other hand at the further end of the Aegean the poets of Lesbos achieved all of these 'iambic' effects with their own very different Aeolic metres. Their songs, line by line, could have neither the monumental solidity of elegy nor the sharpness and thrust that inhered in iambic rhythms, but the brief Lesbian stanzas allowed a series of concepts to be rapidly linked or juxtaposed, then capped with a conclusion not drawn from reason but enforced with all the authority of melody and form.

Because it used folk models and exploited the jokes, assumed personalities and dialogues that we know best in ballads and nursery rhymes, Greek monody is sometimes spoken of as 'naive' or 'primitive'.[14] This, however, is a case of 'simple truth miscalled simplicity', and it is almost as threatening to a true appreciation of early lyric as are the personal and occasional fallacies. Certainly the songs of ar-

---

[12] Presumably a given singer would come to a given collocation equipped with a large repertoire that included the songs of others, old songs of his own (some already performed, some not), new songs of his own, and also potential songs that might be improvised.

[13] See West, *Studies*, 32, on Semonides.

[14] For 'naive', see G. M. Kirkwood, *Early Greek Monody* (Ithaca and London 1974) *passim*; for primitivism, see Dover, *FH* X, 201ff.

chaic Greece did not love decoration for its own sake, for the equilib-
rium of the short poem could not survive the overbalancing effect of
a conspicuously beautiful word or an extended figure of speech. And
certainly again these songs did not love prosy argument,[15] but they
could and often did display complex poetic thought within a consummate economy of means. Sensation and mind, emotion and ethos,
object and essence are not analytically separated in these pieces but
maintain themselves instead in harmonious and indiscriminate occupation of every bit of melody, so that the songs as wholes can lead
their listeners to recognitions that go beyond the merely intellectual.
Sometimes they discover corruption where health seemed evident or
value where it had not been thought to abide. At other times they
force strangeness into the familiar and find out the demonic truth that
dwells in an everyday event. And effects such as these are neither
childish nor rude.

Perhaps the single most important thing to be said about early
monody is that it is dynamic. Each song works, just as a magical chant
or a hymn works, pressing upon the listening consciousness to enforce
some shift in attitude. This active impulse was probably drawn from
more primitive songs that pressed upon nature or the supernatural to
obtain a physical advantage like rain or the death of an enemy, but
it must also have been reinforced by the agonistic temper of the
archaic group. In the symposium, and probably in its female counterpart as well, song was a recognised form of rivalry, the proof of inner
excellence and the test of a certain sort of dominance. One could
reperform an old piece, but any claim to preeminence would have to
be based not only on a new composition but on one that gave a novel
twist to its matter and brought the company into a state of adherence.
'Some men say. . .but *I* say. . .' became a standard pattern in this
ceaseless contest of poetic force, and the formula points to a second
important fact about early lyric which is that it always tried to show
itself wise. Whatever the subject (it might be amatory or military),
whatever the tone (it might be sceptical or reverent), and whatever
the metre (elegiac or one of the mixed systems), wisdom – popular or
esoteric, practical or speculative – was what the singer tried to impose.

Sometimes the element of good but slightly eccentric counsel is
plainly and directly exposed, as it is, for example, in Archilochus' song
about kinsmen drowned at sea (13W); sometimes it is overt but made
a matter of sport, as it is in Sappho's priamel (16V). At other times,
when a song operates in a fully dramatic manner and pretends to be
something that it is not, its wisdom is organic and implicit, as in the

---

[15] This lack of argument is sometimes unreasonably held against the monodists; see,
for example, Snell's criticism of Alcaeus for not 'coping mentally' with the 'anxieties'
that are his subject and for failing to provide 'new meanings for old notions' or to discuss
'social and economic conflicts' (*Poetry and Society*, 33).

case of Alcaeus' curse upon Pittacus (129V), where the power of an oath takes on a demonic reality, and as it is also in Sappho's prayer to Aphrodite (1V), where the truth of divine consolation becomes almost tangible.[16] Finally, the new understanding may be presented as a single logically irreducible emblem, as it is in the mythic ballads of Alcaeus (42, 44, 283, 298V) and in Sappho's song about the girl in Lydia (94V), where the fact that love and Aphrodite are identical shines forth as a moon.

I have tried to treat the songs of Archilochus, Alcaeus and Sappho as poems that happen to come from antiquity, not as antique texts that happen to be poetry. A lyric poem, once made, becomes an event that occurs within its listener's or its reader's time, whenever it is repeated. As an event, it imposes itself according to its own terms, while it also borrows supplementary aspects from whatever context it has found. In its initial manifestations, if these occur soon after the poem's composition, these borrowings are to a large part foreseen and foreordained by the maker of the piece. Later, as the song persists and finds hearers and contexts that the poet could not know, it must itself control changed accretions that are supplied from conditions and sensibilities wholly unforeseen. All of which means that an antique song that occupies a bit of modern time will be an amalgamated event, its essential shape conferred upon a piece of fresh experience in a doubly elaborated form, since it is embellished now with whichever of the old intended elements the new listener can supply, and also with whatever new ones its unchanged substance may elicit. Considered in this way, the revived song has three parts, and the first two of these provide the critic with his task. He investigates the song itself, to find not just its matter and manner, but the balance of energies that keeps its substance suspended and refuses to let it settle into mere inert statement. That is his central and most difficult work, but he must also investigate the poem's own context, trying to reconstruct some at least of the original accretions that were a part of its maker's creative intention. If this job could ever be perfectly done, the elucidated poem could then enter the consciousness of a modern reader and there claim its third part – made up of elements the poet could never have supposed – while it yet remained in essence the same poem that was experienced by its first, intended audience.

In the attempt to ape this ideal critic I have given secondary place to historical questions, though for the sake of convenience they are usually treated first. The life of each poet is considered only as it may have influenced the force of his poems with his audience, and mean-

---

[16] As a third, more difficult example, one might cite Archilochus' eclipse song (122W), where the proverbial wisdom of the saying, ἄπιστον οὐδέν, ὅ τι θεῶν μέριμνα τεύχει (B.3.57) hides in the father's exclamation.

while the primary question is always the inner nature of the surviving examples of his work. I am gratefully indebted to all those scholars who have employed their learning to establish physical texts, for I have exploited their results in every way I could while pursuing the movement, the informing spirit, and the design of the phrases that they have found and made readable. Just here, however, at its centre, a charge of futility can be brought against the present endeavour, for almost every line discussed is in some degree uncertain or incomplete. It must be both presumptuous and foolish to look for 'Gang' and 'Geist' where disintegrating papyrus fibres have destroyed 'Gestalt', but knowing this I have gone ahead because the alternative is to let brute accident rob us of the poetry that it almost bestows. Resistance to this robbery takes the form of forcing the most out of the little that is left, and this has seemed to me to be justified by the fact that lyric song itself directs and encourages an imaginative fulfilment of its every least element.

One of the qualities that distinguishes lyric from epic, ensuring its ability to shape a bit of its listener's actual life, is the self-confirming wholeness that such songs always show. Like an anecdote or a joke, a lyric depends upon its ending, in that the hearer must feel that he has got it *all* (though he cannot restate that 'all') when the poem is done. Unlike the anecdote or joke, however, a lyric produces an ultimate line that closes its movement without in any way solving its sense, for the successful lyric is complete in the way that a pebble or an egg is, not finished after the fashion of a knot untied. It pretends to satisfy only itself and abjures the cheap finality that would make its matter a part of the listener's mental equipment instead of a part of his felt experience. And because he does not depend upon the mechanics of a 'punch line', the maker of such a song must fill its every part with that unparaphraseable 'all' that we are persuaded we possess at the close. In songs of this kind one will almost certainly go wrong in trying to reconstitute a finite portion that has been lost (who, given the opening of the Sapphic priamel, could have divined the absent Anactoria?). On the other hand, one may, in spite of the enormity of the risk, just possibly go right in a search for the direction, the vision, and even the shape inherent in an incomplete passage, and these will in some sense be congruent with the direction, vision and shape of the finished performance. Such, at any rate, is the premise of this book.

August, 1981   A.P.B.
Flavigny-sur-Ozerain

PART I

Archilochus

i

Life

Archilochus belongs to the Aegean and to the seventh century before the birth of Christ. He moved between the island of Paros and its remote colony on Thasos, living as a soldier and composing short songs which the ancient world valued with the books of Homer.[1] Because of his murderous tongue, he was said to have invented the scurrilous iambic mode; he was the first to have 'dipped a bitter Muse in snake-venom and stained gentle Helicon with blood' (*AP* 7.71) and for this he was much admired. Not many of his songs were known, even in antiquity, but the sense was strong that he had been the founder of a genre, and he remained, throughout the Renaissance, as the guardian genius of the European satirist. In recent times, however, Archilochus has been the subject of another sort of admiration, for modishly crude translations have made him the brother of certain contemporary poets, while scholars have set him at the opening of their histories of the so-called Western mind. His bitter songs, it seems, were dictated neither by convention nor the desire to please; they followed rather the pulsing of the poet's own visceral parts, and so Archilochus has been saluted as the first 'individual' of Greek antiquity.[2] Ancient gossip has been revived, and the Parian has been summoned from the archaic world as a figure of full-bodied, romantic realism – a bastard and a mercenary, a bitter pragmatist who hated

[1] Ancient evaluations of Archilochus are to be found in Heraclitus, Diels *Vors.* 22 [12] B42; Plato, *Ion* 531a; Heracl. Pont., *FHG* 11.197.2; at ps. Plut. *de mus.* 5 & 7, Archilochus appears as a musician in the company of Orpheus, Terpander and Stesichorus; see A. von Blumenthal, *Die Schätzung des Archil. im Altertum* (Stuttgart 1922).

[2] B. Snell, *Discovery of the Mind* (Oxford 1953), 50f., 'The depth of the heart ... revealed.' H. Fränkel, *Dichtung und Philos.*[2] (Munich 1962) 149, '... der Begründer der gr. Lyrik.' A. R. Burn, *Lyric Age of Greece* (New York 1960) 159, 'Individual self-expression in poetry bursts into full view with Archilochus of Paros.' G. Kirkwood, *Early Greek Monody* (Ithaca 1974) 23, 'A. is the first voice of the poetry of the individual man.' For a more reasonable statement of Archilochus' connection with the poetry and thought that preceded him, see J. Russo, 'The inner man in Archilochus and the *Odyssey*', *GRBS* 15 (1974) 139ff. More moderate also is the old phrase of Wilamowitz's, in which Archilochean poetry is noticed for its 'frische Subjectivität und goldene Rücksichtslosigkeit' (*Sappho und Simonides*, Berlin 1913, 10).

tradition and sang with the lewd voice of revolt and poverty, a drunkard who fought with both friend and enemy, a rebel against worn-out values, a debunker of aristocratic ideals, a brawling upstart with a vein of music in him.

Fortunately, a few harder facts were provided by a series of stones. For a long time the only archaeological evidence of Archilochus' existence had been a Parian monument from the first century B.C.[3] Once it had honoured the poet with citations from an ancient biographer named Demeas, but unfortunately it had been so badly damaged as to be almost unreadable. This tantalising stone (usually called the Monumentum Archilochi, or else the Sosthenes inscription, in memory of the man who set it up) was, however, unexpectedly reinforced by three more finds that appeared in the 1950s. First, on Paros, a set of inscribed slabs were recognised as belonging to another, older monument likewise dedicated to the poet.[4] These carried an extensive text (referred to as the Mnesiepes inscription, or else as E, for the place of finding, near the river Elitas) which begins with an Apolline command given to a man of the third century B.C. whose name was Mnesiepes. He is ordered to honour the great Parian poet with altars and sacrifices, in a place dedicated to his memory, and the continuing inscription obediently directs itself to that memory. A leisurely life of Archilochus, followed by citations from his works, once decorated the monument, and though the lines of verse have almost all been weathered away a long passage from the early section of the life remains legible. The finding of this inscription was announced in 1952. Three years later an archaic memorial for Glaucus, the friend of Archilochus, was discovered on the island of Thasos, reviving a name that had until then only been known from scraps of poetry.[5] Glaucus proved to be a

---

[3] *IG* XII.5.445; *IG* XII Suppl. p.212 = *FGH* III B 502, p.479ff. = Diehl, *Anth. Lyr. Gr.*[3] vol. 3 (1952), Archilochus no. 51 = 192W. Demeas was a student of Parian chronology who seems to have listed all of the events recorded in Archilochus' poetry, and also the composition of each known poem, according to the order of the Parian archon list. Thus he placed the tale of Koiranos in the time of the first archon, where mythic events presumably belonged. See A. M. Hauvette, 'Les nouveaux fragments d'Archiloque', *REG* 14 (1901) 85–91.

[4] First announced by N. M. Kontoleon in Πρακτικά Ἀρχ. Ἐτ. (1950), 258ff.; see parallel announcements in *BCH* 74 (1950) 310 and 75 (1951) 122, *JHS* 71 (1951) 249. The full publication was by Kontoleon in Ἀρχ Ἐφ. (1952) 32–95, with plates 1–4. See also W. Peek, 'Neues von Archilochos', *Philolog.* 99 (1955) 4–50; E. Vanderpool, 'New inscriptions concerning Archilochus', *AJP* 76 (1955) 186–8; G. Tarditi, 'La nuove epigrafe Archilochea', *PP* 11 (1956), 122–39; A. Kambylis, 'Zur "Dichterweihe" des A.', *Hermes* 91 (1963) 129ff. A hero cult of Archilochus is mentioned by Aristotle (*Rhet.* 2.23), who cites Alcidamas as his source.

[5] J. Pouilloux, 'Glaucos fils de Leptine, Parien', *BCH* 79 (1955) 75–86 (fig. 1 and Pl. III). The inscription reads: 'I am the memorial of Glaucus son of Leptines; the sons of Brentes erected me.' Pouilloux notes (p.85), 'A travers les âges on a continué à célébrer un culte autour de ce monument, culte funéraire et héroïque apparemment, même s'il ne s'agissait

general who had received heroic honours at his cenotaph after his death, and both he and his poet companion consequently grew larger and more real. Then finally, in 1961, a grave-marker turned up on Paros close to the Elitas shrine – a mid-sixth-century column cap, cut to carry a statue and inscribed in fourth-century letters with this dedication:[6]

> Archilochus son of Telesicles, the Parian, lies here
> Where Dokimos son of Neocreon sets up this monument.

The fact that the Parians built a shrine for Archilochus and treated him almost as a demi-god seems to confirm the book-sources in their report that this master of invective was as much honoured as Homer in antiquity. On the other hand, the existence of a public Archilochus cult casts a shade of doubt upon some of the old stories about the poet's rowdy and disreputable life, and so the discoveries of the 1950s have encouraged a sceptical review of all the known biographical materials. These include the fragments of Archilochus' own poetry, the anecdotes that antique scholars told about him, and the bits of the two official Parian *Lives* that survive on the two monuments. The mixture is thus one of self-made notoriety, second-hand inference and worshipful mythologising, but a few minimal facts, with a few further probabilities, can be extracted from it nevertheless.

To begin with, it is strikingly clear that antiquity did not regard Archilochus as a rebel or an iconoclast. The elder traditions do not put him in any way at odds with society; on the contrary, they provide him with the two motifs that were proper to poets of the most august and prophetic kind – divine backing and a supernatural vocation. Late antiquity knew a tradition about an oracle given before his birth, promising him poetic glory (*AP* 14.113; Dio Chrys. 33.12, von Arnim i, 300), and the inscription from the third-century shrine recounts an early version of the same, prefacing it with a folk-tale that makes its hero into a kind of infant Hesiod.

---

que d'un cénotaphe.' See also K. Latte, 'Zeitgeschichtliches zu Archilochos', *Hermes* 92 (1964) 385–90 = *Kl. Schriften* (Munich 1968) pp. 457–63, and for a photograph, G. Daux, *Guide de Thasos* (Paris, 1967) 12, fig. 3.

[6] Announced by A. Orlandos, Ἔργον τῆς Ἀρχαιολ. Ἑταιρ. (1960) 184–5, figs 206, 207; see also G. Daux, 'Chronique', *BCH* 85 (1961) 846–7, figs 24, 25. A white-ground pyxis from Eretria (Caskey-Beazley, *Attic Vase-paintings in the Museum of Fine Arts, Boston*, no. 13, pl. 15; cf. V. Schefold, *Die Bildnisse der antiken Dichter, Redner und Denker*, 57, pl. 1–2) is sometimes mentioned among the Archilochus witnesses; see N. Kontoleon, *Fondation Hardt Entretiens* X (Geneva 1964) 47ff.; see also 85–6. It shows a young man confronted by some strangely clad Muses, and might possibly refer to the tale of Archilochus' vocation, as told in the Mnesiepes inscription, but the identification is far from certain; see the discussion of Peek, op. cit., 23–6. A more certain reference to that story is to be found in the relief of a cow which was found by Kontoleon and identified as part of Sosthenes' shrine; see *BCH* 80 (1956) 333, fig. 11, and 334.

They say [says the stone, E¹ II 22–54] that when Archilochus was still a little boy he was sent into the country by his father Telesicles, in order to bring a cow down to be sold. And so he got up very early and set off while it was still night, though the moon was shining, and fetched the cow to take her to town. When he got to the place called Lissides, he thought he saw a company of women, and supposing them to be country girls on their way from work, going to town for a holiday, he began to tease them. They responded with jokes and foolery, and then they asked him if he meant to sell his cow. When he said yes, they answered that they would give him a fair price for it, but as soon as these words were spoken, both they and the cow disappeared. All the frightened boy could see was a lyre, lying at his feet, but in a little while he came to his senses and understood that these were the Muses who had appeared to him, and that this was their gift. He picked up the lyre and went on into town, where he told his father all that had happened to him, and Telesicles, hearing the tale and seeing the instrument, was filled with astonishment. The first thing he did was to make a search for the cow, throughout the length and breadth of the island, but no trace of it could be found. Later, when he was sent to Delphi by his fellow citizens, along with Lycambes, to ask for oracular guidance, he went the more willingly because he wished to ask about this adventure, and when they arrived, and entered the sanctuary, the god spoke this prophecy to Telesicles:

> Deathless that son is to be, o father Telesicles,
> famous in song among men, he who first gives you speech
> on your return from this shrine, into your native land.

And when they got back to Paros, Archilochus was the first of his sons to meet and to greet his father.[7]

This Simple-Simon tale testifies to a local folk-tradition about Archilochus, just as the appended oracle proves that there was also, in third-century Paros, a more formal version of the poet's life in existence.[8] Both the tale of the cow and the report of the Pythia's words are of course late; both have attached themselves to Archilochus' name long after his own time, as part of his Hellenistic transformation into a hero-poet, but all the same there are inferences to be drawn from this legendary material. First of all, it is plain that the later Parians found nothing in their own remembrance of Archilochus' life that was

[7] On the tale of A. and the Muses, see M. L. West, 'The Muses buy a cow', *CR* 14 (1964) 141–2: H. Maehler, *Die Auffassung des Dichterberufs im frühen Gr.*, Hypomnem. 3 (Göttingen 1963) 49, note 2; and T. Breitenstein, *Hésiode et Archiloque* (Odense Cl. Studies 1, 1971) 9–28, who argues not quite convincingly that the story originated in an Archilochean song. The final chapter, with its oracle, would seem probably to derive from a different source, perhaps some Parian collection of oracles (so Peek, op. cit., 19) or a collection emanating from Delphi (so Tarditi, op. cit., 132). There was a second oracle in circulation in antiquity purporting to deal with the foundation of Thasos (quoted by Steph. Byz. sv *Thasos*) which made no mention of Archilochus, though it named Telesicles.

[8] On typical poet's lives, see Mary Lefkowitz, 'The poet as hero: fifth-century autobiography and subsequent biographical fiction', *CQ* 28 (1978) 459–69; 'Fictions in literary biography: the new poem and the Archilochus legend', *Arethusa* 9.2 (1976) 181–9; *The Lives of the Greek Poets* (London 1981) 25–31.

inimical to the quality of Apollo's sanctity – nothing so disorderly and excessive, so immodest and ugly, as to cause scandal in a Delphic context. Secondly, it is clear that these same later Parians placed the birth of Archilochus before his father's foundation of the colony at Thasos, and that they thought of him as having spent his boyhood on the island of Paros. And finally, the story of the oracle shows that Archilochus' countrymen identified Lycambes, the notorious enemy of the grown-up Archilochus, with an associate of the poet's father in the great aristocratic adventure of founding a Parian settlement opposite the coast of Thrace.

The same wish to connect Archilochus with Delphi is reflected in the literary reports of Archilochus' death, but these, instead of following a typical biographical pattern, seem to have been fabricated from an actual Archilochean song. Scholars of late antiquity believed that Archilochus had been killed in battle by a man named Corax, and they told how the killer went to the temple of Apollo to be cleansed, but was ordered out by the god himself, because the victim had been the Muses' servant (Dio Chrys. 33.12; von Arnim i, 300). Rationalist details were added – the killer was said to have been a Naxian, and he was given the alternate name of Callondas so that this death would sound more like a bit of history. Nevertheless, the enemy named Crow[9] looks extremely suspicious, and the survival of a second bestial name in one version turns the whole episode into an animal fable. According to the report that Plutarch heard (*de sera num. vind.* 17, p. 560E = *Mor.* iii 425s. Paton-Pohlenz), Corax the Crow was enigmatically told by Apollo to seek out the birthplace of the cicada, there to supplicate the soul of Archilochus, and this melodious insect provides the decisive clue. Archilochus on occasion called himself a cicada, because of his ceaseless song (Luc. *Pseudolog.* 1), and evidently he also at some time or other called a harsh-voiced rival of his by the name of Crow (much as Pindar did at *O*.2.88). In a fable addressed to this man he must have reminded his enemy that Apollo honours the sweet insect singer over the raucous bird that knows only how to caw. Probably the preserved line 'You took the cicada by the wing' (223W) comes from this song, but however that may be, its message seems to have been, 'Beware of attacking me, a true poet, for Apollo will protect me!' Lucian knew the piece, or another very like it, and its temper can be judged from his parody, in which he makes Archilochus say to a challenger, 'You unfortunate man, what has inspired you to defy a mouthy poet like me, a man always looking for an excuse to make a bit of fierce iambic verse?' (223W).

With the best known characters from the traditional biography – Lycambes and his daughters – the case for historicity is stronger than

---

[9] Cf. Stesich. 209.9 *PMG*, where the poet calls a rival a crow, and see the discussions of Peek, *Philol.* 102, 172; Tarditi, op. cit., 133.

with Corax; yet they too are obviously creatures of the poet's own fictions and therefore fabulous as well as real. In late antiquity it was taken for fact that Lycambes, a rich and respectable man, had hanged himself, along with various daughters, because of the poisonous attacks that Archilochus had made upon the family, and Hellenistic poets made a game of writing apologies for the girls who were the victims of this killing slander. An epitaph that pretends to be theirs (*AP* 7.351=Gow-Page 1561–2 1555–62: cf. *AP* 7.352) begins:

> Though we suffer such a horrid fame, we daughters of Lycambes
> swear this by the holy oath of all the dead: Never did we
> shame our maidenhood, our forebears, or the steep and sacred isle
> of Paros! Let all gods and spirits testify: Never did we
> meet Archilochus at Hera's temple, or along the city's streets!

The victim's suicide (along with his death by stoning) is the fertilising fantasy of any primitive slanderer, and as an inspiration to her poets Iambe, the eponymous heroine of iambic verse, was said to have hanged herself (Schol. Hephaest., 281).[10]. That would be success: that would be the mark of excellence, and consequently, wherever the artist of abuse is praised, anecdotes of this sort tend to appear. The later iambic poet Hipponax, for example, was said to have been so cruel in his criticism of a certain artist named Bupalus that the poor man hanged himself (see Testimonia, 109–10W). Nevertheless, the ancient biographers who repeated the Lycambes tale took it perfectly seriously.[11] They said that Archilochus had been promised one of the daughters – one named Neobule – but had failed to get her because her father changed his mind, broke his word, and married her to

---

[10] On the suicide motif in iambics, see M. West, *Studies in Elegy and Iambus* (Berlin, New York 1974) 64. The image of the woman who has hanged herself is also important in the iconography of Greek misogyny; see the anecdote that Diogenes Laertius (6.52) tells of Diogenes who, seeing women who had hanged themselves from a tree, said, 'If only all trees could bear fruit of that sort!' Deriving from this is the tale (Cic. *de orat.* 2.278) of the man who keeps cuttings from the tree from which his wife had hanged herself; see W. D. Lebek, 'Dichterisches über den "Hund" Diogenes', *ZPE* 22 (1976) 293, note 2.

[11] The Emperor Julian, however, recognised the tale as false (οἶα ψευδῶς ἐπὶ τοῦ Λυκάμβου Ἀρχίλοχος. epist. 97 Bidez-Cumont = Lasserre 162). The earliest reference to the Lycambids seems to come in an iambic poem of the third century B.C. (Pap. Dublin 193); see G. W. Bond, 'Archilochus and the Lycambides', *Hermathena* 80 (1952) 3–11, and H. Lloyd-Jones, 'Lithos polites', *CR* NS 15 (1965) 246–7. The number of daughters varies; in Horace (*Ep.* 6.11 and *Ep.*1.19.25) it is unspecified; at *AP* 7.69 there are two; at *AP* 7.71 (first century A.D.) there are three; Julian (*AP* 7.69) in the sixth century has two, and the scholiast at Ovid, *Ibis* 54, adds Lycambes' wife to those who are dead. The first identification of the refused fiancée as Neobule is at schol. Horace *Ep.*6.11 (=171W), presumably from the fifth to the seventh century A.D. Eustathius, *Od.* 1684.45, gives no number, but says that according to the old tale the Lycambids hanged themselves because they could not bear the scurrilous force of Archilochus' mockery. As evidence of the busy irresponsibility of fourth-century literati, it may be noted that the comic poet Diphilus made both Archilochus and Hipponax lovers of Sappho (perhaps they contributed to her famous suicide), that Cratinus wrote a comedy called *Archilochoi* and that an *Archilochos* is attributed to Alexis.

someone else. In response the angry poet filled the town with obscene defamations of the old man, the fiancée and all the appended sisters, and hounded them until they chose to die. Indeed, it was this story, rather than any single line of verse, that came to signify Archilochus in antiquity, and it is still the basis, confessed or not, of many a modern assessment of his life and poetry.[12] The ghosts of Lycambes and his daughters haunt each line that is reported from their musical assassin, as every male attacked is identified as the old man, every female as Neobule. Worse yet, the notion of the poet's disappointment and his revenge has become almost a critical principle. It is taken as a proved fact that this singer is one whose love was second only to his hate in its crude ferocity, and it is assumed that he was a poet who used his song as another might a weapon or a tool, for ends that were selfish and immediate. Consequently, any reader of Archilochus is forced, like it or not, to come to grips at some point with this famous bit of gossip.

Certainly there are a Lycambes and a Neobule, though they are not necessarily father and daughter, among the targets of Archilochean verse. The number of their appearances in the surviving lines is, however, strikingly low: four for Lycambes (172; 548?, 57.7?, 71?), perhaps three for Neobule (118W; 206W; Pap. Col.24),[13] and two for unspecified female members of the family (33W; 38W). In addition, there are two fragments that might be thought to bear out the story of the broken engagement ('Father Zeus, I have never held my marriage feast', 197W, and 'That man never gave me a dowry', 200W), but in these there are no proper names at all, and no proof that the poet speaks in his own character. Indeed, the fact that the speaker, in an Archilochean song, is not necessarily Archilochus, leads to the realisation that every person one meets in his lines is to some degree fictional, and this truth has caused some critics to insist that neither Lycambes nor Neobule was ever an actual person.[14] Since an elegiac

---

[12] An extreme example of modern credulity is provided by J. Vendryes, who wrote in the *Revue Celtique* for 1913 (vol. 34, p.96): '. . . it is probably necessary to take the story in a literal sense. Archilochus really condemned Lycambes and Neobule to death; he hurled magical incantations against them from which they could not escape.'

[13] In the case of 206W, Hesychius' citation of one of the words has suggested a possible reference to Neobule.

[14] See C. Theander, Λυκάβης, Λυκάμβης, *Symb. Phil. O.A. Danielsson octogenario dictatae* (Uppsala 1932) 351, on the basis of whose suggestions a theory has arisen, according to which Lycambes is a stock figure in a traditional entertainment, a standard enemy of Dionysus who walks like a wolf, and whom Archilochus has used as the butt of conventional attacks; see M. West, *Studies*, 27ff.; G. Nagy, 'Iambos: typologies of invective and praise', *Arethusa* 9 (1976) 191ff. and *The Best of the Achaeans* (Baltimore and London 1979) 248. No one, however, has attempted a thorough consideration of the ramifications of this theory: who listened to these arcane attacks, and with what response? Why was the old wolf-bogey attacked in a second zoological form, as an Eagle, in 172–81W? How did he find his way into the Parian tradition concerning the settlement of Thasos? (Perhaps it should be noted that West elsewhere seems to take the daughter of the Wolf-Walker, Neobule Newcounsel, as an actual girl.)

poet may write poems to a conventional lover, a satirist may likewise address abuse to a conventional enemy, and proof that these two well-known victims are no more than conventions is allegedly to be found in their almost allegorical names. Lycambes is the wolf-bogey of some village sport, and Neobule is his female counterpart, a disreputable girl (something like the Lazy Mary of Mother Goose?) who stands for all that is new-fangled. According to this theory, then, the enemies that antiquity thought of as human are actually only scarecrows and the poet is no longer to be heard as a man obsessed with his private, physical loves and hates. Instead, he becomes one who still sings the age-old popular concerns of a primitive community.

The transformation of flesh-and-blood enemies into the shadows of effigies thus offers a refreshing release from the excessively personal reading that has been given to Archilochean poetry, and luckily that release may still be enjoyed even by those who would trade the most extreme details of this theory for something more moderate. That some alterations will have to be made seems obvious, for the Mnesiepes stone, after all, tells us that a Lycambes who was associated with the father of Archilochus played a role in the settlement of Thasos. How could the Wolf-Walker figure from a village pantomine have elbowed his way, in less than five hundred years, into the history of the city's proudest adventure? And why, if the name had been made ostensibly human by the attacks of Archilochus, did the chroniclers pair him as an equal in rank and prominence with the father of his famous enemy? Surely it is better to suppose that the man Lycambes did exist just as the later Parians believed, while we nevertheless admit that much of the scorn that Archilochus lavished upon him was of a traditional sort. A man with such a name would be a ready target for an abusive poet who liked to exploit animal fables as a mode of attack, and it looks as if he was used as the frequent representative of whatever masculine failing the poet wished to condemn.[15] Once he had been so defined, female transgressions could of course be attributed to the daughters of such a one, and a system of living ciphers would begin to take shape. Lycambes the man may, in this way, have become Archilochus' private scarecrow, his ideal enemy, the focus of all sorts of calumny, and therefore a natural centre of speculation among the poet's later imitators and biographers.

The nooses that finished off Lycambes and his daughters may have been the free invention of a learned admirer, since they were the final proof of the force of Archilochus' work. It may be, on the other hand,

---

[15] The line between punitive and rhetorical satire is not always sharply drawn; see E. Rosenheim, *Swift and the Satirist's Art* (Chicago 1963) 21ff.

that they originated in a remembered line of poetry,[16] for there is a fragment in which the poet abuses his heart for wanting to hang itself in shame (129W), and this piece of self-reproach suggests the existence of an opposite, aggressive *topos* – a taunt that takes the form, 'You're going to want to kill yourself when I am finished with you' (cf. the actual, 'Now you'll be the laughing-stock of all the citizens', at 172W).[17] Something of the sort, addressed to Lycambes, might have been set down as grisly fact by a literal-minded early biographer, whereupon later antiquity, never having enough of a good thing, will have added the daughters in various quantities. Invented or derived, however, the important thing about these dangling corpses is that they were the vessels in which the fame of Archilochus the satirist was preserved, as Horace well understood when he wrote (*Epod.* 6.11ff.);

> *Cave, cave: namque in malos asperrimus*
>   *parata tollo cornua,*
> *qualis Lycambae spretus infido gener*
>   *aut acer hostis Bupalo.*

> Take care! for I attack what's vile
>   wearing horns that gore, just like
> the son-in-law that false Lycambes scorned
>   or Bupalus' angry foe.

Indeed, they served him so well in this way that Ben Jonson is to be found imitating the Parian's original threat after more than two thousand years:

> I could do worse:
> Armed with Archilochus' fury, write Iambicks
> Should make the desperate lashers hang themselves –
> Rime them to death, as doe the Irish rats
> In drumming tunes.

These parts of the traditional, composite biography – the vocation, the death, and the assassination of Lycambes and his daughters – denounce themselves as unhistorical by their close adherence to a typical biographic form or to the known fashion of Archilochean poetry. There are a few other episodes, however, that seem to be closer

---

[16] Compare 45W: κύψαντες ὕβριν ἀθρόην ἀπέφλοσαν, which possibly represents a similar fantasy vision of self-inflicted death among enemies. If it does, it was probably the inspiration for the phrase, ῥιγηλὸν ὄνειδος/φήμην τε στυγερὴν ἔφλυσεν Ἀρχίλοχος in one of the Hellenistic poems about the Lycambids (*AP* 7.351, 5–6 = 1559–60 GP). Tarditi (op. cit., 126) holds the variant opinion which attributes the invention of this story to the fourth-century writers of comedy.

[17] Note the apparently opposite notion at 168W: 'You're going to like the joke I'll tell you.' This joke may, however, be one on Charilaus, and the singer's assurance may be sarcastic.

to actuality, among them one from the Parian life meant to prove the poet's pre-eminence in the religious development of his native island. In a seriously damaged passage the Mnesiepes inscription states that it was Archilochus who introduced (or reintroduced) the Bacchic worship at Paros,[18] and that he composed lewd songs for the rites of Dionysus (E III 36ff.=89–90W).[19] The garrulous stone goes on to tell how Archilochus was persecuted for his apostleship, how the god answered with a plague upon his persecutors' parts, and how an oracle finally persuaded the citizens of Paros to obey the poet and establish the religion as he advised, however shocking it might seem to be. All this, of course, only repeats the tale of Dionysus himself, at Thebes, of Icarius in Attica, and Pegasus at Eleutherae,[20] and its conformity to the basic myth of the prophets of Dionysus leaves it open to the strongest suspicions. Nevertheless, we must conclude that Archilochus' role in the Parian Dionysus cult was significant enough to make the canonical story appropriate, especially since the rest of Greece likewise believed in the poet's apostolic connection with the god of wine. A collection of hymns called the *Iobacchoi* (311, 323W) was gathered around his name, and though modern scholars doubt that he composed these particular songs, we know on first-hand authority that he put his own stamp upon certain Bacchic rites. In an unknown context he boasted of his own mastery, and then made good his boast by adding (120W; cf. 194W),

ὡς Διωνύσου ἄνακτος καλὸν ἐξάρξαι μέλος
οἶδα διθύραμβον οἴνωι συγκεραυνωθεὶς φρένας.

just as I know how to lead (wits thunderstruck with wine)
the dithyramb, Lord Dionysus' splendid song.[21]

Archilochus was associated in the book sources with two other cults as well, those of Demeter and Heracles. The connection with Demeter is made by Pausanias (10.28.3), who found a man labelled Tellis paired

---

[18] Kontoleon, in discussing where the cult might have been brought from, says, 'sicherlich nicht aus Thasos' (*FH* X, 35), which seems an odd certainty, since there is evidence of a strong early Dionysus cult on that island.

[19] On the Dionysiac anecdote of E III, see G. A. Privitera, 'Archiloco e il ditirambo letterario pre-Simonideo', *Maia* 9 (1957) 95–110, and the comment of T. B. L. Webster, *Dith. Trag. and Comedy*[2], 10. M. Treu takes the stone literally and assumes that there was an actual trial of Archilochus; West (*Studies*, 25) interprets the bits of Dionysiac song that can be culled from the stone as obscene, assuming the grapes and figs to be sexual and translating Oipholios as 'The Screwer', presumably a cult title of Dionysus.

[20] On the apostles of Dionysus, see M. Massenzio, *Cultura e Crisi permanente: la 'xenia' dionisiaca* (Rome 1970).

[21] West (*Studies*, 131) would join this fragment with 118W ('If only I could touch Neobule's hand, as surely as I know how . . . etc.'), and make them come from a drinking song, but to connect them because of the ὡς that appears in each, seems needlessly audacious.

with a certain Cleoboea and a sacred chest, in Polygnotus' painting of the underworld at Delphi. Making inquiries, he was told that these were the grandfather of Archilochus and the priestess who first introduced the mysteries to the island of Thasos; they were represented so far from home because the painter himself was a native of Thasos. Pausanias found nothing unlikely in the explanation, which has indeed a strong probability about it, since it gives this Tellis a son named Telesicles, as well as a famous grandson, and suggests that the political and religious founders of Thasos came from one and the same family.[22] Service in the *orgia* was commonly inherited, but whether or not it passed to Archilochus no one can say; we do know, however, that on Paros he was supposed to have composed a set of choral songs for the Festivals of Demeter (322W; cf. 169W).[23] We also know that Paros was the oldest centre of her worship outside Eleusis itself (the rites may have been brought from Athens as early as the eleventh century) and this means that a family whose names repeat the *telea* that they supervised must have been extremely august in its antiquity. As for Heracles (who also had a strong cult on Thasos where he and Dionysus were honoured together as the Sons of Zeus),[24] the poet's reputed connection with him was so strong that it influenced traditions in distant Olympia, where Archilochus was named as the first to have given the ritual cry that brought Heracles into every victory: τήνελλα καλλίνικε, χαῖρε ἄναξ Ἡράκλεις (324W; cf. Pindar *O*.9.1 and Schol.).[25]

[22] Frazer was sceptical, as was Dieterich (*Nekyia*[2] 1913, 69), and Crusius (*RE* ii, 490) suggested that Tellis and Telesicles were doubles. Others, however, have accepted Pausanias' account; see W. Gober, *RE* sv 'Tellis': 'Im Priestergeschlecht der Kabirischen Demeter kann ein solcher Name sich recht gut vererbt haben'. M.Treu (*Archilochus*, Munich 1959, 250) supposes that it may have been Tellis, not Telesicles, who was the founder of the colony on Thasos, and also assumes that Cleoboea must have been his wife, though this is by no means a necessary conclusion from the words of Pausanias, whose point seems to be that the two are depicted as *young*, though the deeds that brought them fame were done when they were old.) On the Polygnotus fresco, see M. Robertson, *A History of Greek Art* (Cambridge 1975) 266ff.

[23] West, in *IE*, lists the Iobacchoi as spurious, and indeed Hephaestion says that they were 'attributed' to Archilochus (322W); in his *Studies*, on the other hand (p. 24), West seems ready to accept these compositions, or other choral songs of an identical sort, as genuine works of Archilochus.

[24] Pindar, fr. 192, 36–43T, and Apollod. *Bibl.* 2.5.9, reflect the translation of the Heracles cult from Paros to Thasos to Torone. An early fifth-century city gate at Thasos was inscribed: 'The sons of Zeus by Semele and Alcmene of the long veils / Stand guard over this our city' (*IG* XII 8.356). For the cult of Heracles at Thasos, see D. van Berchem 'Sanctuaires d'Hercule-Melqart', *Syria* 44 (1967) 73–109, 307–36, and J. Pouilloux, 'L'Heracles Thasien', *REA* 76 (1974) 305–16, and for the Heracleion, see G. Daux, *Guide de Thasos*, 70ff., who describes the first temple, of 'splendid polygonal masonry', as built in the seventh century. See also D. Lazarides, *Thasos and its Peraia* (Athens 1971) 63, and B. Bergquist, *Herakles on Thasos* (Uppsala 1973) 17–27.

[25] On the victory cry, see Wilamowitz, *Glaube* I (Berlin 1931) 292, note 2, where its authenticity is doubted; also O. Schroeder, 'Archilochos "Tynnichos"', *Hermes* 69 (1934) 352. Archilochean paeans for Apollo were also known in antiquity, and Glaucus of

Hereditary religious duties and an apostolic function in respect to Dionysus prove that Archilochus was an aristocrat,[26] and so, of course, does his family connection with the foundation of Thasos. This colony is hardly mentioned in what is left of Mnesiepes' record, but the book sources confirm Telesicles, the father of Archilochus, as leader of the expedition that first took the northern outpost for Paros. This event occurred round about the year 680 B.C.,[27] and Archilochus will have followed somewhat later, when he was a youth, perhaps with a group of emigrants.[28] Certainly he was there as a young man, for his own mentions of Thasos (20–2, 89, 91–3; 102–4, 228W)[29] and of Thracian skirmishes show that he lived and fought in this second city where he had the honour of belonging to the founding family. At Thasos he was one of the very first men, not only as his father's son but also as the intimate of the effective chief of the place, that Glaucus to whom so many of his poems were addressed. Meanwhile, in the mother city as

---

Rhegium reported that Thaletas imitated them by making them longer and adding cretic rhythms (ps. Plut. *de musica* 10); on this aspect of Archilochus' work, see S. Gerevini, 'L'Archiloco perduto e la tradizione critico-letteraria', *PP* 9 (1954) 256–64, and J. A. Notopoulos, 'Archilochus the Aoidos', *TAPA* 97 (1966) 311–15. Among the surviving fragments, there are in addition four more that seem to be hymns (26, 108, 120, 121) and there are mentions of the following gods: Ares (1.18, 110), Apollo (26), Hephaestus (9, 108), Dionysus (120; c.f. 194), Zeus (98), Athena (94, 98), *daimōn* (210W).

[26] On Archilochus' religious duty and aristocratic standing, see Treu, *FH* X, 155.

[27] For the date of the foundation of Thasos, see Jacoby, *RE* sv 'Thasos' and for Telesicles as founder, Euseb. *Pr. ev.* 6.7.6; Steph. Byz. sv *Thasos*. A. J. Graham in 'The foundation of Thasos', *BSA* 73 (1978) 81ff., puts the date closer to 660 B.C., on the basis of archaeological evidence (see esp. p. 87). Graham brings a bracing scepticism to the tale of the colony's foundation, which he assumes was invented at Delphi in the fourth century. He rejects all testimony connecting Archilochus or his family with the first expedition, and he even approves Tarditi's suggestion that the name Telesicles was a later invention (80, note 184). In the end, however, his own arguments rest on silence, as he admits (77–8), and upon the myth of the Delphian propaganda machine (79f.). There will have been an *oikistes* named in the Parian/Thasian tradition, and it is very hard to see how Delphi could have erased that name and substituted another, whether real or invented. And who can believe that Archilochus' name reached the fourth century without having a patronymic attached?

[28] The Sosthenes stone suggests that Demeas had arranged the order of the events reflected in the fragments in a sequence like this: (1) Koiranos and the legendary past; (2) embassy of Peisistratus' son to the Thracians; (3) victory over the Naxians; (4) Hermes saved me; (5) Glaucus at Thasos; (6) 1000 men and 1000 women (a colonising move?); (7) a Parian-Thasian victory in battle. This order brings Archilochus to military age – as in (4) – before what seems to be a colonising move (6), which might mean that Archilochus was grown before the colony was actually planted, that emigrants went out to Thasos in several waves (so Lazarides, op. cit., p. 17), or that the reference in (6) is to some other move of colonists (that from Thasos to Torone?). Oenomaus of Gadara *FGH* II 373 reports an oracle given to Archilochus, ordering him to Thasos, which suggests a tradition that he reduplicated his father's foundation in his own maturity. For a full discussion of Archilochean chronology, see still F. Jacoby, 'The date of Archilochus', *CQ* 35 (1941) 97ff.

[29] Fragments mentioning Paros: 89, 116; cf. 94, 98W.

in the colony, he was eminent among the nobles.[30] The Mnesiepes inscription tells of membership in embassies, heroic action against the Naxians, and above all of poetic services, for, according to the stone, Archilochus sang his fellow citizens to war, much as Callinus and Tyrtaeus did theirs. For the Parians, his was the voice of the aristocrat's duty (cf. 89–90W), and it was upon Paros that his later fame reflected, as the existence of an Archilocheion there so firmly recognises.

The company he kept and the influence he commanded show that Archilochus lived as a powerful noble in both Paros and Thasos, and consequently the old report of his bastardy[31] loses its credibility. It evidently arose from a misunderstanding of something that the poet himself said, for Critias (one of Athens' Thirty Tyrants) illustrates the foolishness of self-accusation in this way: 'Take the example of Archilochus. If the poet had not told us in his own words that his mother was a slave named Enipo, that he left Paros for Thasos because of poverty, that he made enemies and abused even his friends, that he was lecherous and violent, and finally that he threw his sword away, we would never have known these shameful facts about him!' (fr. 44, ii, p. 396D–K). Obviously the speaker had a particular line of verse in mind, as the source of each of these 'facts', and most of them we too can match with a surviving fragment. There is nothing, however, in the lines that we know to explain the reference to a slavish mother,[32] and one wonders what sort of verse it could be that Critias was remembering. Why would a noble soldier claim to be someone who was not even a citizen? The subject of blood is beyond flippancy, and such a statement would have nothing in common with the bravado confession of cowardice that was meant as a jibe at the hypocrisy of others. A fighting poet might call someone else the son of a slave, but never himself, unless he were quoting an enemy,[33] to whom worse was to be returned. It might be some such deft parry of another's slander that had lodged in Critias' head, but it seems more likely that he was taken in by a characteristic bit of fantasy. The name Enipo, after all, is very close to the Homeric word that means 'rebuke' (*enipē*), and probably the Archilochean song in question was one in which the poet

---

[30] The tradition that Archilochus was a mercenary probably comes from a misunderstanding of 40W, where the poet says with exasperation, 'I shall even be called an "ally" as if I were a Carian' (καὶ δὴ 'πίκουρος ὥστε Κὰρ κεκλήσομαι). Archilochus calls Paros *polis* in the epodes, according to Steph. Byz. sv *Paros*, thus suggesting that he thought of himself as a citizen of that place.

[31] On Archilochus' bastardy (Aelian *VH* 10.13) see the remarks of Tarditi, op. cit., 125, and of Kontoleon and Pouilloux, at *FH* X, 78 and 81.

[32] The Sosthenes stone, B col. iv, has the words μητρὸς αὐτῆς and nothing more.

[33] For a poetic quotation of an enemy, compare Solon 33W. It should, however, be noted that Odysseus could call himself a bastard son of a slave mother when he was inspired by Zeus in the clever deceptions necessary to vengeance (*Od.* 14.202); see the discussion of K. Latte, op. cit., 385–90.

claimed to be the Son of Contumely, a lady who was no Thracian slave but instead the servant of the Muses.[34] If so, the poet did not pretend in any sense to be a bastard, but rather rejoiced in his legitimate connection with the hoary practice of abuse.

His modern admirers have enjoyed presenting Archilochus not only as a mercenary and a bastard, but also as one whose life was crude and dangerous even by the standards of a very primitive time.[35] His poverty, however, seems to have been no more genuine than his bastardy, for it is not true that his two island homelands were backward and miserably poor. Paros was not a sterile bit of marble jutting profitlessly out of the sea, nor was Thasos a mean and uncomfortable spot where colonists were harassed by savages and rival Naxians. On the contrary, the two islands between which Archilochus divided his life were prosperous places, alive to all the explosive changes that marked the half century between 700 and 650 in Hellenic history – the appearance of the alphabet, the acceptance of new ways of knowing and proving, and the proliferation of Near Eastern embellishments.[36] Archilochus' contemporaries were not penurious warriors sunk in a geometric obsession with the past, but men who moved constantly between Thrace and the Cyclades and who knew Asia Minor and mainland Greece as well. They frequented the great religious centres at Delos and Delphi, they visited Eretria, Ionia and the Bosporos, and they shared in the general questing confidence that brought the Greek dark ages to an end.

It pleased Archilochus, in a moment of bad temper, to represent the Parians as a nation reduced to eating figs and fish (116W), but the truth seems to be that the population by no means grubbed for its livelihood. Paros was inhabited by a ruling class of urbane and active merchant-nobles who warred with their neighbours, the Naxians, as much by bribery as by clashing arms. Beneath these men there was a class of artists and artisans who knew the fashions of Ionia and who left their own engaging mark on prevailing Cycladic styles.[37] Their

[34] Compare the likewise allegorical name, Euphemus, given to the father of Stesichorus and see the remarks of J. Vürtheim, *Stesichoros. Fragmente u. Biographie* (Leipzig 1919) 100. On Enipo, see Welcker, *Kl. Schr.* V. 134. West (*Studies*, 28) notes that the name Enipo is 'suspiciously apt for an iambographer's mother'; cf. Nagy, op. cit., 193. G. Tarditi, op. cit., 125–6, would, on the other hand, make this the sacerdotal name of a woman of high rank.

[35] P. Green, *The Shadow of the Parthenon* (Berkeley 1972) 159, speaks of Archilochus' 'harsh, primitive, dangerous existence'.

[36] Compare the statement of Pouilloux, *FH* X, 75: 'Le résultat de cette enquête est encore de nous révéler qu'Archiloque est issu d'une île, où la production artistique et le goût etaient vivants, exigeants. Le poète cesse ainsi d'être un isolé pour devenir le compagnon de ces artisans habiles ...' For Archilochean evidence of prosperity, notice the luxury of Peisistratus' embassy, and the attempt to bribe Thasians with gold, both reflected in 93aW.

[37] On Parian artisans and especially on Parians as the makers of the so-called Melian pottery, see Kontoleon, *FH* X, 57ff., and G. Daux, *Guide de Thasos* (Paris 1967), 158.

pottery, sculpture and bronze veneers are found throughout the Aegean area and on the mainland too, and their sale must have brought considerable profit to the island. When these people were transplanted to Thasos as colonists, they quickly wrought a great change in an island already open to trade,[38] and the city they built there in the seventh century was a rich and sophisticated place where archaeologists have found sanctuaries, elegant walls, ivories from Phoenicia and Ionia, Rhodian gems, Macedonian bronzes, Phrygian fibulae and pottery that shows contact with Corinth and the Cyclades. Thasos was a point from which the opposite Thracian shore could be exploited, but it was no rough military outpost.[39] There is no sign of any major war in the early part of the century, and no reason to think that rival Naxians were operating anywhere near,[40] though there were of course expeditions to the Thracian mainland and perhaps some skirmishing among the colonists themselves. With characteristic ambiguity of emotion and incongruity of image Archilochus likened the island to 'a donkey spine crowned with untamed woods' (21W) and insisted that it was no paradise (22W),[41] but he also said it was where every dissatisfied Greek came looking for a better chance (102W).[42]

Much that has been said about the life of Archilochus has thus had to be modified,[43] and modification is necessary also in some of the descriptions of his poetry that have been hallowed by repetition. We have been asked to listen to an Archilochus who broke out of his own time – one who could send a message direct from an inner, wholly personal 'I' to a 'you' who might be ourselves. Popularisers have made him a 'blazing original' who told dirty jokes, cursed the establishment and loathed all that was stiff and proper, and even scholars have spoken of him as a linguistic rebel and the inventor of a new 'realism'

---

[38] On the wealth of Thasos, see J. Pouilloux, *FH* X, 22, and G. Daux, *Guide de Thasos*, 175. Graham (op. cit. 88ff.) argues that the island's minerals had attracted a Phoenician trading colony in the period just before the coming of the Parians.

[39] There was evidently a siege of Thasos by Thracians, in revenge for the killing of a Thracian chieftain (92W, see below, p. 37), but it is to be noted that the siege was in the end bought off in obedience to an oracle.

[40] On Aegean alliances and rivalries in the seventh century, see G. Huxley, 'Neleids in Naxos and Archilochus', *GRBS* 5 (1964) 21ff., and A. J. Podlecki, 'Archilochus and Apollo', *Phoenix* 28 (1974) 1ff.

[41] The spot that *is* a paradise in 22W is 'the lovely, longed-for, delicious land on the banks of Siris'. This is sometimes thought to be a mythical place perhaps fabulously located in Magna Graecia, but F. Bossi, 'Archiloco et la Propontide', *RFIC* 103 (1975) 129–35, expanding on a suggestion made by L. Braccesi (*RFIC* 101; 1973, 220–4), believes that the reference is to a river in the Propontis, and that the Koiranos myth referred to in 192W is evidence of Parian colonial interest in that area.

[42] 102W: The phrase Πανελλήνων ὀϊζύς might mean Greek men with reason to wail, men bewailed by all of Greece, or men who will call up a wail from Greece; Pouilloux (*FH* X, 13) translates 'la misère du peuple Grec entier'. Compare the τρισοιζυρὴν πόλιν of 228W and perhaps 163W.

[43] The received view is well expressed by Green, op. cit., 155, whose statements do not differ in any substantive way from those made by H. Fränkel and B. Snell.

that was hard and impervious to time. The picture is in its way
attractive, but nevertheless a closer study of the only evidence we
have – the fragments of Archilochus' poetry – must change some of its
outlines. The verse that survives is by no means as iconoclastic or
even as vernacular in tone as it has been said to be, and instead of
strong subjectivity it is marked by a strong professional discipline. All
of which means that just as the bastard mercenary soldier must give
way to a restless merchant-aristocrat, so the insubordinate 'individual'
singer must retire before an artist who works within a proud and
recognised tradition as a poet of blame.

As an elegist, Archilochus conformed to the practices of his contemporaries, producing songs that voice the emotions and needs of his
kind, his group or his community. He eschewed the epic genre because
he had audiences and intentions of quite another sort, but he was
familiar with the Homeric poems, as his frequent borrowings[44]
(already noted and collected in antiquity) show. Oddly enough, his
Homerisms also testify to the traditional nature of his iambic poetry,
for their easy presence in lines where, for metrical reasons, they ought
to be awkward, is a witness to the antiquity of this more popular kind
of song. Only where the second metre was familiar and secure could
these dactylic phrases have been absorbed into an alien rhythm without upsetting it, and the assurance with which Archilochus handles
them proves that he addresses ears well accustomed to the single-
short sound. The ancients of course thought of him as the inventor of
iambics, and certainly he seems to have improved this art, for the
mixed metres and irregular lines that were his speciality are not to
be found before him.[45] Nevertheless, the ease with which his iambic

[44] On Archilochus' use of Homeric language, see D. Page, *FH* X, 126–53. Page's
attempt to show that Archilochus' poetry was orally composed has been dealt with by
Geoffrey Kirk, 'Formular language and oral quality', *YCS* 20 (1966) 172–4. It may be
noted that the Cologne fragment now strengthens the argument against Page, since it
shows how little the poet was tempted to use the dactylic cola of his epode as a lodging
place for Homeric formulae; it is, on the contrary, just in his dactylic phrases that he
is least Homeric, most original; see D. A. Campbell, 'The language of the new Archilochus', *Arethusa* 9 (1976) 154ff. On the conformity of the Archilochean elegy, see A.
Scherer, *FH* X, 90ff.

[45] The word *iambos* makes its first appearance in a fragment of Archilochus (215W),
where it seems to refer either to song in general (in distinction from feasting and other
pleasures) or else to a branch of song that is not meant to give pleasure (in distinction
to a second branch that is pleasureful); see the discussion of K. J. Dover, *FH* X, 186.
Archilochus is praised as the inventor of the iambic rhythm, and as the poet who
brought it to its fullest perfection, at Vell. Pat. 1.5; *AP* 7.674; Cic. *nat. deor.* 3.91; Ovid,
Ibis 53–4, 307; at ps. Plut. *de mus.* 28.1141A he is named as the author of the (presumably iambic) recitation to the music of the pipe called παρακαταλογή. In contradiction,
note the report of the Suda (4.360.7 and 4.363.1) that Semonides was the first to use
iambs for personal abuse. On the antiquity of iambic rhythms, see Page, *FH* X, 150;
Dover, ibid. 204; West, *Studies*, 22–39; G. Nagy, *Comparative Studies in Greek and
Indic Meter* (Cambridge, Mass. 1974) passim. In dissent, see Kirk, op. cit., 172, who
calls the argument for the antiquity of epodic and single short rhythms 'interesting',
but insists that 'no more than a possibility can be regarded as established'.

versification observes a set of subtle rules shows him to be working in a form that has grown flexible with time, and this conclusion is borne out by the appearance of single-short metres in maxims, proverbs and early inscriptions, as well as by their association with certain cult celebrations of great antiquity.[46]

It may be that Archilochus' new song-shapes came, like the orientalising motifs of pottery and metalcraft, from Ionia. His choice of a highly stylised Ionic dialect[47] and his cleverness in excising all the Aeolisms from his Homeric language seem to point that way, but however the question of influence is settled, one thing at least is sure. The iambic songs that Archilochus sang at Paros and Thasos were not the sudden extempore outburst of a music that had not been heard before. Their sound was wholly different from that of a bardic recitation, but it had long been familiar in banquet halls and public places, and their metres had been heard in fields and workshops and temples and sacred groves for as long as men could remember.

Archilochus did not invent iambic metres, nor did he invent the passionate first-person statement that for many critics defines lyric poetry. Popular songs have always used the first person, their singers becoming for the length of the performance identical with an 'I' whose emotion or history is told, and this was a convention that Archilochus often chose to follow.[48] His songs were meant to be repeated at other places and times – they would become part of a permanent repertoire – and so he made use of an assumed or a generalised identity that could be easily passed along. Sometimes his material was frankly fictional and his character wholly assumed, for the rules of banquet singing allowed a man to sing as a lovelorn girl, a youth to imitate an oldster, or an aristocrat to ape a vulgar simpleton.[49] Songs of this sort were so common, in fact, that the poet had no need to proclaim his borrowed identity (though he often did so); he could simply step before his listeners with his 'I' already disguised, and so give them the pleasure of divining whose voice it was that they heard. At other times Archilochus treated feelings or events that had been part of his own experience, but even here his subjectivity was disciplined by a kind of character-drawing, for he spoke always as 'I, the soldier', 'I, the lover',

[46] On the use of iambs in Demeter cult, see Treu, *Archilochus*, pp. 150f.

[47] On Archilochus' Ionic dialect, see Scherer, *FH* X, 93.

[48] On Archilochus and primitive popular song, see Dover, *FH* X, 201ff.

[49] On the occasions for early elegy and iambic song, see West, *Studies*, 11ff. and 31ff., and Nagy, *Arethusa* 9, 195ff. Because he is developing a theory that connects iambic song with Attic drama, West supposes that the references in Archilochus and Hipponax to sexual parts mean that the performer was costumed after the fashion of the padded dancers seen on pottery (*Studies*, 29). By parallel reasoning we would have to say that if a song says 'Glaucus!' Glaucus must have been standing in the flesh at the singer's side. Worse, this notion of costume turns the symposium into a highly complicated affair: did one assume the costume as one took up the lyre or did one dine padded, in the expectation of singing?

or most frequently as 'I, the poet with an abusive tongue'. Such semi-mimetic practices opened the song to repetition, while they also answered the demand of archaic listeners for piquant entertainment, but they were after all only a sharper version of the transformation that occurs whenever anyone announces, by casting his speech into metrical form, that it is no longer an acquaintance, lover, enemy or friend who speaks, but a poet who sings now. Archilochus' songs are his own, but they were shaped by the poet Archilochus, by the other poets who had sung before him, and also by their audience of listening townspeople, soldiers or fellow banqueteers. Some were meant for public ceremonies – funerals, military reviews, or festive rituals – and some perhaps were made for less regular occasions when roaming bands of men used the streets for serenades that might be appreciative or the opposite.[50] Most of his work, however, was sung and resung at table, among a group of companions who amused one another with a ceaseless, bracing anthology of wit and praise and cruelty. Whenever a new song was proposed, it was expected to meet if not to cap the older favourites, and to exploit that archaic style long ago described by Huizinga as 'at one and the same time ritual, entertainment, artistry, riddlemaking, doctrine, persuasion, sorcery, soothsaying, prophecy and competition'.[51]

---

[50] Insulting serenades were customary on Naxos, according to Aristotle (*Naxiōn politeia*, fr. 558R).

[51] J. Huizinga, *Homo Ludens*, tr. R.F.C. Hull (London 1949) 120.

Ares and the Muses

It is true that Archilochus says 'I am', but he completes his sentence with a statement that concerns his profession, not his inner being.[1] What he is, he says, is a man with a double calling and a double set of abilities (1W):

εἰμὶ δ' ἐγὼ θεράπων μὲν Ἐνυαλίοιο ἄνακτος
καὶ Μουσέων ἐρατὸν δῶρον ἐπιστάμενος,

I am servant to Lord Enyalios and also
one who understands the Muses' lovely gifts.

Probably he offered this self-definition in validation of some piece of elegiac advice, but with it he does more than merely claim experience and persuasive power. The lines disclose a paradox, and it is one that the singer is evidently proud of as he insists that he is functionally split between a pair of trades that contradict each other.[2] Enyalios is Ares at his most barbaric,[3] and with this name Archilochus announces that war, as he practises it, is hideous and cruel, but then with his next breath he says that as a singer his deeds are lovely and desirable, a reflection of the Muses' will. He is at once an active lover of discord and a meditative practitioner of harmony; a sceptical soldier and a poet with a stubborn illusion of beauty; a man who lives upon im-

---

[1] Cf. the similarly professional claim of 120W ('I know how to lead the dithyramb . . .')

[2] Page, FH X, 134 would take this split profession as proof of a general archaic social revolution, but his conclusion is based upon his assumption that the Homeric poems, with their integrated men, portrayed actual social institutions. J. Pouilloux, ibid., 26, says of these lines, 'L'homme Archiloque n'est pas double; il se bat à coup de lance, à coup de mots', but the phrase ἐρατὸν δῶρον does not suggest that the poet meant, in these lines, to refer to his special calling as an abusive poet.

[3] R. Harder, 'Zwei Zeilen von Archilochus', Hermes 80 (1952) 381ff. = Kl. Schriften (Munich 1960) pp. 175–9, points out the ugly Homeric associations of the name Enyalios. Other references to Ares are at 3W, 18W (where he is μιηφόνος), 110W (where he is a 'leveller' of men, with reference to Homer's ξυνὸς Ἐνυάλιος at Il.18.309).

mediate opportunity while he searches for the aspects of life that are worth remembering in song.[4]

Archilochus' two vocations were evidently most at ease with one another when he was called upon to compose songs for the whole community, but unfortunately only a few fragments of this sort remain. There is no way of knowing whether these songs that used a public voice were performed at banquets or delivered to the town in public gatherings; all we know is that the Parians who frequented the Archilocheion remembered their poet chiefly as one who had sung them to war with eager, heated advice.[5] Some of the fragments are elegiac and some use the single-short rhythms of cult and popular songs, but in all the scant examples the two aspects of the Archilochean mind can be felt in collaboration. The singer goes to work to create practical courage in the hearts of his listeners, and there is a sense of hard urgency but also of confident artistry as the rhetoric of exhortation is heightened by touches that are sometimes smoothly traditional, sometimes almost crude. One tetrameter piece, for example, rouses its audience to a sense of bitter communality by repeating a popular insult against the non-agricultural Parians and calling out, 'Oh fish-fed fellow citizens, take notice of my words!' (109W).[6] Another (116W) goads its hearers into loyalty by crying, 'Go ahead, give up Paros with her figs and her sailor's life!' In these cases the mode is attack, but there are two other songs, quoted by the Mnesiepes stone, that work in a different way, reminding listeners of successful past actions and attempting, with a dynamic something like that of prayer, to force a repetition of them. The servant of Enyalios, however, cannot bring himself to represent these deeds of the past as wholly glorious; they were merely cases of luck that he would like to reactivate. In one performance (94W) he shows Athena as she 'once more' puts heart

---

[4] The usual notion of a 'double' man was that one half of him must necessarily be false; so, at *Il*.9.312, ἐχθρὸς γάρ μοι κεῖνος ὁμῶς Ἀίδαο πύλῃσιν / ὅς χ᾽ ἕτερον μὲν κεύθη ἐνὶ φρεσίν, ἄλλο δὲ εἴπῃ; cf. E. *Rhes.* 395 and 423; also *AP* 10.95 μισῶ τὸν ἄνδρα τὸν διπλοῦν πεφυκότα / χρηστὸν λόγοισι, πολέμιον δὲ τοῖς τρόποις. On the other hand, note the extended praise of doubleness of power in Pindar's *O*.6.

[5] See the introduction to 89W (from the Mnesiepes stone) and compare the remark of the anonymous metrician who cited 88W as a case where tetrameters were used ἐπὶ τῶν θερμῶν ὑποθέσεων. Demeas called Archilochus 'citizen' and made mention of his reverence and enthusiasm in behalf of his fatherland (*IG* XII.5.445, 2–4). On the songs for the city, see Kontoleon, *FH* X, 39ff., and E. Romagnoli, 'Sulla gnomica Bacchilidea' *SIFC* 7 (1899) 171 for a discussion of Archilochus' influence upon Solon.

[6] This song was evidently much admired in the fifth century, for its opening was parodied by Eupolis (fr. 357), Cratinus (fr. 198 Kock) and Aristophanes (*Pax* 603f). The key word, λιπερνήτης, is of uncertain meaning, but it was taken in antiquity to denote poverty and specifically a want of vegetable food; Aristoxenus (fr. 138 Wehrli) thought that it described fishermen forced to live from the sea instead of off the fat of the land. The epithet caused K. Latte (op. cit., 389ff.) to conclude that the song was addressed only to the poor of the city, but that is to suppose a kind of political situation of which there is no hint in any record.

into 'miserable' Parians who have almost lost their island to the Naxians,[7] and in the other (98W) 'they' (outside the walls, perhaps on scaling ladders and using iron-clad war machines) almost take the city that 'we' defend with javelins; then in the nick of time, with the aid of Athena and Zeus, the enemy is put to flight.

A third song from the stone makes itself formally an imperative call upon an absent commander, Erxias, demanding a relief expedition (89W).[8] It pretends to work upon its distant addressee with a description of immediate disaster (something 'dries in the sun'[9] and men are 'longing to attack the Naxians') that is like the present need section of a cletic hymn. To this there is added a petition for aid (wrath to be suppressed, 'brothers', 'courage') that seems, with its *gnōthi nun* to correspond to the *elthe kai nun* of an epiphany prayer. Meanwhile, of course, the song's actual pressure is being exerted upon its present listeners, the men in need of relief, and for them it is validated by a movement of the poet's own courageous spirit (*tauta moi thumos*, 14) and made effective with reassuring echoes of religious phrasing. The sense created is that god-sent help will certainly arrive.

A similar conceit is used in another tetrameter song that treats a public situation as if it were a private one. The poet this time seems to lay his hand upon the shoulder of the man of the hour, to say (105W):

Γλαῦχ', ὅρα· βαθὺς γὰρ ἤδη κύμασιν ταράσσεται
πόντος, ἀμφὶ δ' ἄκρα Γυρέων ὀρθὸν ἵσταται νέφος,
σῆμα χειμῶνος, κιχάνει δ' ἐξ ἀελπτίης φόβος.

---

[7] Because of the epithet πολύκλαυτος (line 3), Lasserre assumed that the song shows Athena encouraging the Naxians, but would the celebration of a Parian victory include a scene in which Athena visited the battlefield in the interest of the enemy? The continuing emphasis upon land or ground (ἐπὶ χθόνα, 4, and ἐξεχώρησεν γύας, 5) shows that this was a case of invasion, which fact would certainly justify calling the Parians a 'much-lamenting folk'; however, the proper reading in line 3 might be, as Steffen suggested (*Eos* 47, 1954, 57) αὐτὴ γῆς πολυκλαύτου, in which case the occupied land would be 'much-lamented'.

[8] Erxias is also named at 88W: 'Erxias, where does this unfortunate army reassemble?' It is possible that the name hides behind the ερξω that stands at the beginning of 110W, and it is also remotely possible that he was an otherwise unknown hero or god, as West supposes (*Studies*, 126). The simplest assumption, however, is that he was in command of some section of the Parians at Thasos, and that he is asked to gather men from Thasos and Torone and bring them to the aid of Paros. For other interpretations, see West (loc. cit.), who takes the sense of lines 19–20 to be 'some have fallen at Thasos and Torone, others have died at sea', and Lasserre (LB 81), who places the song on Thasos, where he supposes the Naxians to have invaded and split the Parian army. Against Lasserre it should be noted that there is no evidence that Naxians were operating in important numbers in the waters around Thasos; see Huxley, *GRBS* 5, 21ff. and Podlecki, *Phoenix* 28, 1ff.

[9] For corpses drying, cf. 107W and 292W.

Look, Glaucus, how the troubled sea pitches in its depths!
A pile of cloud stands upon the heights of Gyrai, signifying
storm, and fear advances towards us from the unforseen.

Within the fiction of a shipboard scene[10] the singer speaks to Glaucus as a mate might to his captain, pointing out what he knows the other sees.[11] Ostensibly Glaucus is urged to give the commands that will mean that the ship is under control, but the true voice of the poem is that of Archilochus the civic counsellor, and he speaks not to his friend but to the endangered city. He tells the Parians that their commander is present and aware, and he makes them believe that they can meet the skirmish ahead, just as they have so often met foul weather when they were at sea.[12]

The songs so far described have all tried to move the minds and limbs of listeners positively, towards courageous, aggressive action, but there was at least one of the political poems that strove for an opposite effect. This is a piece preserved by Sosthenes about the son of a certain Peisistratus (93aW):

ἄνδρας ‥₍.₎ωλεῦντας αὐλὸν καὶ λύρην ἀνήγαγεν   5
ἐς Θάσον κυσὶ Θρέϊξιν δῶρ' ἔχων ἀκήρατον
χρυσόν, οἰκείωι δὲ κέρδεϊ ξύν' ἐποίησαν κακά—

he led a company that played both flute and lyre
up to Thasos, carrying, as gifts for Thracian dogs,
pure gold, and there for private gain they did much public harm.

Demeas' introduction is in ruins, as are the first four lines of the citation, and the situation described is consequently worse than obscure. It would seem that a group of elegant youths[13] had been

[10] On the allegory of 105W, see F. Adrados, 'Origen del Tema de la nave del estado', *Aegyptus* 35 (1955) 206–10.

[11] There has been some discussion about the location of the heights of Gyrai; Bowra ('Signs of storm', *CR* 54 (1940) 127ff.) put them in Euboea and believed that the poem referred to the Lelantine War. D'Arcy Thompson responded ('Archilochus fr. 56', *CR* 55 (1941) 67) by insisting that no specific locality was meant, while F. H. Sandbach suggested that the heights belonged to Tenos, noting that Cicero was on Delos when he spoke of them ('Ἄκρα Γυρέων again', *CR* 56 (1942) 63). Since the storm is imaginary, and since 'clouds over Gyrai' was probably a proverbial expression for bad weather, the actual location of the spot can make very little difference to the meaning of the song.

[12] If 106W is a continuation of the same song, as West supposes, following Croenert (see *Studies*, 128–9), the singer goes on to urge specific actions ('let's slacken sail') and then turns from his address to Glaucus to make a prayer (to Zeus or Poseidon, presumably) that begs for salvation ('restrain the following wind'). If 106W is a separate song, it is probably likewise allegorical and likewise intended to bring the minds of listeners into a confident readiness for action. These songs should be compared with the similar ship-in-storm poems of Alcaeus; see below, pp. 151–5

[13] On flute-playing as an Archilochean emblem of effeminacy, see F. Lasserre, *Les Epodes d'Archiloque* (Paris 1950) 53–61, where the materials are assembled in support of an argument that is extremely exaggerated.

appointed to carry valuable gifts to the barbarian enemy on the coast-
land facing Thasos, that they misbehaved in some way that has to do
with the gift, and that Archilochus leads his audience in scornful
anger against them. But why was such a gift being sent?[14] At first
glance, this musical embassy from Paros seems to fit into a similarly
shameful episode that was remembered by the erudite Callimachus
(fr.204Pf.=Arch. fr. 92W), one in which some Parians assassinated a
Thracian prince who was named Oisydres. In retaliation for the murder, Thasos was besieged by Thracians who then had to be bought off
by order of an oracle, and it is tempting to identify Peisistratus and
his gift of gold with this rescue of Thasos from the angry tribesmen of
Oisydres. There is, however, a serious obstacle to such an identification, for the Oisydres tale ends with the raising of the siege. The
Parian bribe, in other words, must have reached the proper hands,
and this means that it cannot have been the same as the gold which
is misused by the present melodious ambassadors. If they had any
part at all in the story of Oisydres, they must have been either the
original assassins (the commentary on the stone says that they killed
some Thracians), or else they must have been involved in some subsequent phase of the negotiations – one that they frustrated by their
selfish greed. They may of course have been concerned in some other
episode entirely, but whatever the details of their embassy, it is clear
that the politicians of Paros were paying off the same enemies with
whom the soldiers of Thasos were expected to fight, and that this fact
exacerbates Archilochus' anger against the thieving ambassadors.
Since some of them (according to Demeas) came back to Paros after
their crime and were put to death, the present song might have been
part of the public abuse that preceded their execution, but of this no
one can be sure. It might with equal probability belong to a later time,

---

[14] Before the citation of the Archilochean lines, the commentary from Demeas says
something about a Parian tradition that told of Thracians willingly returning *chrēmata*,
and West, in the attempt to work this into the flute-playing embassy, proposes the
following scenario (*Studies*, 127): the embassy is carrying gold to Thasos where it is
supposed to be put to public use; they take the gold instead to the Thracians and use
it to hire barbarians to perform some deed in their own interest; then they kill their
hirelings and take the money back again, but when they try to make off they are finally
themselves killed. This complicated scheme requires elaborate exegesis for the phrase
'as gifts for Thracian dogs', which in its natural interpretation expresses the intentions
of the Parians who sent the embassy in the first place. And why would money used in
such a way have been returned more probably than money intended as a gift of state?
V. Steffen, 'Ad Archil. fr. tetram. observ. crit.' *Eos* 47 (1954) 51–62 suggested that the
young men did not belong to an embassy at all, but were Naxians in alliance with the
Thracians; an earlier theory was that they were mainland Greeks attempting to buy
their way into Thasos as rivals to the Parians. On these insoluble problems, see A.
Hauvette, *Archiloque* (Paris 1905) 56–8; L. Weber, 'ΣΥΚΑ ΕΦ' ΕΡΜΗΙ', *Philolog.* 74
(1971) 113ff.; C. M. Bowra, in Powell, *New Chapters* Third Series (Oxford 1933) 61–2;
Hiller von Gaertringen, *NGG* 2 Ser. I (1934) 41f.; S. Luria, 'Zu Archilochos', *Philolog.*
105 (1961) 185–7; G. Huxley, op. cit., 23f.

and make use of this notoriously worthless group simply as an illustration. Either way, however, the lines incorporate the defamatory
genius of their poet at its solemn best, for they turn insidiously, from
what seems at first to be only a light charge of effeminacy, to a final
strong condemnation couched in almost Thucydidean terms (for private good they made a public evil). These men have perverted the
ideal, which is to procure the common good, if necessary at the cost of
private suffering, and so, where his other public songs urge their
listeners to make honourable deeds their own, this one demands that
a dishonourable one shall be rejected with a sharp and general scorn.

In the songs for the city the soldier is musical, the Muse practical,
as Archilochus urges his fellow-citizens not to look closely at present
realities but to put their faith in action, leadership, and the gods. In
the songs that treat the actualities of soldiering, however, songs presumably addressed only to his drinking companions, the ambivalence
of the man with a double profession is almost always felt. Here he
takes a sardonic pleasure in considering things as they are, and here
even success can be ugly, as the poet points out in a pair of lines about
a victory (101W):

ἑπτὰ γὰρ νεκρῶν πεσόντων, οὓς ἐμάρψαμεν ποσίν,
χείλιοι φονῆές εἰμεν,

They fled, seven of them fell, and each
of all our thousand claimed the kill!

The enemy are cowards who run from the field, but Archilochus and
his companions are base opportunists who preen themselves on exploits that they have not performed.

Once Archilochus reminds himself that fields grow rich when
corpses lie in their furrows (292W), but he is too intelligent for perfect
cynicism, too angry for resignation, and he would rather insist that
he is surrounded by ugliness because he has chosen it over all alternatives. With the strong pride of the disabused he praises meanness,
discomfort and solitude (and by implication scorns those who value
their opposites)[15] when he sings about life as it is defined by his first

---

[15] The poem reflects a kind of priamel: one man loves bread, another wine, a third
the symposium, but I trade all for the soldier's life. The discussion of the particular
meaning of the phrase ἐν δορί has been endless; Bowra insisted that it had to mean
exactly the same thing in each of its occurrences (*Annales de fil.* cl. 6, 1954, 37ff.) and
much of the consequent discussion has been hampered by this 'rule' (see e.g. Davison,
CR 74 (1960) 1ff.; Pocock *CR* 75 (1962) 179ff.; Ehrenberg, *CP* 57 (1962) 233ff.; Gentili,
Riv. di Fil. 93 (1965) 129ff.). The phrase has been said to mean 'at my spear,' 'on active
service', 'under arms', 'equipped with a spear', even 'on board ship' (reading δόρυ), and
recently G. Giangrande, in 'Archiloque au pilori', *QU* 14 (1972) 37ff., has proposed,
'being a prisoner at the pillory'. Giangrande is right in one thing, at least, and that is

profession (2W):[16]

ἐν δορὶ μέν μοι μᾶζα μεμαγμένη, ἐν δορὶ δ' οἶνος
'Ισμαρικός· πίνω δ' ἐν δορὶ κεκλιμένος.

For me, there's risen bread in my spear, Ismarian
    wine in my spear, and when I drink I couch with my spear.

This ironic nostalgia for what others think of as the worst is not confined to things physical but extends into aesthetic and moral matters as well, as Archilochus makes plain with a broken elegy whose pretended occasion is a storm at sea (4W):

ἀλλ' ἄγε σὺν κώ[θωνι θοῆς διὰ σέλματα νηὸς
    φοίτα καὶ κοίλ[ων πώματ' ἄφελκε κάδων,
ἄγρει δ' οἶνον [ἐρυθρὸν ἀπὸ τρυγός· οὐδὲ γὰρ ἡμεῖς
    νηφέμεν [ἐν φυλακῆι τῆιδε δυνησόμεθα.

Get moving with that cup along the benches of
    this swift-sailing bark; unseal the hollow jars
and pour the wine out to the dregs – we
    can't go thirsty on a watch like this!

In the fiction, the singer urges imaginary men to respond to the chaos of nature with a breach of discipline, and he seems to promise a moment of sublime solidarity as their reward. That moment of drunken defiance of both danger and order is recognised as worthy of the Muse, and it is conveyed to the actual men who listen to the song. They too will feel a perverse joy as they draw together in scorn, not of shipboard regulations, but of certain 'normal' views about the military. The common cup, brought into conjunction with the 'swift-sailing bark' and the 'hollow jars' measures the distance between war as they have tasted it and war as the elder poets described it,[17] and the discrepancy is evidently a source of bitter pleasure to them. Their war is not what Homer reported; it is filthier, and they are proud of the fact.

    The same ironic attachment to a falsely romanticised, truly hideous

---

his reminder that κεκλιμένος has a double sense, since it suggests both the joys of the banquet and the pain of being bent by an exhausting burden. For an extensive review, see D. Arnould 'Archiloque et le vin d'Ismaros', *Rev. de Phil.* 54 (1980) 284–94, where the sense is taken to be 'I eat and drink and sleep on watch'. For a recognition of a shift in the meaning of ἐν δορί, see H. D. Rankin 'Archilochus fg. 2D', *Emerita* 40 (1972) 460–74; N. F. Rubin 'Radical semantic shifts in Archilochus', *CJ* 77 (1981) 6–7.

[16] It is possible that Archilochus means to compare himself with Odysseus, for at *Od.* 9.451 that hero is on the coast of Thrace, at Ismaros, plundering and drinking wine.

[17] Page, *FH* X, 129ff., discusses the tension between epic and non-epic language in this fragment, emphasising the unexpected violence of the imperatives, and paraphrasing, 'Let us attack the casks and grab as much as we can get' (p.130).

profession, is captured in a double-edged description of Parian soldiers as they fight, 'graciously bestowing deadly guest-gifts on our enemies' (6W).[18] Here, a memory of the chivalric encounters of the Homeric poems lends a superb harshness to a phrase that dresses up the act of killing in order to make it more nakedly unpleasant. The Muses, in a sense, have supplied these epic foils that vilify even as they are being repudiated, but Archilochus did not always find their gifts so easy to manipulate, and even in the soldiering poems one can sense the lingering power of certain traditional ideals. Once, for example, he betrays a sense that fighting is not everywhere so ugly as it is with the Parians, and seems to feel something like a longing for an older and more stately form of war. Singing about a real or hypothetical battle on the island of Euboea,[19] he colours his professional interest in foreign techniques with a kind of praise (3W):

οὔτοι πόλλ' ἐπὶ τόξα τανύσσεται, οὐδὲ θαμειαὶ
σφενδόναι, εὖτ' ἂν δὴ μῶλον Ἄρης συνάγηι
ἐν πεδίωι· ξιφέων δὲ πολύστονον ἔσσεται ἔργον·
ταύτης γὰρ κεῖνοι δάμονές εἰσι μάχης
δεσπόται Εὐβοίης δουρικλυτοί.   5

There won't be many bows stretched, nor much fall
    of slingers' stones when Ares and his broil
move upon that plain. Swords will do their shrieking work
    instead, for that's the fight they're devils at,
the war-lords of Euboea.[20]

Euboeans were known for preserving the old ways of war, and Archilochus' admiration for the arcane splendour of their aristocratic sword-work is set off here by his implicit scorn for the modern, bought efficiency of classless light-armed troops. Euboeans drew themselves up on a field and swore to fight like heroes against heroic enemies,[21]

[18] The scholiast at Soph. *El.* 96 specifies these 'gifts' as τραύματα <καὶ> φόνοι. The same conceit is used in 12W, where men lost at sea are called ἀνιηρὰ Ποσειδάωνος ἄνακτος δῶρα; cf. the bitter ξείνιον at *Od.* 9.356f.

[19] Biographers sometimes conclude that these lines prove an Archilochean visit to Euboea and perhaps even that he participated in some phase of the Lelantine wars. Nevertheless, all that can be said for certain is that the poem, as its fiction, assumes a future Euboean engagement by unnamed allies or enemies who are of some interest to the singer's audience. Compare P. Oxy. 2508, an elegiac fragment ascribed to Archilochus that mentions battle, Eretria and Karystos.

[20] The word δεσπότης appears here for the first time.

[21] L. H. Jeffery, *Archaic Greece* (New York 1976) 65 notes that a stele found in Euboea records a pact made between the two armies of Chalkis and Eretria, promising μὴ χρῆσθαι τηλεβόλοις (published by Forrest, *Historia* 6, 1957, 163ff.); cf. the report of Strabo 10.448. Jacoby assumed that the lords of Euboea, like those of Magnesia and Colophon, fought on horseback (*CQ* 35 (1941) 108). For the contrast of bows and slings with hand-to-hand weapons, cf. the scornful words of Lycus at E. *HF*, 157–64.

but Parians, pushing into the barbarian stretches of Thrace or defending themselves from raiding Naxians, were forced, even though they were nobles, to fight like mercenaries.[22]

As a double man Archilochus could never know the complacency either of the nihilist or the idealist, and his difficulty is captured in a famous fragment that ostensibly scorns the outward trappings that glamorised the soldier (5W):[23]

ἀσπίδι μὲν Σαΐων τις ἀγάλλεται, ἣν παρὰ θάμνωι,
 ἔντος ἀμώμητον, κάλλιπον οὐκ ἐθέλων·
αὐτὸν δ' ἐξεσάωσα. τί μοι μέλει ἀσπὶς ἐκείνη;
 ἐρρέτω· ἐξαῦτις κτήσομαι οὐ κακίω.

Some Thracian tribesman flaunts my shield. I left it
 blameless in a bush – betrayed it there unwillingly –
and yet I saved myself, so what's that shield to me?
 To hell with it, I'll buy another every bit as good.

The singer claims to be guilty of an epic 'crime' and he offers its contemporary justification, once again insisting that he rejects false ideals and chooses the real, and yet he allows a nagging ambivalence to rest upon his lines.[24] The shield was abandoned in the disorderly retreat of a man who might have stood his ground to kill or be killed;[25] this much is made certain by a singer who insists that the object itself was unharmed and that its owner acted under duress. The action is thus one that would be called cowardly by anyone with illusions about courage,[26] and the first two lines are made so as to suggest to a listener that he ought indeed to find it distinctly shameful. It was not a noble enemy to whom the shield was lost, it was a barbarian, and on the

[22] Some of the same disenchantment with contemporary ways as compared with older ones is probably the ruling emotion in 216W: 'I shall be called (of all things) a Carian ally!' i.e., a mercenary.

[23] West, ad. loc., suggests that these four lines might represent the whole of the song; Fränkel thought otherwise (*WuF*², 56, note 3, and *DuP*², 152). As a piece of improvisation, it surely might have been launched, as is, for banquet consumption; if the song continued, it may have done so with further four-line units like this one, perhaps adding more examples of gestures of the same sort.

[24] This song used to be taken as a piece of simple, anti-epic iconoclasm; see, e.g., Fränkel, *DuP*², 153. For the more recent assertion of a community of thought between Archilochus and Homer, see H. Lloyd-Jones, *The Justice of Zeus* (Berkeley 1971) p. 39, J. Russo, 'The inner man', *GRBS* 15 (1974) 140ff. and Bernard Seidensticker, 'Archilochus and Odysseus', *GRBS* 19 (1978) 5ff.

[25] Page (*FH* X, p. 286) tried to argue that there was no engagement with the enemy implied, and consequently no question of cowardice raised; he supposed the song to be the poet's record of having carelessly left his shield behind when he moved from bivouac.

[26] The notion of cowardice is increased in the version reported by Sextus Empiricus (*Pyrrh. hypot.* 3.216), where a sense of retreat is lent by the words αὐτὸς δ' ἐξέφυγον at the opening of line 3.

other hand the shield itself was the sort that a noble should bear –
not just a bit of armour but an epic fossil distinguished by the old-
fashioned word *entos*.[27] The shield, in fact, is everything that its owner
is not, and the singer makes this clear by giving it the epithet that a
Homeric hero often wears, making it 'blameless'.

The first couplet thus represents a charge of anti-heroic conduct
levelled by the singer against himself, but the misplaced epithet prepares the song for the turn of thought that follows. A shield carries
the insignia of a noble warrior, but dress it how you will it is only a
thing, and the second pair of lines quickly strips this shield of its
symbolic power, reducing it to a mere object that can be bought and
sold. Survival is clearly more valuable than a piece of ox-hide, or even
of beaten metal, and the present singer is happy to buy his life at the
price of his claim to an outdated form of honour. This, at least, is what
he says in his capping lines, but Archilochus has lent those lines a
jerky flippancy that allows them to defy, but not to destroy what has
gone before.[28] In consequence, the full four-line suite conveys a deeper
impulse than mere rude rebellion against the old notions of battlefield virtue, for its final bravado labels this choice as one that was not
easy to make. The singer boasts that he has separated himself from
the sham of ancient pretensions, but his pride is evidently a mixed
emotion and he does not disguise the fact that it is an inglorious self
that he has preserved.[29] He has exposed a notion of honour that is
dependent upon outward trappings and held principally by cultured
strategists who eat leavened bread and couch on couches to drink. At
the same time, however, the Muse has led him to a final uncomfortable
truth, for what the song in its wholeness says is that actual battle is
sordid in part just because the knightly ideal has been left behind like
the original shield. The soldier may scorn others for not seeing what
war actually is, but the warrior-poet must scorn himself a bit, too, for
still wanting it to be finer.

War was to be stripped of its sham but Archilochus nevertheless
looked for virtues that could cover the actual soldier – (the 'man
bothered by lice' of 236W?) – with his own claim to be good of his kind.
Certain values were pretentious and irrelevant, but there were others
that commanded the respect even of a disillusioned man, and a pattern

---

[27] Page describes the word as 'already moribund' in epic (*FH* X, 110); this, however,
is the earliest occurrence of its singular form.

[28] See, with the contrary opinion, G. Broccia, Πόθος e Ψόγος (Rome 1959) 12, where
the conclusion is that the subsequent *psogos* of the shield drives out the *pothos* for it.

[29] In conjunction with the shield fragment one should read 127W: 'I made a mistake.
I have the impression that others have done the same', and 233W (apparently of a
moment when retreat became necessary): 'feet were of the highest value just there.'

of rejection and acclamation marks four tetrameter lines that were probably sung as part of a banquet's friendly rivalry (114W):[30]

οὐ φιλέω μέγαν στρατηγὸν οὐδὲ διαπεπλιγμένον
οὐδὲ βοστρύχοισι γαῦρον οὐδ' ὑπεξυρημένον,
ἀλλά μοι σμικρός τις εἴη καὶ περὶ κνήμας ἰδεῖν
ῥοικός, ἀσφαλέως βεβηκὼς ποσσί, καρδίης πλέως.

I don't like an officer who struts tall,
shaves, and curls his hair. Give me
a short bow-legged man, a gap between his knees
but steady on his feet and full of heart.

It may be that Archilochus meant this as a double portrait of himself and his friend Glaucus, who is twitted elsewhere for the niceness of his barbering ('Sing, Glaucus of the sculptured curl!' 117W). This is not just fashionable badinage, however, nor is it a simple attack upon military elegance, for the song does much more than assert that a true soldier is not a pretty thing. It brings foppishness into conjunction with physical unloveliness, chooses the second, but then reveals that the reason for this choice has little to do with the looks of either party.[31] The four lines end with the phrase 'full of heart' – this is evidently the essential element in the bandy-legged man and it is a psychic quality that is independent of externals, whether they be fine or crude.[32] In fact, though the form is different, one could compare this witty jibe from Archilochus to the elegiac priamel of Tyrtaeus (9D) in which all the accepted marks of magnificence – wealth, beauty, power

---

[30] For other examples of scolding of friends, see 124W, where Pericles is teased for coming uninvited to the feast; 58W, where someone is reported as singing shamelessly along with the flute girl; and 167W, where Charilas (or Charilaos, cf. 168W) is attacked as a glutton. Probably the witty syntactical *mot* about Leophilus belongs in the same category, though of course its meaning may be political (115W):

Now Leophilus rules, the power is Leophilus',
all belongs to Leophilus, so hear Leophilus!

The last phrase is dubious, since the case must be accusative and all codd. report ἄκουε, which ought to command the genitive. The joke may have lain just here; perhaps it is not the voice of Leophilus that all are to hear, but some bodily sound, so that he himself is the thing heard. The circumstances of 113W may have been much the same, raillery among comrades. There seems, however, to be no good reason to attach it to 112, as West proposes, or to restore the situation of 112–13 after his fanciful manner (i.e. city is besieged, Archus decides to marry, poet reproaches him for ill-timed interest in Aphrodite). It would seem to be just as likely that Archus, in 113, is being taunted for showy, 'Euboean' techniques of warfare, when a simpler use of the ordinary javelin would do the work – all, very likely, with a sexual *double entendre*.

[31] The foppish officer is not a little like Irus, at *Od.* 18.3 (οὐδέ οἱ ἦν ἴς οὐδὲ βιή, εἶδος δὲ μάλα μέγας ἦν ὁράασθαι) while the sturdy man might be compared to Tydeus at *Il.* 5.801 (μικρὸς . . . ἀλλὰ μαχητής). See Lloyd-Jones, op. cit., 39–40 and notes 59–62, 174.

[32] Cf. Russo, op. cit., 143, who likewise finds that the last item shows a 'sudden transference from the physical to the metaphysical plane.'

and athletic prowess – are rejected unless they are accompanied by courage. Archilochus refuses to admire the soldier who is outwardly splendid, but this does not mean automatic praise for his homely opposite, for even short legs are no good unless a man be brave.

A similar process of re-evaluation is achieved in a single line from another, apparently less good-natured song, an elegy that is this time certainly addressed to Glaucus (15W):

Γλαῦκ᾽, ἐπίκουρος ἀνὴρ τόσσον φίλος ἔσκε μάχηται,

Glaucus, an ally is your friend only so long as he fights.

Here the rejected values are unspoken, but by implication they include kinship, political alliance and conviviality – everything that might ordinarily mark another man as dear. The line is bitter in its suggestion that kinsman, ally and boon companion might all prove cowards if life were at stake, but it is once again strong in its assertion of the fighting heart as an absolute good.

Faith among companions is based in action, not in sentiment, according to Archilochus, but one badly damaged fragment suggests that the men who listened to his songs did, after all, recognise bonds of friendship that were not strictly tactical. The poem celebrates the return of a comrade who has been away, as a merchant or perhaps as a pirate, on a lengthy voyage to Crete (24W):[33]

```
              ]νηὶ σὺν σ[μ]ικρῆι μέγαν
πόντον περήσ]ας ἦλθες ἐκ Γορτυνίης
         ]..οτητ.γ.πεστάθη[[ν]]
         ]καὶ τόδ᾽ ἁρπαλ[ί]ζομ[αι]
   κρ]ηγύης ἀφίκ[                          5
         ]λμοισιν εξ[.......].s
         ]χειρα καὶ π[..]εστ[ά]θης
   ]ουσας· φ[ο]ρτίων δέ μοι μέ[λ]ει
         ].ος εἶτ᾽ ἀπώλετο
         ]ν ἐστι μηχανή                   10
```

---

[33] These lines follow the song of the Ant and the City on P. Oxy. 2310, fr. 1 (1) col.I, and some editors, most notably Lasserre-Bonnard and Treu, have tried to make a single song of their combined 39 lines. West (*Studies*, 120ff.) follows Peek (*Philolog.* 1955, 196ff. and *Wiss. Ztschr. Univ. Halle-Wittenberg* V.2, 1956, 191ff.) in reporting two separate songs, the first in dramatic form, with conversation between a man and a woman, ending at line 21; the second a lyric using the poet's own voice and addressed to a masculine friend. For full bibliography, see Treu, 178 and Kirkwood, *EGM*, 218 note 19.

δ' ἂν ἄλ]λον οὔτιν' εὑροίμην ἐγώ

εἰ σ]ὲ κῦμ' ἁλὸς κατέκλυσεν

ἦ   ].ν χερσὶν αἰχμητέων ὔπο

ἤ]βην ἀγλ[α]ὴν ἀπ[ώ]λεϲ[α]ς.

νῦν δ'   ]θεῖ καί σε θε[ὸς ἐρ]ρύσατο   15

].[.]. κἀμὲ μουνωθέντ' ἰδ..

]ν, ἐν ζόφωι δὲ κείμενο⟨ς⟩[

αὖτις]ἐ[ς] φά[ος κ]ατεστάθην.

. . . crossing
a great sea in a small boat, you come from Gortyn
I greet you with pleasure
(3 lines)
. . . cargo doesn't interest me
. . . if it is lost
. . . or if there is some means
. . . I'd not have found another friend
. . . if sea-waves had engulfed you
or if . . . at the hands of armed men
. . . you had lost your glorious youth.
But now . . . a god has rescued you
. . . and me, alone . . .
. . . lying in the shadow . . .
. . . I stand in sun again.

As far as one can tell there is neither irony nor ambiguity in the song
that hides in these desperate remains. There is no hint of any contrived
dissonance of language or outlook meant to suggest dissatisfaction
either with the ideal, for being absent, or with the real, for its present
depravity. Instead, the speaker seems to welcome a friend[34] with unmixed joy, an Antonio to a Bassanio, and the only trick of the song is
that it transforms an ordinary homecoming into a double miracle, for
the traveller returns as if he had been mortally wounded or dead at
the bottom of the sea, to be greeted by a companion who has risen
from a death of despair because of his salvation.[35]

[34] This is the first example of the song-type that is the companion to the *propemptikon*,
a song that greets the returned friend (*prosphōnētikon*). Close to it in function are
Alcaeus 350V (ἦλθες ἐκ περάτων γᾶς) and Sappho 5V. Both of these, however, have an
ironic edge, for Alcaeus teases his returned brother about exaggerating his foreign
exploits, and Sappho (who imitates the form of a prayer) suggests to hers that he might
now begin to provide for her. Sappho's 48V may be a love-song parody of the form; later
examples are Horace O.1.36; 2.7 and Cat. 9; see F. Cairns, *Generic Composition* (Edinburgh 1972), 200.
[35] See D. Bremer, 'Licht u. Dunkel in der frühgr. Dichtung', *Archiv für Begriffsges-
chichte* (Bonn 1976) on the salvation sense of rising from shadow and standing in light.
And for the opposite the concept of 'light darkened', as a motif of lamentation, see E.
Vermeule, *Aspects of Death*, 16.

In the songs for the city Archilochus urged fellow-citizens to have faith in leadership, the gods and the future. They were not to judge but to act, taking values for granted and forgetting the ambivalent nature of things. In the songs of soldiering the same poet put past, present, himself and his particular companions up as objects of ironic scrutiny and suggested that most received notions were in need of revision. The two audiences were thus treated almost as if they inhabited two different worlds, and yet Archilochus demanded loyalty and courage of the second, disabused, group just as he did of the first. Principled action was possible even where cups were common and shields abandoned, and a third set of songs considers the difficult honour of the disillusioned man. Here irony is abandoned along with faith, as the poet urges all men to view the harshness of life as they would an adversary – with aggressive respect. An elegy addressed to one who has lost relatives at sea offers a definitive example of this kind of Archilochean poetry (13W):[36]

κήδεα μὲν στονόεντα Περίκλεες οὔτέ τις ἀστῶν
μεμφόμενος θαλίῃς τέρψεται οὐδὲ πόλις·
τοίους γὰρ κατὰ κῦμα πολυφλοίσβοιο θαλάσσης
ἔκλυσεν, οἰδαλέους δ' ἀμφ' ὀδύνῃς ἔχομεν
πνεύμονας. ἀλλὰ θεοὶ γὰρ ἀνηκέστοισι κακοῖσιν   5
ὦ φίλ' ἐπὶ κρατερὴν τλημοσύνην ἔθεσαν
φάρμακον. ἄλλοτε ἄλλος ἔχει τόδε· νῦν μὲν ἐς ἡμέας
ἐτράπεθ', αἱματόεν δ' ἕλκος ἀναστένομεν,
ἐξαῦτις δ' ἑτέρους ἐπαμείψεται. ἀλλὰ τάχιστα
τλῆτε, γυναικεῖον πένθος ἀπωσάμενοι.   10

Pericles, our wailing grief will not be blamed
by any burgher at his feast, nor will
the city scoff, for they were fine men that
the moaning sea gulped down, bloating out
our lungs with agony. And yet the gods,
dear friend, made stubborn pride the cure
for pains incurable. Evil moves from man to man;
it strikes us now and we lament a bloody wound
but it will turn to others. Think on that.
Forget this womanish complaint. Endure!

[36] Because Tzetzes reported that another fragment (215W) expressed gloom at the drowning of a brother-in-law, it is sometimes said that Archilochus here laments a kinsman, but this conclusion is completely unnecessary since Archilochus wrote a number of shipwreck poems; cf. 7, 9, 11, 12, 13, 107? 212? 213, 214?W. See however F. R. Adrados, *AFC* 6 (1953–4) 225–35, who would attach some of these to the elegy for Pericles.

There are strong epic echoes here,[37] and the advice given sounds much like that of several lesser fragments ('Let us cover Lord Poseidon's painful gifts', 12W, of drowned men, and 'Not by wailing will I cure it nor by feasting make it worse', 11W), but this is no ordinary piece of consolation. It does not bother to praise the dead (beyond the *toious* of line 3) or even to express love for them;[38] instead it turns aggressively against the action, or rather the inaction, of mourning for them.[39] In effect the poet says to his friend, 'Since no one else will blame you for your grief I must, for it is useless.'[40] And then the poem itself imitates the cure it prescribes as it shifts the agony of the drowned men from their corpses to the bodies of their living relatives, and then teaches those survivors to thrust it away from themselves and cast it out upon others.

The initial step of this almost magical healing process is achieved when those who grieve are made to assume the bloated lungs that properly belong to the victims of the shipwreck, and here the similar Homeric phrases[41] serve to emphasise the poet's quiet ingenuity, for if he had sung of swollen hearts or chests according to his epic models, the effect would not have been the same. Only with these painfully

---

[37] For the overall thought, compare *Il.* 24.524: οὐ γάρ τις πρῆξις πέλεται κρυεροῖο γόοιο. Page (*FH* X, 126ff.) identified each phrase that has an epic parallel and concluded with sweeping exaggeration, 'The composition here is wholly of the traditional type; it consists of nothing but epic phrases adapted to the present theme . . . The whole could stand, in just these words and phrases, in a speech by a person in the *Iliad*' (pp. 127 and 128).

[38] M. Treu, op. cit., 167–71 notes the lack of usual funeral motifs of *thrēnos*, praise, biography and love and remarks (in contradiction to Page's conclusion) the complete difference in tone that divides this elegy from the lament for Hector at the end of the *Iliad*. He does not, however, consider the idea that the Archilochean elegy might be other than an actual piece of funeral poetry composed for an actual funeral.

[39] The opening lines of the elegy have often been read as if they said, 'all the city is mourning with you and no one will feast,' but this depends upon a distortion of the meaning of μεμφόμενος, which has to be entirely deprived of its meaning of 'blame' in support of this interpretation. J. C. Kamerbeek, 'Archilochea', *Mnem.* 14 (1961) 1ff. summarised the various ways in which the words have been read as (1) 'Il n'y aura des festins, personne ne s'en réjouira, puisque tout le monde est en deuil'; (2) 'Personne ne trouve à redire à nos manifestations de deuil, personne donc ne se réjouira de festins'; (3) 'Ce n'est pas parce qu'ils font peu de cas de notre deuil douloureux que les concitoyens et que la ville se réjouiront de festins'. Fränkel chose the second of these ('Nicht um die schmerzliche Trauer zu schmälern, wird einer der Bürger, Pericles, oder die Stadt heitere feste begehn', *DuP*, 160) but the third has found an increasing acceptance. Treu (*Archil*, 166) paraphrases: 'Hier ist Leid, dort wird froh gefeiert werden, aber diesen Feiern wird keine Missachtung unserer Trauer liegen; jeder wird uns voll und ganz verstehen.' D. Gerber translates: 'It is not in disapproval that any citizen will take pleasure' (*Euterpe*, ad loc.), citing M. Arrigoni, *GIF* 13 (1960) 134–5, who argued that the position of the participle gives it special emphasis and that it must mean blaming, not grieving.

[40] Cf. J. Borges, 'From an Apocryphal Gospel', 'Wretched are they that mourn, for theirs is the cowardly habit of tears', *In Praise of Darkness*.

[41] The Archilochean phrase is like, but tellingly different from those at *Il.*9.554, οἰδάνει ἐν στήθεσσι (χόλος) and at 9.646, οἰδάνεται κραδίη χόλῳ.

appropriate lungs can the suffering of the drowned men be transferred to the living and then, in the poem's next movement, transformed, as the visceral inner pain is brought outside the survivors' bodies and made into a wound that can be healed. The deaths and the grief they have caused are in this way given a form that is familiar to a warrior, and therefore the poet can next suggest that only women should lament, since a man must despise physical injury. More important, he can control his new image with the answering image of endurance as a poultice or drug that is applied to the 'bloody wound'.[42] It must be noted, however, that this *pharmakon* is in no sense an anodyne; it does not soothe, but is instead a harsh medicine designed only for recovery. The mourner is to stanch the blood and return to action, strengthened by the knowledge that some day he may rejoice again and, perhaps more important, see a like evil strike some other man. There is nothing of the funeral-parlour in this consolation,[43] for it is not resignation or self-control or gentle moderation that the poem urges. Its 'endurance' (the word takes on a special emphasis because it has no Homeric parallel) has daring and power in it, and it denotes a tough, active and even belligerent insistence upon survival.

The elegiac metres of the poem for Pericles emphasise the large, gnomic quality of its advice, but much the same tone is achieved in a tetrameter piece in which the poet addresses his own heart. Such an internal monologue might appear to be a very personal affair, but the poem is in fact a general recommendation of a particular ethical stance, offered to anyone who will listen (128W):

θυμέ, θύμ', ἀμηχάνοισι κήδεσιν κυκώμενε,

†ἀναδευ δυσμενῶν† δ' ἀλέξεο προσβαλὼν ἐναντίον

στέρνον †ἐνδοκοισιν ἐχθρῶν πλησίον κατασταθεὶς

ἀσφαλέως· καὶ μήτε νικέων ἀμφάδην ἀγάλλεο,

μηδὲ νικηθεὶς ἐν οἴκωι καταπεσὼν ὀδύρεο,   5

ἀλλὰ χαρτοῖσίν τε χαῖρε καὶ κακοῖσιν ἀσχάλα

μὴ λίην, γίνωσκε δ' οἷος ῥυσμὸς ἀνθρώπους ἔχει.

---

[42] Alcaeus may have parodied this line at 335.3V, φαρμάκων δ' ἄριστον / οἶνον ἐνει-καμένοις μεθύσθην. M. D Reeve, 'Eleven notes', *CR* 21 (1971) 324, would read κρατερὸν in line 6 and thus achieve 'made pride the strong cure', but this is a wrong removal of emphasis from the concept of *tlēmosynē*. On this concept, see Snell (*FH* X, 114 and 169), who notes that in epic the words of this stem always apply to a physical, not a psychic situation.

[43] This, however, is exactly the quality that the writers of the second sophistic discovered in these lines; Philostratus speaks of the Archilochean advice here contained as demonstrating that endurance is the gift of 'good gods' (*Vit. Ap. Tyana* 7.27); cf. Kirkwood, *EGM* 'a call for balance and moderation', 35. For the opposite view, see R. Pfeiffer, 'Gottheit u. Individuum', *Philol.* 84 (1929) 139.

O heart, heart that seethes with unresisted grief,
rise, fight, thrust a hostile breast
against the ambushed enemy! Stand close,
hold fast and if you win don't boast
to every ear nor, beaten, hide at home
to wail. Welcome joy and yield to pain
without excess – learn what rhythm governs man.

The heart (*thumos*) here addressed is that part of a man where rage and courage, fear and desire are housed. In Hector it was the place where his fury was stored, but it was also the part that shame could threaten, as well as the part that could put the rest of him to shame (*Il.*22.90ff., esp. 122). Odysseus' *thumos* held both bravery and cowardice (*Il.*11.404–10; cf. 6.442–6),[44] and in the same way the *thumos* of Archilochus could at one time dictate a patriotic poem (the call to Erxias), and at another time long to hang itself (129W).[45] This ambiguous organ is the source of any passionate desire to act, but it can be set against itself, causing paralysis, and so the first thing the present poem urges is extreme motion.[46] Gestures of rage will revive true rage, leaving no place for calculation or despair, and with his *thumos* once more single in purpose, a man can confront his enemy cleanly, even when that enemy himself is devious.[47] Heart under attack is thus to respond like a Homeric hero, with unmeasured and open deeds of violent resistance.

Such is the counsel of the first three lines, but in the fourth, where the imaginary conflict is brought to an end, the poem shifts and an opposite rule is given. Heart in battle was to be direct, but heart in victory or defeat is to respond not from its purity but from its essential ambiguity. It will be covert, not overt, and it will show only a diluted emotion of appropriate acceptance. There is something dandified about

[44] In the Doloneia, κραδίη καὶ θυμός urge a Diomedes who has noble motives to volunteer for the raid (*Il.*10.220); soon after, the same organs work the same effect upon a Dolon whose motives are ignoble (10.319). For Homeric *thumos* in general, see J. Böhme, *Die Seele und das Ich im homerischen Epos* (Leipzig, Berlin 1929) 69–83.

[45] In the Cologne fragment, it is the male speaker's *thumos* that urges him to sexual activity (see below, pp. 84). In general, the *thumos* can create a state of mind that is cheerful, eager, agreeable, sound, mighty, enduring, haughty, adamant or cruel; on the other hand it can also foster a temper that is flighty, foolish or womanish; see S. M. Darcus, '-phron epithets of Thymos', *Glotta* 55 (1977) 178ff.

[46] The ἄνσχεο at *Il.*24.549 makes a similar imperative expression at the beginning of line 2 seem probable: ἄνεχε or perhaps ἄνα σύ. On this fragment in general, see Rubin, op. cit., 1–6.

[47] The language of courage is almost formulaic; cf. Tyrt. 11.21 and 31–3. West (*Studies*, 131) discussing ἔνδοκος, which Hesychius says means ἐνέδρα or ambush, asserts that the notion of ambush is out of place here because the heart is urged to fight openly. He forgets that the poem is not a realistic description of actual battle, but is instead an imagistic description of a psychic contest where the enemy, like Pindar's wolf at *P.*2.84, is moving crookedly.

this heat in action followed by coolness in emotional display,[48] and one is reminded that this is, after all, a rule of social deportment. The battle is metaphorical, since it stands for all conflict, and attack may come as frequently from citizen slanderers as from foreigners or barbarians. Whatever the nature of the danger, however, the heart is to be open, pure and intemperate when challenged, but closed, composite and moderate when the challenge is past and there is only triumph or shame to be met. The two parts of this counsel were known separately to the men of Homer's poems, for they could call upon their hearts for domestic rage or battlefield fury (e.g. *Od.*20.18), and they could also suggest moderation, especially to the hearts of others (e.g. *Il.*24.549), but it is only Archilochus who conceives of the two responses simultaneously. His principle, indeed, is almost aesthetic, for he calls upon a man to cast his life into a measured form of alternation (like elegy or epode) in which the pattern can be recognised only when the *thumos* has shown both licence and control.

The 'rhythm' or pattern which a man must know,[49] according to the call to the heart, is that same inevitable shifting of fortune which makes endurance possible in the elegy for Pericles. Another Archilochean fragment gives this familiar notion a further description, again in tetrameter lines (130W):

τοῖς θεοῖς †τ' εἰθεῖάπαντα· πολλάκις μὲν ἐκ κακῶν
ἄνδρας ὀρθοῦσιν μελαίνηι κειμένους ἐπὶ χθονί,
πολλάκις δ' ἀνατρέπουσι καὶ μάλ' εὖ βεβηκότας
ὑπτίους, κείνοις ⟨δ'⟩ ἔπειτα πολλὰ γίνεται κακά,
καὶ βίου χρήμηι πλανᾶται καὶ νόου παρήορος.　　　　5

Fulfilment is the gods' affair.[50] Often when
a man lies helpless on the dark earth they

---

[48] The pecularity of the Archilochean advice can best be appreciated by comparison with the very similar pair of distiches at Theognis 591–4:

A man must boldly endure the gifts of the gods,
easily bearing whatever the portion that's his,
not sickening under misfortune nor, when good things
suddenly come, rejoicing before the end is clear.

With Theognis the rule of coolness is only temporary; when you have at last seen the *telos* of your good or bad fortune you presumably do respond with extremes of emotion.

[49] Bruno Snell, 'Wie die Griechen lernten, was geistige Tätigkeit ist', *JHS* 93 (1973) 172ff., notes a new sense of γνῶναι here. It is, he says, no longer sudden knowledge, imposed by an external object or event, as it is in Homer, but a slowly developed, internally directed recognition based upon a willed observation. Snell believes that here for the first time a Greek poet expresses the paradox 'dass objektive Erkenntnis subjektive Anstrengung erfordert'.

[50] Reading τέλεια (in line 1) with H. Hommel, 'Cetera mitte' (*Gymnasium* 58 (1951) 219. West proposes πείθοι' ἄπαντα 'put your trust in the gods' (*Studies*, 132), but it is hard to believe that lines with such heavy emphasis upon the negative turn of fortune would begin with this sentiment.

set him right again; often too they overturn
the ones who journey at their ease, calling up a swarm
of evils to pursue, and then a man will wander
hungrily, with madness running in his mind.

The thought here is general and its generality is reinforced by the
ruling image of life as a ceaseless journey,[51] but there is no banality
in these lines. The speaker does not say 'One day you're down, the
next day you're up again', but concentrates instead upon the descend-
ing arc of reversal, so that a terse dramatic power derives from the
fragment's swift sequence of decline.[52] Everything is in motion, but it
is motion of three sorts, as the free and purposeful activity of the gods
gives way to the halting progress of even the happiest of men, and
this again to the errant fumblings of the unfortunate. A similar picture
of wretchedness is offered by Tyrtaeus in his description of the coward
in exile (10.5ff.W), but this parallel only makes the special nature of
the present lines more evident. In the Spartan poem the exile is
miserable because he has betrayed his city and is the victim of a
discriminating misfortune that supports secular justice. In this Parian
song, on the other hand, fortune acts in a more mechanical way, for
the creature who is pursued, Io-like, along a senseless path, is not a
deserter but merely one who once was prosperous. In Solon's elegy for
the Muses (13W), an equally disinterested system of overturn is con-
flated with another in which disasters come as just punishments, but
as far as one can tell no similar rationalisation is made by Archilochus.
In his view, fortune's rhythm is autonomous and insensitive to men's
deserts; it is beyond justice and morality, and so a knowledge of its
inescapable pattern offers a grim comfort, not only to the unfortunate
but also to those who are envious, disappointed or sceptical.

According to Archilochus men have mixed natures, their successes
and failures do not reflect their qualities, and even their virtues and
vices are not entirely their own. You may call upon your *thumos* for

---

[51] Note M. S. Silk's analysis of the poem, *Interaction in Poetic Imagery* (Cambridge
1974), 234–4, where it is argued that the lines are made of 'matching clichés' with the
result that no image is felt to be present at all. As demonstration of the deadness of the
journey cliché, however, Silk can only cite materials that are post-Archilochean, and
so he cannot even prove heavy use, in this case, much less his basic assumption, which
is that use necessarily devitalises any image. The one relevant parallel (not cited by
Silk) comes at the end of 24W, where Archilochus uses the image, 'lying in shadow/
standing in sun' in such an emphatic position that we can feel sure he was counting on
its current vitality.

[52] The fine economy of the final line can be appreciated when it is compared to three
Homeric lines that work for the same effect (*Il.*6.200–2): ἀλλ' ὅτε δὴ καὶ κεῖνος ἀπήχθετο
πᾶσι θεοῖσιν, / ἤτοι ὁ κὰπ πεδίον τὸ Ἀλήϊον οἶος ἀλᾶτο, ὃν θυμὸν κατέδων, πάτον ἀνθρώπων
ἀλεείνων.

a courageous action, but you cannot be sure of its response, for it like you is an ephemeral thing (131–2W):[53]

τοῖος ἀνθρώποισι θυμός, Γλαῦκε Λεπτίνεω πάϊ,
γίνεται θνητοῖς, ὁποίην Ζεὺς ἐφ᾽ ἡμέρην ἄγηι.
καὶ φρονέουσι τοῖ᾽ ὁποίοις ἐγκυρέωσιν ἔργμασιν.

The heart of man, o Glaucus son of Leptines,
depends upon each day as Zeus presents it,
and thoughts take shape according to the deeds we chance upon.

Taken out of context, these lines seem to present a familiar, almost hackneyed notion, for the idea that not only men's fate but even their minds are controlled by events is a very old one. Odysseus remarks to Amphinomus that fortunate men never believe in bad times to come, even though they have experienced evil in the past, because the human mind is moulded by the present moment brought by Zeus (*Od.* 18.132ff.).[54] Solon makes much the same observation in more secular terms when he notes that values and ambitions are not formed inside a man but outside, by the sphere that fate has placed him in (13.35ff.W).[55] Indeed, Archilochus seems to take this thought one step further by applying it to the passionate as well as the intellectual side of man. The traditional view, after all, had been that though the thoughtful and the visceral sides of the heart (the *phrēn* and the *kardia*) were open to outside interference, a man's energy for courage or cowardice (his *thumos*) was his own. The gods might tamper with his physical strength (his *menos*, as e.g. *Il.*10.366); they might even translate his whole body to some other spot, but his primal passionate part was beyond their ordinary reach. Sometimes, in fact, it found itself in direct opposition to the will of a god, as Helen's *thumos* was when she resisted Aphrodite (*Il.*3.395), and as Achilles' was, when he had to ignore his own rebellious heart in bending to Athena's will (*Il.*1.217). Is it true, then, that Archilochus here denies this last passionate freehold of mortal independence by asserting not only that thought is shaped by present opportunity, but in addition that even the heart-source of kindness and cruelty, glory and shame, must fluctuate according as one's fluctuating days are fixed by Zeus? We can't be sure, since the full song is lost, but it is notable that in antiquity

[53] The first two lines are cited by Stobaeus (1.1.18), the third by ps. Plato, *Eryxias* 397e. West prints them consecutively but notes with approval Jacobs' suggestion that they be joined. G. Fischetti, 'Tre note greche', *Ist. Ven. di Sci. Lett. ed Arti, Atti* 132, 1–2 (1974) 170ff., considers that the third line belongs to the same song, but that it should not be placed immediately after the initial two.

[54] On this passage, see the discussion of Fischetti, op. cit., 177ff.

[55] On Archilochus and Solon, see E. Romagnoli, 'Appunti sulla gnomica Bacchilidea', *SIFC* 7 (1899) 171, who concluded, 'Non potè Solone, come nessun altro epigono, sottrarsi all'influsso del grande astro di Paro.'

Archilochus was heard to say in this performance, not that intentions accord with deeds but instead the opposite: that deeds take on the quality of the man who does them (ps. Plat. *Eryxias* 397 = 132W). If this is a true reflection of the song, it cannot have been an assertion of moral mutability and an abdication by the *thumos*; instead, it was probably a poem that began with subtly disdainful comments applied (like those of Odysseus) to the general run of humanity, after which it urged a distinguished show of heart (in deeds that reflected intention) upon the listening Glaucus.[56]

Gestures, objects and men's hearts all have qualities that shift with circumstance, according to the songs that Archilochus sang for the whole of his community. A fallen corpse can enrich a field; a spear can destroy or satisfy; a disorderly drink may be a necessity, grief a form of cowardice, and even a fighting temper is not always hot.[57] Judgment by category is impossible in such a world; values can be found only in accomplished deeds, and deeds are the fruit of conflict. Aggressiveness is a man's best part, and it is not his because he is handsome or well-born but because he has exercised and tested a fighting spirit at every opportunity. In each new conflict he discovers his own momentary worth and that of his comrade, just as he discovers what is momentarily worth fighting for, whether he succeeds or fails. Morality, in this world, is constantly being invented afresh; it is not the possession of a single class, it does not depend upon education or attitude or predisposition, and it can never be taken for granted. Virtue does not belong to the splendid and vice to the base, courage may be shown by any artisan as well as a landowner, and it is in demand at all times and in all places, not just in battle. All life is turbulent and complex, and the poet's work must reflect its fragmentation and its fierce responsibilities. A singer cannot simply commemorate the generally glorious because the generally glorious doesn't exist; instead he must find and praise the active, aggressive element in each separate deed, while he strikes out at every show of cowardice

---

[56] Compare Semonides of Amorgos (1D 3–5) where the poet envisages an intellect that could resist the ephemeral nature of life. The alternative possibility is a song that laments some piece of public blindness or rashness with the implication that men ought to be able to live differently. Something like this was the supposition of Gallavotti, 'Archiloco', *PP* 4 (1949) 149: 'Il popolo va con chi commanda.' See also the discussion of L. Massa Positano, 'Nugae', *PP* (1946) 364, who cites in comparison Xenoph. 34D and Heracl. 17D.

[57] The same ambivalent vision is found in the donkey-spine that wears a wreath, an image for the island of Thasos (21W), and likewise in the threatening sea that is yet 'richly curled' (8W). The cruel beauty of the epithet εὐπλόκαμος is peculiarly apt for freshening waves that break into curling caps; nevertheless D. E. Gerber ('Archilochus, fr. 8W', *Philolog.* 121, 1977, 298) has argued that it must belong to an unnamed goddess supplicated in the genitive, and he proposes Artemis because she is εὐπλόκαμος at *Od*.20, 80. But why call upon Artemis when at sea?

or falseness or laxity. And so, like the individual man, this poetry finds its true worth only when it engages in conflict.

iii

Blame

The Parians who made a hero of Archilochus remembered his patriotic poems and his cult songs, but the rest of the ancient world honoured him primarily as a poet of abuse, the first and best, and one whose evil tongue could kill. He was at once the inventor and the most perfect practitioner of blame (Vell. Pat. 1.5) and his loud verses were 'filled with rage and the venom of dread scurrility' (*AP* 9.185), because he had 'sprinkled his harsh Muse with Echidna's bile' (*AP* 7.71).[1] Teachers recommended the study of his modes of attack,[2] and Plutarch records the moment when Cato 'angrily and impetuously turned his energies to the writing of iambics, in which he made a violent attack upon Scipio, using the bitter style of Archilochus and allowing himself to exaggerate and make childish jokes' (*vit. Caton. min.* 7). The tale of Lycambes and his daughters, hounded to death by obscene libels, was repeated again and again to prove the force of the Archilochean genius, and ugly though it was it did not seem to contradict other stories about Apollo's patronage of the poet, for according to later antiquity men had more need of blame than of praise in their poetry (Dio Chrys. *or.* 33.11f.). Archilochus' old calumnies were thus music to the ears of Rome's cynical politicians and dilettanti, but in their own time they had served a far deeper purpose, for the archaic poetry of blame was an instrument of social health, as necessary to a sound community as those complementary songs that put splendour in the air. Abuse was one of the two poetic practices essential to social life, and as such it had its history, its rationale and, in Momus, even its presiding divinity.

Momus, in the time of Callimachus, was a mere personification of

---

[1] Cf. *AP* 7.69, where Archilochus is said to have used 'fierce iambics brought to birth by a tongue of bitter gall'. Callim. fr. 380Pf. has him mix the bitterness of dog's bile with the sharpness of a wasp's sting to make the poison of his tongue.

[2] Students of rhetoric were urged not to neglect their study of Archilochus, that they too might know how to treat enemies (Menander, *Rhet. epideict.* ii 393 (p. 122 Russell and Wilson) = Lasserre test. 35; cf. Hermogenes, 319R).

envy. His voice was that of sterile criticism[3], and with that voice he
passed into the Renaissance as the jealous colleague who tried to
destroy the sublime work of Apelles.[4] Originally, however, Momus
had been a creature much more powerful and more ambivalent than
this, for according to Hesiod he was a child of Night, the brother of
Grief, and one of a host of dark *daimones* who were both harmful and
beneficent (*Theog.* 214). Momus was the natural companion of Death,
since blame was associated with silence and forgetfulness, but he was
as well the friend of Sleep, the Moirai, and the maids of paradise, who
were all forces of order and health. This allegorised blame-figure defined himself in action in the stories of the epic cycle, for it was he
who strongly urged Zeus to prosecute the Trojan War, that the pres-
sures of human population might be reduced (Schol. at *Il.*1.5 =
*Cypr.*1).[5] Momus had always a very low opinion of the value of mankind, which he saw as the worst section of the animal creation (Babrius, *Fab.* 59),[6] and in Stoic diatribe he blamed now Prometheus, now
Hermes, for ever having devised such a species.[7] In this respect he
was a peculiarly archaic deity, for it was his apportioned task to
remind men always of their ungodlike qualities, and so to check their
growing audacity and pride.

On earth, the work of Momus was done by abusive song, which was
thought of as being almost as old as music itself.[8] Combined with
obscenity, poetic attack had become a magical weapon for driving out
demons, and the apotropaic effects of the filthy insult were borrowed

[3] Swift, with the same antipathy, makes the critic the offspring of Hybris and Momus,
in *The Tale of the Tub*.

[4] R. Foerster, 'Die Verleumdung des Apelles in der Renaissance', *Jahrb. der König.
pr. Kunstsammlungen* (1887) traces the Apelles story from Pliny to Alberti's *Trattato
della Pittura* of 1435. However, the Veronese at the National Gallery in London shows
that the renaissance notion of Momus was not confined to this incident, since it included
the erotic blame of jealousy.

[5] Compare the role of Mummu in the Enuma Elish (Tablet 1), the god who counsels
Apsu to destroy the noisy lesser gods (A. Heidel, *The Babylonian Genesis*, Chicago 1942,
19). The name has been doubtfully connected with Aeolic μῦμαρ = αἶσχος by Hesych.
who also explains μυμαρίζει· γελοιάζει.

[6] Athena, Poseidon and Zeus have a contest to see who can make the best thing and
Momus is their judge. Of Athena's house he says, 'Why hasn't it wheels?' of Poseidon's
bull, 'Why aren't its horns under its eyes?' and of Zeus' man, 'Why doesn't his chest
open, that his thoughts may be evident?'

[7] *Stobaei Hermetica Exc.* 23.44–6 (Scott, Oxford 1924); cf. Ferguson, *Hermetica* iv
455–61 and Eustathius 1574–.16; see R. Reitzenstein, 'Die Göttin Psyche', *SB Heidelberg*, PhH K1. 8 (1917) 10. Abh., 76ff. The argument is that man, unfettered, is prone
to excessive *spoudē* and wants to explore the secrets of the gods and even to storm the
heavens, which sounds much like the ἀπέδιλος ἀλκά that Alcman censured in the
seventh century. Earlier expressions of the dangers of *spoudē* are found in Solon 13; cf.
Soph. fr.257: οὐ γὰρ ἐσθ' ὅπως σπουδῆς δικαίας μῶμος ἄψεταί ποτε. This stoic scene
between Momus and a divine friend of man may have as its source the lost Sophoclean
satyr-play called *Momus* (frr. 419–24 Radt).

[8] At *h.Herm.* 54–5 Hermes invents the lyre and at once begins to sing mocking taunts
(κερτομεῖν) as boys do at feasts.

from superstition for use in rites of fertility and in certain rituals of Dionysus and Demeter.[9] Momus, however, was interested in men, not gods, and blame found its widest uses in the secular world, where it was employed in the self-regulation of the primitive community.[10] Individual behaviour was monitored only by the pressure of the group, and opinion had to assume a form that would actually inhibit or encourage those who were censured or approved. Blame and praise not only had to be expressed, they had to be invested with the power of wounding and rewarding, and the magic of metre and melody was exploited to this end. Praise adopted the same choral music that was used for magnifying gods, and eventually it produced that strangely atavistic form, epinician song, while blame chose the monodic forms that belonged to the witch, the healer and the itinerant dealer in purification. It had need of some such magic, since it had to bind and control those absurd and bestial parts of men that Momus scorned from above.

In theory blame was the natural companion of praise, but in the practical world of composition and performance the two sorts of song were inevitably rivals, since they were opposite in spirit as well as in technique. Successful praise magnified its subject; it made use of sweetness, looked only for the noble, and roused a sense of emulating pride in its listener.[11] Blame, on the other hand, made its object small: 'chew', 'chop fine', is probably the meaning of its major verb, *psegein* (though some have supposed that it activates the disgusted exclamation, *pso*).[12] Successful blame was bitter and degrading; it searched out what was shameful, obscene, deformed or grotesque, and it roused

[9] For obscenity in the Athenian Thesmophoria, Apollod. 1.5.1; in the Demeter cult at Syracuse, Diod. 5.4.6; at Pellene, Paus. 8.27.9; and in the cult of Damia and Auxesia at Aegina, Hdt. 5.83. Aristotle, *Pol.* 7.1336b17 testifies to scurrilous abuse called *tōthasmos* as part of the cult practice of his own time. Nilsson believed he could distinguish a divergence in primitive Greek practice, by which phallic reference became appropriate to fertility magic, while gestures and symbols relative to female parts were used to ward off evil spirits (*Gesch. der gr. Rel.* I³, Munich 1967, 118f). In general, see H. Fluck, *Scurrile Riten in gr. Kulten* (Diss. Freiburg 1931).

[10] At *Od.*2.86, just, true and inspired reproaches are meant to fasten blame upon those who have behaved shamefully, but the poetry of attack more usually employed the childishness and exaggeration that Cato copied. The natural cognate acc. of λοιδορέω is τὰ αἰσχρά, as at Hdt. 4.184. On praise and blame in epic contexts see G. Nagy, *The Best of the Achaeans*, 222–42; in general, see M. Detienne, *Les Maîtres de la Vérité* (Paris 1967) 21ff.

[11] The bee of praise fed on *aretē* (P.P.10.53) but the momus-bee avoids the honey-lady of Semonides (7.83) and so by implication feeds on rottenness, being the opposite of the normal insect that, according to Aristotle (*HA* 535a2) πρὸς οὐδὲν προσιζάνει σαπρόν.

[12] Menander (*Rhet. epideict.* ii 3 93, 9f. (p. 122 Russell and Wilson) = LB test. 35) implies that ψέγειν means κολάζειν τοὺς ἐχθροὺς τῇ ποιήσει. For the derivation from Sanskrit *psati*, 'chew up, pulverise, devour', see Boisacq, sv. Prellwitz² 517 suggests that the oldest word is ψόγος from an exclamation ψό, 'Fie!' out of which a later ψέγος and ψέγειν derived.

a laughing scorn,[13] but also a covert questioning of self, within its audience. Ideally, praise created a sense of unity as it mixed one man's virtue into the virtue of the group that had produced him, but blame was necessarily divisive, since it separated the base or unsound man from his fellows and ejected him, almost as if he were a *pharmakos*.[14] Blame was, thus, in the vulgar sense, more political than praise, for its legitimate abuse kept alive the spirit of contention that made cities prosper, and it also acted as a kind of popular review, a *dokimasia* that any man who gained prominence would have to undergo. Its power could even be projected into the future with an inhibitory effect, for the poetry of blame acted, in its potential form, as an effective threat. It was an obvious truth that, in a small city, 'no one who felt the people's scorn as a burden could find much to enjoy' (14W),[15] and this meant that the mere presence of a master of calumny ensured an increase in propriety among the citizens.

The praise poets of a later time equated blame with slander,[16] and Pindar pictured the blame-singer as an ugly creature who manipulated envy and courted the dregs of society. For him, Archilochus was the perfect emblem of everything that song should never stoop to, and he called him by name in his great ode on ingratitude (*P*2.52–6):

[13] Compare the distinctions made by Dio of Prusa (33; I.300.9ff. Arn.) between Homer (as one who ἐνεκωμίασε) and Archilochus, whose work is to ψέγειν καὶ λοιδορεῖν τὴν ἀβελτερίαν ... καὶ τὴν πονηρίαν φανερὰν ποιεῖν. Cf. Plato, *Laws* 11.935 where poets are not to make a man laughable. In that it made its object worse than he was to start with, blame had an obvious connection with the battlefield insult that was meant to make an opponent weak, cowardly, ignoble and womanish; see E. Vermeule, *Aspects of Death*, 101ff.

[14] The idea of the *pharmakos* is explicit in the abusive songs of Hipponax; see 5–10W.

[15] Archil. 14W. This fragment is usually interpreted as a defiance, on the part of the singer, announcing his own superiority to mere public opinion, but the commentator's explanation of ἐπιρρήσις as meaning κακαγορία or ψόγος shows that he had in mind the particular, painful, poet-formed scorn of professional abuse. He could, of course, be proclaiming his imperviousness to attacks from rival calumniators, but it is at least equally likely that he is here boasting of his own power, as a poet of abuse, to make any man's life miserable.

[16] Simonides reads Scopas a lesson, but insists that he is not φιλόμωμος (37/542.33 *PMG*); note also Bacchylides 13 (12) 199ff., where *mōmos* is ready to attack all of men's deeds, but is defeated by an *alatheia* that seems to be identified with sung praise. The ambiguity and innuendo of abuse no doubt contributed to its classification as the reverse of truth, for Hesiod was not alone in believing that ἀμφιλλογίαι were the sisters of lies (*Theog.* 229). Pindar recognised blame as valuable in certain circumstances – when it justly attached itself to excess (*I.* 2.20–1) and when it followed upon a betrayal of honour (*O.*10. 7ff.). Once he even imagined the scattering of blame upon sinners as part of his own responsibility (*N.* 8. 37–9), and once also he demonstrated the effectiveness of potential blame in ensuring virtuous action, for at *P.* 1.82 he counselled himself to work in the way that would minimise surfeit and consequently would minimise blame. At other times, however, he found a mutually exclusive opposition between praise and blame (e.g. *N.* 7. 61–3; fr. 181S).

> I for my part
> must avoid the bitter gall of calumny
> for from a distance I observe Archilochus,
> futile and abusive, growing fat[17]
> on heavy words of scorn.

Such superb abuse from a poet who insists that he is above the practice is the fairest crown that Archilochus could win,[18] but this passage not only fixes Archilochus' reputation, it also provides a reverse description of his profession. Blame is not richly rewarded, according to Pindar, which means that its poet is not the servant of a wealthy patron. Blame fawns upon the populace, by this report, which means that it does not flatter the rich and powerful. Blame is like an ape who pleases children, says the Theban,[19] which means that its poet is a citizen among citizens and understood by all, not a prophet whose deep meaning can be taken only by the few. Blame, then, is an art that is independent,[20] popular and even in the fifth century still so powerful that a Pindar must scorn it, still so reputable that he can do so without spoiling his own dignity.[21]

Blame addressed the bestial part of man because its function was to keep that part from controlling society and offending gods who were

[17] At *P*. 2. 56, with the word πιαινόμενον, Pindar may be playing upon Archilochus' boast that a fight was to him better than a drink (125W), but he doubtless also has in mind the general ancient association made among the concepts of stomach, idleness, parasitism and lies. Phrases using the word γαστήρ are studied by J. Svenbro, *La parole et le marbre* (Lund 1976), ch. 2, and in these the ruling idea proves to be that the man who speaks from his stomach speaks from hunger, wanting food and consequently fawning and using false words (see in particular *Od*. 14. 124–5; Epimenides fr. 1; Hes. *Theog*. 26–7). In an extension of this notion, Aeschylus proposes the figure of the child whose central need for food makes it ready to 'fatten' on almost anything, i.e., ready to hope on the basis of rumour (*Agam*. 276–7).

[18] Pindar in fact pays Archilochus the compliment of imitation, for though he suggests (with his reference to the ape) that animal fables are low, he nevertheless, towards the end of his ode, poses himself as a wolf beside the fox of blame. His word for foxes (κερδοῖ) is the one that Babrius later used, and for his choice of the wolf as his own beast, compare Babrius 53, where the wolf plays Hades to the fox's Sisyphus. Archilochus identified himself as a fox at 174W and 185W, and the later popularity of the notion is reflected at Pl. *Rep*. 365c: τὴν . . . Ἀρχιλόχου ἀλώπεκα ἑλκτέον ἐξόπισθεν (of those who would be sly).

[19] P. *P*. 2.73–4, καλός τοι πίθων παρὰ παισίν, αἰεὶ καλός. This phrase effects the song's return to the subject of calumny. One of the Archilochean epodes concerned an ape (185–7W) who was excessively eager for power, and this Pindar's audience would remember. Nevertheless, the present ape is probably meant more generally, as a figure for lowness, indecency and the imitation of one's betters.

[20] Freedom is the claim of the Archilochus that Lucian pictured; he sings like a cicada, because it is his nature and because he is full of words καὶ ἄνευ τινὸς ἀνάγκης (*Pseudol*. 1).

[21] To appreciate the essential nobility of Pindar's abuse, one has only to compare Sir Car Scrope, abusing Rochester for the same sort of satiric activities:

Sit swelling in thy hole, like a vext toad
And full of pox and malice spit abroad. . .

ready to blame. The singer of defamatory song kept off the lesser demons of presumption and self-satisfaction, and also the greater ones of corruption, pride and injustice, and so in his own view he was as important as any priest or magistrate. He practised an art that was conscious and traditional, one that maintained the health of the community, and consequently it will be egregiously wrong to take the slanders of Archilochus as the mere raw outbursts of an angry man who happened to have a lyre in his hands. Archilochus is fond of saying that anger is a part of his nature, but the statement is meant to validate his professional vocation, proving that his blame is as honest as other poets' praise and that, coming from his *thumos*, it is not for sale.

The three most prominent characteristics of Archilochean blame turn out to be a distance from the object, a consciousness of function, and a manipulation of convention, all of which are evident in the poet's descriptions of himself as a singer of abuse. Standing back to observe the cleanness of his own passion, he can say, 'One important thing I understand – how to answer wrong with wrongs' (126W), or 'I love a fight with you as I love a drink when I'm thirsty' (125W).[22] Anger is generalised and the audience is reminded that attack is a form of artistic activity and also a form of wisdom – the expression of a hard, popular instinct for communal self-defence. 'The fox knows many tricks, the hedgehog just one – but his is a good one!' (201W) is not the boast of a privately angry man. It is instead a programmatic statement from a poet of anger,[23] a very different creature indeed, and it can be found amusingly repeated by another professional, the seventeenth-century Englishman Joseph Hall, who wrote, 'The Satyre should be like the Porcupine/That shoots sharpe qwils out in each angry line' (*Virgidemiarum*, Sat.3.1–2).[24] With his hedgehog, Archilochus announces that his verse is meant to wound, but that it will do so with an Aesopic justice and also with an Aesopic consciousness that its singer shares in the common bestiality of all.

The animal tale was in fact one of Archilochus' favourite weapons when he wished to be abusive, for by the mere choice of the form he could announce that his anger was exemplary. The beast fable was

---

[22] Sir George Etherege, in *The Man of Mode or Sir Fopling Flutter* made his hero (Rochester thinly disguised) say, 'Next to coming to a good understanding with a new mistress, I love a quarrel with an old one'. G. Lanata, 'Archiloco 69D', *QU* 6 (1968). 33–5, discusses the possibility that the μάχη for which Archilochus thirsts is an erotic battle, but concludes that the question is open.

[23] A programmatic statement of a different sort occurs at 134W, where 'It is not honourable to scold the dead', read positively, yields 'It is an honourable thing to scold the living'.

[24] Ed. A. Davenport (Liverpool 1949) 83.

exotic, being an import from Asia Minor,[25] and it was also anachronistic, since it had been invented long ago by people who needed to laugh at creatures more miserable than themselves. Such stories were cruel survival aids that taught men to be proud that they were not animals, while they laughed at themselves because the difference was so slight, and in their primary form they were subversive of all morality since they admired nothing beyond raw success.[26] When they were repeated among more fortunate peoples, certain ethical suggestions sometimes crept into these harsh Near Eastern tales, but as far as one can tell there is still very little of ordinary morality in the fable poems of Archilochus. Instead, the original tendency towards vilification of the entire human race is caught in a very elegant metrical arrangement, and the result is a curious mode in which the singer, his own passion artfully disguised or dissipated, elicits a joyous and almost abstract scorn from his audience.

The fable was a mannerly though vulgar means of attack, for by telling an old beast tale (or what pretended to be one) the poet necessarily muted all emotion and assumed the sardonic calm of the raconteur. He announced, in effect, that his song was an artifact, not a vehicle for personal rage, and Archilochus at these times liked to employ a special two-line stanza whose mixed iambic and dactylic elements reflected his own mixture of insult and narrative.[27] Balance and contrivance were the outstanding characteristics of this epode form, and evidently the same characteristics marked the poems as wholes, for the fables were developed according to proclaimed programmes, and they were introduced by prefaces that stamped them as pieces of dispassionate wit. One begins with a challenge that is positively good-humoured in its confident superiority (172W):

πάτερ Λυκάμβα, ποῖον ἐφράσω τόδε;
    τίς σὰς παρήειρε φρένας
ἧις τὸ πρὶν ἠρήρησθα; νῦν δὲ δὴ πολὺς
    ἀστοῖσι φαίνεαι γέλως.

Father Lycambes, what was this plan of yours?
    Your wits were sound; who's

---

[25] For the derivation of the fable from Ionia, see Morten Nojgaard, *La fable antique* I (Copenhagen 1964) 150 and the bibliography cited there. For the larger Near Eastern background, see W. G. Lambert, *Babylonian Wisdom Literature* (Oxford 1960), 217f. which reports an eighth-century Assyrian tablet with anecdotes containing animal speakers (cited by M. West, 'Near Eastern materials in Hellenistic and Roman literature', *HSCP* 73, 1969, 113ff.).

[26] Cf. Nojgaard, op. cit., 517: 'un raisonnement qui sape de l'intérieur les bases de la morale de la société officielle.'

[27] On the development of these epodic metres, see L. E. Rossi, 'Asynarteta', *Arethusa* 9 (1976), 207ff.

fuddled them? You're going to be
a joke around this town!

The next formal element seems to have been a passage in which the
poet described himself as a terrible adversary, but with obvious self-
irony. 'Why did you want to provoke a garrulous poet like me, one
who's always ready to make more iambics?' is Lucian's parody of one
such transitional phrase (*Pseudol.* 1).[28] After this the victim's 'crime'
might be specified, perhaps with lines like, 'You went back on your
oath and betrayed table and salt', though these words (173W) have an
unwonted earnestness about them. Finally the fable would be given
its official introduction, much as the mythic example is officially proposed in the victory ode,[29] though these stories were far from splendid
(174W):

> αἶνός τις ἀνθρώπων ὅδε,
> ὡς ἄρ᾽ ἀλώπηξ καἰετὸς ξυνεωνίην
> ἔμειξαν,

> People tell the tale, you know,
> of how the eagle and the fox
> went into partnership . . .

In another fragment, the announcement of the fable stands at the
beginning of the song, where it mingles with a challenge built on the
victim's name (185W):

> ἐρέω τιν᾽ ὕμιν αἶνον, ὦ Κηρυκίδη,
> ἀχνυμένηι σκυτάληι,
>
> . . .
>
> πίθηκος ἤιει θηρίων ἀποκριθεὶς
> μοῦνος ἀν᾽ ἐσχατιήν,
> τῶι δ᾽ ἄρ᾽ ἀλώπηξ κερδαλῆ συνήντετο,
> πυκνὸν ἔχουσα νόον.

5

---

[28] Compare Odysseus at *Od.* 9.494: σχέτλιε, τίπτ᾽ ἐθέλεις ἐρεθιζέμεν ἄγριον ἄνδρα;
[29] Compare another offering, addressed ostensibly at least to a friend (168W):

'Charilaus, son of Erasmonides,
I'm going to tell
a funny tale, O best of friends
– one that you'll like to hear.'

Cf. also Pl. *Gorgias* 523A: ἄκουε δή, φασί, μάλα καλοῦ λόγου (introducing a mythic
example). F. R. Adrados, 'Nouveaux fragments d'Archiloque', *Rev. de Phil.* 30 (1956)
30f. discusses the formulaic nature of phrases like αἶνός τις ἀνθρώπων ὅδε (174W).

I'll tell you a story, Kerykides,
  but you won't like my message much . . .
The ape was sent in banishment by his
  companion beasts, once, and went alone
into the wilderness and there the cunning fox
  pursued, because he had a clever plan.

The stories that followed these introductions can only be guessed at. Even their length is problematical, though apparently the tale told in the song addressed to Lycambes stretched out for about thirty lines (172–181W, if all these fragments do in fact belong together). One thing, however, is certain, and that is that these fables, again like the mythic examples of epinician, were dramatic in form and could contain passages of direct speech.[30] A fragment from the Lycambes song preserves the voice of the fox, whose friend the eagle has stolen his cubs and destroyed them (177W).

ὦ Ζεῦ, πάτερ Ζεῦ, σὸν μὲν οὐρανοῦ κράτος,
  σὺ δ' ἔργ' ἐπ' ἀνθρώπων ὁρᾶις
λεωργὰ καὶ θεμιστά, σοὶ δὲ θηρίων
  ὕβρις τε καὶ δίκη μέλει.

'O Zeus, Father Zeus, yours is heaven's rule!
  You supervise the deeds of men,
their crimes and villainies; you care as well
  about the beasts, and whether they are rough
or just . . .'

'Come to my aid now, for I have been wronged' is the obvious burden of the fox's prayer, and in the story his call was answered, for the eagle soon set fire to his own nest with a bit of stolen altar meat. The eaglets fell from their flaming bed and were eaten by the fox in a compensatory feast (179, 180W).[31] But how did a fable like this one function as abuse? Presumably the audience recognised the poet in this fox, and the target Lycambes in this punished bird, but as far as one can tell from the poem's remains, the Lycambes-eagle was never actually slandered. Instead he seems to have flown off at the end, childless but still swift and free (181.10–11W). Lycambes was thus warned that if he enriched his own household by raiding those of his friends he would eventually harm himself, but this is hardly damaging to his reputation, nor would it have

[30] This use of direct speech within the narrative (not just for the triumphant quip or résumé at the end) is unlike the usual Aesopic form, and may have influenced the later Babrius; see Nøjgaard, op. cit., 451.
[31] The development of events in the tale of the fox and the eagle can be reconstructed from the Aesopic fable (1 Hausrath and Perry = 3 Chambry); there is full bibliography at West *Studies*, p. 132, note 4.

provoked scorn on the part of the listener. Further, since according to the ancient explanation the actual Lycambes did not take anything from Archilochus but offended in the opposite way, by refusing to give, the story seems to be no more apt than it is devastating.[32] If we use the ancient gossip and press hard for meaning, the tale can be made to yield a slightly stronger paraphrase, since it may be saying that, just as Lycambes took the fiancée of Archilochus, so Archilochus will in return devour (i.e. slander) the child of Lycambes, who happens to be that same fiancée. Even in these terms, however, the fable does no more than repeat the opening threat of the song, while it postpones the very defamation that it promises.

Instead of conveying anger, the fable in this case deflects anger from a song that in itself attaches no shame to its victim, and the only possible conclusion is that direct personal abuse was never a part of the poet's true purpose here. He seems rather to be engaged in creating a double fable, wherein a typical poet and a typical Lycambes reduplicate the typical fox and eagle, and where the listener is asked to scorn, not a particular man, but a general trait that may even be one of his own. Probably the real aim of the song was achieved through its satire of humanity, for this is the impulse most evident in the animal prayer that was cited above.[33] As a suppliant, the Archilochus-fox shows an obvious touch of Xenophanes' later scepticism as he calls upon a god who is concerned about beasts exactly as the gods of Homer and Hesiod were about men, and yet it is not the gods who suffer *meiōsis* here. The poet-fox, in spite of his grief, employs the rules of rhetoric and, proceeding Aristotle-fashion, he divides all of creation into its human and its bestial species, allowing to each a double set of characteristics. Beasts, it seems, may behave either with violence or justice, while men's deeds likewise fall into one or the other of two classes – the Villainous or the Unlawful![34]

The fable that was addressed to Kerykides (perhaps a punning name since it means 'herald's son') concerned the fox and the ape (185W), and if its contents were like those of Aesop's tale of the same pair (Chambry 31) it must have been a bit more insulting than the Lycambes fable was. The later story, at any rate, tells of an ambitious

---

[32] K. Latte, 'Zeitgeschichtliches. . .' *Hermes* 92 (1964) 387, note 2, concluded that the fable of the fox and the eagle could not belong to a song attacking Lycambes: 'Die fable wäre schlecht gewählt, da Lykambes dem Archilochos nichts geraubt, sondern nur etwas nicht gegeben hatte.' He noted that the papyrus versions show no traces of Lycambes' name and that it was in fact Diehl who attached the fable fragments to the lines addressed to Lycambes.

[33] Prayers offered by animals also occur in a Sumerian proverb and a Babylonian tale (Ebeling 22.1.14), both cited by Nojgaard, op. cit., 452.

[34] Reading κάθέμιστα in line 3 with the ancient witnesses. West, following Liebel, writes καὶ θεμιστά, on the assumption that the realms of men and beasts must be parallel; it is his belief that the elaborate distinctions made here are useless decoration with no real point at all.

ape who had attempted to rule over the other animals but had been rejected by them. The fox went to him in his exile and promised to reinstate him,[35] but he was a creature of wily plans and he did just the opposite. He played upon the greed of the ape, got him into a trap, and displayed him to the others in a posture that showed him to peculiar disadvantage, calling out, 'And you thought you were somebody, with a bare ass like that!' (187W). Perhaps Kerykides was a striving power-seeker, perhaps he was a private enemy (or friend) lampooned with a charge of effeminacy, but in either case one notable fact remains the same. The fable does not itself make a genuine attack upon him, but instead it depicts the poet in the act of attack, describing a blame-maker who does not devour this time but instead denudes the object of his scorn.

Animal fables paradoxically allowed the poet to maintain a tone of cool superiority even as he descended to the bestial level assigned to his victim; it was as if he said, 'In crudeness too I can outdo you!' They also gave his abuse a mark of conscious and traditional artistry that set it apart from mere ephemeral rage. The fable, however, was not the only instrument for achieving these ends, and in two fragments we find Archilochus using the wise-man's gnomic manner so as to get exactly the same effects of coolness, irony, and generality. In an iambic trimeter that starts out like an old saw, the poet says (25W):

>]τις ἀνθρώπου φυή,
> ἀλλ' ἄλλος ἄλλωι καρδίην ἰαίνεται.
>].τ[.].μελησα[...]. σάθη
>]ε βουκόλωι Φαλ[...]ιωι.
> τοῦτ' οὔτις ἄλλος μάντις ἀλλ' ἐγ ε ἰπέ σοι·   5
>]γάρ μοι Ζεὺς πατὴρ Ὀλυμπίων
> ἔ]θηκε κἀγαθὸν μετ' ἀνδράσι
> οὐ]δ' ἂν Εὐρύμας διαψέγο[ι

Man's nature is [a various thing;]
each takes his pleasure in his different way.
... Melesander, for example, loves a cock
just as Phalonius, the bumpkin [likes a bit of ass.]
No minor prophet tells you this
but I, [endowed with Zeus' sacred gift...]
so well-renowned a seer
even old Eurymas couldn't fault me.

---

[35] The formula 'two beasts, having become friends ...' is typically Aesopic, as is also this praxis, by which whatever the fable-world finds anomalous is expelled; see Nøjgaard, op. cit., p. 452. Aristides II 397, 2 Dind., reports that the apes of Archilochus are πανοῦργοι καὶ ποικίλοι ...περὶ οὗ γέγονεν αὐτοῖς φιλονεικία βασιλείας. Another possible allusion to this song occurs at Pl. *Rep.* 265c.

Exactly what Phalonius prefers to the *sathē* favoured by Melesander is not clear (the translation follows a suggestion of West's), but his choice is obviously indecent, for the trick of these lines lies in their substitution of a list of sexual practices for the list of vocations or values usually proposed by poets in the priamel.[36] The time-honoured pattern, 'One man chooses wealth, another power, but I . . .' as a rule produced a final term of elevated importance – courage, health or beauty – but this priamel seems to be an Aristophanic joke. After the singer's overblown self-validation – probably a jibe at the praise-poet's habitual boast of inspiration – a last term will be produced and, though it may swerve from the sexual realm, we can guess that it will be triumphantly base.[37] The singer's favourite pleasure will surpass those of Melesander and Phalonius, but it cannot, after such a start as this, offer them any solemn correction. The blame that attaches to them is only incidental, anyway, for the central purpose here seems to be to ridicule a pompous way of thinking. In effect what the poet apparently says is that those laudable values so often discovered by singers are not in fact the ones that shape men's lives. Man's nature *is* everywhere the same in that it is everywhere absurd and obscene, and this is why all stand in need of the poetry of blame.

Four iambic lines survive from another poem that likewise parodied the priamel. Aristotle says that the poet here put his lines into the mouth of a fictitious person, a carpenter called Charon, because he did not want to take their excesses upon himself, but we do not know

---

[36] The interpretation of this song is obviously highly conjectural, but it was known in antiquity as a parody of the *topos* familiar from *Od.*14.228 (ἄλλος γάρ τ' ἄλλοισιν ἀνὴρ ἐπιτέρπεται ἔργοις) and E. *Oeneus* (fr. 560N²), to which examples the long sequence beginning at Solon 3.39, Pindar. *O.*1.113 and E.*Ba.*905ff. are the most obvious additions. See the discussion of the priamel, pp. 281ff. below.

[37] K. Latte, op. cit., 387, restored [φίλον σὲ] at the beginning of line 6 and in line 7 [νῦν δ' αὖθ' ἅ γ' οὐ]δ' ἂν Εὐρύμας διή[ν]ετο. . . He paraphrased the resulting poem as being something like the Strasburg curse (Hipp. 115W), a reproach to a faithless friend: 'Was selbst Eurymas nicht fertig gebracht hatte, das hat ein Zwischenträger oder irgendwelche Umstände erreicht. Zeus hat den Bund gestiftet, weil der Eid bei ihm bekräftigt hat. So erscheint der Bruch des Vertrauens als Vergehen gegen den Gott.' What this would have to do with the opening of the song is not clear. West, *Studies*, 122, recognised Archilochus' essential statement as, 'There's no accounting for tastes', but supposed that the singer went on to describe his own father's love for a slave girl (though elsewhere he doubts the reality of Enipo)! He would begin line 6 with τὸν πατέρα and read, 'but I, whose father Zeus established as noble and good in social terms'. It is obvious, however, that the strong emphasis upon 'I' in line 5 is not meant to be thrown away on someone else; this 'I' is going now to speak about himself, not his father or his friend, and he is probably going to specify his own favourite pleasure as that of slandering. This, at any rate, is the strong suggestion of the heavily emphasised name 'Eurymas'; in Homer (*Od.*9.509) Eurymas was the ur-mantic, the father of all prophecy, but Pherecydes reported him as a master of blame, one who tried to stir up trouble between the Dioscuri with his slanders (fr.164 Jac = FGH³; see Latte, *Gnomon* 27, 1955, 493). If the poet is in a position in which Eurymas, the master, οὐδ' ἂν διαψέγοι, the activity he will claim as his favourite is probably that of διαψέγειν.

what the imaginary situation was, why the poet made his speaker an artisan, or how the sequence came to an end. All we have is a voice that mimics a common man in order to say (19W):

"οὔ μοι τὰ Γύγεω τοῦ πολυχρύσου μέλει,
οὐδ' εἷλέ πώ με ζῆλος, οὐδ' ἀγαίομαι
θεῶν ἔργα, μεγάλης δ' οὐκ ἐρέω τυραννίδος·
ἀπόπροθεν γάρ ἐστιν ὀφθαλμῶν ἐμῶν."

'Gyges' gold[38] is no affair of mine –
I don't want it, and I don't envy gods
their deeds, or dream of tyrants' thrones:
that's further than I look . . .'

Wealth, eternal life, and worldly powers are all rejected for a final object which is what the speaker emphatically *does* care for. We have no clue as to what this ultimate value was; it may have been public or private, political or erotic, decent or obscene. Possibly this 'carpenter' announced with rude exactitude just what he and his tools would like to do to an enemy whom the audience could easily identify, but however that may be two things at least are sure. One is that the fourth term was extremely shocking, since otherwise the mask of Charon need not have been assumed. And the second is that the mask was in no way an actual disguise, but was instead an announcement of intention. By speaking as Charon, Archilochus said to his audience: This is the kind of song that one pretends to disown!

There was a second song that followed the same convention, according to Aristotle (*Rhet.* 1418b28) and likewise put its blame into the mouth of another. This time a fairly elaborate fiction was set up and the remaining fragment shows that the singer's formal distance from his target was actually established thrice over: by impersonation, by irony, and by the employment of a showy figure of speech. The imaginary situation is extremely obscure, but seemingly a father is speaking about a daughter whose hand is being sought in marriage,[39] though she is either ugly or lewd. In his astonishment he addresses her suitor with these sarcastic words (122W):

[38] A late Roman metrician, Juba, reported a poem about Gyges composed by Archilochus but this is the only mention of him in the surviving fragments; see O. Crusius *RE* sv 'Archilochus', 489.

[39] The scholiast at Ar. *Rhet.* 1418b28 attempts to explain the fictional situation of this song in various ways. According to one of his theories the father is answering someone who has said that his girl is evil and ugly by saying, 'Considering that anything can happen, what is surprising about my having an ugly daughter?' According to another theory, the father speaks to an impoverished suitor, encouraging him to hope, either for money or for the girl. Since the abuse, according to Aristotle, ought to be in the mouth of this 'disguised' speaker, the first of these theories is discredited, and since it ought to be as excessive as possible, the second seems very unlikely.

"χρημάτων ἄελπτον οὐδέν ἐστιν οὐδ' ἀπώμοτον
οὐδὲ θαυμάσιον, ἐπειδὴ Ζεὺς πατὴρ 'Ολυμπίων
ἐκ μεσαμβρίης ἔθηκε νύκτ', ἀποκρύψας φάος
ἡλίου †λάμποντος, λυγρὸν† δ' ἦλθ' ἐπ' ἀνθρώπους δέος.
ἐκ δὲ τοῦ καὶ πιστὰ πάντα κἀπίελπτα γίνεται   5
ἀνδράσιν· μηδεὶς ἔθ' ὑμέ̩ων εἰσορέ̩ων θαυμαζέτω
μηδ' ἐὰν δελφῖσι θῆρες ἀνταμείψωνται νομὸν
ἐνάλιον, καί σφιν θαλάσσης ἠχέεντα κύματα
φίλτερ' ἠπείρου γένηται, τοῖσι δ' ὑλέειν ὄρος.
                                   Ἀρ]χηνακτίδης   10
                                   ]ήτου πάϊς[
                                   ]τύθη γάμω̣ι[

'Nothing is too odd or wonderful,
nothing is beyond belief since Father Zeus
made night from noon, hid away the sun
and laid a shrinking fear on men.
From that time all things were possible
and so no man should marvel if
the forest beasts remove to dolphins'
salty fields, finding roaring waves
a sweeter home than land, while fishes plunge
high up on wooded mountain slopes.'

'Nothing is too odd', he seems about to conclude, 'and yet this is indeed
a wonder – a man who wants a girl like mine!'

One's heart goes out to the creature whose own father is made to
scorn her – whose wedding can only be explained as a reversal of all
of nature's laws – and yet the arresting thing about these lines is
their freedom from explicit calumny. Perhaps there was a direct attack
in some other part of the song, but here at least the famous Archilochean poison is entirely contained within a fastidious form of ridicule.
As the song descends from misplaced planets[40] to misplaced beasts,
and then with exquisite bathos lights upon the man who intends to
misplace himself in this young person's bed, no further syllable is
needed, for the girl has been beautifully rendered hideous.[41]

In the song of the ugly girl, the direct speech that embellished the

[40] The eclipse referred to is generally thought to be that of 648 BC; see F. Jacoby,
'The date of Archilochus', *CQ* 35 (1941) 97ff.
[41] It has been frequently asserted that this father is Lycambes, this daughter Neobule,
as if no other father and daughter existed in Paros or Thasos; F. Lasserre, 'Le fr.74',
MH 4 (1947) 5ff. believed them to be the father and sister of Archilochus! The appearance of the name Archenaktides in line 10 does nothing either to support or to destroy
either identification, though Treu (op. cit., p. 223) is convinced that this unknown must
be the rival to whom Neobule was given. For a contrary argument, see S. Luria, 'Zu
Archilochos', *Philolog.* 105 (1961) 183.

fables appears with a new function, for here, instead of merely supporting a narrative, it is itself the substance of the song. In this particular case we don't know whether or not the suitor also spoke, exciting the old man's answer, but there are other Archilochean songs in which two-way exchanges do certainly occur. In recognising these it would be pleasant to hail Archilochus as the first writer of non-epic dialogue, were it not for the fact that the ubiquitous question-and-answer rhyme of children's games existed in early Greece[42] and was common enough in Sappho's time to be exploited in her song for two players, the bride and her maidenhood (114V).[43] There are in truth conversational songs in most folk repertoires, and so Archilochus must not be thought of as an inventor because he sometimes gave his songs this shape. He was, however, as far as one can tell, the first to expand the simple challenge and response ditty into a discrete scene[44] something like those of his later imitator, Theocritus.[45]

In the true game songs no words are uttered outside the direct speeches, but in Archilochus' archaic idylls the singer employs epic formulae to mark a change of speaker ('So he spoke. I answered . . .'), and one such poem displays a narrative close. The Hellenistic imitations suggest that there were sometimes brief introductions as well, either in the third person or in the poet's first person, with perhaps an address to a friend.[46] (Something of the sort can be seen at the opening of a banquet anecdote that is offered to Glaucus for his amusement, 48W). The expository frame was evidently minimal, however, leaving the body of the poem to voices that were still typical – not to the eagle

[42] For Greek songs of play, cf. ποῦ μοι τὰ ῥόδα (Athen. 14.629E = 19B) and the Tortoise (Pollux 9.125, Eust. 1914 = 21 B); see the discussion of T. B. L. Webster, *The Greek Chorus* (London 1970) pp. 60–1. For elegiac dialogue, note Theognis, 577–8, and see West, *Studies*, 17–18. In Egypt and the Near East there was a genre of poetic debate that produced exchanges between Winter and Summer, Olive and Laurel, Stomach and Head, which seem to have influenced the Aesopian debates; see M. West, 'Near Eastern materials in Hellenistic and Roman literature', *HSCP* 73 (1969) 119 note 21. Compare also the Babylonian satiric dialogue between master and slave reported by Lambert, *Babylonian Wisdom Literature*, 139ff.

[43] Another example is the song for the voices of Sappho and Alcaeus that survives in the Sapphic corpus (137V); cf. S.102V and Alc. 10V. Alcman 107 *PMG* apparently represents an exchange for bride and groom: see T. Nissen, 'Zu Alkman frgm, 95D', *Philol.* 91 (1936–7) 470ff. At Hipp. 25W a man and woman exchange curses; cf. Hipp. 92W, which seems to be an anecdote with direct speech reported. West would classify Archil. 33W as a dialogue song, too, but there is no proof that the voice of the daughter of Lycambes was there presented directly.

[44] Sappho used almost the same structure in her fr. 94; see below, pp. 290ff.

[45] Compare especially Theocritus 27. Their Hellenistic imitations have caused some scholars to doubt the authenticity of the Archilochean dialogues; see Gelzer and Theiler, 'Ein wiedergefundenes Archilochos-Gedicht?' *Poetica* (1974) 490.

[46] Cf. Theoc. 6, 8, 13, 18, 20, 23 for third person; Theoc. 2, 11, [21] for first person; Theoc. 6, 11, 13, [21] for address to friend; the exx. of Theoc. 11, 13 and [21] suggest that these songs could also begin with a gnome, to which the dialogue was appended as a demonstration.

and the fox, now, but to human creatures who were generalised by a very formal mode.

No Archilochean dialogue poem survives in full, but two long papyrus fragments represent the mode, one in trimeters and the other an epode. In the trimeter song only the last speech can be read, but nevertheless it is clear that a small but complete scene is being played, one in which an action (that of persuasion) is depicted not in narrative but in dramatic form. The purpose of the song is not, however, simple entertainment, for three familiar elements mark it as an exercise in the art of blame: an Aesopic touch, an extended figure of speech, and a plain statement of injurious intent. A man and a woman have been set in conversation, and the woman has just ceased speaking when the song becomes legible (23W):[47]

.].[ ]ρ.βα.........δε..[[ω]]ρ ἠμειβόμ[ην·
"γύνα[ι], φάτιν μὲν τὴν πρὸς ἀνθρώπω[ν κακὴν
μὴ τετραμήνηις μηδέν· ἀμφὶ δ' εὐφ[ρόνηι,
ἐμοὶ μελήσει· [θ]υμὸν ἴλ[α]ον τίθε̲ο̲. 　[
ἐς τοῦτο δή τοι τῆς ἀνολβίης δοκ[έω
ἥκειν; ἀνήρ τοι δειλὸς ἆρ' ἐφαινόμην[,
οὐ]δ' οἷός εἰμ' ἐγὼ [ο̲]υ̲τος οὐδ' οἵων ἄπο. 　[
ἐπ]ίσταμαί τοι τὸν φιλ[έο]ν̲[τα] μὲν φ[ι]λεῖν̲[,
τὸ]ν̲ δ' ἐχθρὸν ἐχθαίρειν̲ τε̲ [κα]ὶ κακο̲[
μύ]ρμηξ. λόγωι νυν τ[ῶιδ' ἀλη]θείη πάρ[α.
πό]λιν δὲ ταύτη[ν ...]α[.... ἐ]πιστρέ[φεα]ι̲[
οὔ]τοι ποτ' ἄνδρες ἐξε[πόρθη]σαν, σὺ δ̲[ὲ
ν]υ̲ν εἷλες αἰχμῆι κα̲[ὶ μέγ' ἐ]ξήρ(ω) κ[λ]έος.
κείνης ἄνασσε καὶ τ[υραν]νίην ἔχε̲·
π[ο]λ̲[λοῖ]σ̲[ί θ]η]ν̲ ζ]ηλωτὸς ἀ[νθρ]ώπων ἔσεα̲ι̲."

　　　　I answered her:
'Madame, do not let this vulgar calumny
distress you. Pleasure is my care
so make your heart propitious . . .
Did you think I'd sunk to such a state
of wretchedness – did I seem so cowardly?
I'm not that kind, nor were my ancestors!
This I understand–how to love my love

---

[47] In spite of language, metre and a typical piece of abusive self-identification, the Archilochean authorship of these lines has been doubted; see C. Gallavotti, 'P.Oxy.2310', *Philol.*119 (1975) 153–62. K. Latte (*Gnomon* 27, 1955, 494) reported a single song that continued through 24W (as did LB and Treu) and resumed the situation as follows: someone has gone on a pirate expedition to Crete and has brought back a treasure, but the city to which he has returned is full of rumours against him, perhaps because the treasure originally belonged to it; a woman has also been brought back from Crete.

and how to hate my enemy and do him harm,
for I'm an Ant – *that* tale at least is true!
This city that you now explore
men have never sacked; you have taken it
by storm and you shall have its fame.
Rule it now, as tyrant of the place;
be envied by that multitude of men!'

Because of the disappearance of the poem's opening, the fictional situation is painfully opaque. The speaker's simplest assertion seems to be that a city is open to the woman's rule because it has not fallen to others, but this fairly plain statement is preceded by a balancing but seemingly irrelevant claim of personal innocence, and the two passages are joined (or divided) by an exclamation about an ant![48] The sequence is so bizarre that it has inspired at least a half-dozen different reconstructions of the inner drama that is here proposed, some of them quite elaborate. Certain scholars, struggling with a conviction that city-sacking is not a proper pastime for a woman (and also with the fact that the adjective 'envied' in the final line shows a masculine form),[49] have supposed that actually there was a cast of three, so that the present speaker may turn from his female companion to a male soldier or regent in the course of his remarks. Others suggest a conversation between two men in which our speaker is reporting to his masculine friend yet *another* conversation which he had at another time with a woman. Still others have insisted that the speaker's companion is not the mistress that she seems to be[50] but instead a female potentate from the Near East,[51] the wife of a friend named Ant,[52] or a male acquaintance whose predilections cause him to be called 'Madame' in derision.[53] Those who do not wish to face this wealth of suggestion prudently set both the fiction and the fragment aside and call them both 'baffling'.[54]

[48] Line 16 has been read in various ways, but West's isolation of the word μύ]ρμηξ is surely right. Like Theognis at 347 (ἐγὼ δὲ κύων), the speaker is making an animal boast with this single nominative; see R. D. Murray, 'Theognis 341–50', *TAPA* 96 (1965) 277ff.

[49] It should be noted that Euripides twice uses this same masculine adjective for a woman, at *Androm.*5 and *Med.*1035.

[50] F. Adrados, 'Sobre algunos papiros de Arquiloco', *PP* (1965) 38–41, identified the woman as the poet's mistress, as did also F. Lasserre, 'Un nouveau poème d'Archiloque', *MH* 13 (1956) 226–35, who went on to assert that she is Neobule. According to the interpretation here proposed, she is imagined as the speaker's mistress.

[51] Treu, *Arch.* 181ff. proposed a woman ruler who would take an actual city but is afraid she will be criticised; to her the speaker says (like Clytemnestra to Agamemnon): 'Go ahead. You will never be envied if you do not dare'. See also J. C. Kamerbeek, 'Archilochea', *Mnem.* 14 (1961) 9ff., and Kirkwood, *EGM*, 29.

[52] See W. Peek and O. Lendle, *Sammelband Politeia und ResPublica*, Palingenesia iv (Wiesbaden 1969) 47, and G. Schiassi, 'De novo Archilocho', *RFIC* 85 (1957) 151–66.

[53] See D. L. Page, 'Various conjectures', *PCPS* 187 (1961) 68–9 and K. Latte, loc. cit.

[54] Kirkwood, *EGM*, 29: 'Little more than chaos has issued from the study of this baffling fragment.'

Baffling it certainly is, but there are nevertheless two important observations to be made. First, these lines contain, not an attack but its counterpart, a complete speech of defence made in response to slanders that have probably been recounted by the previous speaker. And secondly, since this defence ends the poem and cannot be amended or contradicted, its final reassurance must fix the emotion which is the abiding achievement of the song. With this speech the speaker refutes his enemies and wins a verbal victory, and so his triumph under attack, mixed with that warmth of heart that he asks the lady for, is what is left behind when the song is done. This one speech is preserved in full; it is short and it was successful, which means that every one of its elements must have had a clear and vital significance, both as poetic matter and as persuasive rhetoric. Its two parts – its argument from character and its assertion about the city – must therefore be closely bound together in the service of the single end of refutation. In short, these fourteen lines must contain within themselves the calumny that they would resist, and consequently it should be possible to elicit from them the substance of the attack that provides the imaginary occasion for the song.

The first point in the defence is pleasure or well-being,[55] and this suggests that the defamatory rumour had somehow denied the speak-

---

[55] The interpretation here offered depends upon taking εὐ[φρόνηι in line 9 as if it were εὐφ[ροσύνη, the experience of one who is εὔφρων. (Otherwise line 9 would mean 'night-time is my care', which is how West takes it, *Studies* p.119; also J. Henderson, 'Early Greek erotic poetry', *Arethusa* 9 (1976) 162–3; cf. H. J. Mette, who read εὐφ[ρόνων as a contrast to the ἀνθρώπων κακῶν above, and translated 'I only pay attention to well-wishers'.) We do not know when εὐφρόνη first began to be used as a euphemism for 'night', nor do we know when, if ever, it took this secondary meaning as its exclusive signification. Hesiod, *Op*.560, speaks of the restoring μακραὶ εὐφρόναι of the winter season, where he could as well mean long pleasure-times (when darkness made work impossible) as long nights, and Simonides, 519 I ii.2 PMG has εὐφρόνα in what seems to be a festive context. Aeschylus, *Agam*. 264, uses the word for 'night', but indicates that to his ear it is still figurative by causing it to echo with εὔφρων, placed just above. (Such at least was the understanding of Sidgwick, Verrall, Schneidewin and many more recent scholars, though it is termed a 'doubtful' interpretation by Fraenkel, ad loc.) Later, Aeschylus shows the same consciousness of the basic meaning of the word by playfully writing the phrase ὦ φέγγος εὔφρον at *Agam*. 1577. Pindar, *N*.7.3, chooses εὐφρόνη in a happy passage in which he would avoid any of night's sinister associations and he adds the epithet μέλαινα to establish the term as the opposite of light. Sophocles makes a similar poetic use of the double connotation of εὐφρόνη at *El*.17, μέλαινά τ᾽ἄστρων ἐκλέλοιπεν εὐφρόνη (so Kaibel, who translated 'die schwarze Sternheiterkeit', and Housman, who rendered it 'the festal gathering of the stars' and argued that εὐφροσύνη was still the first meaning of εὐφρόνη, *CR* 2, 1888, 244; J. Vahlen, *Opusc*. 11.507, while rejecting Kaibel's understanding of the Sophoclean passage, still assumed that the 'original force' of *euphrone* was *hilaritas*). The Orphic hymn for Selene (9.8) treats *euphrone* as parallel to *hesuchia*. The situation is summed up by Hesychius, who reports: εὐφρόνη νὺξ καὶ εὐφροσύνη. In the present case, the ἵλαον that follows in line 10 strongly suggests that *euphrone* here carries its oldest and simplest meaning and that the poet was roughly paraphrasing *Od*. 6.156: μάλα πού σφισι θυμὸς αἰὲν εὐφροσύ-νησιν ἰαίνεται Cf. *Od*. 17.531; *h. Aphr*. 102; *h*.30.4 (where the θυμός is εὔφρων).

er's interest in, or power to provide, joy and satisfaction. 'On the contrary', he insists, 'that is all I care about.' His enemies' denial of his hedonism would, if believed, trouble the woman and cause her to harden her heart towards her friend, but under the influence of his opposite assertion she is to become warm and gracious.[56] She too is therefore interested in pleasure.

The next point is that whatever the speaker was accused of is something that one might be brought to if one were wretched, or cowardly, or of a certain 'sort'. In dealing with these suggestions, the speaker is at first realistic – 'I was never that hard up' – and then proud – 'I'm not that sort, nor is anyone in my family'.[57] As further evidence that he is not the kind who would behave as charged, he claims to be one who (like the abusive poet) deals in sincere and appropriate hatred and love. The slander is false because he knows how to pleasure his friends and give real pain to his enemies.

Once he has established himself as a man of just emotions, the speaker turns to a city which he says is open to the woman's rule. The evil gossip evidently reported that it had been sacked and was therefore worthless, but this he simply denies. The woman is its single conqueror, and yet he offers it to her as if it were his own, marking his proprietary sense with a touch of complacency. It has never fallen, but many have coveted it and when she takes possession she will be envied by a multitude of men. Under the influence of the evil report, the woman has evidently refused the city as unworthy of her, but with his reassurance she will change her mind and accept it, for the song ends with a prospective vision of her happy tyranny in the unspoiled stronghold where her friend will place her.

The two sections of the song thus in effect duplicate each other, for in each of them the woman is persuaded to receive something of value that the speaker has to give: first pleasure and then dominion. These two offerings have both been smirched by a single slander, then cleared by a single defence, as the speaker's claim to justice in his loves and hatreds worked a simultaneous enhancement on them both. In a passage as short as this, such perfect parallelism necessarily brings the two parts of the speech into conflation as the woman is begged to make her heart receptive to delight and then straightaway begged again to receive the rule of an envied place. Delight and rule overlap and mingle in their close similarity, and in consequence the

---

[56] In the *Iliad* (9.639 and 19.178) one who consciously gives up anger and sets himself to receive friendly overtures 'makes his *thumos* ἵλαος'. At Hes. *Op.* 340, the phrase is used of gods happily receiving sacrifices; at *h. Dem.* 204 it describes Demeter's action as she relinquishes her sadness and agrees to know pleasure, urged on by Iambe's bawdy gesture.

[57] Cf. West, *Studies* 120: 'So you take me for a low person and mistake the true class of the man before you and of his background . . .'

lover is heard to urge just one action to which, like a psalmist, he has
given two consecutive descriptions. 'Oh take pleasure in your friend,
exercise power over your town' is the pattern of his plea, and when it
is recognised the song loses its incoherence. It is plain that the city
the lady is to rule is identical with the friend – no political community
but her lover's body – and that the pleasure she is asked to take is
identical with a power that is not military but erotic.[58]

Once the metaphor of the city is recognised, the nature of the rejected slander becomes apparent. The rumour that disturbed the
woman and made her ungracious asserted that this man who would
be her lover, being poor and a coward, interested in money rather
than pleasure, and unable to discriminate between friend and enemy,
has allowed his 'city' to be sacked. His enemies have been saying, in
other words, that he has sold himself, their accusation being not unlike
that of Archilochus himself when he says elsewhere, of female prostitutes, that their sexual parts are 'places of no pleasure' because they
work for hire (263W). Presumably he has been slandered as one who
served men[59] (it would be difficult for a man to sell himself in any
other way, where women had no money and no freedom) and this suits
the standard *topos* of abuse for effeminacy. Archilochus had made that
charge against Melesander, though with tongue in cheek, in the Eurymas song, and again with friendly derision in the line 'Sing Glaucus
of the sculptured curl' (117W).[60] He had given it the ruder form of the
ape fable as well, if the point there had to do with shaving the body,
and later antiquity knew songs of his aimed at a certain flute-player
whom the poet presented (by means of the epithet 'blower of horns')

---

[58] Adrados, op. cit., suggested that the city might be an erotic metaphor, but he was
covered with scorn by Kamerbeek, op. cit., 11: 'Archiloque n'est pas un poète de basse
époque. Il est libidineux, obscène même à ses heures, mais jamais poète ne fût plus
exempt de mièvrerie et d'autre part de gongorisme que lui.' Kamerbeek of course did
not know of the garden = pubis, gateway = vagina figures that appear in the Cologne
fragment, but he might have remembered the woman = field of 188W, the fig-tree =
prostitute of 331W, or the hose and pail of 46W. To such a list West would add woman
= mountain landscape, in 190W, but nothing makes this expression necessarily metaphorical or if metaphorical necessarily sexual in its application. (W. pretends that
unless it is metaphorical the line would express an un-archaic delight in mountain-
walking, but there is no explicit delight here, and the line at any rate may have come
from a speech in a fable). The idea that the city represents the body of the speaker is
accepted by West (*Studies*, 119), who adduces Theognis 951 (=1278c) as a parallel
metaphorical conquest, though there the city is not erotic.

[59] It is merely ἄνθρωποι who are repeating the slander in 1.8, and πολλοὶ ἄνθρωποι
again who will be jealous in the future, but at line 18 the city's reputed spoilers are
specified emphatically as ἄνδρες in the speaker's denial.

[60] Unless the more correct translation is 'Sing Glaucus the horn-moulder', in which
case the line is explicitly obscene; cf. 239W and 240W, both comic words apparently
applied to effeminate hair styles, and 217W and 265W, references to bodies shaved to
make them more elegant (like the unfortunate ape of the fable for Kerykides).

as a kind of eponymous hero of male homosexuality (270W).[61] When the occasion arose, Archilochus was perfectly ready to lay a charge of perversion upon an enemy, but in the present case he has chosen another stance and has pretended to repulse such an attack, as if he himself were the victim of calumny.[62]

Such indirection suggests that this song was meant for friends, not enemies – that it was a piece of that childish banquet raillery that Hermes' original singing had ordained. Its riddling dialogue supposes an initiated audience that knows the history, or pseudo-history, of this and many another battle of abuse. The song has more than this to offer, however, and its larger meanings likewise address a group of companions to whom the poet presents, not an enemy for scorn, but himself, for approbation. In the fiction a lover, attacked as a male whore, persuades his mistress to reject the slanders of his enemies and receive him; in the speaker's metaphor, a city rumoured to have been sacked persuades its conqueror to take it as unspoiled. The little drama is consistent and complete, and yet there is obviously another level to the poet's intentions, for the speaker is portrayed not just as a lover but also as an artist in blame. 'I am an ant!' he announces in a moment of high rhetoric, and this homely insect, standing alone and unexpected at the beginning of line 16, almost destroys the dramatic illusion. The ant doesn't suit a plea to a disdainful mistress, and yet he has obviously been carefully chosen, since he brings into the defence a true *logos* that will outweigh the lying *phatis* of the speaker's enemies.[63] People were wont to say, 'There's wrath, even in an ant' (schol. Ar. *Birds* 82), and when they did they referred to a fable in which Ant bit a bird-catcher who was about to entrap his friend Dove (Aesop, Chambry 242).[64] The doughty little ant thus provides an illustrative commentary upon the words that have just been uttered ('I understand

---

[61] According to ancient report, Archilochus attacked homosexuals as 'the lowest of the low', (294W) and Julian (*epist.* 80, 97, 19B-C) claimed to know an Archilochean work in which Laius was abused, presumably on the score of Chrysippus (see Wilamowitz, *Kl. Schr.* iv 363). In addition, two Renaissance forgeries (327 and 328W) prove that such attacks were later thought to be typical of his work; see G. Tarditi, 'Due carmi giambici di uno ps. Archiloco', *RCCM* 3 (1961) 311–16 and A. Garzya, 'Varia Phil. IV.5', *BPEC* 9 (1961) 44–5. Compare also Hipp. 148W.

[62] Note that there is an attack upon himself by an imaginary enemy among Solon's tetrameters (33W), and that the song of Alcaeus contained in P.Oxy. 2506, fr. 77, likewise seems to be a poetic rebuttal of a piece of slander; see below, p. 169.

[63] West, *Studies*, 119, supposes that this *logos* is contrasted with another *logos* of the speaker's which the woman has rejected as untrustworthy. For *logos* in the sense of a proverb, cf. Aesch. fr. 235N; *Sept.* 225; Pindar *O.*7.21 (of the received version of the Tlepolemos tradition) and *P.*1.35 (of the proverb about fair beginnings and fair ends).

[64] Another proverb about the ant exists, not quite so apt to the present context: [Theoc.] 9.31 has τέττιξ μὲν τέττιγι φίλος, μύρμακι δὲ μύρμαξ 'each to his kind'; compare Dio Chrys. 40.32 (von Arnim ii 54) of ants: οὐδέποτε ἠνώχλησαν ἀλλήλους ἀλλὰ πάνυ πρᾴως ἐντυγχάνουσι καὶ παριᾶσι καὶ βοηθοῦσιν ἀλλήλοις. See W. Morel 'Die Ameise bei Archilochus', *ZPE* 8 (1971) 143–4.

how to love and hate . . .') and in addition, by specifying the harm
done to enemies as a bite, the work of his mouth, the insect turns the
speaker's boast into a motto for the profession of blame.

The ant of this poem thus joins the cicada, the fox and the hedgehog
as one more animal figure for the poet of abuse, and with his bite (and
his ability to love) he is perhaps the most telling of the four. He proves
that the male speaker here is a version of Archilochus, and he likewise
proves that, to the fable's announcement, 'I am dreadful when I attack
others', this song now adds the complementary claim, 'When others
attack *me*, I am impervious'. On this level, the blame-poet, slandered
as having been for sale, persuades his audience to listen to him as the
very best of his kind, indeed a prince of blame. Nevertheless, because
his service is to Momus, his own claims must be deflated and deprived
of any tendency towards pomposity, and here again the ant is useful
to him. The ant has allowed the lover to refute the charge that he sold
his love, while he let the poet deny that his hate was for sale; he has
in addition allowed the singer-speaker to threaten his slanderers with
retaliation, and yet no one can deny (and the singer least of all) that
when this poet-ant is set beside his other self, the lover-city, the
resulting disproportion is desperately ridiculous. Because of the ant,
the man who views himself as an acropolis faces his conquering mistress on the field of eros, where no one should suffer *meiōsis*, as an
insect of the smallest sort.

Archilochus thus uses his two metaphors to laugh at himself more
artfully than ever his enemies could, and in so doing he refutes other
more serious charges that might have been brought against his profession of calumny. The woman is mere *staffage*, a mouth-piece for slander which likewise becomes incidental as the poet promises his fellow
citizens that they will be gratified by his unbought anger, just as the
lady will be by his unbought love. He fully understands (*epistamai*,
14) how to honour and how to scorn because he has none of the self-
righteousness or hypocrisy that might have turned his biting blame
into spite or jealousy, and in demonstration of this fact he sets his own
ant to attack his own citadel. Both of them in consequence suffer from
absurdity, for Archilochus is here practising the self-satire that is for
the abusive singer what self-praise is for the maker of epinician odes
– a proof of the infallible precision of his song.

iv

Obscenity

Indecent language was proper to archaic blame, formally because it
had belonged to the primitive rituals from which iambic metres had
devolved,[1] and rationally because it served the central purposes of
Momus and acted to check the presumptions of mankind. As an instrument of mortal humiliation, obscenity was the more efficient counterpart of the animal fable, since a single word or gesture could reduce
all men to a state of equal bestiality. It was less artful than the fable,
certainly, but still it had its own variety, and it could be used in either
of two ways, according to the mood and the sophistication of the poet.
If he were in a primitive mood, the blamer could attack a given victim
and accuse him of lewdness, fixing some laughable sexual activity
upon him. In this case sex was treated with derision and given a
negative evaluation, so that the imaginary result of the song was the
defeat both of the man and his practices: like a demon attacked with
apotropaic obscenity, he would be evicted from society, taking his
lewdness with him. In another mood, however, the poet could praise
obscene actions, much as the old fertility magic did, but with the
added satiric suggestion that indecency was more true and more
admirable than the pretentious behaviour generally accepted by society. In this second form, the poet's attack was made broadside upon
all the complacenies of his community, but he did not need to condemn
or justify, for an open and joyous use of forbidden words pressed his
charge more strongly than reasoned argument could.

Not much of Archilochus' obscenity has survived and what exists is
extremely fragmentary, so that it is not easy to discriminate between
these two impulses in his work. No one can say, of words for sexual
parts (male, 82.4; female, 40, (in the plural), and perhaps 48.8 and
67.11W) and an isolated phrase for an erection (66W), whether they
were used to celebrate or denigrate, though one pair of lines seems to
represent a joyous attack upon 'decency': 'His cock overflowed like that

---

[1] See the bibliography and summary of J. Henderson, *The Maculate Muse* (New Haven
1975) 14–18.

of a barley-fed ass from Priene' (43W).[2] Other expressions, however, link the notions of cutting and climax with an effect that is far from joyous (222W,[3] 67W), and a phrase like 'out of the hose and into the pail' (46W) can hardly be anything but vilification of the heterosexual act. Even less ambivalent in their scorn are two lines about a slightly different encounter (42W):[4]

ὥσπερ αὐλῶι βρῦτον ἢ Θρέϊξ ἀνὴρ
ἢ Φρὺξ ἔμυζε· κύβδα δ' ἦν πονεομένη.

Like some Phrygian or Thracian sucking beer
through a straw, she bent and drank him off.

The prostitute[5] was a special subject for Archilochean blame and for his obscenity was usually employed in its negative form. The whore is attacked as a symbol of degeneracy and greed, because she makes public what ought to be private (she is *dēmos* 207W):[6] she is attacked because she is like an animal (*bous ergatēs* 35W) and does her work for hire (she is *ergatis* 208W, and *drēstēs* 119W),[7] wasting the money that men collect with such difficulty (302W);[8] and finally she is attacked because she is a receptacle that collects all the defilement of a community (she is *musachnē*, 209W). She is loathsome and she makes her clients loathsome too, as the poet says with his taunt

---

[2] Compare the very different ἁπαλὸν κέρας at 247, where the striking oxymoron may perhaps be used in praise, though scorn is equally possible.

[3] In 222W Henderson, op. cit., 21, reads as if the verb were ἀπεθρίασε instead of ἀπέθρισε, and translates, 'she peeled back the fig-leaves of my manhood', but the true meaning seems to be something much more like 'she cut the stalk of my sex'. At 67W the idea of cutting (τομῆι,1) is placed in proximity with that of an erection figured as a growth.

[4] Cf. Hipponax 22W, where Arete is similarly bent, and for discussion see R. Lattimore, 'Notes on Greek poetry', *AJP* 65 (1944) 172ff. and D. E. Gerber, 'Archil. Fr.42 West', *QU* 22 (1976) 7–14.

[5] See Hans Herter, 'Die Soziologie der antiken Prostitution im Lichte des heidnischen u. Christlichen Schrifttums', *Jahrb. f. Ant. u. Christ.* 3 (1960) 70ff., for general discussion.

[6] This publicity becomes the point of later topoi in which the prostitute is a figure for a literary form, e.g. Callim. *Ep.* 28 Pf; Horace *Epist*.1.20. 1–5, 7–8 and 10–13; Ovid *Amores*, 3.8ff.

[7] Compare 263W, where Hesychius reports that Archilochus called a vagina ἀηδονίς, because it was a place of work, not pleasure. On ἐργάτις and ἐργαστήριον in this sense, see A. D. Knox, *Herondas, The Mimes and Fragments, with notes by Walter Headlam* (Cambridge 1922) 417. It is possible that 34W refers to a prostitute's demand for her wage.

[8] In 302W both money and lust seem to be compared to a snake: not hard to catch but hard to hold on to. The figure is conceptually related to that of the eel in 189.

for a whore: 'Many's the blind eel you've taken in!' (189W).[9] Some
fragments, however, suggest that a prostitute might be admirable, if
she enjoyed her work (see 41W, where she flaps her wings in pleasure,
perched upon her partner), and there are two lines, not always
accepted as genuine,[10] in which Archilochus pays tribute to a famous
madam with an ironic but perhaps friendly pun that plays on the
promiscuity of her name (331W):[11]

συκῆ πετραίη πολλὰς βόσκουσα κορώνας,
εὐήθης ξείνων δέκτρια Πασιφίλη.

Fig-tree on the rocks, feeding all the crows,
obliging every guest, hospitable Pasiphile!

Abuse of the prostitute embraces abuse of her guests and their lusts,
and the fragments about whoredom suggest that Archilochus attacks
such women because they teach a man to 'fall into a hard-working bag

[9] West would attach 189 to 188, but such a conjunction would weaken both the
woman=field image of 188 and the penis=eel here; on this figure, see D. E. Gerber,
'Eels in Archilochus', QU 16 (1973) 105–9. In the Anthology prostitutes are often
represented as women who practise special sexual arts, and this may be the point of
44W.

[10] Page (FH. X, 136–7) judged the lines to be a 'forgery' because the density of their
verbal play was not 'oral', and he objected specifically to εὐήθης, as not having a second,
ironic meaning until the fifth century. In response it could be urged that this punning
play on a name is much like that in the address to Kerykides (185W) or the lines on
Leophilus (115W), and that the Cologne fragment also shows usages that otherwise do
not appear until the fifth century, most notably ἐς κόρακας, μαίνολις, δίπλοος, ἐπήλυσις;
see D. A. Campbell, 'The language of the new Archilochus', Arethusa 9 (1976) 151ff.; E.
Degani, 'Il nuovo Archiloco', A&R 19 (1974) 125. West (Studies, 139ff.) argues against
the authenticity of the Pasiphile fragment in two further ways. First he says that the
Cynics would not have taken up the comparison without acknowledgment of its source,
if it had come from Archilochus; to which one might answer that the comparison may
well have become a locus communis (or even have been one, when Archilochus used it).
West's second objection derives from the words of Athenaeus, who cites the lines by
saying about a fourth-century courtesan, '. . . the Ionians called Plangon "Pasiphile".
And Archilochus talks about her in these lines . . .' (594cd). Accordimg to West, Athenaeus is referring the couplet to Plangon, which means that it cannot have been
rightly attributed to Archilochus, and so he corrects Athenaeus' ascription to read
'Archias' (cf. CR 20, 1970, 148). This criticism, however, seems to ask far too much of
Athenaeus' syntax, and it seems better to allow him a bit of imprecision and understand
him as saying, 'The Ionians called Plangon "Pasiphile" (after the famous Pasiphile) and
Archilochus talks about her (the original) in these lines . . .' In favour of the ancient
attribution to Archilochus one might note the typical parody of Homer's Σκύλλη πετραίη
(Od. 12.231), which becomes Συκή πετραίη, and the double meaning of δέκτρια, which
is exactly like that of ἔδεξω in 189W; see Gerber's discussion of this verb, op. cit., 106.

[11] Pasiphile's name may be compared with that of the bride Πασιχάρηα at Alcman
107 PMG. The joke about Pasiphile's 'reception' is much like the one made about a male
prostitute at Theoc. Epig.14, where the boy is likened to a bank. On figs and their
sexual symbolism, see V. Buchheit, 'Feigensymbolik im antiken epigramm,' RhM 103
(1960) 200ff., who notes the σῦκα πέτραισιν ἐπ᾽ ἀκρολόφοισι at AP 12.185, eaten by
vultures.

and strive there, belly to belly and thigh against thigh' (119W).[12]
Whores make men their equals and encourage them to betray other,
less sordid forms of sexuality. Archilochus is not, of course, a poet of
romantic love, but he does have some lines that begin to sound, in
spite of their traditional phraseology, like later love songs. In his own
or someone else's voice he says somewhere in an epode (191W):

> τοῖος γὰρ φιλότητος ἔρως ὑπὸ καρδίην ἐλυσθεὶς
>   πολλὴν κατ' ἀχλὺν ὀμμάτων ἔχευεν,
> κλέψας ἐκ στηθέων ἁπαλὰς φρένας.

> Desire for love crouched at my heart,
>   so strong it poured a cloud of mist
> upon my eyes and stole my feeble senses
>   from my breast.

Sexual longing is here first imaged as a grovelling suppliant who
might be spurned by a proud heart, but then it is transformed to
become a metaphysical force. In the second line it exercises a power
like that of death and causes the lover to suffer exactly as a fallen
warrior might, in a Homeric battle. In another fragment the poet
repeats this comparison of love with death which was to become an
amorous commonplace (193W):[13]

> δύστηνος ἔγκειμαι πόθωι,
> ἄψυχος, χαλεπῆισι θεῶν ὀδύνηισιν ἕκητι
> πεπαρμένος δι' ὀστέων.

> Wretched and full of desire, I lie
> lifeless, pierced to the bone
>   by this divine and dreadful pain.

A strong emotion that makes a man weak is a paradox for Archilochus
(as simple lust never is), and a sense that love is both tyrannical and

---

[12] The *askos* of the first line is obviously a receiving female organ, in spite of the
arguments of D. Korzeniewski, 'Die erste Satire des Persius', *Wege d. Forsch.* 228 (1970)
394. At E. *Med.* 679, the *pous* or spout of the wineskin figures the penis, but here the
whole receptacle is meant, and is feminine. The characteristic ugliness of Archilochus'
lines can be sharply felt if one compares to them their sugary imitation at *AP* 5.128:
στέρνα περὶ στέρνοις, μαστῷ δ᾽ ἐπὶ μαστὸν ἐρείσας / χείλεά τε γλυκεροῖς χείλεσι συμπιέσας,
κτλ. Compare also Theoc. *Id.* 2. 140f., and see D. E. Gerber, 'Archilochus Fr. 119W',
Phoenix 29 (1975) 181–4.

[13] For this agony that is and is not death Archilochus uses a new epithet, ἄψυχος,
which gives the line an almost Hellenistic sound; for desire, he employs πόθος, which
occurs in the *Odyssey* and in late epic, as well as in elegy, but not in the *Iliad*. In
connection with the phrase πεπαρμένος δι' ὀστέων, it might be noted that some ancient
theories located the source of semen and so of virility in the marrow; so Hippon (DK⁶
38A12), Hippocrates, *de genit.*2, Plato, *Tim.* 73B; see Onians, *Origins of European
Thought*² (Cambridge 1954) 108–9. In general, on association of ideas of love and death,
see E. Vermeule, (op. cit., pp. 151ff).

absurd in a man of action is expressed in a single line where the dissolute epithet *lusimelēs*[14] is juxtaposed with a verb of dominance (196W):[15]

ἀλλά μ' ὁ λυσιμελὴς ὦταῖρε δάμναται πόθος.

but oh, my friend, weak-kneed desire so masters me . . .

Blame of ugly lusts and prostitutes implies the existence of better pleasures and of women who are chaste, but these alternatives are not subjects that a derisive poet likes to treat. Archilochus for the most part admitted to seeing only corruption and its potential – only false virgins and real whores. The girls provokingly drove men away (47W) while the professionals knowingly led them on, but in truth they were all the same; each prostitute had once been pure, but each untouched girl knew how to arouse desire, and all of them were insatiable (246W). Beauty and decency were mere appearances, for paid entertainers could appear to be lovely (48.5–6W),

τροφὸς κατ.[ͺἐσμυριχμένας κόμην
καὶ στῆθος, ͺὡς ἂν καὶ γέρων ἠράσσατο.

so perfumed as to hair and breast
they might have made an old man lust,

and a girl who was now common property had once seemed as un-stained as any pre-Raphaelite maid (30–1W):[16]

ἔχουσα θαλλὸν μυρσίνης ἐτέρπετο
ῥοδῆς τε καλὸν ἄνθος.
                    ἡ δέ οἱ κόμη
ὤμους κατεσκίαζε καὶ μετάφρενα.

a sprig of myrtle, long ago, or an open rose
was all her joy, and her hair's deep shadow fell
below her shoulders, where her back was small.

---

[14] With λυσιμελής compare *Od.*18.212 λύτο γούνατα, where the subject is eros; λυσιμελής is an epithet of eros at Hesiod *Theog.* 121, 911; Alcman 3.3.61 has λυσιμελεῖ δὲ πόσῳ. In none of these cases, however, is there a verb of strength or domination.

[15] This is the second line of a couplet that may have begun with an expression of desire for military, sympotic, or abusive activity which must be given up because of love's effects; see West, 'Two notes', *ZPE* 26 (1977) 44–8, where Γλαῦκ', οὐκέθ' ἱρῶν οὖτ' ἰάμβων μοι μέλει (cf. 215W) is proposed as the opening.

[16] Two separate fragments were joined by Bergk to make this much admired sequence. Synesius reports that the hair of the second fragment was praised 'although it belonged to the body of a prostitute', but critics nevertheless often pretend that the lines must describe Neobule. See B. Marzullo, 'La chioma di Neobule', *RM* 100 (1957) 68–82 (reprinted in E. Degani, *Poeti Greci Giambici ed Elegiaci* (Milan 1977), who believes that the two fragments are not from the same poem, but that both describe girls currently practising prostitution.

All in all, woman was a perverse being who cheated men by creating passion and then extinguishing it, either with a chill rejection or with a response that was much too hot (184W):[17]

τῆι μὲν ὕδωρ ἐφόρει
δολοφρονέουσα χειρί, θἠτέρηι δὲ πῦρ.

In one hand this deceitful creature
carries water, in the other, fire.

Women betrayed the promise of their beauty. All were like prostitutes, corruptible where they should have been pure, and the decay of their flesh – an outward sign of their true state – was a thing Archilochus liked to mark. One old lady is assumed to be looking for a whore's work (205W)[18] 'else why should a crone like you smear herself with scent', and another is the butt of a catalogue of destroyed parts that ends '. . .*and* fat ankles, the promiscuous drab' (206W).[19] Worn-out women were proof that what one most valued in one moment could become hateful in the next, but they had a positive function too, in this poetry, for when the masculine singer and his friends laughed at such creatures they felt a cynical vitality. Through the crone and the drab they could reject old age as well as illusions and Archilochus shows them how, in lines ostensibly addressed to a lady of the town (188W & 478b *SLG*):[20]

[17] Demetrius (35.6), making this citation, likens its woman to Tyche, who brings both hope and fear. The epithet δολοφρονέουσα seems to establish a relationship between her and Aphrodite (see below, pp. 251ff.), but Treu (*Archil.*, 183) believes that the figure has a political meaning.

[18] Compare Rochester's abuse of an overaged beau: '. . . to paint thy grizly face, to dance, to dress . . .'

[19] The woman's age is indicated by these fat ankles since girls were conventionally slim-ankled (τανύσφυρος). In addition, the word παχεῖα evidently held an imputation of promiscuity, either because it could mean 'pregnant' or else διὰ τὸ πολύτροφον, according to Eust. in Hom. p.1088.38.

[20] The word ὀπώρα was frequently used of a sexual harvest (Ar. *Pax* 530: cf. Aesch.*Supp.* 997–8; 1015: P.*I*.2.7; *N*.5.11; *AP* 9.563) and came to be a favourite nickname for a prostitute, as in Alexis' comedy of that name (1644 = K11.1.358); see Buchheit, op. cit., 208. On this fragment, see S. M. Medaglia, 'Archiloco, Orazio e il secondo epodo di Colonia', *QU* 25 (1977) 7–15. The fact that this song appears on the Cologne papyrus immediately following the poem that abuses Neobule might indicate that the copyist believed it to refer to her also.
To this satiric contrast of a woman's age to her youth, one might compare Rochester in 'Corinna':

Gay were the hours and wing'd with joy they flew
When first the town her early beauties knew.
Courted, admired and lov'd, with presents fed,
Youth in her looks and pleasure in her bed . . .
. . .
Diseas'd, decay'd, to take up half a crown . . .

οὐκέ]θ' ὁμῶς θάλλεις ἁπαλὸν χρόα, κάρφετα[ι γὰρ ἤδη
ὄγμοι]ς, κακοῦ δὲ γήραος καθαιρεῖ
.....], ἀφ' ἱμερτοῦ δὲ θορὼν γλυκὺς ἵμερος π[ροσώπου
πέπτω]κεν· ἦ γὰρ πολλὰ δή ς' ἐπῆιξεν
πνεύμ]ατα χειμερίων ἀνέμων ⟨ ⟩ πολλάκις δε[

No more does your soft flesh bloom, its folds
have given up their fruit and ugly old age
[– hoe in hand –] comes to clear the ground. . .
The sweetness of your face is gone; it's plain that many gusts
of winter wind have swept it bare, and often . . .

It is any old woman who is attacked, for the extended figure serves to
generalise the abuse, abuse that is none the less harsh as the lines
swiftly replace an image of flowers with one of withered stubble in
preparation for whatever charge is to follow the broken 'and often
. . .' The woman is finished, but her observers are not, for the satirist
(unlike Mimnermus when he sang of lost youth) here separates them
from the process he describes. Instead of identifying himself with a
debility that is the common fate, as the elegist does, he stands aside
here, chooses a figure of the opposite sex, invests her with age and
ugliness, and then gets rid of her by scourging her with song.

In antiquity Archilochus was most famous for the lewd attacks he
made upon the daughters of Lycambes, but until a short time ago the
nature of these could only be guessed at. There were two scraps of
verse that seemed to praise – 'If I could but touch the hand of Neobule'
(118W)[21] and something about the voice of a daughter of Lycambes
(33W) – and another that mentioned the 'upper' or 'elder' child of
Lycambes as being 'alone' (38W), but nothing else referred certainly
to these notorious girls.[22] The poet had called the Lycambids obscene
and promiscuous, according to later epigrams that playfully took up
their defence (e.g. *AP* 7.351), but only two dubious words of this sort
survived, in a notice of Hesychius (206W) which reported that Neo-

---

[21] Compare Hipp. 119W: εἴ μοι γένοιτο παρθένος καλή τε καὶ τέρεινα which may
represent an invidious wish inspired by an opposite actuality.

[22] 54W, which seems to be a sexual narrative containing a 'she', may be addressed to
Lycambes (see line 8) and likewise 57.7W may refer to him, since the restoration
Δω]ιάδεω would give his patronymic; 71W again may contain his name, but the nature
of these fragments is unknown. West, in *IE* and also in *Studies*, gives the impression
that there is much reference to the Lycambids, for he takes everything that may
possibly refer to prostitutes and presents it as if it were necessarily attached to this
family; his fragments 30–87 are thus described as 'de Lycambae filiabus', although only
two of the 57 items are specifically so identified.

bule[23] was called 'fat' or 'pregnant' (*pacheia*) and a 'professional' (*ergatis*) by the poet Archilochus. Then, in Cologne in 1973, a bit of inscribed papyrus was taken from a mummy, and when it was read it was found to carry lines of verse that abused Neobule with supreme ferocity.[24] The slander itself held no surprises, for the woman was berated as a worn-out whore in terms familiar from other Archilochean passages. Wholly unexpected, however, was the setting of the attack, for much more than simple rage appears in this rediscovered song. Its twelve lines of abuse are placed within a dramatic speech, and that speech in turn is placed within a dialogue scene that ends with a narrative of delight and praise. Indeed, the abuse is ostensibly only incidental to the poem as a whole, for Neobule and hatred appear in the midst of a conversation between a man and a girl, an 'I' and a 'she', who meet in a rustic spot in the beginning, and who become lovers before the song is done.

The girl has evidently had the first long speech, and the Cologne papyrus becomes readable just as she delivers her final lines (Pap. Col.7511 = *SLG* 478):

πάμπαν ἀποσχόμενος·
ἶσον δὲ τολμ[2
⟨———⟩
εἰ δ' ὦν ἐπείγεαι καί σε θυμὸς ἰθύει,
ἔστιν ἐν ἡμετέρου
ἢ νῦν μέγ' ἱμείρε[ι   5
⟨———⟩
καλὴ τέρεινα παρθένος· δοκέω δέ μι[ν
εἶδος ἄμωμον ἔχειν·
τὴν δὴ σὺ πένθ[8
⟨———⟩
τοσαῦτ' ἐφώνει· τὴν δ' ἐγὼ ἀνταμει[βόμην·
"Ἀμφιμεδοῦς θύγατερ
ἐσθλῆς τε καὶ [περίφρονος   11
⟨———⟩

---

[23] It is possible that Hesychius has here wilfully substituted Neobule's name for the πόρνη of the other commentators.

[24] A papyrus from the first century A.D., first published by R. Merkelbach and M. West, 'Ein Archilochos-Papyrus', *ZPE* 14 (1974) 97–113; more on its date by Merkelbach, 'Nachträge zu Archilochos', *ZPE* 16 (1975) 22ff. The poem is generally accepted as Archilochean, although T. Gelzer argued that it was a Hellenistic imitation; see 'Ein wiedergefundenes Archilochos-Gedicht?' *Poetica* (1974) 490ff. and 'Köln pap. 7511', *MH* 32 (1975) 12–32. A select bibliography of the early discussion of the fragment is given by J. Van Sickle, 'The new Archilochus texts', *Arethusa* 9 (1976) 149–50; see also his general report in 'The new erotic fragment of Archilochus', *QU* 20 (1975) 123–56.

γυναικόc, ἣν νῦν γῆ κατ' εὐρώεcc' ἔ[χει,
τ]έρψιέc εἰcι θεῆc
πολλαὶ νέοιcιν ἀνδ[ράcιν   14

⟨———⟩

παρὲξ τὸ θεῖον χρῆμα· τῶν τιc ἀρκέcε[ι.
τ]αῦτα δ' ἐπ' ἡcυχίηc
εὖτ' ἂν μελανθη[17

⟨———⟩

ἐ]γώ τε καὶ cὺ cὺν θεῶι βουλεύcομεν·
π]είcομαι ὥc με κέλεαι·
πολλόν μ' ε[20

⟨———⟩

θρ]ιγκοῦ δ' ἔνερθε καὶ πυλέων ὑποφ[
μ]ή τι μέγαιρε, φίλη·
cχήcω γὰρ ἐc πọη[φόρουc   23

⟨———⟩

κ]ήπουc. τὸ δὴ νῦν γνῶθι· Νεοβούλη[
ἄ]λλοc ἀνὴρ ἐχέτω·
αἰαῖ πέπειρα δ .[26

⟨———⟩

ἄν]θοc δ' ἀπερρύηκε παρθενήιον
κ]αὶ χάριc ἣ πρὶν ἐπῆν·
κόρον γὰρ οὐκ[29

⟨———⟩

..]ηc δὲ μέτρ' ἔφηνε μαινόλιc γυνή·
ἐc] κόρακαc ἄπεχε·
μὴ τοῦτ' ἐφοῖτ' ἀṿ[32

⟨———⟩

ὅ]πωc ἐγὼ γυναῖκα τ[ο]ιαύτην ἔχων
γεί]τοcι χάρμ' ἔcομαι·
πολλὸν cὲ βούλọ[μαι πάροc·   35

⟨———⟩

cὺ] μὲν γὰρ οὔτ' ἄπιcτοc οὔτε διπλόη,
ἡ δ]ὲ μάλ' ὀξυτέρη,
πολλοὺc δὲ ποιεῖτα[ι   38

⟨———⟩

δε]δοιχ' ὅπως μὴ τυφλὰ κἀλιτήμερα
cπ]ουδῆι ἐπειγόμενος
τὼς ὥσπερ ἡ κ[ύων τέκω."   41

⟨————⟩

τοc]αῦτ' ἐφώνεον· παρθένον δ' ἐν ἄνθε[cιν
τηλ]εθάεccι λαβὼν
ἔκλινα, μαλθακῆι δ[έ μιν   44

⟨————⟩

χλαί]νηι καλύψας, αὐχέν' ἀγκάληιc ἔχω[ν,
δεί]ματι π..[.].μένην
τὼc ὥcτε νέβρ[47

⟨————⟩

μαζ]ῶν τε χερcὶν ἠπίωc ἐφηψάμην
ἧιπε]ρ ἔφηνε νέον
ἥβηc ἐπήλυcιc χρόα·   50

⟨————⟩

ἅπαν τ]ε cῶμα καλὸν ἀμφαφώμενος
λευκ]ὸν ἀφῆκα μένος
ξανθῆc ἐπιψαύ[ων τριχόc.   53

⟨════⟩

'. . .

holding off entirely.
Risk an equal. . .

Or, if you're pushed by pressing lust,
there is a girl among us
who already yearns . . .

a soft and pretty maid whose beauty
I call blameless.
[Take her to be your love!']

Such were her words, and I in answer said:
'Amphimedo's child, daughter
of that [wise] and noble

lady held within broad earth's embrace,
the goddess has provided many
pleasures for young men

other than the sacred act, and one of these
will satisfy. Such matters, in tranquillity,
until [the day] grows dim,

shall you and I with heaven's help discuss!
I promise to agree as you propose
[although I long to pass]

beneath the arch and through the portal there,
and you, my dear, be not ungenerous –
for I will stop

within your grassy garden plot. And learn this well:
Neobule another man may take!
She's [doubly] ripe . . .

the bloom is off her maidenhood,
the charms she had are gone, for she
can never get her fill . . .

but, frenzied, shows the measure of her shame.
Crows take her! and
may [Zeus ensure]

that I shall never be the butt of neighbours' jokes
for having one like her!
It's you I want

for you don't deal in lies or treachery,
where she is sharp and takes
a hundred [friends] –

indeed I fear she'll bear litters premature
and blind, for she's as eager as
the fabled Bitch.'

So much I said. I took the girl and couched her
where the blossoms opened full,
wrapped her soft

inside my cloak and put my arms about her.
[She trembled] like a fawn in fear
[but then grew still]

beneath the soothing hands that claimed her breasts
where Hebe's touch was openly displayed
upon her new-made flesh,

and then my fingers learnt her lovely body well
before I let the white sperm go,
touching golden hair.[25]

[25] Notes on text (which is that of Page, *SLG*, 478) and translation:

   2 Perhaps τόλμησον παθεῖν (Ebert and Luppe); she means to be chaste and he
     should attempt the same.
   5 Assuming something like λέχεος at the end of the line.
   8 Reading τὴν δὴ σὺ ποίη[σαι φίλην (Koenen).

Taking the Hellenistic imitations as rough models, we can suppose that this song began with a short first-person narrative in which its pastoral scene was set.[26] There might have been a conventional

15 The question between the two is not marriage (nowhere mentioned) but inter-course, as is proved by Hesych. π 839 Schmidt: παρὲξ τὸ θεῖον χρῆμα· ἔξω τῆς μιξέως; see E. Degani 'παρὲξ τὸ θεῖον χρῆμα nel nuovo Archiloco di Colonia', *QU* 20 (1975) 229, where the Hesychius gloss was first pointed out.

20 Perhaps ἐ[ποτρύνει πόθος . . . ὑποφθάνειν

21 Cf. E. *Cycl.* 502, θύραν τίς οἴξει μοι; in an erotic context; see also Ar. *Thesm.* 60, cited by Austin.

23 Cf. E.*Cycl.*170–1, καὶ παρεσκευασμένου / ψαῦσαι χεροῖν λειμῶνος. He will 'put in at' (σχήσω 23) the grassy plot and 'hold off from' (ἀποσχόμενος 1) the further regions that are reserved to the 'sacred act'. She on the other hand must not be too fussy about the πάμπαν (1) of her original request.

26 West ('Two notes', *ZPE* 26, 1977, 44–8) cites Hesych. δὶς τόση· τῆι ἡλίκιαι· Ἀρχίλοχος, and restores δὶς τόση, which he takes to mean, 'she is twice as old as you are'.

28 Cf. *AP* 5.273.4, τὴν πρὶν ἀφῆκε χάριν; also *AP* 5.21.4.

39 For the 'I fear lest . . .', cf. Alc. 119V.

40 Reading ἐπειγομένη and τέκηι with Gronewald; Treu and Koenen suggest -μένοις. S. R. Slings, 'Archilochus. The Hasty Mind and the Hasty Bitch', *ZPE* 21 (1976) 286ff., well sums up the arguments against allowing this male speaker to give birth, even in a hypothetical metaphor. For an attempt to confound Slings and defend ἐπειγόμενος, see J. Van Sickle, 'Archilochus: the hasty emen-dation', *BASP* 15 (1978) 171–3.

45 The notion of 'one cloak that covers two' later becomes an erotic commonplace; cf. e.g. S. *Trach.* 539f.; Eur. fr. 603.4 N²; Theocr. 18. 19; Asclep. *AP* 5.169.3f., and see Pearson on S. fr. 483.

46–7. Reading δεί]ματι . . . ἐκ φυγῆς with the first edd. because in the Homeric passages about fawns the idea of flight is almost always present. For the in-transitive expression, cf. E.*El.* 1108, ἐκ τόκων παυσαμένη. Otherwise one might conceivably read ὥστε νεβρίον τρέμειν, as was suggested by Merkelbach, *ZPE* 16, 221.

50 Reading ἐπήλυσιν with the pap. Youth's 'approach to her young flesh' would signify the marks of puberty (cf. *AP* 5.268.3) but the word ἐπήλυσις may also have a magical meaning, in which case a translation might be 'the sorcery of her youth' (so Degani, *A&R* 19, 197, 121, 'incanto di giovinezza'); cf. N. J. Richardson on ἐπηλυσίη at *h.Dem* 228 and 230. Hebe suggests the eroticism of extreme youth; at *h.Apol.* 194–6 she appears among the Charites; Philodemus περὶ εὐσεβ. seems to know a Sapphic fragment in which a goddess who was probably Hebe was called χρυσοφάης and θεράπαινα Ἀφροδίτης.

53 With ξανθῆς some word for 'hair' is certain, and it is most natural to suppose that pubic hair is meant (O. Taplin cites E.fr. 1106 and proposes χνοός). This would explicitly confirm the speaker's promise to halt in the 'grassy plot' and not to 'pass beneath the gate'. It is, however, also possible that the speaker refers to the free-flowing, uncut hair of the head which was a sign of a girl's virginity (cf. 31W; E.*IT* 1144–51; Callim. *Hymn* 6.5 and Schol.; Schol. at E.*Or.* 1267, and see J. W. Fitton, 'The οὖλος / ἴουλος song', *Glotta* 53, 1975, 233). Either τριχός or χνοός will produce a final stanza in which all three lines end in -ος, which might be felt as an argument in favour of κόμης.

[26] The convention of opening an amorous encounter with the situation of a girl picking flowers is illustrated fully by W. Bühler, 'Die Europe des Moschus', *Hermes Einzel.*13 (Wiesbaden 1960) 77–82; 109–15; see also J. M. Bremer, 'The meadow of love', *Mnem.* 28 (1975) 268–80.

address to a friend or enemy,[27] or a gnomic summary of the meaning of the episode to come, but there may also have been only the sketchiest of statements – something like the 'Eunika laughed at me, when I tried to kiss her, she scolded me like this . . .' that opens one of Theocritus' Idylls (20). At any rate, the speaker is by some brief means brought into converse with a girl in a country spot.[28] He accosts her as a lover; she demurs; he persuades on special terms, and in the end he has his way. In this résumé it sounds like any amorous ballad, but two things in particular distinguish this ancedote of conquest – the burst of fury that produces a diatribe against another woman, and the carefully circumscribed sexual act that brings the poem to its close. The love, in this small erotic drama, is somehow curtailed, while it is made to depend upon its opposite, an unbridled hatred, and each of these passions – the moderate and the excessive – is associated with a different girl. One is embraced while the other is reviled, and the song cannot finally be said to belong to either of them, for this is not just the tale of a lover and his lass, invaded by invective, any more than it is a simple poem of abuse incomprehensibly decked out as a valentine. Rather, the poem achieves its purposes when it has engineered and given structural emphasis to an astonishing confluence of abuse with lyric eroticism, of crude insult with sensual detail.

This, however, is not the way the song is generally read. Ancient tradition insisted that Neobule, the faithless beloved, had broken her word to Archilochus and had been hounded by his retaliatory verses until she hanged herself, along with her sister(s) and their father Lycambes. Consequently, when Neobule's name was found, the present piece was taken as an example of that killing music that had destroyed the poet's enemies. It was read as a crude instrument of destruction – an artifact, not a work of art – and its Neobule was regarded, not as a projection of poetic emotion, but as a target external to the song. This reading meant that the second girl, too, was part of its machine of slander, and so she was quickly identified as Neobule's younger sister, and a victim of rape. The result was a song in which the reputation of Lycambes' family was forever obliterated by a poet who violated one girl with words and the other with deeds, a poet who was a 'serious pyschopath', as one of the first editors morosely observed.[29]

---

[27] The song might conceivably have been addressed to Lycambes, as at 54W. West would put 38W into this opening section, and would have the erotic encounter take place in the *temenos* of Hera, following the hints of Dioscorides at *AP* 7.351.8, οὐθ᾽ Ἥρης ἐν μεγάλῳ τεμένεϊ κτλ. H. Flashar and K. Maurer, *Poetica* (1974) 5 propose an introduction like that of Propertius *El.*2.26a, which would make the whole episode a dream (they cite also *AP* 5.2, 237, 243 and 9.286), but it would seem that the actual episode of Ovid *Amores*1.5 would provide a better model.

[28] The most economical supposition is that the poem proposed two balanced speeches, triggered by the lovers' initial words, which may or not have been directly reported.

[29] Merkelbach, *ZPE* 14, 113.

Such a song might well have left the father and his daughters ready
for their fabled suicides, and yet, the more the actual poem is read,
the less does it seem to be merely a brutal act of double defamation.
To begin with, the nameless girl can only be made into Neobule's
sister if excessive weight is given to the words 'among us' (*en hēme-
terou*, 3),[30] for in fact the expression means only that the two girls
belong to the same household or group, and does not make them kin.
Again, the sisterhood can only be maintained by overlooking the divisive effect of the lines that emphasise the name of the mother of this
girl, for she would have been called 'daughter of Lycambes' if she were
so in fact and if the poem were an attack upon the family. This address
by a mother's name is almost unparalleled,[31] and probably it echoes
a remark that the girl has made in her lost speech – perhaps it is her
dead mother[32] who has taught her to value her chastity – but even so
the failure of a patronymic and the insistence upon the mother's name
ought to mean either that the father is not known in the poem's
community, or else that the mother is in some way notorious. Perhaps
this mother who was all the girl could claim was presented as a
foreigner or a slave, or again she may have been supposed to be a
woman of professional standing – a midwife, a mantic, a musician or
a teacher.[33] One thing is certain, however, and that is that she is *not*
proposed as the wife of Lycambes or as the mother of Neobule.

Such are the arguments against making the girl a Lycambid; they
are strong, but they are external to the poem, and better ones exist
within the song. To begin with, if the two girls are sisters, why is the
recommendation of Neobule in lines 4–7 given with such distant

[30] Hesychius, who knew of this song, has ἐν ἡμετέρου· παρ᾽ἡμῖν, ἐν ἡμῖν, cf. Hdt. 1.35.4;
7.8.50; 7.85.1. The parallel ἐς ἡμετέρου appears at *Od*.2.55; 7.301; 17.534; cf. *h.Herm*.
370. Clearly the phrase could apply to a specific place ('our house', 'here'), to a region
('our city'), or to a population group ('our *thiasos*'). For a similar view, see J. Ebert and
W. Luppe, 'Zum neuen Arch. pap.', *ZPE* 16 (1975) 223ff.; B. Gentili, in a review of Page,
SLG, *Gnomon* 48 (1976) 749–50; E. Degani, 'Il Nuovo Archiloco', *A&R* 19 (1974) 122.

[31] Schol. *Il*.11.750: οὐδέποτε δὲ Ὅμηρὸς ἀπὸ μητρὸς σχηματίζει. Elsewhere, however,
divinities are occasionally so identified; cf. *h.Dem*. 75; Hipp. 32.1W, where Hermes is
addressed as Μαιαδεῦ, and Hdt.1.173, who mentions that in Lycia children are named
from their mothers. There are mother-names in the magical texts, and one is reminded
also of the mysterious Aenesimbrota at Alc. *Parth*.73, who almost gives her name to
her girls. L. Koenen, *Poetica* (1974) 500 suggests that Lycambes had two wives, first
the mother of Neobule, then Amphimedo, the mother of this second girl, but this would
not explain the failure to name Lycambes (though it might justify the emphasis placed
upon Amphimedo's name).

[32] Ebert and Luppe, op. cit., 227 suggest that the juxtaposition of the notion of the
mother's death with that of Aphrodite's pleasure gives the lover's speech the air of a
carpe diem exhortation, but this is certainly not the way it strikes the ear, for it seems
to express the speaker's recognition of the girl's plea for postponement.

[33] The fact that the dog-woman of Semonides 7.12ff. is child only of her mother
suggests as well that this might be a way of saying that the girl was just like her
mother, in which case we should pay attention to this woman's name, which might be
taken to mean 'guardian'. If the name was invented and used for its significance, then
the speaker will be calling the girl 'guardian child of a guardian mother', but if this is
his intention it is hard to see why the poet should specify that the mother is dead.

admiration, and what purpose does this naive tribute serve in a song meant to assassinate both its female characters? Again, if the aim of the song is to show that both girls are lewd and neither can lay claim to her virginity, why does the lover so elaborately assure one of them that he will do her no harm, and why are the closing words so ambiguous that there is still argument about her final state? If the song is meant to ruin both, it must show this girl deflowered and identical with her sister in the end, whereas, even supposing (for the moment) that she *is* ravished in the last line, it is clear that the lover's speech will work against such calumny, since his broken promises will prove that this second sister was unwilling, not lewd, and that she was taken by deception. The poem will, in other words, present her with a kind of apology, which is not defamation as Archilochus understood that art. All of these, however, are lesser objections to taking the girl as a second target of abuse; overarching and confirming them is a major one that arises from the song's emphatic doubleness of temper. Why should a piece that was meant to vilify two sisters alike so exercise itself to discriminate between them? Why should it make the turn from one to the other a turn from the gutter towards a kind of paradise, and why should its closing words strike a lyric note of peace and satisfaction?

The fragment cannot be restored to any harmony by forcing the unknown girl into harness with Neobule, and so it will be best to forget the scant and probably false information that we have about the Lycambid family. The poem must be allowed to define itself, and since it does not make the details of its fiction clear, that fiction must be left alone as we turn to the form of the piece, no longer asking who this unknown girl is, but asking instead what the poet makes her do for his song.

The Cologne poem is fashioned as a miniature drama and it imitates the moment in which the speaker makes a choice. His action has two objects, since choice includes refusal, and these appear as two women, Neobule and the girl. They are the matter upon which he exercises his discrimination, and so the song shows him rejecting one and claiming the other, cursing one and persuading the other, vilifying one and making the other beautiful. Indeed, everything in the lines that we have has been made to serve the delineation of these two opposite equivalents – two women who come from a single house or band of friends, but who stand at the two furthest poles of femininity. Their opposition is clearly fixed in the speaker's explicit announcement of choice, for there he states that what Neobule is, the girl is certainly not (1.24).[34] At this point the girl's positive qualities are only implicit

---

[34] The statement is much like that at Theogn. 1367, where Boy and Woman are similarly compared: παιδός τοι χάρις ἐστί · γυναικὶ δὲ πιστὸς ἑταῖρος / οὐδείς, ἀλλ᾽ αἰεὶ τὸν παρεόντα φιλεῖ.

– Neobule is faithless, double and sour in her cunning, and so the girl must be faithful, true and sweet in her simplicity. In the next passage, however, the chosen one is given her own description, and it is one that, point by point, makes her the virgin who contradicts the whore.[35]

Physically, Neobule is overripe (26)[36] but the girl's flesh is new (49);[37] the flower of Neobule's maidenhood is long since gone, but the girl brings hers to her couch of flowers (*anthos . . . partheneïon*, 27; *parthenon d'en anthesin*, 42) and she is likened to green grass; the seductiveness that graces the young no longer lies upon Neobule (28), but the girl has all the enchantments of youth (50). Neobule's spirit is avid and for her not even excess is enough (29),[38] but the girl refuses love and offers a substitute (5). Neobule is in constant motion, frenzied with lust (30), but the girl is almost paralysed and trembling with fear (46); Neobule makes a public show of her sexual need[39] (*ephēne*, 30), while the girl's youth is made manifest (*ephēne*, 33) only to her lover. Neobule is hasty and eager (40), while the girl will 'consider in tranquillity' (16–18). Neobule is aggressive and expansive – she takes her lovers in quantity (38) – but the passivity of the girl is proved grammatically, for she is the object of all but one of the verbs of the final passage. She is indeed as quiet as a living corpse in the poem's last lines, for it is her *sōma*[40] that her lover learns by touch.

All of these strongly drawn oppositions are summed up in the bitch and the fawn, a pair of beasts whose images fix the listener's final response to Neobule and the girl. The mention of the bitch comes first; it stands as the penultimate word of the invective against Neobule, and though it has been prefaced by the reference to promiscuity just above (38), it comes as a dubious surprise to the modern ear. Just where a superb and specific insult is expected, the speaker seems to fall back weakly upon a common proverb, and one is inclined to object

[35] Cf. Semonides fr. 7, where the Bee-Woman stands over against all the others, much as the girl here does against all of Neobule's vices. See H. Lloyd-Jones, *Females of the Species: Semonides on Women* (London, 1975) and W. J. Verdenius, 'Epilegomena zu Sem.fr.7', *Mnem.* 30 (1977) 1–12.

[36] Note the imitation at Anacreon 87B=432 *PMG*: κινζή τις ἤδη καὶ πέπειρα γίνομαι σὴν διὰ μαργοσύνην.

[37] If line 17 is read εὖτ' ἄν μελανθῆ[ι σοι τρύγη, 'until your grape grows dark', i.e. until you are mature (so Ebert and Luppe, *ZPE* 16, 223), then the girl's flesh is likened to that of a green grape, as girl-flesh is at *AP* 5.124f., 5.20, and Theoc. *Id.* 11.21; see Gow ad loc. where Nonnus 1.71; 48.365 and 457, and Aristaenetus 2.7.21 are also cited.

[38] Compare Rochester of the Duchess of Cleveland:

When she has jaded quite
Her almost boundless appetite
She'll still drudge on in tasteless vice
As if she sinned for exercise.

[39] The contrast holds, whether we read ἄσ]ης μέτρ' with Page, or the oxymoronic ἄτ]ης μέτρ' favoured by other editors.

[40] In Homer the word denotes either a dead body or else the yet living prey of a beast.

that no one yet drew blood with a phrase from La Fontaine. In fact, however, this animal reference is more mordant than it seems. The bitch with her blind pups belongs to a fable (Perry 223) in which she engages the sow in an argument about their comparative fecundity. The bitch is getting the worst of it, and so she brings in the tangential claim of speed in delivery – she is as forward in bearing as she is in conceiving her young. 'Yes,' says the sow, 'but your pups are born blind!'[41] The dog of the fable thus proves that haste makes waste, and the urgency of Neobule's lust provides the point of contact between Archilochus' poem and this bestial debate. Beginnings presage endings, and to judge by Neobule's bitch-like mating habits, her offspring should be bitch-like too.[42] Nevertheless, it is not really the Aesopic moral that Archilochus exploits. What he wants is the full natural aroma of the canine female, and this he can take from the fable in a heightened form, since the tale adds to the usual image of a shameless bitch[43] all of the malodorous associations that her friend the sow can bring. The dog of the fable is a lewd and quarrelsome female creature compounded of dirt and dugs and crawling newborn things, and she cannot even properly perform the one function that might justify her repulsive existence, for as a mother she is beaten by the sow. She thus sums up centuries of misogyny, and through her the speaker can bring his final accusation since, among humans, children who are blind and premature suggest the presence of demons and disease in the womb that held them. Such, according to the lover, is the nature of the bitch-woman Neobule.

The fawn is the song's alternate icon of femininity, but it is notable that this second beast is introduced with an appropriate modesty. It does not come labelled like the bitch as a proverbial example, but slips in instead as a graceful simile. The fawn brings suggestions that are epic and legendary, rather than popular, and unlike the comical creatures of fable, it is also touched by the solemnity of ancient cult association. Deer as a species were fleet and magical, glimpsed and

---

[41] Contrast the pro-bitch cuneiform fable cited by S. N. Kramer, *History Begins at Sumer* (London 1961) 185: 'Thus speaks the bitch with pride, whether I have fawn-coloured pups or brindle, I love my young.'

[42] That we must read ἐπειγομένη in line 40 is unintentionally proved by the interpretations proposed by those who attempt to apply the breeding bitch to the lover instead of to Neobule. See, e.g. N. F. Rubin, 'Some functions of the enclosed invective', *CJ* 74 (1978/9) 139, who explains that the lover fears that if he rushes he will spoil his relationship with the girl or else will return to Neobule!

[43] The usual associations are wonderfully exploited by Rochester in his lines on the Duchess of Cleveland:

Full forty men a day
    provided for this whore
Yet like a bitch she
    wags her tail for more.

lost, sacred to hunters, and so the special property of Artemis,[44] and through that goddess they came to represent untouchable virginity. This is why the nymph Taÿgeta was changed into a hind when she would escape from Zeus, and why Heracles could not keep that other, sacred hind that she later dedicated to her goddess-saviour.[45] The notion of the chastity of the doe may also have derived from actual observation, for Aristotle notes that she submits to the stag only under compulsion and rarely allows him to complete his act of engendering (*HA* 540a6).[46]

A second set of the associations derived from the solicitude that deer showed for their young, and attached itself particularly to the fawn. The dappled creature that trembled at its mother's side seemed to epitomise youth in its vulnerable tenderness, and this is probably why it became a figure for the infant Dionysus. The fawn was one of the victims of the *ōmophagia*, and the fawnskin shawl marked the nurse-maid Maenads as initiates to eternal youth, themselves fawns that 'played at childish games in the meadow's green delight' (E.*Ba*. 866).[47] The fawns that appear in Homeric similes[48] are always childlike nur-selings; they belong in the soft natural beds that are found in thickets and grassy glades, and their essential quality is fear, as they flee (or else lie trembling, panting or wounded) before their conventional ene-mies, the lion and the dog.[49] They have neither courage nor force.[50]

The pervasive system of oppositions that is resumed by the fecund bitch and the fearful, childlike fawn creates a separation between virgin and whore which is, within this poem, absolute. Each confron-tation with the fresh girl makes the Neobule figure filthier, and in this way each comparison serves the abusive function of the song.[51]

---

[44] For Artemis Elaphos and Elaphebolos, see Farnell *Cults* ii 433. Theoc. *Id*.11.39 pairs fawns and bearcubs as symbols of virginity; see Roscher I.2200 for a b.f. vase with Artemis and a hind.

[45] Taÿgeta appeared on the Throne of Amyclae (see Paus.3.18.10); Pindar, in *O*.3, associates her fleeing deer with the olive and so with ideas of virtue and imperishable fame; cf. Callim. *Hymn* 3.100.

[46] Compare Oppian *Cyn*. 2.187–205, where stags must copulate while running on their two hind feet because the doe always flees.

[47] For fawns in Dionysiac rites, see Farnell *Cults* v.164ff.; in the omophagia, Phot. sv νεβρίζειν. Note also Hesych. Ἐρίφιος˙ Διόννσος, and for fawns on Dionysiac monuments, see K. Kerenyi, *Dionysos* (Munich 1976) 254, pl.64c, and 319, pl.102. L.Deubner, *Abh.d.Pr.Ak.ph.h.kl.* 7 (1943) 9, interprets the cult title Κεμήλιος as 'to whom the deer is sacrificed'.

[48] *Il*.4.243f., 22.1f., 8.248ff., 22.189ff., 21.29, 15.579; *Od*.4.336, 17.127ff., 19.230ff.; cf. Theogn. 949=1278c.

[49] E. Vermeule, *Aspects*, 84–5, suggests that the pair, Predator and Grasseater, figures the other pair, Death and He-Who-Dies.

[50] *Il*.4.243; cf. Theogn.949 and Arist. *HA* 676b25, where they have no χολή.

[51] It is the view of J. Ebert and W. Luppe, op. cit., 232, that this is her only function: 'Man darf vermuten, dass das gefühlvoll geschilderte Erleben mit jenem Mädchen – das mit seiner Unmittelbarkeit unserem Empfinden nach auch ein selbständiges Ged-icht hätte bilden können – hauptsächlich nur als Kontrast zur Verdeutlichung des Neobule-Bildes sollte.'

This is obviously one mechanical purpose of the virgin foil, but the introduction of this figure has deeper effects as well, for the presence of the girl broadens the poem's narrow slander into a theme that is universal. Since Neobule is foul, the girl is necessarily fine, and just as the woman is clarified by abuse until she is almost an abstract representation of corruption, so the girl is ever more carefully defined until she appears almost as the idea of purity, and the result is that, between them, a seemingly irresolvable enigma is framed. It is a problem that is set here in sexual terms, but it is one that can occur in any realm of human experience where there is a mind that longs for perfection. The pure example, whatever it may be, when recognised arouses desire in such minds, but possession mars its purity and therefore the act of obtaining becomes an act that destroys the object of desire. Idealists are thus doomed to disappointment, 'Sure if they catch, to spoil the Toy at most', as Pope said in the *Characters of Women*. When it is sensed in its absolute form, this paradox is agonising and insoluble, but fictions were made to deal with just such cases and Archilochus is able to solve the problem of how to have what will disappear in the having by means of his finite tale. By the grace of the gods, life provides what philosophy forbids – quibbles and evasions – and in this case it provides a form of sexual activity that will allow chastity to survive though its owner is possessed, thereby permitting a desire that is neither belittled by renunciation nor defeated by its own victory.

One of the implicit charges against Neobule has been excess: her actions are extreme, mad, and dictated by lust. This means that the poem's rejection of what she stands for can be kept intact even when the speaker's own lust is fulfilled, if the final deed is minimal, moderate, and one in which desire is not given free rein but mastered instead. If, in other words, it is one of those pleasures 'other than the sacred thing' which the man is made to propose as the subject of the amorous 'discussion'. And so the poem's closing lines describe a lover who behaves with artful restraint, pleasing himself while he yet honours the girl's inviolate virginity. Their act of love is reported in an extended and cadenced account[52] that places all its emphasis upon the tranquillity (the promised *hēsuchia* of line 16) and the healing gentleness of the lover's gestures towards the passive girl. She is couched, covered and given a chaste embrace; the speaker's hands move first to her breasts, then to all parts of her body, knowingly, like a warrior's hands with his weapons. Then, after this controlled preface, he finds his satisfaction as he had said he would, without entering 'the gate'. He spills his force in the 'grassy plot' and in this way testifies to the

---

[52] There is a formal sequence from throat to breast to flesh to body; compare the like erotic sequence at Sappho 94V, from head to throat to breast to possession (see below, pp. 296ff.).

strength of his desire for what is pure, taking what he wants without destroying it.[53] If the girl had been cold and obdurate, she would not have been perfection of her sort; if the lover had renounced his conquest, he would have shown his own desire to be less than perfect, and his asceticism would have cast a doubt upon the final beauty of flesh and its attainment. And of course, if he had simply taken the girl in an everyday way, he would never have obtained *her* at all, but only another Neobule. All of which dangers are prepared and then avoided, as both virgin and poem are saved by a lover who imposes order and measure upon an act of love, and yet manages to prove a new pleasure that is both physical and dream-like, at the poem's close.[54]

His final moderation in love presents an absolute contrast to the speaker's excess, when he is moved by rage, and the difference reminds one of the Archilochean advice to the heart (128W), for this is a perfect example of unmeasured violence in 'battle' and temperance in 'victory'. The Cologne poem's formal discovery of worth in one member of a species while it devalues a rival example makes it also a little like the song of the foppish lieutenant (114W), and where it discriminates between two kinds of behaviour it might even be said to resemble the advice to Pericles (131W). Nevertheless, this song of dramatic abuse and praise is very different from those plainer performances, for here the mode is not one of reflection or exhortation: here the poem itself moves and does. In so far as it is abusive, it is a gesture of persecution against Neobule (whether she is a particular woman or an encompassing general figure), fulfilling the same fantasy that Lord Rochester amused himself with so many centuries after, when he wrote:[55]

I'll make her feel my scorn and hate;
Pelt her with scandals, truth or lies,
And her poor cur with jealousies,
Till I have torn him from her breech,
While she whines like a dog-drawn bitch;
Loathed and despised, kicked out o' th' town
Into some dirty hole alone,
To chew the cud of misery
And knows she owes it all to me.

[53] In connection with the delicate and ambiguous phrasing of the final line, one should remember that this is the poet who can, if he wishes, describe a fulfilled heterosexual act with the explicit crudeness of 46W.

[54] Compare Rochester's 'Platonic Lady' (Veith, *The Complete Poems of John Wilmot Earl of Rochester*, Yale 1968, 25):

I'd give him liberty to toy
and play with me and count it joy.
Our freedom should be full complete
And nothing wanting but the feat.
Let's practice, then, and we shall prove
These are the only sweets of love.

[55] 'A ramble in St. James Park', Veith 46.

The peculiarity of the Archilochean poem, however, is that the gesture is double, for it defeats its ugly Neobule while at the same time it causes the influence of Amphimedo's child to prevail. In modern terms the lover frees himself from fear of the feminine by the filth and rage of his anger; in allegorical terms Lust is evicted before Love is entertained; but what Archilochus has done, in terms of his own time and society, is make a paradigm for the uses of calumny. He has employed the old magic associated with the single-short rhythm and has exorcised the Neobule-woman with obscenity, as if she were a demon, taking the whip of animal allusion to drive her out like some polluted *pharmakos*. The song does not stop there, however, but, like a Thasian door inscription that refuses famine while it welcomes plenty,[56] it goes on to receive another figure got up to represent youth. From what is worn out the song derives freshness, taking purity from filth, calm from violence, love from rage, and this is why, when its abuse is finished, the satirist can drop his ordinary mask of disillusionment to salute a sexuality that is neither lewd nor obscene.

[56] See P. Bernard and F. Salviat, 'Inscriptions de Thasos', *BCH* 86.2 (1962) 608–9. According to the theory which holds that Lycambes and Neobule were never real people but instead stock characters in a debased version of Dionysiac ritual abuse (see above, p. 21 note 14), the song would say: 'I reject Fickleness, daughter of Wolf-Walker, Dionysus' enemy, and take to myself an unravished daughter of a lady guardian.

V

Archilochus and Hipponax

The bitterness, even the rage, of Archilochus was expressed always with a clean pride that can best be appreciated when his work is set beside that of the poet who was his closest imitator. The ancient world named Hipponax of Ephesus as second after Archilochus in the composition of iambics, and certainly the sixth-century iambograph had a great deal in common with his Parian master. Like Archilochus, he used first-person narrative with strong self-identification ('These things Hipponax knows, better than any other man . . .' 17W; cf. 79.9, 32, 36, 37W),[1] and like Archilochus he was an inspired practitioner of obscene attack. He too was said to have destroyed his victims physically, for supposedly he had a pair of enemies (sculptors who made humiliating statues of him) and he hounded them into nooses almost as famous as those of Lycambes and his daughters.[2] In spite of these likenesses, however, the two bodies of verse are wholly unlike in temper and style, the difference between them being finally equal to the difference between collaboration and resistance, in the face of a reality that both poets saw as contemptible.[3]

The iambics of Hipponax have their own artistry, but in them all the poet's skill is spent upon recreating an ugly reality that in no sense implies an ideal, and their abuse is of the sort that rejoices in depravity. If there were city poems, none of them survive,[4] and the only songs for the gods are gross parodies of prayer in which the singer sulks and complains because food, clothing and greater success in

---

[1] As one of his editors says, 'se intende per lirico il poeta che mette in primo piano il proprio io, nessuno fu piu lirico di Ipponatte', A. Farina, *Ipponatte* (Naples 1963) 25.

[2] Callim. fr. 191.1–4; *AP* 7.405.1–3; Pliny *HN* 36.11; Luc. *Pseud.* 2; ps. Acron ad Hor. *Ep.* 6.14; Suda ii 665.16; see West, *IE*, 109–10.

[3] Note, however, that Clement classed them together as equally shameful and beneath imitation (*Strom.* 1.116.94).

[4] That he had some sort of political life is suggested by the fact that he was, according to the Suda, banished by the tyrants Athenagoras and Komas, after which he went to Clazomenae to live.

thievery have not come his way.[5] The world that his songs create is one where no illusion has ever been entertained; heroic notions do not exist even to be scoffed at (though there is a burlesque epic that would sing the gluttony of a certain Eurymedontiades, 128W), and ugliness is met, not with scorn, but with a sniggering admiration. His characters are engaged only in brutish attempts to survive, and among them the poet pretends to be perfectly at home. He is no embittered debauchee who would humiliate his senses, nor is he a soldier looking for the oblivion of vice, and he certainly does not present himself as an observer who might discover the rhythm of experience. Instead, Hipponax chooses to sing as if he and his companions were all of them depraved and stupid men with concerns obsessively physical – equal citizens of the lowest depths.

Archilochus is fond of masks, and by wearing now one and now another, he keeps his listeners conscious of his assumed posture as a performer, and conscious too that each poem is a made thing, not just a snatch of speech. Hipponax, on the other hand, has only one disguise – that of the boor – and he gives his songs as nearly as possible the voice of an actual boor.[6] His vocabulary is gutter-polyglot;[7] his rhythms strive to be vulgar;[8] his obscenity lingers on the scatological (61W; 92W; 135W), and neither he nor anyone he describes will take the trouble to be witty, ironic, or even cynical. Instead they quarrel, drink from buckets and copulate in puddles of beer.

Archilochus smiles and belittles himself as an ant, but he also sees himself as an acropolis, whereas Hipponax tries to persuade us that he is a buffoon who whines about warm cloaks and dishes of gruel. An animal reference from him is exactly that – the mention of a crocodile (155W) or an ape (155aW) – for he has no use even for so simple an artifact as the fable. Archilochus stings with poisoned words, but Hipponax boasts that he will cudgel (*kopsō* 120W; 121W) his enemies, using both his hands. Archilochus likens a man to an ass from Priene (43W), a woman to a wine-sack (119W) or a barren field of stubble (188W), but Hipponax coins the Greek version of 'mother-fucker' (*me-*

[5] Hermes is his favourite god (32W; 34W, cf. 3aW) but apparently he even dares to ridicule the dogmas of Eleusis, saying, 'I'll hand myself over to the damned if you don't send me some barley for a *kykeon*' (39W).

[6] On this voice, see West, *Studies*, 29. N. Terzaghi, 'L'Odio di Ipponatte ed il primo epodo di Strasburgo', *SIFC* NS 17 (1940) assumes that Hipponax was in fact a nobleman who actually led the life of which he sings: 'era caduto tanta in basso da non vergognare della compagnia del ladro'. This would seem to be something like supposing that the friends of Theocritus were actually cowherds and shepherds.

[7] On Hipponax's use of foreign and plebeian words, see West, *Studies*, 30; Farina, op. cit., 25–9, and O. Masson, *Les fragments du poète Hipponax* (Paris 1962) 29–32. For comical compounds, see West, op. cit., 148.

[8] On the metres of Hipponax, West notes (loc. cit.) 'a deliberate crashing incorrectness emphasising the clumsy uneducated character that is being projected'. For analysis, see Masson, op. cit., 21–9 and Farina, op. cit., 29–38.

trokoitēs, 12W; cf. 70W)[9] and calls a woman a 'muck-hole' (*borboropē* 135b), a 'cock-shaker' (*anaseisiphallos*, 135; cf. 135aW) or 'the sister of shit' (*bolbitou kasignētē*, 144W). Archilochus describes the battlefield indignity of losing one's shield, but Hipponax gives us the squalid humiliation of a man who has lost his potency and seeks its revival at the hands of a filthy sorceress who is surely not on the up-and-up (92W; cf. 78W).[10]

Only in the so-called Strasburg Ode[11] does Hipponax voice something like the scorn of an Archilochus, and even there the differences are notable. The song is a parody of the good wishes for a happy voyage that noblemen customarily sent off with departing friends, and the fragment begins just as the singer has reached the climax of the bad wishes which he offers, almost as a curse, to someone who has evidently been named in the opening lines (115W):

κύμ[ατι] πλα[ζόμ]ενος·
κἂν Σαλμυδ[ησσ]ῶι γυμνὸν εὐφρονε.[5
Θρήϊκες ἀκρό[κ]ομοι
λάβοιεν—ἔνθα πόλλ' ἀναπλήσαι κακὰ
δούλιον ἄρτον ἔδων—
ῥίγει πεπηγότ' αὐτόν· ἐκ δὲ τοῦ χνόου
φυκία πόλλ' ἐπέχοι,   10
κροτέοι δ' ὀδόντας, ὡς [κ]ύων ἐπὶ στόμα
κείμενος ἀκρασίηι
ἄκρον παρὰ ῥηγμῖνα κυμα....δρυ·
ταῦτ' ἐθέλοιμ' ἂν ἰδεῖν,
ὅς μ' ἠδίκησε, λ[ὰ]ξ δ' ἐπ' ὁρκίοις ἔβη,   15
τὸ πρὶν ἑταῖρος [ἐ]ών.

...beaten by the waves.
In Salmydessus let 'well-meaning'[12]
   top-knot Thracians
seize his naked body (he can get his fill
   of evil eating slavish bread)

---

[9] In the nineteenth century, Bergk and Ten Brink proposed to see this term as a reference to Cybele; cf., however, 70W, where someone is mentioned as one who would rape his mother – while she was asleep.

[10] Evidently the process is something like that described by Petronius in ch. 138 of the *Satyricon*; see B. Lavagnini, *Da Mimnermo a Callimaco* (Torino 1950) 56–66, and West, *Studies*, 144–5.

[11] First published by Reitzenstein, *SB pr.Ak.Wiss.* 45 (1899) 857ff., where it is attributed to Archilochus.

[12] If Diels' εὐφρονέ[στατα is right, the word is meant with heavy sarcasm, which might be paralleled by the μητρότιμος in 122W, if it is applied to Bupalus, the μητροκοίτης (see Farina, op.cit., 130, note 3). However, others may be closer to the original when they restore a phrase made with εὐφρόνη (e.g. εὐφρόν[ης σκότει, Schulthess, or εὐφρόν[ης μέσης).

rigid from cold! Let seaweed
    rise from scum and bind him!
Let him grind his teeth, lying
    spent and muzzle down,
dog-fashion in the surf. . .!
    These things I long to see
because he wronged me, walked upon his oaths,
    who was once my friend.

The lines are vigorous and full of anger, and they be betray none of
the usual Hipponactean buffoonery (unless the reference to 'eating
slavish bread' echoes some previous abuse on the score of gluttony).
Indeed, the passage is so proud in its tone that a number of scholars
have persuaded themselves that it must have come, not from the
loutish Hipponax but from his more splendid predecessor.[13] Nevertheless, closer study of this cruelly meant *propemptikon* shows that, however unlike it may be to the rest of Hipponax, it is even more dissimilar
to anything that Archilochus has left us. Archilochus is, to begin with,
lucid, controlled and not given to excited parentheses, whereas here
much of the power comes from an unabashed exploitation of the potential illogicality of poetry as images of ship-wreck, drowning, death,
capture and slavery pile up in rapid disorder. Archilochus, again, is
fond of concrete generality, whereas here it is the tangible precision
of the detail that gives the song its flavour of magical effectiveness.[14]
The closest Archilochus gets to this scum and seaweed is with his
metal cup, in the fragment about drinking on watch (4W), and there

[13] The fragment is followed on the papyrus by a song in which the singer seems to
call himself Hipponax (116W), and consequently is most naturally to be attributed to
the same poet. Nevertheless, there has been, from the beginning, an imposing number
of scholars who wanted it for Archilochus; Eduard Fraenkel spoke for them when he
said, 'I must not be guided by my strong conviction that this glorious piece . . . belongs
really to Archilochus', and nevertheless was so guided (*Horace*, Oxford 1957, 31, note
2). The fullest arguments (which involve assuming an anthology) were advanced by R.
Cantarella, 'Gli Epodi di Strasburgo', *Aegyptus* 24 (1944) 1–112 and by G. Kirkwood,
'The authorship of the Strasburg epodes', *TAPA* 92 (1961) 267–82, where bibliography
is cited; Treu, H. Fränkel (*DuP*², 157), Gerber (*Euterpe*, 412–13) and others treated the
song as indisputably Archilochean (see also S. Commager, *Odes of Horace*, New Haven
1962, 123ff.). The authorship of Hipponax was meanwhile defended by G. Perrotta, 'Il
poeta degli epodi di Strasburgo', *SIFC* 15 (1938) 3–14; N. Terzaghi, op. cit., 217ff; O.
Masson (in contradiction to his earlier opinion), op. cit., 158–60; Farina, op. cit., 163–
83; W. Medeiros, *Hipponactea* (Coimbra 1969) 86–90; and West, *Studies*, 136 takes it as
beyond discussion. An unpersuasive attempt to argue that the ode was the work of
neither poet was made by G. Coppola, 'Archilocho o imitazione ellenistica?', *SIFC* 7
(1929) 155–68 and C. del Grande, 'Ancora sul età di composizione', *CIF* i (1948) 255ff.

[14] We cannot know how closely the Strasburg song followed the pattern of actual
curses since the opening section, where demonic powers of enforcement would normally
be named, is missing. It should be remembered, however, that even if such powers were
named, the song would be merely *like* a curse, it would not actually be a curse (*pace* E.
Fränkel, who believed that it was literally meant to destroy and that it 'realised its
primary function in actual life', op.cit., 30). For other Hipponactean curses, cf. 25W,
where a man and a woman exchange imprecations.

the word *kōthōn* is employed, not for purposes of realism, but rather as salt to the heavily epic language that surrounds it. And when does Archilochus ever engage in undisguised gloating over the itemised agonies of an enemy? Not when he pictures Lycambes as the bereaved eagle; not when he sees the marriage of the ugly girl as a reversal of nature; not even when he images Neobule as the eager bitch. 'You are going to be laughed at' is what he says again and again to his victims. He may also have said, 'You are going to want to put a noose around your neck', but nothing that remains suggests that he ever would have added, 'and how I should like to see your purple swollen face, as you dangle there!'[15]

The one song of Archilochus that does in any way resemble the Strasburg Ode is the Gortyn fragment (24W, see above, pp. 44ff.), but the likeness here is a formal one that is perfectly balanced by a total dissimilarity in tone. The Hipponax piece is a version of the *propemptikon*,[16] but a perverse one in which destruction is wished upon a departing ex-friend, while Archilochus' song is technically a true *prosphōnētikon*[17] that rejoices in a companion's safe return.[18] The one is an undisguised expression of hatred, the other a rare Archilochean expression of love, but the reverse parallelism goes deeper than this, for where Hipponax wishes two cruel disasters upon his victim, Archilochus names the same two (in hypothetical form) as events that would have destroyed him too, had they destroyed his friend. The two pieces also show characteristic differences in style, for where the Strasburg song has sharp physiological detail – rigid body, chattering teeth, muzzle in the sand – the psychic suffering of the trimeter song is given the insubstantial image of 'lying in shadow', while revival becomes 'standing in the light'. The epode implies, through its negations, the same positive evaluation of brute comfort – food and clothing and warmth – that the other Hipponactean songs express,[19] but the Gortyn song explicitly rejects and devalues material things as a way of marking the value of a friend.

In Archilochus' view, bread comes from one's spear, not from a

---

[15] The emphasis upon the oath is also worth noting, for the song seems to identify kept oaths with civilisations and safety, broken ones with barbarism and catastrophe. This kind of thinking is not typical of Archilochus, and there is nothing in his fragments to suggest that he subscribed to anything like a faction or a system of personal alliances confirmed by oath. The oath that he mentions in 173W seems to have had a very particular content, and is usually equated with Lycambes' promise of his daughter.

[16] See the discussion of F. Cairns, *Generic Composition* (Edinburgh 1972) 55–7.

[17] Cairns, op.cit., 20ff.

[18] Both songs have a strongly literary quality. To line 13 of the Gortyn song, one might compare *Il.*19.63, 11.827 and 15.289; to line 14, *IG* I Supp. 446a; to line 15, *Il.*15.290. To line 4 of the Strasburg Ode, *Od.*5.389 may be compared; to line 6, *Il.*4.533 (also Soph. *Ajax* 494); to line 15 *Il.*4.157.

[19] Compare the poet's own state at 32W; cf. 10W, 26W, 26aW, 117W, 118W, and note the slavish bread at 39W.

conniving Hermes. Misfortune is met with defiance, not with base complaints, and society is cleansed of corruption by a poet's scorn, not by a supernaturally wrought catastrophe. Never, so far as we know, does he attack as if he meant to bring magic into play; instead he indulges in indirection and various forms of poetic dalliance, discussing his own powers and asking that they should be admired as well as feared. He sees his song as a benefit to the city and an honour to the gods, and he expects it to influence the understanding of men, not the mechanics of the demonic world. He will wisely offer the gnomic proposition that others will have to suffer as his friends suffer now; he will coolly boast that he knows how to give back harm for harm, and he will arrange for his characters to curse one another, inside a framework of fiction, but he will not breathe out bare imprecations upon his enemies.

About the soldier's life, the city's dangers, or the sources of courage, Archilochus sang with a marked ambivalence, but he nevertheless betrayed one or two positive convictions, strongly held. Friendship and faith were not ordinarily his subjects, and his praise of dead comrades might be limited to a terse 'such men' (13W), but even the hard statement, 'Glaucus, an ally is your friend only as long as he fights' (19W), hides a love of loyalty within its cynicism. In the songs of blame and obscenity he led his city in attacks upon ugliness and age and unwholesomeness, but he also reminded the community of its own human tendencies towards 'the villainous and the unlawful' (177W). The justice of honouring one's kin and one's word was not openly upheld in his songs, but outrages upon that justice were discovered and denounced, and in the same way his attacks upon prostitutes constituted a defence of sexual pleasures that were neither bought nor sold. There is, in other words, a set of principles lurking in the seemingly anarchic work of Archilochus, and this is why he can be called a satirist.[20]

Like satire, Archilochean verse often mediates between a perceived reality that is base and a suppressed ideal that is fine. Because of the ideal, the poet is angry at the deviation and the deformity that he discovers, but having seen these flaws he becomes angry with himself as well, for ever having entertained visions of another kind, and angry with those visions, too, as being perhaps nothing more than illusion or cant. Anger is thus his most familiar muse, but he mitigates it with wit and exaggeration because he is himself among the objects of his disillusioned regard. His work is serious, but he wears a comic mask as he unmasks the world, for if he were solemn and candid he would

---

[20] This is exactly contrary to the conclusion reached by G. Highet, *The Anatomy of Satire* (Princeton 1962), for he believed that Archilochus lacked any norms, failed to distance himself from his own hatreds, and consequently could not be called a satirist (p.40f.).

himself be open to attack, either as a romantic simpleton or else as one who pretends to exemption from the general depravity. Nonetheless, Archilochus occasionally slips into something like praise (as Hipponax never seems to do), for he admires fierce aggressiveness and honest sensuality. He will sometimes voice an earnest admonition, and he always combines the currents of his scorn with the patterns of his verse so as to produce judgment and thought.

PART II

Alcaeus

i

Life

The poetry of Alcaeus comes from a time not severely separated from that of Archilochus, for the Lesbian was at work as the seventh century turned into the sixth. Both poets were singers for companies of soldiers and both had a penchant for abuse, but nevertheless the two bodies of song are far apart in both impulse and tone. Lesbos lay close to the shore of Asia Minor, and Mytilene was a far more luxurious city than those that Archilochus knew, but the difference is not simply one of geography. Archilochus spoke as Archilochus, while Alcaeus sang always as a member of the Lesbian nobility; Archilochus was a split creature, part poet and part soldier, but in Alcaeus the singer and the aristocrat were one. Archilochus viewed the public realm with sour objectivity while his passions were engaged by failures of private morality, but for Alcaeus life was led in an open arena of duty and power where public and private could not be separately defined. Like Archilochus, he was exercised by a discrepancy between the real and the ideal, but he believed that they had diverged only because of a quirk of events and that they might be reunited in a community that was properly arranged. This conviction and the moment in which he lived made his poetry political, but since he fought to revive an idealised past, his politics were in a sense poetical. His love, his rage and his hatred were spent in an attempt to impose a polished and traditional order upon society, and so he was able to make political verse without prettifying even the crudest sentiments and also without spoiling the measure of his song.[1]

Alcaeus sang for men whom he believed to be like himself, and his

---

[1] Dionysius of Halicarnassus, περὶ συνθέσεως ὀνομάτων, 24, characterises Alcaeus' poetry as μεγαλοφυὲς καὶ βραχὺ καὶ ἡδὺ μετὰ δεινότητος. Athenaeus, however, makes a kind of apology for him (14. 626), saying that if he is not the most musical of poets this is because he put the expression of *andreia* ahead of mere artfulness. Nevertheless, there is general agreement that Alcaeus provides a strong exception to Goethe's rule that political poetry must be bad poetry. A modern critic reports that Alcaeus contemplated his own political passions and idealised them with fantasy (G. Perrotta, 'Alceo', *A&R* 4, 1936, 323), but surely it would be more accurate to say that he idealised them with form.

music was meant to ready them for action by reaffirming the unity and permanence of their common convictions. His songs make no claim to novelty,[2] but are characterised instead by the craft of their fashioning[3] and the confidence of their assertion that one lives, as one sings, by a set of principles. Their physical sound is fixed by the soft Lesbian dialect and the short lines of the folk-songs of that island, while the potential banality of their lilting rhythms is controlled by phrasing as direct as common speech. They are melodious because the singer was a natural metrician, pure and economical because the convention would not allow any superabundance, and they are touched always with a peculiar zeal that belongs to Alcaeus alone. Strong emotion fills measures that are fragile and sensuous, whether the song is a hymn, a mythic piece or a bit of vilification, and an elegant virility results from this easy adjustment of turbulent matter to an exquisite form.

It is not hard to understand why Alcaeus idealised the past, for the present – the period between 620 and 570 B.C. – was a time of anarchy when Mytilene, having broken its ancient constitution, became a prize that one faction after another tried to gain. The men of Lesbos were notorious as drinkers, horse-breeders, adventurers and mercenary soldiers; they were also, according to ancient report, proud, luxury-loving, magnificent and confident.[4] The nobles were divided into at least four great clans,[5] all presumably sharing these characteristics, but nevertheless the island lived under the titular domination of just one group, the Penthilids, until the period of Alcaeus' birth.[6] This family claimed supremacy with the boast of descent from the union of Orestes with a daughter of Aegisthus, and it had supplied kings who commanded the nobles in time of war. The Pentihilid rulers seem also to have acted as judges of last resort, appointing magistrates to decide lesser

[2] This lack of novelty becomes a subject for reproach with Snell, who complains (*Poetry and Society*, Bloomington 1961, 33) that Alcaeus' thinking is inadequate, that he 'provides no new meanings', and that 'only Solon will lead us ahead'.

[3] Moderns often overlook the craft of Alcaeus; see, for example, Perrotta, op.cit., 240, who reports that his work is 'tutto impulso e istinto', or Fränkel's invidious comparison with Sappho, in which she is given all the discipline and finesse while Alcaeus is described as 'fahrig and ungleich' (*DuP*, 228).

[4] Athenaeus 14.624e, quoting Heraclides Ponticus.

[5] In addition to the family of Alcaeus, we know of Penthilids (472V; cf. 70.6V), Cleanactids (112.23; 468; cf. 63.3 and 306a.13V), and Archeanactids (112; cf. 444V). Sappho refers to Cleanactids at 98bV; Strabo mentions the presence of Archeanactids at Sigeum (13.1.38) and names Cleanactids among those whom Alcaeus attacked (13.2.3). S. Mazzarino, 'Per la storia di Lesbo nel VI secolo a.C.' *Athen.* 21 (1943) 54, note 4, supposes that ὠγεσιλαΐδα at 130bV is equivalent to ἐγὼ ὁ ᾿Αγεσιλαΐδα and consequently identifies the poet's clan as Agesilids, but the phrase is much more probably a vocative one, naming a friend.

[6] On ths history of Lesbos at the end of the sixth century, see Mazzarino, op. cit., 38–78; C. Gallavotti, *Storia e poesia di Lesbo nel VII–VI secolo aC. I: Alceo di Mitilene* (Bari, 1948); D. Page, *Sappho and Alcaeus* (Oxford 1955) 149–243.

questions of justice among the arms-bearing landholders who counted as citizens,[7] and since the king's treasury drew in the incomes, such as they were,[8] of this archaic state, the government could be classed as a monarchy. It was however modified by strong oligarchical elements, for the heads of the great families met regularly in council, and all of the nobles gathered from time to time in the agora,[9] to approve or disapprove royal policies. These, at any rate, were practices that Alcaeus thought he could recall.

Alcaeus himself belonged to one of the noble families that were essential to this traditional order, but he came of age just as the monarchy collapsed and with it the regular functions of the nobility. Colonialism, campaigns in the Troad,[10] and the beginnings of merchant activity had made the aristocrats richer and more restless, increasing their ambition and rendering the dominance of the Penthilids intolerable, and meanwhile the royal family had grown more repressive and more debauched as it became more unpopular. An initial aristocratic conspiracy led by a certain Megacles,[11] perhaps from the Cleanactid family, failed to destroy the monarchy, but a second uprising (about 620 B.C.) finally killed the last Penthilid king.[12] The regicide wrought a revolution, but it seems not to have been a truly political act, for Aristotle reports it as the vengeance of a man called Smerdis whose wife had been raped by the king (*Pol.* 1311b).[13] The story, of course, may be no more than gossip, but the aftermath of the assassination suggests that no organised impulse had been at work. Instead of inaugurating a new form of government, the fall of

[7] These magistrates may have been called *basileis*; this, at any rate, was the practice in the fourth century (*IG* XIII. 2.6; 2.18²), and it has been argued that the title existed three centuries earlier and was the basis of the report that Hyrras, Pittacus' father, was *basileus*; see J. C. Kamerbeek, 'De novis carminibus Alcaei', *Mnemosyne* Ser. iii 13 (1947) 161ff.

[8] At Cyme the government was already levying port taxes and controlling shipping, sometimes through tax-farmers who became extremely rich (see A. R. Burn, *The World of Hesiod*, 179); this may also have been done at Lesbos, but there is no documentation to prove it.

[9] See Alcaeus 130V and compare Xenophanes fr. 3D², where there is mention of the regular parade of about one thousand Colophonian aristocrats in the agora. The Thessalians, too, had a 'free', i.e. non-commercial, agora where only magistrates and nobles might go (Arist. *Pol.* 7.11.2/1331a 30–5).

[10] For war with Erythrae, see 444V, where Archeanactids are visited by Apollo on the battlefield.

[11] Megacles evidently acted with other members of his faction, μετὰ τῶν φίλων (Arist. *Pol.* 1311b23).

[12] If Pittacus' wife was the daughter of this Penthilus, and if he married her in the 600–595 period, she should have been born *c.* 615 and Penthilus could not have been killed much before. If, on the other hand, she was the daughter of this king's namesake grandson, then the assassination will have to be pushed back to the middle of the century, which would seem to leave too much time before the campaign at Sigeum.

[13] Note, however, that Gallavotti (*Storia*, 14) argues on the basis of the name, Smerdis, that this was a revolt of the people.

the Penthilids marked the beginning of a quarter-century of aristocratic strife on the island of Lesbos.

The nobles of Mytilene, experienced though they were, were unable to give their kingless city a stable government, probably because nothing in their previous history had caused them to recognise themselves as a single class with common interests. They had seen nothing beneath themselves, since they had not yet been challenged by any bourgeoisie, and nothing above, since their king was one of their own kind, and consequently they had no sense of their own position. They were the *damos*, the true substance of the state, but in their own eyes they were united only by habits of honour and rites of pleasure, and each one of them knew himself not as a noble but instead as a member of one particular family. A man was a Cleanactid or an Archeanactid before he was a man of Mytilene, and this fierce sense of clan was reinforced by a system of *hetaireiai* – clubs that associated cousins, brothers and more distant kin in one another's constant society.[14] The almost sacramental experience of drinking together moulded such groups into bands of soldiers bound to courageous performance by a seamless web of pride and shame, self-love and love for one's admired companions. It is easy to see that in war-time companies of this sort would be invaluable (they had mottos like 'It is a fair thing to die for Lord Ares', 400V), but it is equally easy to see that within a small city, when they were not at their military work, such groups would harass one another, especially in their youthful ranks. And in fact, in the years just after Penthilus' death, Mytilene seems to have been a rougher version of the Verona of Mercutio and Tybalt.

Before long, the disorder became so great that a tyrant was called for and a man named Melanchrus began to rule much as the old kings had done. He was evidently the creature of an unsteady clan alliance, however, not the representative of any new political element (Alcaeus later described him with words that could only apply to an aristocrat),[15]

---

[14] On *hetaireiai* in general, see E. Ziebarth, *Das gr. Vereinswesen* (Leipzig 1896) pp. 95 and 141ff. and *RE* sv *hetaireia* viii 1373ff.; K. Kircher, 'Die sakrale bedeutung des Weines im Altertum', *RGVV* 9 (1910) 48–59; G. M. Calhoun, *Athenian Political Clubs* (Austin, 1913) 15; N. Terzagho, 'L'Odio di Ipponatte', *SIFC* (1941) 223–8; F. Sartori, *Le eterie nella vita politica ateniese* (Rome 1957); P. von der Mühll, *Anhang zu Xenophon. Das Gastmahl* (Hamburg, 1957) 79–109 = *Kl. Schr.* 483–505. For the clubs of Alcaeus' time, see C. Talamo, 'Per le origini dell' eteria arcaica', *PP* 16 (1961) 297–303 and J. Trumpf, 'Über das trinken in der poesie des Alkaios', *ZPE* 12 (1973) 139ff.

[15] See 331V: Μέλανχρος αἶδως ἄξιος ἐς πόλιν, where the description means that he was the kind of man in whose presence one would watch one's own noble behaviour. This fragment is usually dismissed as 'inscrutable' (so Page, *S&A*, 151) or else as 'ironisch gemeint' (M. Treu, *Alkaios*, Munich 1952, 157) but the easiest way to take it is to suppose that Alcaeus means, 'M., though worthy of *aidōs*, yet did (something) to the city . . .' (older commentary is discussed by Mazzarino, op.cit., 40, note 1). It might be noted that in spite of this fragment V. Steffen has assumed that Melanchrus was a representative of the plebs and an opponent of the nobles; see 'Die politische Krise in Mytilene in der Zeit des Dichters Alkaios', *Scripta Minora Selecta* i (Warsaw 1973) 136.

and the one thing known about him is that he was soon removed. Like his regal forerunner, he was assassinated, perhaps about 612 B.C.,[16] but this time the act was fully political, the fruit of a conspiratorial plot that had been made inside Alcaeus' own clan (DL 1.4.74). The death of Melanchrus thus opens the period of Lesbian history that belongs peculiarly to this poet, and it introduces as well the man who was to be the subject, or rather the target, of so much of his poetry. Pittacus was later to become the tyrant of Mytilene and the focus of Alcaeus' passionate hatred, but in this early time he was the close friend of the heads of his clan and the man whom they chose to kill their enemy. Supported by the poet's older brothers, Pittacus succeeded, and for the moment he must have been the hero not just of a boy still too young for military service, and not just of his friends, but of all the noble factions that had not belonged to the tyrant's party.

Pittacus was daring, ambitious and intelligent; he was capable of killing with great style, as Phrynon's corpse would soon testify, but capable also of the kind of pithy reflections that are made by a thoughtful man who is well-pleased with himself. He was clearly stronger, both as soldier and as conspirator, than any of the hot-heads around him, and yet with all his extraordinary powers it took him something like twenty years to progress from the assassination of the original tyrant to his own assumption of the tyrant's role. Melanchrus was dead, but neither he nor his allies moved to take control in the immediate aftermath of the killing, and soon most of the nobles, the young Alcaeus among them (401BbV), left the city under Pittacus' command to meet the Athenians at Sigeum (Hdt. 5. 94–5; Strabo 13.38). They were not able to put a permanent stop to Athenian activity in the Troad, but nevertheless the campaign was memorable for Pittacus, like some epic avatar,[17] called out Phrynon, the enemy commander, and killed him in single combat (DL 1.74; Strabo 13.38; Plut. *Mor.* 856; Suda sv *Pittakos*, placing the event in the 42nd Olympiad, 612–608 B.C.). He was now not only the notorious tyrannicide and the ally of one of the leading families, but also the recognised saviour of the city, yet once again he took no political action, and his restraint seems to prove that absolute power was not the simple and obsessive aim of every noble party. It also strongly suggests that Pittacus had no numerous cabal of kinsmen behind him, and that

[16] Herodotus (5.94) was in some confusion about the date since he had both Periander and a son of Peisistratus take part in the Athenian defence of Sigeum; for a résumé of the discussion of the question, see Kamerbeek, op. cit., where the traditional dates are defended against Mazzarino's later Herodotean chronology. On the date of the Sigean war, see also Schachermeyr *RE* sv 'Pittakos' and Page, *S&A*, 152ff.

[17] The same epic mentality is reflected in the tradition that made Archeanax fortify Sigeum with stones from Troy; see Strabo 13.1.38.

perhaps some of Alcaeus' later insults about the quality of his blood were based in truth.[18]

Whatever the reason, the fact is that it was not Pittacus but a man named Myrsilus who became the second tyrant of Mytilene. It used to be thought that his unexpected rise, in a moment when Pittacus rode so high, was due to a shift of social and economic power – that Myrsilus was a non-aristocrat who appealed to the rich merchant classes against the oligarchs, and who had the backing of commercial Lydia.[19] This explanation has a pleasantly modern sound, but it is discredited by a fragment from a song of Alcaeus (305aV) which proves that Myrsilus had been at some point allied with Alcaeus' own noble faction. He had been in exile, probably during the time of Melanchrus, and had been smuggled back into the city by a certain Mnamon whom Alcaeus later claimed as a friend. The episode is obscure, but it proves that Myrsilus was no bourgeois anti-aristocrat, but rather a Mytilenean noble engaged in the same factional struggles that occupied all of the great Lesbian clans. This means that he must have been brought to power by the same men who might alternatively have raised up Pittacus – he must, indeed, have had the active support of the hero of Sigeum

---

[18] It is often supposed that Pittacus' father was a Thracian; this was reported by Diogenes Laertius (1.74), who cited Douris as his witness (cf. Diod.Sic. 9.12). A Byzantine note that may go back to Dicaearchus' Life of Alcaeus (S. Dion. Thrax = Hilgard 368.15) names the father Hyrras and calls him *basileus*. This foreign derivation would explain Alcaeus' practice of calling Pittacus a *kakopatrid*, but it makes the tyrant's early association with Alcaeus' brothers hard to understand, and so it is usually assumed (after Wilamowitz, *S&S*, 173) that his ancestors had been noblemen in Thrace (Pittacus is the name of a Thracian king at Thuc. 4.107.3). It has been suggested in addition that his mother may have been a member of the Lesbian aristocracy (so Mazzarino, op. cit., 50; Burn, *Lyric Age*, p.243, where the connection is presumed to be with the Archeanactids; Treu, *Alk.*, p. 110 and Page, *S&A*, pp.170–1). A. W. Gomme, however, denied the possibility that Thracian ancestry, noble birth, and a father who was a *basileus* could have characterised a Pittacus whom Alcaeus called *kakopatrid*, and after a somewhat confused résumé of Lesbian history he concluded that the term, which he thought meant bastard or son of a slave, was used in slander against a man who was in fact a member of the middle class ('Interpretations', *JHS* 77, 1957, 255). Meanwhile, V. di Benedetto had argued that ὑρράδιος was not a patronymic at all but a word for 'bastard' and in consequence he had likewise rejected the Thracian connection altogether, positing a Pittacus who was the illegitimate son of an Archeanactid ('Pittaco e Alceo', *PP* 41, 1955, 97ff.). The Penthilid marriage, however, would seem to destroy both the middle-class and the bastard hypotheses and in the end the soundest position seems to be that of Kamerbeek (op.cit., 171), who argued that a *kakopatrid* was the opposite of a *eupatrid* and that even in violent abuse such a term would have to be used with a certain accuracy. With it, Alcaeus most probably referred to Pittacus' known non-Lesbian parentage. It should be added that his father seems to have been a landholder, if one can trust the anecdote at Diod.Sic. 9.12, where Pittacus and his brother both inherit Lesbian property. In later times of course Pittacus was claimed as a Lesbian and given a tomb inscription in which a maternal Lesbos weeps at the grave of her son (DL 1.79).

[19] So Gallavotti, op.cit., 24–5.

when he first moved into a position of dominance.[20]

Myrsilus ruled the city in the period that immediately followed the campaign against the Athenians – the period in which Alcaeus came fully of age – and in spite of their original complaisance Pittacus and the poet's family soon actively opposed the tyrant's power. Myrsilus was too much like his predecessor (Alcaeus saw him as a 'second wave', (6V), and so they planned a second conspiracy that was doubtless meant to fulfil itself, like the first, in an assassination. The leaders of the faction swore to return the city to the *damos* – the landholding citizen body – or die in the attempt, but at the last minute Pittacus dextrously dissociated himself from the plot and it was discovered before any move was actually made.[21] Indeed, it seems very likely that Pittacus did more, for his subsequent position as the tyrant's second-in-command suggests that it was he who actually denounced his erstwhile friends to Myrsilus. He stayed in the city of the tyrant and they, in order to avoid retaliation, fled from Mytilene and hid in the back-country, unable to resist as their honours were absorbed and their properties exploited by their enemy and their own former hero, the two strongest men of the moment, allied now in absolute power.

For a time Myrsilus and Pittacus ruled together, but what their relations were we do not know. Pittacus may have been counsellor, philosopher,[22] vizier, chief of secret police, or head of the élite guard. Possibly Myrsilus was in need of a younger arm, possibly he thought it safer to keep a tyrant-killer under his own eye, but whatever his reasons for taking up with one who had recently opposed him, the alliance seems to have been a success. Sappho remembered these years

---

[20] The marginal note at 112V may indicate that Myrsilus was a Cleanactid, and he is reported as certainly so by Treu, Burn and Bowra (who makes him the brother of Melanchrus). Mazzarino, (op.cit., 56ff.) builds an elaborate picture of a Cleanactid commercial faction led by Myrsilus and closely allied with Lydia, but this depends upon his own special reading of the problematical Sappho fragment, 98bV. Page sensibly remarks that the entire Cleanactid connection is 'insufficiently attested' (*S&A*, 174), but one thing would seem to be certain and that is that Myrsilus cannot have been of the same clan as Melanchrus, in the light of Pittacus' position of trust at Myrsilus' court.

[21] The commentator at 114V speaks of 'the first exile' as occurring ὅτ᾽ ἐπὶ Μύρσιλον κατασκευασάμενοι ἐπιβουλὴν οἱ περὶ τὸν Ἀλκαῖον κ(ατα)φαν[ ]φθάσαντες πρὶν ἢ δίκην ὑποσχεῖν ἔφυγον εἰς Πύρραν (cf. 129 and 130bV). Another scenario might put Pittacus' defection a bit later: conspirators denounced (by an unknown); whole faction goes into exile, there swears to return to power; Pittacus sneaks off and returns to Mytilene and Myrsilus. This sequence is favoured by those who believe that the oath referred to in 129V must have been taken in the place referred to in that song, but there is nothing to bear out this belief (see below, pp. 157ff.) and on the face of it this second reconstruction of events seems much less likely than the first, since it would be very hard to understand why Myrsilus gave such high honours to Pittacus if he had actually taken part not only in the initial conspiracy but also in the exile, with its (presumed) further conspiracy.

[22] For Pittacus the philosopher who advises a tyrant, see Plut. *sept. sap.* 147 = *Mor.* 1. 302.

(if this was the time she refers to in her song about a head-band for Kleïs, 98bV) as a period of easy commerce and modish life, but for the exiles it was a time of bitterness. What Alcaeus saw from the country was a brace of rulers who devoured the wealth of the city and made poor men of the ancient nobility, and he was filled with self-disgust at his own impotence (130V).[23]

Myrsilus died, apparently of natural causes, about the year 597 B.C.,[24] and his death marked the end of the first exile of Alcaeus and his friends. Singing, 'Now a man must drink and drink intemperately, for Myrsilus is dead!' (332V), they came back to the city expecting a return to the old hurly-burly of aristocratic politics.[25] Pittacus alone seemed to offer no threat of further tyranny, and the notorious nature of his former activities appeared to disqualify him even for the ordinary games of politics. His youthful assassination of Melanchrus had alienated that tyrant's clan forever; his more recent defection from the Alcaic faction had made him the object of obsessive hatred among his first allies; and meanwhile he could not be viewed by the family of Myrsilus as anything but a rival to one of themselves for the place that their kinsman had held. At least three clans were thus necessarily opposed to him, and there is no sign that he had any powerful relations of his own. Nevertheless, Pittacus did have *panache*, and at this difficult moment his strategy was impeccable: he married a Penthilid (5, 70, 75, 296V).[26] With the support of that ancient family and its retainers he could once more influence the council, and it looks as if he courted both the poor and the land-owners with policies that were now subtly anti-commercial. He also seems to have tried to weaken his aristocratic opponents by encouraging nobles of fighting age to go off on mercenary expeditions (69V), and as an alternative he procured

[23] We do not know whether the exiles, on their return, were allowed to recover their lands by payment of *poinai*, but if they were in some cases, this will have been a source of negotiable wealth for the tyrants' treasuries.

[24] H. Berve, 'Wesenszüge der gr. Tyrannis', *Hist. Zeit.* 177 (1954) 8, notes that none of the tyrants known to us died in battle or by suicide, and since there is no sign of a successful conspiracy against Myrsilus, it may be that he died a natural death; see Gallavotti, 'La Morte di Mirsilo', *Studi in onore di L. Castiglione* i (Florence 1960), 319–29, where the author proposes joining 206V to 332V, but sheds no new light on the circumstances of the tyrant's death.

[25] There were probably several years of factional jostling at this time; Gallavotti ('Nuovi testi letterari da Ossirinco', *Aegyptus* 22, 1942, 111) assumed a brief period of Cleanactid-dominated oligarchy (to correspond with Sappho 98bV); Mazzarino (op.cit., 70) supposed a short term of joint rule by Pittacus and Deinomenes, whom he identified as a Cleanactid. Kamerbeek (op.cit., pt.2, 166–7), who believed that Pittacus represented the common people, saw this as a time of 'Lutte déchainée ... entre aristocrates et démocrates'.

[26] DL 1.81 makes the royal wife a shrew. For the Penthilid marriage, see below, pp. 171ff. The event cannot be certainly dated, but 70V seems to place it after the time of Pittacus' joint rule with Myrsilus.

sentences of exile against his worst enemies, among whom Alcaeus and his brothers soon figured conspicuously.

Once again Alcaeus' faction went up-country, but this time they seem to have combined with some of the other clans, intending to force their way back into the city, and Pittacus was able to demand extraordinary powers as Mytilene's defender against these dangerous exiles. 'The crowd with great cheers set base Pittacus up as tyrant of their unlucky lily-livered city' is the way Alcaeus saw this decisive turn in Pittacus' career (348V).[27] Officially in command again, the hero of Sigeum led his army out and defeated the banished men in an encounter 'at the bridge' (306AeV).[28] Some of the exiles were killed (Antimenidas, the poet's brother, may have been among them) and the others were forced now to leave the island in a third and more stringent exile. Some went to Egypt, some to Asia Minor, to mainland Greece and even to Sicily, and we know that Alcaeus 'fled from lovely Lesbos' (296b12V) and wandered at least as far as Boeotia (325V) during this period of banishment.[29]

The position of Pittacus was now secure and he remained in power for many years; a suspiciously Solonic tradition has him hold the office of *aisymnētēs* for exactly a decade (595–585 B.C.) and then return voluntarily to the status of a private citizen (DL 1.74). He made no changes in the constitution, according to Aristotle (*Pol.* 1274b18), so presumably he continued to call occasional meetings of council and agora, though it is hard to see just who was left to attend. Perhaps he worked some enlargement on the citizen body; at any rate, the repeated emphasis upon land lots in the anecdotes told about him suggests that there was some confiscation and redistribution of the exiles'

[27] This would not, of course, be 'the crowd' in the modern sense, but instead a mass meeting of those arms-bearing men who were still in the city; see Page, *S&A*, 239; Burn, *Lyric Age*, 243. Aristotle (*Pol.* 1285a) cited Pittacus as an example of a tyrant elected to his tyranny, saying that he was 'chosen by the Mytileneans to act against the exiles who were led by Antimenidas and Alcaeus the poet' (cf. DL 1.75).

[28] On the 'muster at the bridge' (306AeV), see Page, *Oxy.pap.* 29 (1961) 45; M. Treu, 'Neues über S.u.A.', *QU* 1 (1966) 30ff.; W. Barner, 'Zu den Alk. fg. von POxy 2506', *Hermes* 95 (1967) 1ff. The commentator mentions that Antimenidas took part in the action at the bridge, but that Alcaeus did not die there but lived to enjoy the third return from exile, because of something about a war between Astyages and Alyattes. This 'battle', if such it was, would seem to offer the one chance for Pittacus to have taken Alcaeus prisoner and then to have let him go, as Diogenes Laertius reports (1.74); there is, however, no need to believe that the anecdote is historical, since it serves as a frame for one of Pittacus' maxims.

[29] For Alcaeus in Boeotia, see 325V, where Athena seems to have the titles that she had at Coronea, and perhaps also 306AcV. The Marmor Parium takes Sappho to Sicily, and Dicaearchus seems to have believed that Alcaeus knew the west (462V); whether Strabo, 13.2.3, with his mention of Egypt, refers to this time is not clear. Treu (*Alk.*, 61) believes that Alcaeus went to Aenos, a colony at the mouth of the Hebrus, and also to mainland Greece; at *QU* 2 (1966) 30ff., he also puts Alcaeus in Asia Minor as a mercenary with Alyattes at some point during the exile.

property.[30] With or without a noble council, he legislated against private warfare and passed various regulations aimed against debauchery, including a system of double punishment for crimes committed while drunk (DL 1.74; cf. Ar. *Rhet.* 1402b12). Among his sumptuary laws were restrictions upon funeral expenditure, and since the funeral was the defining experience of the ancient clan this may have been tantamount to an attack upon the aristocracy,[31] but nevertheless as time went by Pittacus began to permit the return of his banished enemies. 'Pardon is better than punishment,' he is supposed to have said (DL 1.76) and, more to the point, he knew that Mytilene could not survive without its warrior class.[32] When the amnesty became general, Alcaeus and those of his party who were still alive came back to the city, probably some time before 585 B.C., and as far as we know the poet spent the rest of his life there, in more quiet than he had ever known before. We have no date for his death, but Pittacus, who was his elder, was supposed by later tradition to have died in the year 570/69 B.C.

Almost everyone who reads the poems of Alcaeus is tempted to pass some kind of judgment upon the part that the poet played in these events. In the nineteenth century, especially in Italy, his restless career of resistance was romanticised and Alcaeus was praised as the enemy of tyranny and the first singer of liberty. More recently, however, historians have pointed out that the *damos* Alcaeus swore to defend was not the people but a handful of hereditary landholders,[33] and in addition they have reminded us that Pittacus, the tyrant whom Alcaeus most hated, was no Franco or Mussolini but instead a wise and moderate man whom the ancient world counted among its Seven

---

[30] According to Diogenes Laertius (1.74) the Mytilenaeans gave Pittacus land, on which he put up a shrine called the Pittaceum; Diodorus Siculus (9.12) reports that the citizens gave him land and that he divided it into equal lots, saying that equality was greater than having the greatest share.

[31] It is usually assumed that his policy was frankly anti-aristocratic; see, e.g. A. Andrewes, *The Greek Tyrants* (London 1956), 97. There is, however, nothing to show that Pittacus made any special appeal to the lower classes, and it seems reasonable to suppose that laws against luxury would be anti-commercial and therefore unpopular among the bourgeoisie. Consequently Mazzarino (op.cit., 52) insists that Pittacus' policies retained an essentially upper-class character and were no more than 'una forma nuova in cui la vecchia etica aristocratica si revelava, criticando se stessa'. After the retirement of Pittacus, the Lesbian state evidently continued as an oligarchy, and since nothing suggests that violent changes were needed to restore its institutions, they must have been at least formally maintained during the tyranny.

[32] It looks as if Pittacus was, towards the end of his period of power, moving towards closer relations with Lydia; the traditions about him include a meeting with Croesus (Suda sv *Pittakos*) and Plut., *sept. sap.* 153e, brings him into contact with Alyattes. It is nevertheless hard to see any merit in Treu's attempt to fix Pittacus' death as having occurred in battle, in Lydia, where the ex-tyrant was supposedly fighting as an ally of Croesus ('Neues über S.v.A. POxy 2506', *QU* 2, 1966, 30ff.); for a corrective, see Barner, *Hermes* 95 (1967) 16ff.

[33] See Page, *S&A*, 177; Andrewes, op.cit., 94.

Sages. This poet was interested in liberty only for his own class, perhaps only for his own faction – such is the disillusioned conclusion of most contemporaries. Those who are Marxists hear Alcaeus' songs as the music of repression and reaction,[34] and others see him as a foolish fanatic who could only look backwards into the past. He should, they feel, have recognised those tendencies in tyranny that would in time liberalise Hellenic politics by broadening the citizen base. He should have welcomed the first signs of democracy, they say, and often they find themselves forced to dismiss Alcaeus as one who lacked vision and intellect.[35]

Since the events under consideration are more than twenty-five centuries old, and since their social context is entirely unknown, judgments such as these are of a somewhat dubious value. Fortunately, however, they are quite irrelevant to the poetry of Alcaeus, since what matters there is not our view of the poet's time but his own, and his own is perfectly clear. Alcaeus did recognise the changes that were taking place and he disliked them, for he saw in them a threat to all that he valued in life. He could see the tendency towards a more democratic state and it was exactly that tendency that he hoped to halt. He took his oath that no *kakopatrid* should be allowed to assume the functions and the powers that were by custom the exclusive possessions of the nobility (those whose fathers had been on the island 'from the beginning' 67V),[36] and the fact that his word *kakopatrid* could mean 'one who harms his fatherland' as well as 'one who has a base father' perfectly expresses his deepest thought.[37] Any upsurgence of the non-noble elements would, to his mind, be harmful to the state, since it would necessarily change the ancient and awesome structures that had forever defined the Lesbian community.

What Alcaeus seems to have wanted was a headless version of the destroyed monarchy – a city administered by a council of nobles who

---

[34] E.g., V. Steffen, op.cit., 135ff., who sees Lesbian 'Volksmassen' who turn to the tyrants for relief from the oppression of nobles like Alcaeus.

[35] Andrewes, op.cit., 96, calls him 'empty-headed' and complains that he 'resisted the change that was coming over the world' (92). Page speaks of his political ideals as being 'at least suspect' (*S&A*, 176), and Kirkwood concludes (*EGM*, 59): 'Alcaeus was certainly on the wrong side.' Perhaps the most extreme is Mazzarino (op.cit., 63, note 2), who insists that all the aristocrats were alike, and all wished absolute power for their own party; the only exception he will recognise is Pittacus: 'Pittaco sta su un piano politicamente assai piu elevato.' For a more moderate discussion, see Kamerbeek, op.cit., 161ff.

[36] The expression seems to stand in 67V as οἰ ἀπ᾽ ἀρχαω[. Note however that some would read Ἀρχαω[, and so make this a place name that identified a particular group of exiles after their return from banishment; see Gallavotti, *Storia*, 102ff.

[37] J. Wackernagel, 'Gr. Miszellen', *Glotta* 14 (1925) 50–1 = *KL. Schr.* ii 858–9, cites φιλοπατρία (at Ar. *Vesp.* 1265 as 'love of father') and φιλόπολις, the normal epithet of a patriot, and concludes that in the early case of Alcaeus both 'plebeian' and 'unpatriotic' are possible meanings for *kakopatrid*, and that a choice between them can be made only on subjective grounds.

would be assisted at times by a full assembly of those who owned land and defended the city by bearing arms.[38] These, the best of men, licensed to act according to their natural virtues of good faith, bravery, wisdom and love of what is fine, would produce the best of governments. Of course they were not all equally endowed; practical leadership, especially command of the army, would devolve now upon one man and now upon another, according to the moment and the task, and through the performance of these tasks certain men would gain a manifest importance. They would be *phaneroi* (67V) and would win the fame that excellence always strives for (the *kudos epēraton* that is misplaced at 70.13V), but they would have been chosen from those who were already respected as free and propertied soldiers – those who had a natural affinity for honour (compare 72V, where those who are *eleutheroi* and *esloi* are the normal recipients of *doxa*).[39] Above all, they would be ever open to challenge from their equally honour-loving peers. Such was his ideal, and Alcaeus believed (or pretended to believe) that it had existed in the past and that his grandfather and father had known and supported it. He also believed (or acted as if he believed) that it could come into being again if only the nobles would forget their feuds and their exclusively factional aims (70V). A city governed in this way would be one that a man might long for almost as one longs for a lover (130b.3V), for in such a place the enemies would all be abroad and everyone within would feel the tie of ancient cult and common history.

Alcaeus seems to have become an opponent of tyranny precisely because he did sense the inherent dynamism that so often made this form of government a prelude to deeper constitutional change. Probably he and his friends began by approving first Melanchrus and then Myrsilus because they both seemed to be leaders like the early Pittacus – men whose eminence had been tested and proved in noble competition. Soon, however, such a one became interested in power, not in Lesbos and its aristocracy; maddened by a desire for absolute authority, he would turn the city upside down (141V). Because he refused to recognise any challenge to his pre-eminence, the *turannos* or *basileus* would look outside the arrogant nobility for his support and engage in acts of evil *hubris*,[40] thus making his power illegitimate

---

[38] In a fragment about old age (39V) the mysterious phrase πολιάταν ὄλιγον appears; it might possibly refer to an aristocratic duty, one that devolves upon the old, or can no longer be performed by them.

[39] Alcaeus of course knew that not every man of blood and property was truly 'noble'; see 391V, where he calls upon ὄττινες ἔσλοι / ὐμμέων τε καὶ ἀμμέων, the 'you' and the 'us' being surely both groups of aristocrats.

[40] The word occurs in 306gV. For early meanings of *hubris* as the violent opponent of the order of *dikē*, cf. Hes. *Erg.* 213ff. and also 275, where *dikē* is forgetting βία; see the discussion of W. Barner, *Neuere Alkaios-Papyri aus Oxyrhynchos*, Spudasmata xiv (Hildesheim 1967) 84.

as he tried to establish what Alcaeus called a *monarchia*.[41] Such a one was a ruler, not a leader any more, and the consequences of his rule were the slaughter of the aristocracy, the confiscation of property and the promotion of men who had no family. Naturally, the fact that a tyrant might be chosen by the clamour of a crowd only made him the more illegitimate, since the mob had no place in the city's government. Such a ruler endangered the position of the landed even when he was himself one of them, and if there was some flaw in his heredity, as there evidently was in the case of Pittacus, he became (in Alcaeus' eyes) a savage beast who gobbled up the Lesbos that ancestors and gods had created. The city, under his command, was no object of love, but a thing to be despised as unfortunate and cowardly (348V).

Ordinarily men were to be ruled by the nobles, the nobles by custom and ceremony, rivalry and honour, and also by the fear of one god who was all-powerful, for Alcaeus saw Olympus as a monarchy.[42] He salutes many other gods, praising them as the sources of various kinds of graciousness, but he honours Zeus as their king, and he seems to have been the first to call him *basileus*.[43] The title is not offered lightly or in passing, but appears four times in the fragments that survive (38a; 296a; 308; 387V), and once Alcaeus insists upon the absolute cosmic control of this heavenly king with the (perhaps fresh-coined) term *pambasileus* (308V), a word that would not appear again until Christian times.[44] The Zeus of Alcaeus is a eupatrid who has come to power legitimately (though after some factional strife!) as his father's son, and this the poet proclaims by giving him his patronymic each time that he proffers the title *basileus*. He also takes care to make him the Cronian one in passages where the universal extent of his power is emphasised (200; 112; 306g9V). This king of heaven is allied with *moira* (39a10; 206V); he is the overseer of all (306g9V) in whose hands are the completion and the fulfilment of everything (200.10V),[45]

---

[41] Myrsilus' government is elsewhere called a *monarchia* (6.27V, unless this refers to its doublet, the government of Melanchrus that constitutes the 'first wave'). On the illegitimacy of the tyrant, note the οὐ κὰν νόμον (129.25V) of Pittacus' collaboration with Myrsilus; Barner (ibid. 105) supposes that the γεγρα- in line 27 of that fragment makes this a reference to written law, but this seems highly unlikely. The *nomos* in question may be simply the custom of honouring oaths; a custom on which aristocratic politics were based.

[42] C. del Grande, *Hybris* (Naples 1947) 43, proposes their common belief in Zeus' absolute power as a supreme god as the single point in common between Alcaeus and Hesiod.

[43] After Alcaeus, Zeus is βασιλεύς at Theog. 856, P.O.7.34, etc.

[44] The feminine version, παμβασίλεια, appears at Ar.Nub. 357 and 1150, obviously as a term of exaggerated respect.

[45] In 200V, the will of Zeus is represented as the opposite of chance (δαίμων, 4, usually bad luck in Sappho and Alcaeus). A friend seeks to understand an event that has called both justice and faith into question (see lines 7 and 8), and Alcaeus responds with the statement 'Zeus, son of Kronos, himself controls the fulfilment of every object.' Hesiod (Erg. 669) had said that Zeus was the fulfilment of both good and evil, in support of

whether in nature (338V) or in the minds of men (361V). Not a hair falls from an old man's head (39aV), not a scheme prospers among the nobility (361V) without his having decided that it should be. Himself a ruler, his power is naturally felt in political affairs, and he determines the vicissitudes of the city (269a; cf. 69V), protecting it with his aegis (*aigiochos*, 343V), receiving its suppliants (*antiaos*, 129V), and hearing the curses of those who have been betrayed in the fight for the *damos* (129; cf. 112V). As son of Cronus, this Zeus is the guardian of an order that goes back to creation, an order expressed in all the boundaries that fate and custom and class have fixed – an order that Alcaeus used his life to defend and his song to define.

---

advice in favour of taking risks; Semonides (1.1ff.W) likewise asserted that Zeus held the ends of all things, as a rationalisation for his conviction that men are all blind fools (cf. Archil. 298W, which is also assigned to Euripides). Alcaeus is thus the first known poet to associate the idea of Zeus' control of *telos* with that of justice, whether by *dika* he means a specific judgment or punishment, or whether he refers to some larger balance in men's affairs. See the discussion of Barner, *Neuere Alk. Pap.* 102–12.

Ideal Companionship

Alcaeus' songs were performed for an audience that was more than fraternal, since it was made up of brothers, cousins, uncles and friends whose kinship was outwardly displayed in common military action, inwardly affirmed by rites of sociability and, on occasion, by formal oaths.[1] These men fought side by side when Mytileneans were engaged abroad, and within the city they were a closed contingent that operated as a single unit in political matters. Linked with the whole of the nobility by their common duty to defend the city, they were yet more tightly bound to one another by inherited alliances and by constant social intercourse. They dined together as regularly as possible,[2] at home, on campaign, or in exile, and for them the term *sumpotēs* was invented (perhaps by Alcaeus himself)[3] because wine, banquet, and garlands were the sanctifying signs of their fealty and their fighting solidarity.[4] Met together for pleasure, they celebrated common cults and entertained one another with songs of every sort – hymns and exhortations, but also riddles, jokes, abuse, and salutes to the victories and defeats, departures and reunions, as well as to the sexual adventures, that made up their mutual life.

[1] Compare the observations of G. Perrotta, 'Alceo', *A&R* ser.3.4 (1936) 222f., and see the bibliography cited above, p. 110, note 14. No one knows just how the membership in these groups was determined. B. Snell, *Poetry and Society* (Bloomington 1961) 30, studies the later indications of Herodotus (5.71) and [Plato] (*horoi* 413c) and concludes that they were based in a given initiation class, but this would yield a group of men all of the same age drawn from all the clans, and this was clearly not the case in Mytilene, where Alcaeus can meet his elder brother Antimenidas at a gathering of the *hetaireia*.

[2] Snell (op.cit., 32) gives no reason for his statement to the contrary.

[3] See 306Ab.27V, συμπόταις; cf. 70.3 and 368.2V, συμπόσιον; 401(b)V σύμπωθι. Theognis 298 has συμπόσιον as the place for a talkative man; cf. P.N.9.48; O.7.5; I.6.1. For a discussion of the other συν- compounds in Alcaeus as a sign of a new sense of community, see Snell, loc. cit.; Fränkel *DuP*, 71, note 22.

[4] See especially Trumpf, *ZPE* 12 (1973) 139ff. The wine of the symposiasts' libations recognised the presence of the gods, as at Athen. 5.192b and in so many victory odes (e.g. P.O.3.40; N.9.48ff.); the crowns were a reminder of Promethus' subjection to Zeus (see Von der Mühll, *Das Gastmahl*, 87 = 486); the music signified the aristocrat's understanding of measure and harmony, and so of government (as at P.P.1.70; cf. the Molpoi of Miletus, a group of singing aristocrats who governed the city).

It is impossible for us, now, to define the Alcaic faction more precisely than this, and it would have been difficult, no doubt, even for one of its own number, for the functions of the group were social and spiritual as well as military and political, and even the membership, being traditional, was open to fluctuation. Common conviction and a common impulse – perhaps what Alcaeus calls the *noēma* of the group (361V, cf. 392V) – were essential, but a sense of definition, in such a company, is neither natural nor dependable, and this is why music was almost as important as wine to their gatherings. Wine was the mirror of each man (333V), but music, or at any rate the music of Alcaeus, was the mirror of the fraternity, a reflection in which it might study itself and learn its own outlines. Singing as if his voice were indistinguishable from theirs, Alcaeus gave the multiple consciousness of his audience a form that was composed and memorable, and he offered his friends a common image of themselves. Or, to be more precise, he offered them two such images, for in Alcaeus' songs the faction saw itself sometimes as a noble replica of the Homeric band of *hetairoi*,[5] sometimes as the ignoble forerunner of the political cabals that Thucydides and Isocrates would later describe.[6] When he asked them to idealise themselves, Alcaeus addressed his audience as a gathering of comrades who shared an unspoken system of values and an unquestioned sense of function. These were noblemen whose mutual trust was as plain as the marks upon their shields,[7] and to them he sang sometimes of battle, sometimes of wine and love and the safe harbour of comradeship, but always with an easy pride. When, on the other hand, Alcaeus held up a more critical glass, his songs addressed the same audience as if it were a faction in the later sense of the word – a group shaken by shifting allegiances and split by new ambitions (141V) that interfered with the old aims of aristocratic honour. To this second audience (in personnel more or less identical with the first), Alcaeus sang of plots and treachery, of wine misused

---

[5] At *Il.* 1.179; 16.170, 268, etc. the word is used of the companions of Achilles who will follow him without question. It should be noted, however, that the company of epic *hetairoi* may include men of low birth; at *Il.*4.294 Nestor's 'companies' include *kakoi* as well as *esthloi*. A particular situation can create a particular companion relationship, as that between Diomedes and Odysseus in *Il.*10, between Odysseus and one section of his party at *Od.*9.172, or among the transformed men at *Od.* 10.320. Alcaeus himself calls the men of his group *hetairoi* in connection with their having taken an oath enjoining common action (129.16V); he uses the word once more, but in an unidentifiable context (156.4V). On the meanings of *hetairos* in epic and later, see N. Terzaghi, *SIFC* NS 17 (1940) 217ff.

[6] Hdt. 5.71; Thuc. 3.82; Xen. *Hell.* 5.2.25; Isoc. *Nik.* (3) 54; cf. Plato *Rep.* 365d. The distinguishing signs of these later factions were meetings at night, presumably in secret, and a tight organisation under a single leader to whom members were bound by special oaths. The word is also used by Plutarch (*de gen. Socr.* 13. 583a) to describe the special associations of the Pythagoreans.

[7] Note Barner's comment on the boar ensign of 179V: 'Vielleicht hat A. es als Sinnbild der Hetairie gesetzt; kraftvoll und jederzeit zum Angriff bereit' (*Neuere Alk.-Pap.*, 62).

and oaths that failed to fix the doubtful loyalty of the group. And to them he expressed anger, outrage and shame.

At times Alcaeus says to his friends, 'You are splendid: be what you are!' At times he says, 'You are despicable: change!' and these two forms of exhortation, implicit or explicit, invest all of his work except for the art songs. One set of performances idealises the *hetaireia* and attempts to enhance its certain virtue, while another censors it as a disintegrating faction, but this does not mean that the two sets must necessarily belong to different moments or to altered objective situations. It would be naif to suppose that early untroubled symposia were followed by later banquets that were themselves the victims of stasis, and equally ingenuous to think that tranquillity came to the poet and his friends only after their final return to Mytilene. Ease may be felt in exile, discomfort at home, and the choice of a particular song will have been dictated, on any given evening, by the need to contest or surpass the performance just ended, while its tone will have been produced by the state of the poet's illusions, at the time of composition. Quite possibly Alcaeus addressed his friends within a single hour, now as a perfect company of gentlemen, now as a conjuration given over to treachery and internal intrigue. And quite possibly, too, he composed songs of amity one day, songs of enmity the next, according to his mood. To separate the two sorts of song is thus to defy both the probabilities of chronology and the actualities of the sympotic experience, but nevertheless they will be so separated in the discussion that follows. The songs that assume a noble solidarity within the *hetaireia* will here be considered before those that address a dubious and fragmented virtue, because the poet's disillusionment is the creature of his ideal, and this means that we who do not belong to his company can only take his blame correctly after we have heard his praise.

The *hetaireia* that Alcaeus loved was a band of noble friends whose hereditary profession was war. They drank together by night because they fought together by day, and Alcaeus made battle and banquet one by reminding his idealised comrades that he sang, and they listened, in the presence of their arms (140V):[8]

$$] \ldots [$$

μαρμ⌊αίρει δὲ ⌊μέγας δόμος
χάλκωι, π⌊αῖσα δ' "Α⌊ρηι κεκόσμηται στέγα
λάμ⌊πραιϲιν ⌊κυνίαιϲι, κὰτ
τᾶν λεῦ⌊κοι κατέπ⌊ερθεν ἵππιοι λόφοι 5

---

[8] Compare the passage of Herodotus (1.34.3) cited by Page (*S&A*, 222) in which the men's halls of Lydia are described as hung with arms. It is possible that this hall is meant to be that of Alcaeus' family, and Fränkel may thus be right to translate: 'Von Erz funkelt mein weites Haus' (*DuP*, 214, note 1). There is, however, no reason to suppose (as F. does at *WuF*, 55) that Alcaeus here sings only for himself, using the first person plural in lieu of the singular.

νε‚ύοιϲιν, κεφά‚λαιϲιν ἄν-
  δρων ἀγά‚λματα· χ‚ά‚λκ‚‚αι δ‚ὲ παϲ⟨ϲ⟩άλοιϲ
κρύ‚πτοιϲιν ‚π‚ερικεί‚‚μεναι
  λάμπραι κνάμι‚δεϲ, ἔρκ‚οϲ ἰϲχύρω βέλεοϲ
θόρρακέϲ τε νέω λίνω   10
  κόιλαί τε κὰτ ἄϲπιδεϲ βεβλήμεναι·
πὰρ δὲ Χαλκίδικαι ϲπάθαι,
  πὰρ δὲ ζώματα πόλλα καὶ κυπάϲϲιδεϲ.
τῶν οὐκ ἔϲτι λάθεϲθ' ἐπεὶ
  δὴ πρώτιϲτ' ὑπὰ τὦργον ἔϲταμεν τόδε.   15

The vast room gleams with bronze,
     each wall enhanced for Ares' eye
with sheen of casques and nodding sweep
     of pale dependent plume,
the gear of brave men's heads. Bright
     greaves of bronze that foil
the arrow's bite disguise
     the pegs they hang from
and new-made linen vests and hollow shields
     are thrown pell-mell upon the floor
along with swordblades from Chalkis,
     along with belts and tunics in a heap.
These things no one of us forgets – not
     since we first took up this task.

Unlike Archilochus, Alcaeus can easily see the utensils of war as beautiful, and the fragment begins as if to salute the beauty of the weapons it describes, holding them at a distance with Homeric vocabulary, polishing them with long phrases, and listing them apparently for the sheer pleasure of making a list. For a moment[9] these arms seem to hang up in idleness, catching cobwebs like the trophies in Bacchylides' paean to peace, but then a careless, almost violent word causes everything to change. The corselets and shields of lines 10 and 11 have not been decorously hung up, they have been thrown down (*beblēmenoi*, 11) in haste and their actual disorder is confirmed by a sudden drop from exalted syntax to a swift, rough summary in anaphora (*par de . . . par de*, 12 and 13). The sword blades that follow are mentioned with the everyday, not the epic, word (*spathē* not *xiphos*) and qualified with an epithet that is practical instead of heroic. They take a good edge, because their metal was tempered at Chalkis. After the swords, belts and non-Homeric tunics appear without any adornment at all, and then the narrowing poem reaches its goal in

---

[9] Fränkel thought he recognised a tranquil satisfaction that pervaded the entire fragment (*DuP*, 215 = *Early Greek Poetry*, 189).

the flat and wholly de-poeticised 'work' of these gathered weapons and men – the *ergon* of the final line.[10]

Short as it is, the series of distiches has wrought a change upon its weapons, and what is more, it has achieved a kind of transportation as well, for it has taken the arms off the walls and placed them in the minds of the listening men. Arms that begin as externalised objects end as a common obsession, even as the compensatory stylistic change produces phrases ever more urgent and terminology increasingly technical and terse. Hung up to be observed, these weapons are splendid, antique and defensive,[11] but when they move into the thoughts of the men who gather among them they grow more ordinary, more modern and better suited to killing. The splendour is still upon them, still to be seen all about the banqueteers, but it does not merely decorate the poem any more than it does the hall. The poet has changed magnificent but lifeless things into a vivid apprehension of their potential, his music working to transform their beauty into aggressive energy. His performance thus joins in the 'task' that is set for the *hetaireia*, since it fosters an essential process of 'not forgetting'. It is, like the visible arms, an active sign that the symposium is not an escape from martial work, but rather an extension of it.

Because of its internal dynamic, the song of the hall of arms has the effect of an exhortation,[12] but it is in comparison with the generic call to action that the peculiarity of Alcaeus' relation to his audience can be appreciated. Ordinarily there is a strong tension between an exhorting singer and his listeners, as the poet stands apart in real or assumed anger and says 'Go! Be! Do!' or 'How long will you refuse . . .?' Here, by contrast, all is harmony and confidence. Alcaeus does not employ a voice of separate wisdom; he does not address error or even the inevitable human inertia that needs to be roused with insults, and he does not use the imperative. He sings instead with the integrated and depersonalised voice of all those who listen to him, and he

[10] The last clause is often taken to have a future sense (cf. e.g. Bowra, *GLP*, 147, 'so soon as we undertake this task', and 148, 'the fight has not yet begun'). The verb, however, is perfect, and Page (*S&A*, 210, note 3) translates 'warlike preparations are for ever in our minds, from the moment we have undertaken this task'.

[11] Page discusses the weapons at length (*S&A*, 211–22) but because he takes the poem to be simple reportage he ends by supposing that the actual equipment of Alcaeus' companions was absurdly outdated and 'eccentric' (211), like that of the song (compare the similar conclusion of A. M. Snodgrass, *Early Greek Armour*, Edinburgh 1964, 183). Probably there was enough actual bronze decoration to justify its mention, but the important point is that Alcaeus here characterises the Lesbian weapons as romantic, heroic and in imagination assimilable to the arms that were carried by Homeric men. This is made perfectly clear in the highly reminiscent phrase that embellishes the greaves: ἔρκος ἰσχύρω βέλεος , based upon the Homeric ἔρκος βελέων (or ἀκόντων).

[12] The song's rapid turn from tranquillity to an almost hortatory note is also observed by G. Maurach, 'Schilderungen in der archaische Lyrik', *Hermes* 96 (1968) 15ff. He, however, finds at the poem's close no 'selbstzufriedene gemütliche Freude, sondern eine grimmige Lust am Kampfgerät' (p. 20).

assumes an audience so secure in its common courage that it can indulge in a common taste for elegant poetical effects. He appends an implied 'Let us remember to be what we are!' but his central statement is indicative and filled with conscious pride: 'What we are is men in whose hands epic weapons fit – in whose deeds past and present meet.'

The members of Alcaeus' armed faction approached the gods as a body, even as they did the enemy, and the poet seems often to have brought his audience into a common posture of worship by singing hymns for them. Judging from the few that survive, the Alcaic hymns did not merely enforce moments of simultaneous praise, however, for all of them encourage the gathered warriors to think of themselves in a particular way – as young men, fresh from initiation, on whom the gods will naturally smile. The most famous of such songs was the Hymn to Apollo, and though nothing remains but its invocation ('Lord Apollo, child of great Zeus', 307aV; cf. 303AbV), a very good idea of its contents and temper can be taken from a summary made by the sophist Himerius (*Or.* 48, 10–11 = 307aV rest.):

I'll tell you a story that Alcaeus sang in making a paean for Apollo . . . When Apollo was born, Zeus decked him out in a golden crown and gave him a lyre and a chariot to drive, a chariot drawn by swans. He sent him off to the Castalian streams at Delphi, where he was to proclaim human and divine justice to the Greeks, but Apollo climbed into his car and ordered the swans to fly him up to the Hyperboreans instead! When the people of Delphi heard of this, they performed the paean and set choruses of young men dancing round the tripod, calling on the god to come to them out of the north. He, however, stayed up there for a whole year, making law for the Hyperboreans, and only when he judged it the proper time for the Delphic tripods to have music did he command the swans to take him away again and down to them. It is summer – high summer – when Alcaeus brings Apollo down from the Hyperboreans. And because summer is shining forth and Apollo is come home, the lyre softens itself into a kind of summer-mode, just for the god. Nightingales sing for him, the way birds do in Alcaeus, and swallows and cicadas too – not to announce their own sufferings to mankind, but voicing each note in honour of the god. By his poetic art Castalia flows silver and Cephisus rises in waves of purple, imitating Homer's Enipeus, for Alcaeus, like Homer, makes even water able to perceive the presence of a god.

There is no knowing how much of this tale was actually told in the Alcaic hymn, but Himerius leaves no doubt that nature's joy at the arrival of Apollo was represented by the poet as a burst of music. Alcaeus, in other words, used his sacred myth in part as an aetiology, and though he showed the whole earth as making spontaneous melodies, it is plain that man-made music was, according to him, the special gift of Apollo.[13] Song, in this hymn, comes to the community of Hellenes along with a young god who is fresh from a season of boyish disobedience,[14] and it therefore serves, like that god, as a proof that rebellion and order, youth and maturity, can meet and mix. Alcaeus addresses Apollo as 'child of great Zeus' but he evidently calls him *anax* as well; he makes him a god of freedom and insubordination, but also a god of law who joins inchoate bodies of men (Hyperboreans, Delphians or Mytileneans) into societies that have a common sense of what is right and just.[15] Violence and discipline are reconciled in such a god, as they are also in song, and in the *hetaireia* when it functions as it should.[16]

The idea that youth and rebellion have their place in society – a notion that seems to emanate from the rites of initiation – was evidently expressed in at least two other hymns. One, addressed to Hermes, tells yet another childhood tale of unreproached divine naughtiness that is paradoxically related to a larger system of law. The song begins with a traditional invocation (308V):

Χαῖρε Κυλλάνας ὁ μέδεις, σὲ γάρ μοι
θῦμος ὕμνην, τὸν κορύφαις' ἐν αὔταις
Μαῖα γέννατο Κρονίδαι μίγεισα
    παμβασίληϊ

Cyllene's guardian, hail! My heart would sing
to thee whom Maia bore upon the mountain top
because she'd mixed in love with Cronus' son,
    the king of all creation.

Nothing more remains of the original, but fortunately Horace made a stanza from the Lesbian hymn (*Carm.* 1.10, 9–12),[17] and from his commentators we learn that Alcaeus showed the youthful Hermes as a consummate pickpocket. The story was evidently that of the Homeric hymn, but in this Alcaic version the precocious godlet not only steals

[13] There appear to have been three branches of music distinguished: that of nature (birds, insects, rivers, etc.): that of ritual (danced flute-music, as at the tripod): that of the individual (sung lyre-music). Ps. Plutarch, commenting on this hymn, reported Apollo as the originator of both flute and lyre playing (*de mus.* 14).

[14] Apollo's defiance of Zeus' command seems to have been the invention of Alcaeus, and therefore it can be recognised as a motif particularly important to his purpose; see the discussion of Page (*S&A*, 249).

[15] The idea that some sort of customary law is important in a band of fighting men may be expressed at 328V, where Athena seems to assemble a scattered army and breathe νόμισμα into their ranks. On this fragment, see B. Marzullo, 'Hesychiana', *Helikon* 5 (1965) 483, a discussion of the meaning of ἐπιπνεῖν.

[16] A local cult of Apollo had special significance for the members of Alcaeus' faction, as is proved by the fact that the oaths of 67.3V were sworn at his altar.

[17] Identified as Alcaic in origin by Porphyrion, who comments at line 9: fabula . . . ab Alcaeo ficta.

Apollo's cattle, he manages to pinch his brother's quiver from his shoulder, during his own arrest. Apollo laughs, exchanges his rod for the infant's lyre, and Hermes is accepted into adult Olympian society.

A hymn for Dionysus told a story of much the same sort – that of a young god's reception as 'one of the Twelve' (349eV) – and again it made the change of status follow upon an episode of rowdy misbehaviour. Hephaestus with great disrespect had fixed Hera in her magic throne and gone off to earth, 'so that no one on Olympus could loose her without him' (349bV). Ambassadors were sent, but it was finally Dionysus who softened him with drink and brought him back, thus securing both Hera's freedom and his own entrance into the divine establishment.[18] The story traditionally ended with a banquet in honour of the returned miscreant and the new god, and though the shape of Alcaeus' hymn is beyond reconstruction, it is clear that the poet has once more chosen a tale in which something wonderful enters the community with the restored initiate. It is wine, this time, instead of music, that comes in from the wilds with the youngsters, bringing an element of prankish juvenility to the gatherings of their responsible elders.[19]

The three lost hymns were thus all marked by motifs of youth, exile's end, joy and divine largesse, and they seem to have been meant to persuade their audience that gods often smile, especially upon groups of smiling young men who make use of the gifts of song and wine. Whether or not this same hilarity was expressed in the prayer to the Dioscuri is hard to say, but certainly its divinities are youthful, and certainly its major theme is rescue (34V):

Δεῦτέ μοι νᾶ]cον Πέλοπος λίποντε[c
παῖδεc   ]ιμοι Δ[ίοc] ἠδὲ Λήδαc
.....ω]ι θύ[μ]ωι προ[φά]νητε, Κάcτορ
    καὶ Πολύδε[υ]κεc,   4
—

[18] This beneficial association between Dionysus, the releaser, and Hera, the sponsor and foster-mother, was probably a favourite Lesbian notion; at any rate, it seems to have been expressed in cult as well as myth, for Alcaeus knew a shrine dedicated to Zeus, Hera, and Dionysus (129V); see below 157ff.

[19] Note that Alcaeus somewhere (447V) made Hermes the wine bearer of the gods. The hymns to Hermes and Dionysus thus use the same motifs and express the same ideas as the later satyr plays that staged these same fictions; see F. Brommer, *Satyrspiel*[2] (Berlin 1959) 29ff; D. F. Sutton, *The Greek Satyr Play* (Meisenheim 1980) 43ff., 70–1. On the notion that the motif of trickery was especially suitable to ephebes, see the remarks of P. Vidal-Naquet on the Apatouria, 'Chasseur noir', *Annales ESC* 23[2] (1968) 947ff.

οἲ κὰτ εὔρηαν χ[θόνα] καὶ θάλασσαν
παῖςαν ἔρχεςθ' ὠ[κυπό]δων ἐπ' ἴππων,
ῥῆα δ' ἀνθρώποι[c] θα[ν]άτω ῥύεςθε
    ζακρυόεντος   8

 —

εὐϛδ[ύγ]ων θρώϲκοντ[εϲ ..] ἄκρα νάων
π]ήλοθεν λάμπροι πρϙ[   ]τρ[....]ντεϲ,
ἀργαλέαι δ' ἐν νύκτι φ[άος φέ]ροντες
    νᾶϊ μ[ε]λαίναι·   12

        ]υε[
        ]ϙϲ[
⟨   desunt fortasse octo versus   ⟩
    ]..ανδ[
    ].ων [⊠   16

Come, leave the island of Pelops,
you vigorous children of Leda and Zeus!
Appear with glad heart and be gracious to me,
    Castor and Pollux!

Mounted on swift-footed horses you roam
easily over the land and the sea
where, rescuing men from a chill
    watery death,

you leap to the crow's nest and high above
run through the rigging like fire,
carrying light in the night's dark fear
    to the black ship.

Castor and Pollux were the patrons of aristocratic friendship,[20] and
so the three stanzas that seem to have followed these may have asked
their protection for a comrade about to go to sea. However, since the
pair also brought aid in battle, it is equally possible that Alcaeus here
figured the whole faction as a ship in need of help. A third possibility
is that the twins are simply invited to join in the present banquet,
much as they are at the end of Pindar's third Olympian ode, but
whatever the stated purpose of the song, the artfulness of its invocation gives a promise of instant success. With a perfect understanding
of the petitioner's science, the poet catches his gods in a tightening
spiral that limits their enormous circlings of all creation, first to the

[20] The Dioscuri, because of their horses, were thought in many places to be specifically
linked with the nobility; at Megara (Theog. 1087ff.; Hdt. 6.127), at Athens (Ar. fr.
310D), at Agrigentum (P.O.3.1). See Bethe *RE* sv 'Dioscuren' 1087, and also S. Luria,
'Adnotationes Alcaicae', *PP* 26 (1947) 82, who would change ζακρυόεντος (surely the
telling word) to δακρυόεντος in order to give the song the flavour of the battlefield!

sea (between lines 6 and 7), and then to a ship on that sea which itself
shrinks from an exemplary plural to a specific singularity at the end
of stanza three. A very few words focus a cosmic force upon a single
point of human experience, thus creating a sense of startling speed,
and meanwhile the force itself is shown to be of a wonderful sort, for
the power of these gods is opposed to toil, difficulty, cold, darkness and
death, and its outward sign is the fairy-miracle of St. Elmo's fire.[21]
With helpers like these, the men of the *hetaireia* could begin any
enterprise with boyish confidence.

Other hymn fragments address Ares, 'through whom rending fear
is felt' (inc. auct. 6V),[22] Zeus, whose daughter is to oversee the petitioners' 'work' (310V),[23] and curiously enough an Athena who belongs
to a local cult of Boeotia (325V).[24] However, since the *hetaireia* was
built upon common pleasures as well as common toil, there are in
addition songs addressed to the sweeter aspects of divine force. One of
these called out to the powers that watch over adolescence with a neat
suggestion that boys must grow into warriors – 'Ye nymphs that
sprang from aegis-bearing Zeus' (343V) – and another addressed Eros,
a divinity always present in the archaic symposium. This figure of
love in boy-form is invoked (327V) as,

δεινότατον θέων,
⟨τὸν⟩ γέννατ' εὐπέδιλος Ἴρις
χρυσοκόμαι Ζεφύρωι μίγεισα

. . .most dreaded of the gods,
whom fair-shod Iris bore, having mixed
in love with golden-haired Zephyrus.

Part wind and part rainbow, according to this fanciful report of his
parentage,[25] the Eros of the Alcaic faction is quick, bright, soft and
certainly inconstant. Another emblem of their shared delight was the
lyre, and Alcaeus, his own instrument in his hands, addressed it in a
hymn parody as 'Child of rock and foaming sea!' and specified its
powers with mock seriousness in a final line of praise: 'You soften the
wits of boys, oh sea-born tortoise shell!' (359V).

A further step away from the true hymn, but still a mirror for the

---

[21] Cf. Perrotta, op.cit., 238: 'Qui Alceo precorre Pindaro, che trascorrera veloce, come
spinto da una forze invincibile, la variopinta materia del mito.'

[22] Reading with Treu, *Alk.*, 26, who takes the fragment to be Alcaic.

[23] Following Diehl[2] and presuming that 'your daughter' implies an address to Zeus.

[24] The citation is from Strabo 9.2.29, who is scornful of Alcaeus' knowledge of Boeotian
geography.

[25] Zephyrus is a close associate of Aphrodite's (*h. Aphr.* 2.3; Callim. *Ait.* 4 fr.110.53ff.)
and in Locrian and Tarentine reliefs he can be seen with Iris pulling Aphrodite's
chariot; see E. Simon, *Die Geburt de Aphrodite* (Berlin 1959) pp.27, 28, 37, abb. 13, 14,
22.

light-hearted symposium, is a song that addresses a river known to all who had campaigned near the Lesbian colony of Aenus, in Thrace (45V):

Ἔβρε, κ[άλ]λιστος ποτάμων πὰρ Α[ἶνον
ἐξί[ης cθ' ἐς] πορφυρίαν θάλασσαν
Θραικ[... ἐρ]ευγόμενος ζὰ γαίας
 .]ιππ[.].[..]ι·   4
[—]
καί cε πόλλαι παρθένικαι πέ.[
....]λων μήρων ἀπάλαισι χέρ[cι
....]α· θέλγονται το.ρν ὢc ἄλει[ππα
 θή[ἴο]ν ὕδωρ   8
—

Hebrus, you flow out at Aenus, there
to meet the purple sea, the fairest,
[though] you've thundered down through Thrace
 . . . horses . . .

Maidens bathing in your streams
[soothe pale] limbs with tender hands
[that cup] the magic water's
 sacred balm . . .

Traditional as it is in form,[26] this song is steeped in a peculiarly Alcaic charm, the sources of which are not hard to find, for these two stanzas show a violence that produces serenity. The first sets the pattern (what was fearful has turned fair) by finding a rough up-country torrent just behind the superlative estuary that it hails, then fixing an impression of noise, speed and explosive power in the lightly touched image of a Thracian horse. After this, the second stanza proposes its counter-image – bathing maidens – and causes the thundering sounds of the river to be replaced by the touch of wet skin in the listener's sensual response, as the giant stream is reduced to tiny quantities confined in the soft palms of girls. In just eight lines, a panoramic view of a whole rough continent has been replaced by an intimate genre piece, and with this change a sense of blessing is enforced. Actually the Hebrus is eternally double, having a destructive force like that of a volcano

[26] The river is addressed in the vocative, like an immortal being; it is given an epithet (κάλλιστος) and placed in a favourite locality; its *dunameis* are specified with the eruptive participle of line 3; its cult described in what seems to be a ritual bath. Fränkel thought that this rite was an actual one that commemorated the colonists' first bath upon taking possession of the spot: 'Wenn wir aber annehmen dass die Badenden als Lesbierinnen zu verstehen sind, erkennen wir jetzt die Bedeutung dieses Bildes. Alkaios gibt seiner Freude darüber Ausdruck, dass sich Siedler aus Mytilene in der lieblichen Gegend von Ainos festgesetzt haben' (*Antike Lyrik*, ed. Eisenhut, Darmstadt 1970, 50). Gallavotti (*Storia*, 99ff.) suggested that the song describes a rite of propitiation.

(*ereugomenos*, 3) as well as a favouring grace that heals and soothes, but Alcaeus, by letting his song move with the river's stream, has suggested that nature is finally kind. Moreover, he has shown (just as he did in the other hymns) that excess and disorder are among the elements necessary to quietude, or, to follow the imagery of this song, that wild horses and delicate girls may share the same stream.[27]

The mirror of sympotic song showed the banqueteers as warriors and as worshippers, but it also urged the *hetaireia* to recognise itself as a drinking group. Wine was a pledge as well as a looking-glass, and the singers kept up a steady refrain of 'Drink!' 'Rejoice and drink this ... Come, drink with the rest!' (401a,bV), 'Drink, Melanippus!' (38V), 'Drink, why wait for the lamp?' (346V), 'Let's drink, the star now shows in the sky!' (352V). In a more elaborate vein, this kind of exhortation could expand to 'Plant no tree before you plant the vine!' (342V), and it could work to justify drink in any season. So, with playful blasphemy and a witty reference to political activity, Alcaeus could sing (338V):

Ὕει μὲν ὀ Ζεῦϲ, ἐκ δ' ὀράνω μέγαϲ
χείμων, πεπάγαιϲιν δ' ὐδάτων ῥόαι
〈   ἔνθεν   〉
〈   〉   4
κάββαλλε τὸν χείμων', ἐπὶ μὲν τίθειϲ
πῦρ, ἐν δὲ κέρναιϲ οἶνον ἀφειδέωϲ
μέλιχρον, αὐτὰρ ἀμφὶ κόρϲαι
    μόλθακον ἀμφι〈   〉 γνόφαλλον   8

Zeus rains and from heaven above
comes a great storm; quick-flowing streams
stand frozen . . .
    . . .

Resist the storm – take it by fire!
Pour the sweet wine into our cups (don't
spare it) and tuck a soft cushion
    here at my back.

Laughingly described as rebellion against winter, drinking proves to be a part of the warrior's work, and even a pillow becomes a weapon in this indoor campaign of passive luxury.

Summer, however, is equally a time to drink, and Alcaeus greets it by singing, 'Flowering summer is on its way ... quick, fill the cups with sweetest wine!' (367V). He also amuses himself by translating

----

[27] The Hebrus was the river down which the severed singing head of Orpheus floated (Verg. *Geor.* 4.523ff.) but nothing in the surviving lines suggests that this idea influenced the present song.

Hesiod's Boeotian lines about summer (*Erg.* 582–8) into his own softer language (347V):[28]

Τέγγε πλεύμονας οἴνωι, τὸ γὰρ ἄστρον περιτέλλεται,
ἀ δ' ὥρα χαλέπα, πάντα δὲ δίψαις' ὐπὰ καύματος,   2
ἄχει δ' ἐκ πετάλων ἄδεα τέττιξ . . .
ἄνθει δὲ σκόλυμος, νῦν δὲ γύναικες μιαρώταται   4
λέπτοι δ' ἄνδρες, ἐπεὶ < > κεφάλαν καὶ γόνα Cείριος
ἄσδει   6

Wet your lungs with wine, now the dogstar shows,
for summertime is harsh, and heat makes all things thirst.
The cicada sings now, sweetly from the bush
. . . thistles bloom and women putrefy, but men
are delicate, for Sirius makes dust of knees and head.

The passage is not perfectly preserved, and the Hesiodic lines may have been altered later, under the reverse influence of Alcaeus, all of which makes comparison a dangerous process. Nevertheless, it is a rewarding one, for some of Alcaeus' most characteristic motifs have been introduced here as improvements upon the tradition. Most obvious is the fact that Hesiod's cool observation that some things (goats and wine) are at their best, while others (men and women) are at their worst in summer, has here been transformed into a warm call for drink. Alcaeus has added a word for thirst (*dipsais'*, 2) and has brought the concept of heat into initial prominence (*opa kaumatos*, 2; cf. *Erg.* 588). He has also imperceptibly lightened and prettified his picture of nature by substituting many leaves (*petala*, 3) for a single exemplary tree, and by calling the cicada's song 'sweet' instead of 'shrill' (*ligura*, *Erg.* 583). Most interesting, however, is the invidious contrast which he has arranged between the women and the men of his song, for where Hesiod classes them together and so measures the two extremes of disordered sexual appetite, Alcaeus includes his women with the thistle that prospers in the heat, and so sets his men apart from all the rest of nature as the only ones to be debilitated. His women, however, thrive to the point of rottenness; they are not simply lusty, as they are in Hesiod (*machlotatai*, *Erg.* 586), they are 'polluted', 'overripe', or 'repulsive' (*miarōtatai*, 4).[29] And meanwhile his men are

[28] See, however, the discussion of J. T. Hooker, *The Language and Text of the Lesbian Poets*, Innsbrücker Beiträge z. Sprachwissenschaft 26 (Innsbruck 1977) 60. He supposes that the oldest form of this passage was an Aeolic song in epic meters which Alcaeus followed directly and which Hesiod recast into the language of Homeric epic; he is refuted by R. Kassel, *ZPE* 42 (1981) 11ff.

[29] J. U. Powell, 'Conjectures', *CQ* 20 (1926) 185, argued that the sense of pollution and rottenness was impossible and gallantly proposed an emendation, φιαρώταται 'plumpest'.

no longer frankly impotent (*aphaurotatoi, Erg.* 586) but are instead described by a word that may carry a positive aesthetic judgment; they are 'small', 'fine' or 'delicate' (*leptoi*, 5). The summertime women, in other words, are treated with conventional misogynist scorn, while the wry euphemism that produces 'heads and knees' as the men's destroyed parts lets them off with an indulgent, infra-masculine joke that verges on self-praise.

For the ordinary man, wine induced forgetfulness and so was a healer of pain, but for the men of the *hetaireia* who could never forget their 'work', the doctrine of wine was not quite so simple as this. Of course, the conventional view could be expressed and the symposium could be seen as a refuge from age and toil, as it evidently was in a song that began (50V):

Κὰτ τὰς πόλλα πₗαθοίςας κεφάλας κάκχεέ μοι μύρον
καὶ κὰτ τὼ πολₗίω ςτήθεος   2

—

πωνόντων, κάκα[
ἔδοςαν, πεδὰ δ' ἄλλω[ν   4

Drench my weary head with myrrh,
pour it on my grizzled breast
. . . of drinking men . . .

Another time, Alcaeus repeated the usual definition of wine as a divinely given escape from care, as he insisted on a breach in the usual etiquette (346V):

Πώνωμεν· τί τὰ λύχν' ὀμμένομεν; δάκτυλος ἀμέρα·
κὰδ δ' ἄερρε κυλίχναις μεγάλαις, ἄϊτα, ποικίλαις·   2
οἶνον γὰρ Ϲεμέλας καὶ Δίος υἶος λαθικάδεα
ἀνθρώποισιν ἔδωκ'. ἔγχεε κέρναις ἔνα καὶ δύο   4
πλήαις κὰκ κεφάλας, ⟨ἀ⟩ δ' ἀτέρα τὰν ἀτέραν κύλιξ
ὠθήτω   6

Drink! Why wait for the lamp?
– only a finger of day lasts.
Take down the large elaborate cups
for wine was given to us by the son
of Zeus and Semele, so that we might
put all our cares to sleep. Pour it
out double strength – to the brim!
and keep a second in readiness
to urge the first cup along.

Other songs, however, develop the notion that drinking is not an alternative but a necessary support to military activity. One brief exhortation hides this message in a metaphor by saying (335V):

Οὐ χρῆ κάκοιϲι θῦμον ἐπιτρέπην,
προκόψομεν γὰρ οὐδὲν ἀϲάμενοι,
ὦ Βύκχι, φάρμακον δ' ἄριϲτον
οἶνον ἐνεικαμένοιϲ μεθύϲθην   4

It's wrong for our minds to dwell upon care
for no man, heartsick, marches ahead.
Bycchis, the finest tonic for man is
    to bring out the wine and get drunk.

Life's essential business is an advance, a progress along a difficult route where the way must be cut (*prokoptein*, 2); such an advance is hindered by thoughts of danger or misfortune, but favoured by the wine that fills a man's heart with thoughts of an opposite sort. Drinking is thus an active form of resistance against the brooding that would otherwise invade a warrior's empty hours and sap his strength. To refuse its aid is to pretend to powers greater than those of other men, or, in plainer terms, it is to be a sanctimonious fool, and Alcaeus uses a mythic example to make this perfectly clear (38V):

Πῶνε[. . . . . . .] Μελάνιππ' ἄμ' ἔμοι. τι[. .].[
†ὅταμε[. . .] δινάεντ'† 'Αχέροντα μεγ[2

ζάβαι[ϲ ἀ]ελίω κόθαρον φάοϲ [ἄψερον
ὄψεϲθ', ἀλλ' ἄγι μὴ μεγάλων ἐπ[4

καὶ γὰρ Ϲίϲυφοϲ Αἰολίδαιϲ βαϲίλευϲ [
ἄνδρων πλεῖϲτα νοηϲάμενοϲ [6

ἀλλὰ καὶ πολύιδριϲ ἔων ὐπὰ κᾶρι [δὶϲ
δινάεντ' 'Αχέροντ' ἐπέραιϲε, μ[8

α]ὔτω⟨ι⟩ μόχθον ἔχην Κρονίδαιϲ βα[ϲίλευϲ
μελαίναϲ χθόνοϲ. ἀλλ' ἄγι μὴ τα[10
[—]
'].ταβάϲομεν αἴ ποτα κἄλλοτα.[
. .]ην ὄττινα τῶνδε πάθην τα[12
[—]
. . . . . . ἄνε]μοϲ βορίαιϲ ἐπι.[

Drink, Melanippus – expect no return
after you cross wild Acheron's flood!

You won't see the clean light of the sun
down there, so don't [be a prude.

Remember King Sisyphus, slyest of men,
Aeolus' son – how he thought to cheat

death, but in spite of his wit passed twice
over the eddies of Acheron! Think too

how in the end the Cronian lord decreed
toil for him, under the deep black earth.

Come, we must not, [while we are young
. . . whatever there is to suffer . . .

. . .north wind . . .

The shared wine of the Alcaic *hetareia* represented the unity of men
who willingly pledged their common loyalty, but the loves that were
likewise shared represented another, unwilled unity that derived from
common blood. Love for one's comrades was a version of that kin-love
which gave an orderly and effective pattern to the aristocratic world,
and it was this general love for brothers and uncles and cousins that
was reduplicated and re-enforced in the particular sexual affairs that
occupied the members of the group.[30] There is no way to know whether
these affairs were exclusively contained within the group or whether
one might pursue and praise a boy of another class, but the details of
actual Mytilenean practice are not our concern. The important fact is
that, according to Alcaeus, one loved as one fought, in the midst of a
band of friends devoted to a task that all held in common.

The love-song meant to flatter a favourite must have been standard
musical fare at these Lesbian banquets, and it may be that the fragment that begins, 'Wine, dear boy, and truth . . .' (366V) went on to
apply its paradoxical non-forgetfulness (*alatheia* instead of *lēthē*) to
the subject of the dear boy's charms. Nevertheless, there is almost
nothing in the remnants of Alcaeus' work that seems to come from a
simple first-person love-lyric.[31] We find the opening to a conventional

---

[30] Cf. Xen. *resp. lac.* 2.13, where the lovers in the Spartan *agelai* are said to represent
the love of father and son or brother and brother.

[31] A line from a *kalos* song, and a few more from a song of erotic reproach are cited
by the commentator of P.Oxy 2506; see 306AbV. In addition a damaged fragment with
an oddly Japanese flavour may perhaps represent the lament of a singer who has failed
to make himself someone's first lover (43V). The sense is thoroughly uncertain, but the
lines seem to say: 'Using my head, I came with the cranes and wrapped myself in a
cloak for the first voyage of spring, but may I never . . . such a . . . nor . . .' (The *νω* of
the first line may however represent a plural first person pronoun in the dative case;
so Wilamowitz, *NJA* 33 (1914) 243.) Another song that looks like a love complaint
(130aV) begins, 'My mind is in pain and neither friends nor . . .' and goes on to mention
a 'hollow heart' and something about grapevines. Nevertheless, erotic content is made
doubtful by its final legible term, which is τεῖχος βασιλήϊον 'the royal wall'. This 'wall'
could of course be figurative, in which case it would belong in the same category as
Archilochus' 'city', but it is also possible that the song expresses professional or political,
not erotic, distress. The marginal comment specifies τὸ τῆς Ἥρας, which led Gallavotti
to classify this as a poem of exile; see 'Nuovi Testi', *Aegyptus* 22 (1942) 111. (The one

door-step serenade ('Take me in, a reveller, take me, I beseech you, I beseech you again!', 374V) and a scrap that says, 'I fell by the tricks of the Cyprian born' (380V), but neither of these need have been sung in the poet's own voice. Judging from one smart couplet, love was regularly offered, not to its object but to the group, as a convivial joke, for Alcaeus once sang (368V):

Κέλομαί τινα τὸν χαρίεντα Μένωνα κάλεccαι,
αἰ χρῆ cυμποcίαc ἐπόναcιν ἔμοιγε γένεcθαι

Let someone call in pretty Meno
if this party means to pleasure me!

Like Sappho, Alcaeus put sexual pleasure always in a context of general festivity, and so the moment when a friend first fell under the spell of a certain boy becomes part of a ceremony (117bV). Either it happened so, or else this was the way that the *hetaireia* liked to see its love affairs: 'Lovely ... desirable sight ... you undertook the nimble race ... fresh ripe gourds ... he bore on high ... being pale and tender ... nights ... he poured it in libation ... good ... destroy ... profit ... of Zeus and the blessed gods...' Such easy mixing of ritual and eroticism was natural to a group that was constantly welcoming fresh members as they reached the age of war (and love), and another of Alcaeus' songs celebrates the newly available beauty of such a boy (296bV):

Κ]υπρογένη', ἔν cε κάλῳι Δαμοανακτίδ[
].πὰρ ἐλάαιc ἐροέccα[ιc] καταήccατο
]cύναιc· ὡc γὰρ ὀ⟨ε⟩ί[γ]ρντ' ἔαροc πύλ[αι
ἀμβ]ροcίαc ὀcδόμενοι[.]αιc ὕπαμε[4
]χήλαδε.[ ]ν[
]ριδε...[ ]'[   ]...[
] ρὐκ ο.[....]θ'· α[..]αυ[..] νεανι[
].ξιαχ[...]ῳ cτεφαγῳμενοι[8

Cypris, Damoanactides watches for you
in a perfect [spot] where breezes blow
sweet pleasures through the olive grove,
for now the gates of spring are opened wide

Royal Wall famous in antiquity was at Sardis; see Charon *FGH* 262F10 = Plut. *de Herod. malig.* 681d). Two further fragments may come from love songs though they may also derive from art songs: these are 317aV ('and you shall be the keeper of your own youth') and 255V ('he drew the bones from me'). Lobel identified the addressee in the first as Endymion, and Page (*S&A*, 274, note 3) argued that the second referred to a magical, not a sexual process.

... youths divinely scented ...

...

... young men crowned with hyacinth ...

Perhaps an actual rite inspired these lines; more probably the poet chose to salute the beginning of Damoanactides' erotic life with an imagined ritual,[32] but in either case the song makes use of images that are ceremonious and communal. One boy, viewed by a poet who seems to belong to a throng of spectators, is surrounded by countless others, all of them touched with ambrosia and carrying the sign of Apollo's love for Hyacinth,[33] as they move out of a temple of spring. Their new maturity is confirmed by Aphrodite and so is now a public affair, which means that the song can present one of them, Damoanactides, to older companions who are now licensed to admire. As the song continued the singer may have led them in such admiration, describing his own particular response to this boy – brother, cousin, nephew or beloved – but it is the youth's new relation to the entire company that has been established in this breezy olive grove.[34]

Love is an aspect of that same assertion of youth and vitality that the hymns so confidently make. It may be proposed as an alternative to anxiety, as it is in a scrap that says (362V),

ἀλλ' ἀνήτω μὲν περὶ ταὶς δέραις⟨ι⟩
περθέτω πλέκταις ὑπαθύμιδάς τις,
κὰδ δὲ χευάτω μύρον ἆδυ κὰτ τὼ
    cτήθεος ἄμμι

---

[32] The 'gates of spring' seem to belong to poetic imagery, not to any actual building; they are paralleled by the 'gates of song' that open at P.O.6.27 (cf. B.fr.5.3) and more significantly by the doors of the chamber of the Horae that Pindar causes to open in spring in connection with Semele's marriage (fr. 75.14S). Nevertheless, the conceit is usually rejected as too baroque for archaic song, and scholars consequently suppose that the physical doors of some material temple are described as opening in some actual ritual; see the discussion of Barner (*Neuere Alk.-Pap.* 21–2) which unfortunately was written before the discovery of the Cologne fragment of Archilochus, with its metaphorical gateway.

[33] Reading ἰακ[υνθ]ω in line 8, with Page. On Hyacinthus, see M. J. Mellink, *Hyakinthos* (Utrecht 1943) 111ff. and I. Chirassi, *Elementi di cultura precereale nei miti e riti Greci* (Rome 1968) 159ff.

[34] The association of season with advancing sexuality seems to be repeated in 397V: 'the delicate bloom of midsummer ripeness'. This place where a boy first meets Aphrodite is strikingly like the shrine to which Sappho calls the same goddess (2V; see below, pp. 259ff.). Here, *euphrosunē* (or ἀβροσύνη, γαθοσύνη) is wafted in the air, there a somnolent spell drifts down from the trees; here there are olives, there apples; but in both places youthful mortals are brought into contact with the ambrosia of the goddess. Compare also Alcaeus 41V, where the scene seems to be a *temenos* of Aphrodite and where words for softness (ἀβρο-, 2), wine (11), heart (θυμ-, 14), and lyre (15) appear, combined with what seems to be a reference to women (γυν-, 21). For another example of a song that welcomes a boy into the group of potential *erōmenoi*, see Alcman 58 *PMG* and on it P. E. Easterling, 'Alcman 58 and Simonides 37', *PCPS* 200 (1974) 37.

rather let garlands of dill fall
over our shoulders, let myrrh pour
  sweetly upon our breasts . . .

but in effect it is like wine – a cure that keeps the *hetaireia* strong. Such is the tenor of a pair of songs that use the opposition of sea and shore to represent the dangers of active life as they are opposed by the consolations of the symposium. One of them (58V) is now almost illegible, but it is evidently addressed to a companion in what is imagined as some temporary camp where death, open water and perhaps oars are present. 'Let's be sparing of the sea,' the singer urges, as he counsels an opposing generosity in the use of wine ('Dip the ladle into the jar', 9), song ('sing to me as you drink', 12, cf. 24), and fire. Men are to be cheerful and hearts bright while cups are emptied in a single gulp. The second song again places the singer and his companions in a refuge on the beach. The ship that has brought them is ready to sink,[35] its cargo must be abandoned, and all in all the situation is what a man might wish upon his worst enemy, but nevertheless the poet suggests that, like the men of Odysseus, they should all forget the voyage home (*Od.* 9.97), rest where they are, and prove their youthful strength with ceremonies of love and fellowship (73V):

πὰν φόρτι[ο]ν δ . . [

    δ' ὄττι μάλιϲταϲάλ[2

καὶ κύματι πλάγειϲ[αν
ὄμβρω⟨ι⟩ μάχεϲθαι . . [
φαῖϲ' οὐδὲν ἰμέρρη[ν, ἀϲάμωι]

    δ' ἔρματι τυπτομ[έναν   6

[35] There has been much discussion as to whether or not this dispirited ship is allegorical, and in spite of Wilamowitz's pronouncement to the contrary ('Hier ist es ausgeschlossen in dem Schiff ein allegorie zu sehen', 234, *Neue Jahrb.* 33 = *Kl.Schr.*i. 383) most scholars agree that this is some version of the Ship of State, perhaps a Ship of Faction; see Theander 'Lesbiaca', *Eranos* 41 (1943) 162; R. Merkelbach, 'Literarische Texte', *Arch.f.Pap.forsch.* 16 (1958) 91ff.; J. Trumpf, op.cit., 141. The question was for a time confounded by a commentary (306iV) that seemed to identify the ship as a figure for a prostitute (a notion that Page reversed to make this an actual ship being compared to a figurative professional lady, *S&A*, p. 195), but G. L. Koniaris pointed out that the commentary in fact refers to two separate poems with ships in distress; see 'Some thoughts on Alc. fragments D 15, X 14, X 16', *Hermes* 94 (1966) 385ff. It is the second ship – one that is rotten and refuses to come into harbour – that represents or is represented by the prostitute, but that rotten vessel is entirely separate from the ship of 73V, which is threatened by a reef, and it is mentioned by the commentator only as part of a learned digression. After making this essential distinction, Koniaris concluded that the ship of 73V could refer to the Alcaic faction but that the purpose of the song was more probably erotic, which is also the opinion of Barner (op.cit., 144), who calls it a celebration of youth.

κῆνα μὲν ἐν τούτ[
τούτων λελάθων ὠ.[
cύν τ' ὔμμι τέρπ[..]α[⟨]άβαιc⟩
    καὶ πεδὰ Βύκχιδος αὐ..[10
—
τὼ δ' ἄμμες ἐς τὰν ἄψερον ἀ[μέραν
αἰ καί τιcαφ[...]..αντ..[
δείχνυντε[

. . . hammered by the waves . . .
They say she won't resist the storm
but longs to strike a [hidden] reef
    and broken, sink upon it.

I'd leave her to her [miseries,
forget the journey back, [stay here
among you all in mingled youth and joy
    with Bycchis at my side.

Should someone, on some future day
. . . we'll show him . . .

There has been much discussion about whether this ship is or is not allegorical, but the important thing to notice is that ship and singer, in these eight lines, have been placed in parallel positions – each refusing to brave further foul weather, each longing for rest, one upon a sunken rock, the other with his love.[36] The quick responsion of clausula to clausula fixes 'reef' and 'Bycchis'[37] in identical melodic phrases, and in conflation they produce the submerged image of the Reef of Love, recognised here by an ancient commentator who knew a parallel from Anacreon (306i, col.i, 11V; the citation is unfortunately lost).[38] The sequence of the lines thus abandons the despairing ship to its version of repose, as the singer takes her place, transforming surrounding wind and waves into rejoicing friends and replacing the oblivion of the sea's depths with that of sexual satisfaction. Love can bring forgetfulness of the worst disasters; it offers a kind of lotus-land for all, one to be found within the *hetaireia* when outer ventures

[36] There is perhaps a voyage = love affair metaphor in 43V; see above, note 30. Compare the erotic 'ship of love' at Theog. 1361; cf. Ar. *Wasps* 1343 and Crat. at Pollux 5.143; for discussion, see S. Luria, 'Adnotationes Alcaicae', *PP* 2 (1947) 82.

[37] Bycchis is associated with Pyrrha and so with exile in the comment on 60V, and consequently all the songs that mention him are sometimes lumped together as Songs of Exile (335V; 306cV and 73V). This, however, is a reasonable procedure only if we assume that Bycchis was an actual boy who would be addressed only during the period of his actual brief youth. Barner (op.cit., 145) notes that the known exile poems seem to express a very different mood from that of 73V.

[38] Cf. Theog. 1361, where a boy-ship has missed the harbour of the poet's love and hit a rock.

capsize. Perhaps Alcaeus is urging his friends to restore themselves in the face of some actual moment of unpleasantness; perhaps, on the other hand, the shipwreck is only the poetical counterpart to those winter storms that one fought with soft pillows. The song may be specific or general in its application, but one thing is certain, and that is that love and pleasure, like wine, belong to the 'harbour of comradeship'[39] and bring their gift of forgetfulness within the context of the gathered band.

A congregation of men bound together by ties that were semi-religious had, in theory at least, a considerable psychic power, and Alcaeus can often be found using music to direct that power inwards, in positive or negative form, upon the group itself. The company could bless and the company could curse; it could also laud and criticise and otherwise whip itself into shape, and all these things it did by means of song. To begin with, the indissoluble unity of the *hetaireia* could be asserted whenever a member was to be temporarily gone, and just enough remains from a *propemptikon* to show the sort of white magic[40] that Alcaeus, at such a time, could practise on behalf of all (286V). Actually, it is not clear whether the object of this happy spell is thought of as present, just departed, or about to return,[41] but what is certain is that a comrade, somewhere, is launched upon the sea with well-omened words that are meant to attract divine favour and keep evil away. The singer specifies, and so in a sense summons, a season that is 'spring with its countless flowers', and then like a magician he takes care of the opposing powers by making sure that storm winds and 'shuddering frost' are penned up 'beneath Tartarus'[42] (cf. Vergil, *Georg.* 4.51f.), while 'smiling calm rides on the back of the sea' (*gelanna* is restored, in line 5, from the scholium).[43] Only when these favourable circumstances have been poetically established does the song set the traveller upon his way by saying, 'May you attain prosperous safety!' (*eusoiais tuchois*, 6). A song of this sort, performed in

---

[39] Cf. the nostalgic phrase of the Sophoclean Ajax, ἐταιρείαις λιμήν (S. *Ajax* 682).

[40] This is the kind of song that the singer of the Strasburg ode is so pointedly *not* performing; note the striking κρύερος πάγος here (3), in comparison with the ῥίγει πεπηγότα of the Hipponax song (115.9W).

[41] Barner, op.cit., 12, note 3, concludes that sending off a present friend would be 'more natural', but admits that archaic poetry shows a developing sense of 'geistige Gemeinschaft' that can stretch out to those who are absent; he cites Sappho 96V, to which one might add Stes. 209 *PMG*. On *propemptika* in general, see F. Cairns, *Generic Composition*, 50ff.

[42] Tartarus is probably mentioned as the source or even the father of these winds (not, as Page supposed, with some vague reference to the Persephone myth, *S&A*, 289); at Hes. *Theog.* 869 the storm winds arise from Typhoeus as his children, when he is cast into Tartarus, and the scholiast at Alcaeus 77A Col.Ia2V (glossing Tartarus) says οὐ τὸν πατέρα τῶν ἀνέμων λέγει, as if this would have been the natural assumption.

[43] Since it was a company of lovers who offered these good wishes it is perhaps not irrelevant to note that Aphrodite had cults as Euploia and Galaneia (Euploia, Paus. 1.1.3; *AP* 9.144; Galaneia, E.*IA* 546; *Hel.* 1456).

the sympathetic multiplicity of the fraternity, meant that a man went forth as if with an ancient tribal talisman to guard him.[44]

A singer could also lead the Alcaic group in auspicious greetings when a wanderer returned, but the usual form of such songs must be adduced from an example that is surely not typical. In it, Alcaeus welcomes his brother and congratulates him on his safe homecoming after a season of foreign service, but he lets his joy take the form of friendly raillery and the song is salted with a pinch of blame (350V):

ʼΗλθες ἐκ περάτων γᾶς ἐλεφαντίναν
λάβαν τὼ ξίφεος χρυσοδέταν ἔχων
τὸν ἀδελφὸν ʼΑντιμενίδαν . . . φησιν ʼΑλκαῖος Βαβυλωνίοις cυμμαχοῦντα τελέcαι
ἄεθλον μέγαν, εὐρύcαο δ' ἐκ πόνων,
κτένναιc ἄνδρα μαχάταν βαcιλη⟨ί⟩ων   5
παλάcταν ἀπυλείποντα μόναν ἴαν
παχέων ἀπὺ πέμπων

So, you're come from the ends of the earth
with a gold-chased ivory hilt to your sword!
. . .
You've fought a great fight, you've saved
[Babylonian friends] from grief, and you've
killed a man who missed being five cubits high
just by a palm!

These lines have attracted a wealth of commentary on their probable date, their reference to one or another Babylonian campaign, and their possible connection with one of the exiles of Alcaeus' family.[45] There is a standard note, too, on the statistical frequency of giants in the Persian army.[46] To the historian of literature, however, the song is chiefly remarkable as an example of the kind of affectionate scorn that could be voiced inside the self-applauding *hetaireia*. The song is clearly not unique, for its effects are easily arrived at by a poet who

[44] Whether the lines of fragment b belong to the same song is not known, but if they do, it may be that the piece used a past episode in which the addressee triumphed over danger (perhaps on land in a hunt, if line 3 says 'You killed a beast') as a guarantee of similar triumphs in the future, after the pattern of the hymn reminders. On the other hand, the lines may belong to a separate song, perhaps one with mythic content.

[45] There were three campaigns that Antimenidas might have taken part in: (1) that of 601 B.C. when Palestine was occupied; (2) that of 597, the punitive expedition against Jehoiachin because of his father's revolt; (3) that of 588–586 when Jerusalem was taken a second time after an eighteen-month siege. It is usually assumed that Antimenidas would only have enrolled with the Babylonian army if he were in exile; if one respects the traditional dates of Pittacus' power (595–585) and likewise the tradition that Alcaeus was recalled to Mytilene before the end of that time and that Antimenidas had died earlier (perhaps at 'the bridge' before the third exile even began), the last of these three campaigns becomes irrelevant, and the song will refer either to 601 or to 597.

[46] Cf. e.g. Page *S&A*, 223, note 4, with ref. to Hdt. 7.117.

knows how to offer gross exaggerations with a transparent irony. As an ally of the Babylonians, Antimenidas will have been fighting in one of the punitive expeditions against Jerusalem (II Kings 24–5), which means that 'the ends of the earth' were no further off, in unembellished fact, than Palestine.[47] The 'great fight' will have been the capture of a small provincial city by an enormous army, and the Babylonians 'rescued from grief' will have been representatives of an aggressive empire engaged in quelling a minor rebellion. Antimenidas' accomplishments are thus inflated with an appearance of sympathy, only to be punctured in the end by the final distended item of the list – an enemy more than eight feet tall. Only a Goliath could figure in the kind of tale this man tells, and once the giant is mentioned we realise that the fancy sword-hilt was likewise greeted with genial contempt, as a bit of foppery typical of this all too glorious brother.[48]

Blame of this loving and ironical sort was easily practised and easily accepted because it was an intra-mural sport in which satirist and satirised might change places at any moment. Where the company felt itself to be one, poetic attack was always a form of self-scrutiny, and Alcaeus could find pretensions in himself as well as in his brother. He takes care of the pride he felt in his first campaign with a conscious flourish of self-denigration, adapting the famous lines of Archilochus about his shield and singing as if from Sigeum (401BaV):[49]

Ἄλκαος cάοc †ἄροι ἐνθάδ᾽ οὐκυτὸν ἀληκτορίν†
ἐc Γλαυκώπιον ἱρον ὀνεκρέμαccαν Ἄττικοι

Alcaeus is safe but his weapons are not; Athenians
hang them in grey-eyed Athena's shrine.

Here the obvious literary reference proves that the poet is not quite serious either in his bravado or in his confession, while it announces his admiration for the great practitioner of abuse. Even as he pretends to be a Parian, however, Alcaeus shows his innate romanticism, for

[47] Mazzarino, op.cit., 77, noted the exaggeration of calling Palestine 'the ends of the earth' but concluded that the poet must consequently mean that Antimenidas had been all the way to Babylon.

[48] There is another fragment that seems to make fun of dress, asking (345V): 'Who are these birds of Oceanus, come from the edges of the earth – motley, speckle-necked and long of wing?' The mood of taunting the super-militant evidently recurs also at 372V in the phrase, Ἄρευος cτροτιωτέροιc.

[49] The lines are supposed to have been sent to a friend at Mytilene (so Herodotus 5.95), and Strabo cites them in his account of the campaign of Pittacus against Phrynon at Sigeum, which probably would have been Alcaeus' first military experience. Strabo's report leaves the text extremely uncertain and it has been restored in various ways; see W. Schubart, 'Bemerkungen zu Sappho, Alkaios und Melinno', *Phil.* 97 (1948) 311ff., where an iambic version is proposed. The unreadable οὐκυτὸν in the first line may contain κύτος = shield (cf. A. *Sept.* 495).

where Archilochus saw his shield as a mere utensil now in degrading use among barbarians, the young Lesbian imagines his lost weapons in a kind of apotheosis, treasured by noble enemies and kept in a famous temple.[50]

One further song may represent this same music of friendly attack (119V), but its tattered condition makes it very hard to interpret. The singer begins, Archilochus-fashion, with a deprecating question: 'Who told you, you villain, to blame fate where fate is not to blame?' He urges his unadmirable comrade to stop complaining (evidently about the good things he has lost) and to size up the possibilities of the actual situation, but then, where an old saw or a mythic example might have re-enforced this good advice – where Archilochus would have put a fable – Alcaeus employs a common wisdom-tale in a new and perverse way. The vine-trunk that seems to be dead but nevertheless puts out new shoots was a familiar didactic emblem and it was used in stories like that of the Master and the Husbandman to prove thut one should not give up hope. Alcaeus, however, does not intend to console, and he uses his vine-trunk only to prop up his victim so that he can take another swipe at him:

coì μὲν [γ]ὰρ ἤ[δ]η περβέβα[τ]αι χρό[νος
χ]αὶ χάρπος ὄcc[ο]c ἦc cυνα[γ]άγρετ[αι
τὸ χλᾶμμα δ' ἐλπώρα, χάλον γά[ρ,
    ο]ὖκ ὀλ[ί]γαιc cταφύλαιc ἐνείχη[ν   12
[—]
....]ψ[.], τοιαύτας γὰρ ἀπ' ἀμπέ[λω
....]υc γ......ι cχρπιάμ[
τά]ρβημι μὴ δρόπ[ω]cιν αὔταιc·
    ὄμφ]αχαc ὠμοτέραιc ἐοίcαιc.   16

Your time is gone; what fruit
you bore has all been cut. True,
the new shoot, being fine,
    gives hope of many clusters

(but beware:) Derived from such a vine

. . .
they'll pluck the grapes still green
    and take them sour, I fear!

The wit is evident, even if the sense is not, as the optimistic old commonplace is twisted to produce a bitter result and what seems to be praise turns into blame. 'Because you had the season you did, your

---

[50] G. Perrotta, op.cit., 221, thought that he perceived a note of sadness, in comparison with the Archilochean joy of survival, but given the state of the lines only a superhuman sensitivity could make out their 'note'.

followers will miss theirs, for too much will be expected of them, and too soon' – such is the underlying prophecy that the man addressed receives.[51] And behind it a larger warning stands, offered to the entire audience on the subject of the fruits of this man's deed: 'Look out – these grapes are sour!'[52] Perhaps the song applies to some notorious beauty and his younger brother, nephew or son. Or perhaps the new generation is only figurative, the fruitful season a season of deeds that now have consequences, but whatever the particular meaning the faction is taught to smile somewhat cruelly at one unit of its membership and to be the stronger for its self-ridicule.

The ideal faction's impulse towards auto-criticism was matched by another towards self-advising but, judging from the remains of his poetry, Alcaeus did not find the gnomic mode much to his liking. A certain amount of sententious counsel was sure to be offered wherever Greek men drank together, and Alcaeus was aware of the importance of common sentiment within a band of fighting men (cf. 361V), but

---

[51] The similarity of the vine-cane to Archilochus' figure of the cleared field might seem to suggest a female object of attack – a mother and daughter or a madam and her professional successor – but the sense of cowardice and knavery in the word πονηρός ordinarily limits its application to men. One may also note the masculine participle of line 5, though it does not certainly apply to the person addressed.

[52] There have been various political interpretations of this song. Some critics suppose that the 'new shoot' must be Pittacus, from which it follows that the old fruits were previous rulers (the various Penthilids and Melanchrus and Myrsilus) and also (and most improbably) that the 'you' of the song is the whole city of Mytilene (so C. Theander, 'De Alcaei poematis in Hyrrham, Pittacum, Penthilidas invectivis', *Aegyptus* 32 (1952) 190, and G. Perrotta, op cit., 231). Page (*S&A*, 242, note 3) tentatively suggested the idea that the 'you' was Pittacus himself, his 'season' being his time as *aisumnētēs*. This, however, makes the 'new shoot' represent Pittacus' political legacy and this is unlikely since concepts of this sort do not appear in archaic poetry. Bowra at one point suggested that the pickers of the future (1.17) were called γεώμοροι, and supposed a political double meaning that referred to a distribution of land (*GLP* 182 and 445), but the term he wished to restore is not proper to Lesbian speech (see Page, loc.cit.). If a political meaning must be found, one might suppose a reference to the daughter of Penthilus who, because of her father's season of royal splendour, is about to be prematurely plucked by a greedy Pittacus. This would make the 'you' of the song her (presumably absent) brother, which is far-fetched, but no more so than its equation with a likewise presumably absent Pittacus, and less so than its equation with the city. (For songs about Pittacus' marriage, see below, pp. 171ff.). At the opposite extreme from those who find a precise political meaning are those who would make the song completely general in application, its 'you' being every member of the audience, its message being simply 'seize the day, the season of ripeness is short' (Wilamowitz, *Gl.d.Hell.* 2, 112, note 1; Bowra 'Zu Alkaios u. Sappho', *Hermes* 70 (1935) 240). This, however, ignores the perverse and vindicative tone of the fragment and reduces it to banality. All in all, it would seem most probable that the intention here was private and the reference erotic, as H. Fränkel suggested (reviewing Lobel's Sappho and Alcaeus, *GGA* 1928, 275) and as Treu attempted to confirm by pointing to a possible double meaning in the πονήμενοι of 1.17 (*Alkaios*, 166ff.). In this case the song would continue the Archilochean tradition by joshing an over-aged male beauty and suggesting that his younger brother, nephew or son will suffer from this predecessor's notorious success.

this was evidently not his normal vein.[53] Somewhere he warned, 'If you speak according to your own pleasure, you'll listen to your displeasure' (341V), and somewhere he repeated the comic proverb, 'The man who moves a stone without securing it will have a headache soon' (344V). He announced that 'nothing comes from nothing' (320V), and he resumed some statement or other with the phrase, 'as the ancient saying has it' (339V), but whether these lines came from fully sententious songs or stood as isolated gnomes in contexts of another sort, there is no way to know.[54] Alcaeus does, however, seem to have meditated musically on the subject of old age, for the line 'the heart is the last part of a man to grow old' appeared in one of his songs (442V),[55] and another desperately mutilated fragment still gives off a faintly Mimnerman perfume (39V). A bitter sequence of broken phrases is all that remains, but it sounds as if even here the gnomes somehow fail, for the standard counsels of noble resignation seem to be overcome, in the end, by a particular and unappeased apprehension of death: '... me, old age... to forget lovely things ... of tender [boys] ... song ... what is fated ... our ancestors ... if a man be wise and equipped with dense wits ... in opposition to Zeus' apportionment, not a hair ... with sickening agony ... to be carried deep ...'

Poverty was another subject that drew generalised comment from Alcaeus, for to his way of thinking poverty among the nobility was the central evil of his time. The city depended upon its warriors, but armed men could come only from those who held land, and consequently when these grew poor, because of encroaching commerce or the confiscations of civil war, the entire state was in danger. This idea is expressed in almost allegorical terms in a pair of lines made heavy with dactyls (364V):

ἀργάλεον πενία κάκον ἄσχετον, ἂ μέγαν
δάμνα λᾶον ἀμαχανίαι σὺν ἀδελφέαι

Dire Poverty's evil, she can't be resisted; with
Weakness, her sister, she masters the fighting force.

Loss of noble fighting power meant loss of noble influence; men whose wealth came neither from land nor military exploits rose to pre-eminence and impoverished aristocrats found themselves without politi-

---

[53] Note Fränkel, *DuP* 223, who complains that the few surviving Alcaic gnomes are neither original nor meaningful.

[54] The ancient world admired a saying of Alcaeus' about the importance of men in battle ('Men are a city's defensive wall', 112.10V), but when the song from which this neat sentence derived was found, it proved to be a chant of rage that was anything but meditative. On this fragment, see below, p. 150)

[55] Or perhaps, 'Anger is the last part ...', cf. S. *OC* 954–5.

cal weight.[56] The same shift was occuring everywhere, as Theognis was to testify, and Alcaeus once at least enlarged his bitter view of it into a gnomic generality (360V):

ὡc γὰρ δή ποτ' 'Αριcτόδα-
μον φαῖc' οὐκ ἀπάλαμνον ἐν Cπάρται λόγον
εἴπην, χρήματ' ἄνηρ, πένι-
χρος δ' οὐδ' εἶc πέλετ' ἔcλοc οὐδὲ τίμιοc

When Aristodemus told the Spartans,
    'Money makes the Man', he didn't
miss the mark: a pauper never meets
    with honour or with noble treatment.[57]

It is perhaps characteristic of Alcaeus that when he wished to be sententious he had to borrow a saying from someone else. The resigned and inhibiting self-knowledge of the true gnome was not a thing he sought and only on the subject of sex does gnomic pomposity seem to come naturally to him. In that area his wisdom was his own, and he converted it easily into pithy advice, as can be seen in a song about the effects of wine upon the young which is really a statement of the seducer's impasse. The piece is built on a rhetorical structure of alternatives (If the boy drink lightly/ If the boy drink heavily), and its opening section evidently noted that when a youth takes a bit of wine his charms are enhanced but his willingness disappears and he is apt to grow surly. When, on the other hand, he drinks more, he becomes contrite and available, but no longer has much to offer (358V):[58]

]οιδ' ἀρις[.....]νμεναιτ[..]ονω[...]δε κενη[....]c.   1. 2
  πε˻δάcει˩ φρέναc οἶνοc οὐ †διωτεοc.
κάτω γὰρ κεφάλαν κατί-   4
  cχε[ι] τὸν Ϝὸν θάμα θῦμον αἰτιάμενοc,
πεδαλευόμενοc τά κ' εἴ-
  πη· τὸ δ' οὐκέτι [....].εν πε[δ]αγ[ρέ]τω

---

[56] Burn, *Lyric Age*, 246 for some reason reports these sayings as showing Alcaeus' sympathy with commerce and the new rich, but Treu is surely more accurate when he describes them as the poet's complaint against the appearance of new values (*Alk.*, 172).

[57] One who is τίμιος is in receipt of outward marks of honour, and this prepares for the external sense of ἔσλος, one who is treated as a noble. Hesiod is more subjective when he says (*Erg.* 347),Ἔμμορέ τις τιμῆς ὅστ' ἔμμορε γείτονος ἐσθλοῦ.

[58] Demetrius Lacon, who cited the lines, perceived a double meaning in the head that hangs, to which Page hardly did justice when he called it a metaphor for surrender (*S&A*, 317). One might compare the 'heads and legs' dried out by the summer sun in 347V. On the citation, see A. Vogliano, 'Spigolature Ercolanesi', *Acme* 1 (1948) 262.

...But if the wine once
soaks into his wits, he isn't worth the chase.
His head hangs down, he blames himself
repeatedly and takes back all he's said, but –
that certain thing is gone, and can't be had!

Another song seems to have contrasted two sorts of pleasure, praising one, which must have been love with a boy, and condemning the
other, which is explicitly love with a whore. Of the initial section
nothing can be known,[59] but the final passage can almost be followed,
as it transforms a commonplace warning into a strangely moving
evocation of wretchedness. The turn from boy to prostitute is accomplished with an old saw ('but the man who gives money to a whore
might as well toss it into the sea')[60] and the following stanza begins
with the same tone of sagacious pomposity (117b28ff.V):

'̓]πε[..]ε.ιϲ τοῦτ' οὐκ οἶδεν, ἔμοι π[ί]θην,
ὃ]ϲ π[όρν]αιϲιν ὁμίλλει, τάδε γίνε[τ]α[ι·
δεύε[ι] μα[.] αὔτω τὼ χρήματοϲ [ἄψερο]ν
α]ἴϲχοϲ κα[ὶ κα]κό[τα]τ' ὠλομέγ[αν   31
[–]
πόλλαν.[....]'[.]των, ψεύδη δε[.....]ϲαι
.]αι[.]λέ..[....] κάκων ἐϲχατ[.....].[]
]νδεμ[.].η ψύχαν ἀκατ[   ].   34
..]αίει δάκ[ρυϲι]ν· ἀ δ' οὐ[.]εϲο.[   ].

Hear me, if you don't already know:
he comes to this, the man who frequents
prostitutes – money gone, a wealth of shame
and mortal ills to finish him ...

Here the text almost dissolves, but the succeeding lines do produce a
sequence of words and phrases charged with an unexpected subjectiv-

---

[59] The papyrus seems to contain more than one song, and it is impossible to say where
this one began; in line 24, however, the words πόλλα χαρίϲ[ματα (or [ϲατο, [ϲαϲθαι)
testify to a positive passage preceding the negative lines about prostitutes. This means
that if the lines still further above, at 21ff., stood in an earlier part of the song under
discussion, there must have been a kind of ring pattern: whores, boys, whores. Alternatively, the lines around 21 belonged to another song on the subject of prostitution. It
should be noted that in either case, the phrase νᾶα ποήμενοι at 22 seems to refer to
those who frequent whores, since the scholiast glosses it with ϲυνουϲιάζοντεϲ, and the
singer seems to separate himself from them with his οὐ γὰρ ἔγω at 23. The same figure
(prostitute = ship) is known from the papyrus commentary on 73V (306iV); the
woman-ship, though ancient, swollen and eaten by sand (= leprosy) yet refuses to be
permanently beached. See bibliography cited above, note 35. The isolated word πόρνα
is also to be found at 299.8V.

[60] Cf. Archilochus 302W and Theognis 1367–8. On this fragment, see S. Luria, op.cit.,
81ff. H. Fränkel (*GGA*, 1928, 276) supposed that it belonged to Sappho, and was
addressed to her wayward brother!

ity: '... lies ... evil's furthest reach ... soul ... he laments with tears, but she ...' Evidently Alcaeus has not emphasised the woman's ugliness, as Archilochus would have done, but has followed her client instead, making him a monitory example something like the cowardly man whose misfortunes Tyrtaeus relates (10W). Here, however, there is a note peculiar to Alcaeus, for the contrast between the man's suffering (which somehow involves his soul) and the woman's prosperity seems to ask for the non-gnomic, non-archaic emotion of fraternal sympathy.

In all the songs discussed so far Alcaeus has taught the *hetaireia* to look inwards, confirming its own vigour through worship, strengthening it with pleasure, and defining it by censorship. Nevertheless, the same singer who called for cups and a cushion at his back, choosing wine and shore over sea and storm, could also urge the idealised band to look outwards, and to remember actively that task which in truth forgetfulness could never touch. The difference between a nobleman and an ordinary man of courage was that the nobleman had to live up to his ancestors as well as to himself, and Alcaeus liked to remind his friends of the generations that had preceded them,[61] and of the ancient Lesbian founders sprung from the heroes of Troy.[62] At other times he asked them to recall their own previous deeds, as he does, for example, in a damaged fragment that yields only the words (179V): '... broke through with violence ... of ours ... bright ... shield ... where the boar ensign ... iron struck lightning ...'[63] Such an evocation of an old exploit may have been placed in a hortatory frame that called for similar panache in a present encounter, or it may have been offered as a more general reminder of the virtue that their pledged fellowship enshrined. In either case, however, the song works to recapture the achievements of the past not just for the sake of fame, but in order to transform them musically into the kind of energy that could express itself again, in deeds of equal brilliance.

---

[61] See 169a5–6V, where there seems to be a call to remember men of old who are perhaps the Aeolian founders of Mytilene; cf. the reference to the founders at 129.1–4V; 39.8V seems to mention ancestors; 167.17V, fathers.

[62] See 129.1V. Elsewhere (206V) the poet, in a context of drinking, refers to Athena and courage and says, 'of these things I would remind you'; on this fragment, see C. Gallavotti, 'La morte di Mirsilo', *Studi in onore di L. Castiglioni* (Florence, 1960), 322ff., and also W. Barner, op.cit., 93ff. In two other cases the remembering is of a different sort, for at 6.11V the audience is perhaps asked to remember a disaster, and at 75.5V the singer remembers (or doesn't) the fall of Penthilus.

[63] The mention of this spear should be noted since Page, in commenting on 140V made much of the presumed fact that Alcaeus' 'eccentric' companions used only the sword. For a detailed discussion of 179V, see Barner, op.cit., 52–62. There is battle reminiscence also in 330V and 382V, though in the latter it is not clear whether this wonderful revival of courage was experienced by Alcaeus' faction or by an enemy, since the opening ἦ ποι may very well be sarcastic; see B. Marzullo, 'Hesych.E. 5091–4', *Helikon* 5 (1965) 481, who discusses this as a case of 'divine afflatus', and assumes that the source of the *nomisma* is a divinity, possibly Athena.

The fact that there was a kind of magic in songs like these is demonstrated by another fragment that evidently began with a chain of gnomes, then mentioned events of the past, and finally shaped itself into a curse upon enemies who belonged to rival clans (112V). The details of this extensive song are provokingly hard to grasp,[64] but the fearful effect of its diminishing focus – from timeless generality, through past experience, to present and specific imprecation – is manifest even in the broken phrases that remain. The sequence is something like this: '... bad times, my boy, because of foolishness ... not even Zeus can undo what is done ... contest full of woe ... warlike men are the city's walls[65] ... fate ... Zeus ... formerly; now I pray only for this ... [that these shall no more see] the sun's light ... Cleanactid ... Archeanactid ... honeysweet ... they destroyed ...'

In a song of this sort the singer shaped the single but manifold hatred of his audience so that it should press upon the demonic world with an effect exactly opposite to that of the inward-looking, self-cherishing *propemptikon*. Soft spells for good weather accompanied one of themselves, but with the prayer turned aggressively outwards, harsh curses could pursue their common enemies, and this was not the only reversal of mood that the faction was capable of. When necessary, Alcaeus could lead the company into a perfect contradiction of its hedonistic choice of shore over stormy sea. Their unforgettable work was war and in a song that this time seems to have a clear political reference, Alcaeus imagines a ship that is now not to be left to its miseries, and a shore that means – not fire and song and love – but the desperate work of refitting and re-embarkation, in spite of a raging storm (6V):

[64] Even the curse at the end is not indisputable; the sense seems to be 'May x, y, z be deprived of the light of the sun since they destroyed a', but the singer might conceivably say instead, 'while I look on the light of the sun, I vow to ... (do something to) x, y, z since they destroyed ...' Diels made a full and fanciful reconstruction (ending with a curse) which Treu sardonically translates (*Alk.*, 39); a more cautious rendering was proposed by Schubart (*SPAW*, 1902, 316ff.); see also Mazzarino, op.cit., 60, who restored βίαν Κ]ίκιδος ὤλεσαν in the last line, and made this Kikis (cf. 414V) a brother of Alcaeus and a victim of the enemies here named. See also G. Perrotta, op.cit., 227, who represents the close in this way: 'Che non possa mai piu vedere la luce del sole alcuno dei malreditti Cleanactidi ni alcuno degli Archeanactidi, ne alcuno degli Irradi!' However, since the marginal commentator identified some of the objects of the singer's hatred as individuals (τὸν Μύρσιλον, at 1.23 and τὸν Φίττακον at 1.24), and since the latter gloss cannot possibly apply to the Archeanactid mentioned in the part of the line that survives, it seems most probable that four individual enemies were mentioned here: Myrsilus and a Cleanactid in 1.23, Pittacus and an Archeanactid in 1.24 (*pace* Mazzarino, op.cit., 56 and Page, *S&A*, 174, who assume that the gloss proves Myrsilus to have been a Cleanactid). For further discussion, see J.C. Kamerbeek, 'De novis carminibus Alcaei', *Mnem.* iii 13 (1947) 168).

[65] On the topos of the warrior as rampart of the city see O. Longo, 'Ad Alceo 112.10 LP', *Boll.dell Ist.di fil.gr. a Padova* i (1974) 211–28.

Τόδ' αὖ‍ͺτε κῦμα τὼ π‍ͺρͺοτέρͺω 'νέμω
cτείχει,‍ͺ παρέξει δ' ἄͺμμι πόνον π‍ͺόλυν
ἄντλην, ἐπͺεί κε νᾶͺοc ἔμβαι
      ].όμεθ' ε[4
      ]..[..]·[
[   ]
φαρξώμεθ' ὠc ὤκιcτα[
   ἐc δ' ἔχυρον λίμενα δρό[μωμεν,   8
—
καὶ μή τιν' ὄκνοc μόλθ[ακοc
λάβη· πρόδηλον γάρ· μεγ[
μνάcθητε τὼν πάροιθε γ[
   νῦν τιc ἄνηρ δόκιμοc γε̣[νέcθω   12
—
καὶ μὴ καταιcχύνωμεν [
ἔcλοιc τόκηαc γᾶc ὔπα κε̣[ιμένοιc
οἴ] τᾶνδ[
   τὰν πό[λιν   16

This wave moves in, a new one
much like that other – harsh
toil for the bailers if it should
    break into the ship.

. . .

            . . . let's
build up a bulwark at once . . .
   race for safe harbour –

no soft shrinking now, for
danger is high and clear.
Remember the last time: let each
   be fit for his work,

let none dishonour his noble kin
lying beneath the ground . . .

An ancient critic explains that in this song a fearsome present event
was figured as a wave[66] and Heraclitus goes on to suggest that the
threat was the burgeoning power of Myrsilus, about to crest in a coup
like that of the earlier tyrant, Melanchrus.[67] Critics of our own time,

---

[66] Heraclitus, *quaest. hom.* (All.5a 1–9): 'Who wouldn't have thought this a real mariner's fright?' ἀλλ᾿ οὐχ οὕτως ἔχει· Μύρσιλος γὰρ ὁ δηλούμενός ἐστι καὶ τυραννικὴ κατὰ Μυτιληναίων ἐγειρομένη σύστασις.

[67] This is the usual understanding of Heraclitus' remark e.g. Gallavotti, *Storia*, 26, 89ff., Kirkwood, *EGM*, 76); Barner, however, suggests (op.cit., 136) that Heraclitus might mean that the old wave was Myrsilus, in which case the present one might refer to the growing power of Pittacus. On the other hand, if at lines 10–11 Alcaeus says something like, 'Remember our action in the last crisis', he may be calling for an

however, have felt that if these are indeed its circumstances, the song is insufficiently defiant, and some have concluded that it must in fact be the signal for the first exile. The conspiracy has been discovered and the poet, lyre in hand, has stood up to cry 'Sauve qui peut!'[68] These, however, are the reactions of moderns who believe that a small ship, if it is to behave with nobility, must defy gigantic waves and attempt to ride out a crushing storm on the open sea. Alcaeus' actual audience of experienced seamen had no such romantic notions, but they did know weather, and they also knew Homer, where the coming of a storm meant that one took down sail and rowed for land (*Od.* 9.67ff.).[69] This poetical wave, following upon another, would have reminded them of the series of waves that towered over Odysseus and shattered his raft just off the Phaeacian coast (*Od.* 5.296; 313; 327; 366; cf. 9. 273), and in that case, even with the help of a goddess, there was nothing to do but swim for shore.

What the song actually says is 'Defy the wave in the only way that a wave can be defied!' – by keeping both ship and men safe until they can venture out again. In much the same way Aeschylus, who obviously knew these lines, figured Xerxes' army as a terrible wave, the Greeks as a worthy and capable (*dokimos*) man who stood on shore and tried to save himself by strong fencing.[70] This is the kind of practical resistance that brings salvation, and it is worthy of the deeds of brave ancestors,[71] for it means hard and tireless work and a readiness for the next dangerous exploit. In psychic terms, it means fighting

---

assassination plot like the one that killed Melanchrus, and in that case the song would most probably belong to the time before the break with Pittacus, and also before the taking of special oaths against Myrsilus. Such a time would suit the tone of stern optimism that seems to pervade the lines; see the somewhat florid description of B. Marzullo: 'Lo splendido fr. 6V ... un tambureggiante inno allo resistenza, contro la monarchia, nella conclusione verbalmente esorcizzata' ('Lo smarrimento', *Philol.* 119, 1975, 36). The word *monarchia* in line 27 could of course describe the rule of Myrsilus or of Melanchrus – perhaps even the government that Pittacus intended – and therefore does nothing to fix the date of the song.

[68] Cf. Theander, op.cit., 160.

[69] Compare also Archil. 105W and adesp. 999 *PMG*: φεύγει μέγα λαῖφος ὑποστολίσας ἐρεβώδεος ἐκ θαλάσσας.

[70] Aesch. *Pers.* 70ff., where the Persian elders are the authors of the figure and mean of course to suggest that, to such a wave as they describe, there can be no resistance: δόκιμος δ οὔτις ὑποστὰς / μεγάλῳ ῥεύματι φωτῶν / ἐχυροῖς ἔρκεσιν εἴργειν / ἄμαχον κῦμα θαλάσσας. Aeschylus may have been thinking also of the figure at *Il.*5.90, where Diomedes in his fury is likened to a storm-swollen river which no sort of dike can hold. His particular phrase would seem, however, to refer to actual barriers put up on shore to defend beached ships, houses, etc., from driving waves, and this is close in sense to Alcaeus' practical φαρξώμεθ' – let's build a temporary reinforcement of the ship's sides, to keep the water out.

[71] The word δόκιμος early came to be used like εὐδόκιμος (Hdt. 1.152; 7.117) but basically it meant 'receivable' as a coin might be because of its evident worth, or because it had passed some test of genuineness (Ar. *RA.* 718f; [Demosth.] 35.24 ἀργύριον . . . δόκιμον); Hesychius defines it as χρήσιμος. For a general discussion, see Koniaris, op.cit., 393.

off the mood of some of the other Alcaic songs, for these seamen must be eager to re-embark, and so must not be overcome by that soft reluctance (cf. the *molthakon . . . gnophallon* at 338.8V) which might make them think they had had enough of the sea (*thalassas pheidom-eth'*, 58, 13V) and would do better to drink and rejoice in one another's youthful company (cf. 73V).

This safe harbour is to be a place of work, not warmth and pleasure, and yet if we try to give it a more allegorical meaning (a process which necessarily reduces the force of the song) it seems once more to represent the gathered faction. However, since the hall of arms is a place where one remembers deeds, even while forgetting anxieties, this 'shore' can have two aspects, just as the symposium can give itself up sometimes to love, sometimes to politics. Some storms are best ignored, but this one calls for action, and consequently this symposium will turn from pleasure to politics, as it prepares to 'launch the swift ships' once more into the sea of danger.[72]

That the ship itself represents the faction in its essential fighting capacity is suggested by a second fragment that shows a vessel caught in an unnatural storm. A bit of commentary once again tells us that the storm is political, but this song shows no tendency towards exhortation. It does not address an imaginary audience of fellow sailors, but reproduces instead the internal voice of a single voyager who discovers a scrap of hope in the constitution of the vessel itself (208V):

ἀcυν⟨ν⟩έτημμι τὼν ἀνέμων cτάcιν,
τὸ μὲν γὰρ ἔνθεν κῦμα κυλίνδεται,
τὸ δ' ἔνθεν, ἄμμες δ' ὂν τὸ μέccον
    ναῒ φορήμεθα cὺν μελαίναι   4
χείμωνι μόχθεντες μεγάλωι μάλα·
πὲρ μὲν γὰρ ἄντλος ἰcτοπέδαν ἔχει,
λαῖφος δὲ πὰν ζάδηλον ἤδη,
    καὶ λάκιδες μεγάλαι κὰτ αὖτο,]   8
χάλαιcι δ' ἄγκυραι, ⟨τὰ δ' ὀήϊα⟩]
[   ]
·[...].[−]
   τοι πόδες ἀμφότεροι μενο[ ]   12
ἐ⟨ν⟩ βιμβλίδεccι· τοῦτό με καὶ ϲ[άοι]
μόνον· τὰ δ' ἄχματ' ἐκπεπ[.].ἀχμενα
··]μεν.[.]ρηντ' ἔπερθα· τὼγ[...].
   ]ϲνοιc.[16

[72] The phrase comes from the hortatory close of another song, 167V, which seems to be urging action against Pittacus, after he has broken his oath; see discussion of Barner, op.cit., 62–73.

I'm witless in this strife of winds;
the waves come rolling, now from starboard,
now from lee, and we in this black ship
    slough along between

exhausted by the heavy storm.
Bilge engulfs the mast-step and
light fills the tattered sail-cloth where
    long rents appear.

Both halyards droop, the rudder. . .
   . . .
   . . .   may
    both the feet remain

caught fast by cringles – this alone
can save me. Cargo shifts . . .
   . . .

The style of this song has been described as 'Stoffhongrig',[73] as if
the singer's chief pleasure lay in his knowing use of nautical terms,
but here as always an urgent passion orders and subdues every detail.
After a subjective beginning that announces this storm as a thing to
be felt, not observed,[74] the song glances outwards at the cause of
confusion – the wild uproar of the sea – and then returns to examine
the chaotic state of the imagined ship. Water has invaded it, and the
technical word *istopeda* measures both its depth and its danger, since
a mast that stands in bilge will not stand much longer.[75] The sail lets
light, and so wind, pass through it, and the loosened lines[76] mean that
the yard will soon be beyond control. There is no question of changing
course, anyway, for the rudder oars have apparently been broken. All
the contrivances that make a ship one of the proudest of man's inventions have been rendered quite useless, and it looks as if the perverse
storm will destroy both vessel and crew. Nevertheless, the viewpoint
of the song is that of a single man, perhaps the captain, and through
him its focus narrows to a single bifurcated element of hope. Some-

---

[73] Fränkel, *Stileigenheit*, 52.

[74] The verb ἀσυννέτημμι occurs only here and has perhaps been invented for the song;
it means literally 'I am without intelligence' or, within the allegory, 'my marine science
is gone'. Compare 67.2, where the target of abuse is accused of conscious deception, i.e.
tactical intelligence, and is said to be οὐκ ἀσύννετος.

[75] On the term ἰστοπέδα, see E. Assmann, 'Nautisch-archäologische Untersuchun-
gen', *JAI* 7 (1892) 45, figs 3 & 4. The mast-step may also be termed the λῆνος, and in
English sometimes the 'tabernacle'.

[76] The papyrus has ἄγκυραι 'anchors', which cannot grow slack, and so the word is
usually emended to ἄγκοιναι, which have been defined as 'forestays' (so Cecil Torr,
Ancient Ships, Chicago 1964, 80–1). Nevertheless, L. Casson would have ἄγκοιναι refer
to the 'bent' lines that stretched on each side from deck to mast and back to deck,
allowing the yard to be set; see *Ships and Seamanship in the Ancient World* (Princeton
1971) 262.

thing that can be called 'feet' are still fast in their bindings (*en bim-blidessi*) and as long as they remain so, salvation is conceivable.

These feet are sometimes thought to be the voyager's own, bound or tangled in the lines so as to keep him from being swept overboard. But why, in that case, should there be such emphasis upon *both* of them (*amphoteroi*)? A person tied against a storm is tied 'hands and feet' like Odysseus against the Sirens (*Od.* 12.178–9) and he has hope as long as any one of his members – any single foot – is still attached. By contrast, the 'feet' of a sail (whether the term indicates the two lower corners or the two ropes that hold those corners)[77] are frequently specified as *amphoteroi* because one is useless without the other.[78] In addition, there seems to be an echo of battle elegy in this phrase about the feet,[79] and it lends a paradoxical support to the nautical, rather than the anthropomorphic, reading of the line, since a torn but upright sail could be asked to stand firm on its two feet more appropriately than a fettered sailor on a slippery deck. As long as the fastened[80] sail still tries to use the wind, the ship remains man's invention, not nature's toy, and the voyager may hope for survival, even in the storm's mad turbulence.[81]

The storm is certainly figurative, and the ship is consequently in a sense the same ship that was to be brought into harbour in the previous fragment. It is the ship of faction and its battle with the storm figures the work of the *hetaireia* as it is carried on outside the banquet hall. Perhaps the contradictory waves indicate that civil, rather than foreign, wars are in question; perhaps the loose cargo signifies the danger of confiscation that threatens any defeated party. There is no way of knowing how far to press the allegory, but one thing is perfectly clear. Alcaeus, in this song, makes the faction – however threatened – the one conceivable conveyance through the political storm, and he suggests that as long as it holds together, as long as it uses the storm as a sail uses wind, each individual member may hope to escape being engulfed in the striving sea.

[77] The word πούς means 'sheet-rope' at *Od.* 5.260; Eur. *Or.* 706–7; *Hec.* 1263; Hyperides, fr. 181; Luc. *Jup.tr.* 47; Cic. *ad Att.* 16.6.1; Ovid. *Fasti* 3.565, Lucan 5.427–8. It means 'sail-corner' at *Od.* 10.32; *P.N.*6. 55; *S. Ant.* 715–17. At Luc. *Charon* 3 it could mean either, as also apparently, at Catul. 4.19–21; Sen. *Med.* 320–2; Pliny 2.48.

[78] Luc. *Jup. tr.* 47; Schol. Ar.*Av.* 35; Ar 2.930; Quint. Smyrn. 9.438.

[79] See G. Cerri, 'Una espressione tirtaica in un contesto allegorico di Alcaeo', *QU* 14 (1972) 65, where reference is to Tyrtaeus 7.31 and 8.21.

[80] The method of fastening the lower corners of the sail to the sheets that held them can be admired on a cup of Nikosthenes: the cloth is folded back on itself, the turned-up corner bound in place with fine cord, so that the sail itself offers a loop through which the rope may be passed; see Casson, op.cit., 70 and fig. 90.

[81] Note the opposite interpretation of Marzullo, op.cit., 35, who reads line 13 as meaning 'this will save me and only me', and then identifies the sentiment as an 'antieroico istinto di conservazione' which is perfectly selfish and perfectly opposed to what he finds to be a splendid call to arms, in fr. 6V. Because he believes he has found complete despair in 208V, M. dates the song to a time just after the defection of Pittacus.

The Disintegrating Faction

All the songs so far considered were meant to offer pleasure and strength to a set of fighting noblemen whose banquets symbolised a courage based in love and solidarity. Even the abusive songs enhanced this sense of unity as they asked assembled friends to scoff together, delight in common wit, and defend shared sentiments against a playful attack. There are, however, other songs that imply an audience of another sort – still kinsmen and allies who fight side by side during the day and drink together after sunset, but kinsmen suspicious of the firmness of their ties, and friends in need of stronger assurances of faith. The daylight struggle of these men is against domestic rather than foreign enemies, and more important, it is not imagined as a struggle for glory, but instead as a defensive fight against exile and a loss of hereditary position within the city. These songs do not celebrate pleasure within the walls and danger without; they depict instead strife and distrust inside the *hetaireia*, and hatred and desperation beyond. And whatever the historical truth may have been, for Alcaeus this second audience of restless, threatened and invidious friends was the creation of the erstwhile hero, Pittacus – the man who had exchanged the sympotic motto, 'Wine is the mirror of man', for his own ambitious saying, 'It's power that shows the man' (DL 1.77).

For Alcaeus the imaginary ambience of the healthy symposium was the great hall of arms, and consequently he saw the disintegration of the *hetaireia* as the moving of certain members' arms into alien halls. The permanence of traditional alliances seemed to be gone; men shifted from one faction to another, careless of kinship and old bonds, and if they moved once they might do so again. With bitter sarcasm Alcaeus asks, of men who had once shared wine and weapons with him, whether they have been true to their new factions (383V):

Ἦρ' ἔτι Διννομένη⟨ι⟩ τὦι Τυρρακήω⟨ι⟩
τἄρμενα λάμπρα κέοντ' ἐν Μυρcινήωι;

Do the bright arms of Deinomenes and Hyrras' son[1]
still hang in the Myrsileion?

By Myrsileion, he may mean the tyrant's *salle d'armes* or the tyrant's tomb,[2] but whatever the nature of the place, the question is clearly rhetorical, and the answer is 'no!' Once Myrsilus was dead, Pittacus and his friend formed new alliances, for men such as these are not even faithful to their breaches of faith. They move their arms from hall to hall.[3]

The hymns that Alcaeus made for the idealised *hetaireia* seemed to belong to a band of young men engaged in happy pranks, men sure of divine indulgence for their own group, and of divine justice for outsiders who opposed them. When, however, he called upon the gods in the name of the divided faction, Alcaeus expressed a very different sense, both of the petitioners and of their divinities. The men are angry with one another, and the gods are called upon, not in the genial attempt to render them joyous and favourable, but rather for the particular punishment that they may bring to those whose ambition is destroying the fraternity. Pittacus, as usual, precipitates the change, which can be observed in a long 'hymn' that becomes an abusive curse before it reaches its end (129V):

>].ρα.α τόδε Λέcβιοιι
> ...].... εὔιδειιλον τέμενοιc μέγα
> ξῦινον κά[τε]ιccαιν, ἐν δὲ βώιμοιc
> ἀθανάτων ιμακάιρων ἔθηικαν   4
>
> —
>
> κἀιπωνύιμαccαιν ἀντίιαονι Διίαι
> cὲ δ' Αιιολήιαν ι[κ]υδαιλίμαιν θιέοιν
> πιάιντων γενέθλαν, τὸν δὲ ιτέριτοιν
> τόνδε κεμήλιον ιὠινιύμαιcc[α]ν   8
> ⟨—⟩

[1] Reading Ὑρραδήωι[ι], as first proposed by J.F.A. Seidler, 'Uber einige Fragmente', *RM* 3 (1829) 153ff.

[2] Reading Μυρσιλήωι in l.2 with Seidler. The -ειον suffix denotes a place where something happens, especially of a festive or cult nature, and consequently Alcaeus may have chosen to call Myrsilus' hall a Myrsileion as a way of suggesting the tyrant's excessive pretensions. On the other hand, he may also refer to an elaborate tomb of some sort, in which case his question would be figurative, as well as rhetorical. Compare the Pittaceum that Pittacus was later said to have built for himself (DL 1.74).

[3] Probably Mazzarino is right to locate this song in the period of double rule by Pittacus and Deinomenes that followed upon the death of Myrsilus (Athen. 21, 1943, 69–70). At this period Pittacus seems to have abandoned his connections with the clan of the dead tyrant, and to have consolidated those with the Penthilids. Compare 70V, where Pittacus' lyre seems now to be located in an alien symposium, probably that of the Penthilids.

Ζόννυcον ὠμήcιταν. ἄ[γιι]τ᾽ εὔνοοιν
θῦμον cχέθοντειc ἀμμετιέρα[c] ἄραc
ἀκούcατ᾽, ἐκ δὲ τῶιν[δ]ε μόιχθων
    ἀργαλέαc τε φύγαc ῥ[ύεcθε·   12

⟨—⟩
τὸν Υ̓́ρραον δὲ πα[ῖδ]α ιπεδελθιέτω
χήνων Ἐ[ρίννυ]c ὤc ποιτ᾽ ἀπώμιννιιμεν
τόμοντεc ἄ..[ʹ.]γ·ιγι
    μηδάμα μηδ᾽ ἔνα τῶν ἑταίρων   16

⟨—⟩
ἀλλ᾽ ἢ θάνοντεc γᾶν ἐπιέμμενοι
κείcεcθ᾽ ὑπ᾽ ἄνδρων οἳ τότ᾽ ἐπικ᾽..ην
ἤπειτα κακκτάνοντεc αὔτοιc
    δᾶμον ὑπὲξ ἀχέων ῥύεcθαι.   20

⟨—⟩
χήνων ὁ φύcκων οὐ διελέξατο
πρὸc θῦμον, ἀλλὰ βραϊδίωc πόcιν
ἔ]μβαιc ἐπ᾽ ὀρκίοιcι δάπτει
    τὰν πόλιν ἄμμι δέδ[.]..[.].ί.αιc   24

... precinct Lesbians made of old,
conspicuous and broad. They
consecrated altars here
for the blessed gods

naming Suppliant Zeus and
you, Aeolian Mistress, famed
mother of all, and thirdly
making dedications to

Kemelian Dionysus, Omophage.
Now hear our prayer, you three,
with favour: rescue us from shame
and from this sordid exile!

Send the oath's indwelling curse
after Hyrras' son – the Fury
we invoked the day we swore
not one of us would bend

but all would rest in earth
where foemen laid us, or
would kill and save the people
from their misery.

That was a covenant the Paunch
refused to keep within his heart.
Instead, he walked upon his words
and wolfed the city down.

(Two more stanzas follow, with a mention of Myrsilus.)

The singer pretends to stand in a sacred precinct as a suppliant, addressing a Suppliant Zeus, and the situation that he imagines is one that is familiar from tragedy, where the weak so often take refuge at altars when they are pursued by the strong. In this case the reference seems to be to the moment when the Alcaic faction, its conspiracy against Myrsilus discovered, was hiding in the country to escape prosecution.[4] The need for sanctuary was, or had been, very real, but nevertheless this poetic prayer contains a kind of trick, for it is not what it seems to be. It begins as a suppliant petition but then, instead of asking gods to be kind and begging for escape from pursuit, it looks for angry gods and begs them to inflict a dreadful injury. What is more, the punishment here demanded is not supposed to strike the tyrant who pursues these suppliants, but instead one who ought to be with them – a traitor who was once their friend. All the members of the faction, with Pittacus among them, had sworn to overthrow Myrsilus,[5] and then Pittacus had defected – probably it was he who had

---

[4] See the marginal comment at 114V. Arguments about the location of the shrine usually depend upon: (1) identifying it with the shrine of 130bV and of Sappho 17V; (2) assuming that all of the exiles were hiding there. J.D. Quinn, 'Cape Phokas, Lesbos', *AJA* 65 (1961) 391–3 and plates 128–9, proposed Cape Phokas, as being prominent, visible and far from the city, yet close to the sea so that the Atridae might have landed there; L. Robert, 'Inscr. de Lesbos', *REA* 62 (1960) 285ff. proposed Mesa, presumably the traditional meeting place of Lesbian aristocrats, at sea level, with space for many refugees and fresh water for them; C. Picard, 'Ou fut, à Lesbos ... l'asyle ...', *Rev. Arch.* (1962) 2, 43–69, objected that Mesa was too close to Mytilene and too open to attack, and that anyway its temple remains seem to belong to Aphrodite; he pointed to Lesvori as a better location. Treu (*Alk.*, 142) says he has visited all three spots and found Phokas too small and providing evidence only of a cult of Dionysus, Mesa the best possibility. The whole question, however, has been confounded by a reading of the present poem that is at once too literal and not close enough. Nothing necessarily connects the shrine of the triad with that of 130bV (which the poet, incidentally, imagines as occupied by himself alone aside from the women), for one is a broad, common and conspicuous place, the other a place in which one may hide. And nothing, even in the fiction of the present song, necessarily indicates that a large number of exiles are to be thought of as settled in its vicinity.

[5] It is sometimes assumed that the oath referred to was a general and original one that constituted the *hetaireia* in the first place; so Mazzarino, op.cit., 40, note 4. There is, however, no evidence at all for the use of such oaths in the aristocratic factions of Lesbos which had presumably been constituted generations before; oaths of general constitutive sort seem to belong to a later time and an Athenian context, judging from passages that make συνωμοσία a synonym for *hetaireia* (e.g. Ar. *Eq.* 476; Pl.*Rep.*365d; Demosth.*contr. Mid.* 21.20; *contr. Eratosth.* (12) 43). Alcaic references to other oaths (306(9)V; 167V; 77 col. iiV) suggest, on the other hand, that when a special exploit was to be attempted, a special oath might be taken, and A. Andrewes remarks of such oaths that they would have been sworn only among leaders who were one another's strict equals – the heads of the families who were agreeing to collaborate (*Greek Tyrants*, 73). Barner, *Neuere Alk Pap.*, 91, associates the oath of the present poem with that of 67V, taken at the altar of Apollo, thus at least reminding us that there is no reason to assume that the oath of 129 must have been sworn in the same locale in which the singer now pretends to sing. The oath of 67V, however, bound those who swore it to keep *kakopatrids* from power, and consequently it can hardly be identified with the present oath, by which men swore to overturn a government already in power. Barner

denounced the intended plot – and now he sits in comfort in Mytilene, close to Myrsilus (70.7V), while the rest must hide to escape retaliation. Worse, since all were bound by oath either to kill the tyrant or themselves to die, they have all become oath-breakers, thanks to this friend who chose his belly over his word. Because of him the faction has failed itself, and so shame joins disappointment and defeat, and a whirlwind of hatred is unleashed upon the absent Pittacus.

The song turns itself into a solemn curse – 'Let the Erinys attack him!'[6] – and though it is in actuality a sympotic performance, not a ritual denunciation, the poet has found ways to give it a sense of

---

may nevertheless be right in attaching 306(9)V to 67V, since both refer to Apollo; see his discussion of 306(9), op.cit., 86ff. It is just possible that the present oath, apparently taken specifically against Myrsilus, is the one associated with a millstone thrown into the sea, in 77 col. iiV, where the commentator seems to attach the action to the tyrant, calling the oath-makers τοὺς περὶ τὸν Μ(ύρσιλον); see E. Diehl, 'Lyrici Gr. redivivi', *RM* 92 (1944) 23.

[6] It is usually assumed that the Erinys of line 14 must derive from dead comrades, and consequently the κήνων of that line is treated as if it referred to corpses, though nothing of the sort has been mentioned. Kamerbeek ('De novis carminibus Alcaei', *Mnem.* 13 (1947) 105) desperately proposed that, though the dead were not noticed in the song, they were literally present to the audience, making this a kind of funeral song! The problem, however, is historical as well as syntactical, for it is hard to see why there should have been any dead at all, when the conspiracy was denounced before its attempt was made. (Had this not been so, the conspirators would never have been allowed to leave the city.) Burn, *Lyric Age*, 241, calls in the scholiast at fr. 60 and reconstructs an encounter between the Alcaic faction and the body-guard of Pittacus, occurring somewhere between Pyrrha and Mytilene, but this, of course, is completely hypothetical. Further complications arise when the second κήνων, at line 21, is coordinated with the first, for there corpses are even harder to accommodate: Gallavotti translated 'con l'animo di loro' (the dead) 'non sintratenne affabilmente il panciuto' (*Aeg.* 22, 1942, 111); Deubner, 'er kümmerte sich nicht darum, was ihnen' (the dead) 'am Herzen lag' ('Zu den neuen Bruchstücken' *Abh. Pr.Akad. Wiss.*, ph.hist.kl. 7, 1943, 8ff.); Kamerbeek, 'Eorum voluntatis rationem non habens', explaining, 'Clam sociis P. consilia cepit' (loc.cit.). Dead comrades who give this much difficulty and who are never directly mentioned are best abandoned. A. Luppino, 'Per l'interpretazione del nuovo Alceo', *PP* 5 (1950) 206–14, suggested that κήνων in both passages should be heard to refer to the gods, though this produces the difficult concept, the 'erinys of the gods'; 'Ma l'Erinni dei celesti perseguiti...' and 'Coll'animo dei celesti non parlò il panciuto ...' More recently, B. Gentili (*Polinnia*, 1965, 204) has proposed understanding the second κήνων as referring to living comrades, among whom Potbelly did not speak sincerely, which at least properly attributes the *thumos* to the subject of the sentence. Page and Treu recognised that the κήνων of line 21 must be neuter, its case commanded by the verb of remembering, its reference being to what has gone before, but since they still would find dead comrades as the source of the Erinys in line 14, they ended by denying the effect of an obviously contrived repetition. The present translation is based on the notion that κήνων in both passages refers to the oaths, the ὅρκια that are implied by ἀπώμνυμεν in line 14 and by τέμοντες in line 15 (which resumes the expression τέμνειν ὅρκια) and that are named below, in line 23. These oaths are plural only because many swore, and when broken they produce the *single* Fury of line 14 (as a number of dead men never could); these oaths are what Pittacus refuses to take to heart in line 21, and tramples upon. This reading is not unlike that of Fränkel at *DuP*, 219: 'die Erinys dessen was wir zu jener Zeit hochheilig schwören.'

supernatural efficacy. First among these is a sharp intensification of emotion, as a grand and generalised awe is rapidly compressed into a vortex of rage and then concentrated upon a victim who is specific and mean. The technique here is something like that of the Hall of Arms poem, for the final urgency is derived from an opening passage that is slow and deceptively quaint.[7] The venerable *temenos* has three adjectives, its gods are not only deathless but blessed, its ancient founders establish altars and also confer cult names, and this redundant expansiveness continues through an address to gods who are generously equipped with epithets. Then, with the word 'exile' in line 12, a sudden change is made, for this proves to be the last decorated term. From this point on, the diction is as utilitarian as that of a contract; not a sound is wasted, and the only thing that resembles embellishment is the ugly nickname given to the enemy.

By such means Alcaeus achieves a fearful concentration of energy, while at the same time he builds a song that seems to contain its own fulfilment. To begin with, he addresses his pseudo-petition to three divinities who by their very existence on Lesbos prove that he and his friends are not meant to feel shame. These gods are the patrons of the aristocracy, their cult having been brought by the founders of the island, their *temenos* being the oldest common possession of that noble community (the *damos*) that the conspirators had meant to save.[8] These three gods must have despised a base and disloyal Pittacus, even if no oaths had been sworn and no Erinys created, and conversely, these three would listen to the descendant of one of the founders of their shrine, no matter what he asked. Alcaeus stands in an almost priestly relation to them, but nevertheless he doesn't trust to his blood alone as he addresses them. Instead, he captures their favour with a poem built on the magic of their own number, three.

First, the prayed-for revival of the faction is acted out in a triple series of verbal gestures, for Zeus is addressed from a posture of mortal humility, as Antiaios; Hera from a stance of racial pride, as the birth-source of all; Dionysus from a mirroring position of noble feroc-

---

[7] Compare the report of A. Luppino, op.cit., 207, who finds in the first part, 'il senso d'immenso stupore davanti alla divinità,' and in the second, 'il tono bladanzoso e sicuro di chi vede profilarsi il trionfo della giustizia divina'.

[8] On this combination of divinities, see C. Picard, 'La triade Zeus Hera Dionysus', *BCH* 70 (1946) 455ff., and G. Tarditi, 'Dioniso Kemelios', *QU* 4 (1967) 107ff. Picard relates the group to a pre-Hellenic triad reflected also in the Heracles-Hera-Dionysus group at Samos, and assumes that this Lesbian Hera is a kneeling childbirth goddess (cf. Eitrem, *RE* sv 'Hera', 401). Tarditi likewise sees Dionysus as a version of the boy-consort of Hera-Ge, and if this is correct, the Lesbian cult will have been peculiar in its substitution of a powerful, chthonian Zeus of Suppliants for the second consort, usually likewise a youth.

ity, as Omestes.⁹ To these three divinities the ever more confident song makes a threefold petition: listen to our prayer; save us from suffering and exile; see to it that the Fury pursues the oath-breaker. In the same way, the oath itself is specified as threefold: no one would abandon the plot; all would die and be buried in the ground they fought for; all would live as saviours of the traditional constitution. And meanwhile the song as a whole moves through three phases of tradition, reality, and fantasy as it evokes first numerous but insubstantial ancestors in quiet acts of worship, then a smaller group of contemporary men engaged in a rite of swearing, and finally a single beast-man in the act of devouring. Because of this pervasive triadic organisation, the song seems to reflect and repeat the nature of its divinities; it seems indeed almost to emanate from them, and to be filled already with their active power.

Alcaeus calls upon the three Lesbian gods to send the Fury who is to devour Pittacus, but meanwhile he does her job himself, destroying the man in his own way with a final image that is grotesque, base and detestable. He makes him a bloated cur; one that gobbles up the city like a stray; a creature who is all distended belly, ugly and perhaps diseased; a man who is dangerous only as a dog might be. All this he does by combining the bestial verb *daptei*[10] with the inspired denomination of Pittacus as *ho Phuskōn*, the swollen one, the Paunch.[11] Shocked critics have complained that the poet is guilty of a crime against taste, but this crude term is the necessary agent of the poet's own fury as he banishes the deserter from the noble company

---

⁹ On ὠμήστης, note *Il.*24.207, where Hector calls Achilles ὠμήστης because he is pitiless and does not honour pledges. The epithet may possibly be a reminder of an abandoned rite of human sacrifice; so Clement, *Protr.* 3.42.5, cited by E. R. Dodds, *Bacchae*,² xix. The previous epithet was evidently less vengeful, though its exact meaning is in doubt. L. Deubner, op.cit., 9, proposed a derivation from κεμάς, -άδος, as at *Il.* 10.361, a male fawn. K. Latte, 'Zu den neuen Alk. Bruchstücken', *MH* 4 (1947) 144 = *Kl. Schr.* pp. 485–91, objected that the form ending in -ηλιος should mean 'deriving from'. As an exception, B. Gentili mentioned Ar. *Lys.*290, where κανθήλιος comes from κάνθων ('Note ad Alceo', *Maia* 3, 1950, 256), but nevertheless Deubner's explanation has generally been rejected. Bowra followed Beattie in emending to τὸν Σεμελήϊον (*GLP*², 142); Kamerbeek (loc.cit.) suggested κειμήλιον or possibly εὐμήλιον, as the opposite of ὠμήστης, but all of these are impossible for metrical reasons. More recently, G. Tarditi, loc.cit., has connected the ke-me-ri-jo of the Pylos tablets with Hesychius' definition, καμαν· τὸν ἄγρον· Κρῆτης, and concluded that the epithet makes this a Dionysus of the fields.

¹⁰ The verb δάπτειν is used in Homer only of animals; cf. e.g. *Il.*11.474.81, of lions or jackals; *Il.*16.156–63, of wolves; *Il.* 23.182–3, of dogs. The plundering ruler of epic is a δημοβόρος βασιλεύς, *Il.*7.231.

¹¹ The essential meaning is of swelling, either with food or with wind, but the presence of δάπτειν in the passage fixes this as a charge of gluttony. It is interesting to note that a standard motif in Jewish tales of tyrants is that they swell up until they burst; see F. J. Foakes-Jackson & Kirsopp Lake, *The Beginning of Christianity* i (London 1933) 22–30, and Pierre Benoit, 'The death of Judas', in *Jesus and the Gospel* i, tr. B. Wetherhead (London 1973) 189–207.

he has betrayed. They are descendants of founding Achaeans, worshippers at antique shrines, men of honourable and tragic purpose who know how to make a prayer. He is a greedy animal.

Another pseudo-prayer full of real anger strikes an Archilochean note, as Alcaeus calls upon Zeus to witness a different sort of treachery (69V):

Ζεῦ πάτερ, Λῦδοι μὲν ἐπαιϲχάλαντεϲ
ϲυμφόραιϲι διϲχελίοιϲ ϲτά[τηραϲ
ἄμμ' ἔδωκαν, αἴ κε δυναίμεθ' ἴρ[
    ἐϲ πόλιν ἔλθην,   4

̄
οὐ πάθοντεϲ οὐδάμα πῶϲλον οὐ[δὲ]ν
οὐδὲ γινώϲκοντεϲ· ὁ δ' ὡϲ ἀλώπα[
ποικ[ι]λόφρων εὐμάρεα προλέξα[ιϲ
    ἤλπ[ε]το λάϲην.   8

Father Zeus! The Lydians grieved so
at our calamity that they assigned
two thousand staters to us, should we
    take the holy city –

knowing nothing of us! never
having had a favour from us! – and he,
that wily fox, predicted ease and hoped
    we would be duped.

Most of those who have looked at this song have taken it as a bit of history, then scorned it as the prosy record of an unpatriotic alliance between Alcaeus' exiled faction and a major foreign power.[12] The Lydian offer is supposed to have been actually made and actually accepted; the 'holy city' is identified as Mytilene, the 'wily fox' as Pittacus, and then the invocation to Zeus is discovered to be almost irreverent, since it is followed, not by a prayer but by a factual statement about a sum of money spent in some shameful and abortive attack upon the mother city.[13] This line of interpretation is fruitless in every sense, however, for the critic cannot explain what happened to the foreign-backed expedition; he cannot explain how a Pittacus at

[12] Fränkel found the piece to be typical of 'the new realism' with its detailed reporting, but concluded, 'there is nothing of poetry in it' (*Early Greek Poetry*, tr. Hadas and Willis, New York 1975, 193).

[13] See, for example, Andrewes, op.cit., 93, who speaks of 'financial support on a large scale from the Lydians'. For Mazzarino (op.cit., 74, note 2) this subsidy from a foreign court is final proof that Alcaeus himself was potentially the worst sort of tyrant, one who would destroy his own city for the sake of absolute power there, but Kamerbeek (op.cit., pt.2, 176) is more generous: 'Il est blamable, mais à un reproche il aurait sans doute répondu qu'il ne combattait le tyran que pour sauver sa patrie.'

home could try to influence his enemies in exile; and above all he cannot explain why a song about a failed attempt to force a return home should be marked by abusive scorn.[14]

It will be best to start again, very simply, and with the song itself. What the singer does in this performance is denounce an enemy who has tried and failed to trick the members of his audience, and he clearly means to elicit an emotion of triumphant contempt from his listeners as he offers the enemy's failure, and consequently their own success, to the notice of Zeus. The trickery evidently lay in the anomalous, unexpectedly specific sum of money that is named, and it is worth noting that the words *statēras* (2) and *alōpax* (6) were sung to the same musical notes. The two thousand staters are at the core of the poetic situation, and the problem is to adjust the song's tone of scorn to this so explicit amount, for it is certainly not a niggardly one. With only one thousand staters, Croesus raised an army; with two, the Athenians bought back the rich city of Rhoeteum,[15] and it has been calculated that in the first decades of the sixth century two thousand could have kept a force of five hundred men in the field for several months.[16] Far from being contemptible, the figure is more than princely, and it is assuredly out of all proportion to anything that the Lydians might have spent to support one faction against another, in the miniature rivalries of the Lesbian civil war.[17] Indeed, it is out of

---

[14] Mazzarino, loc.cit., thought that the exiles, with this Lydian support, were such a threat that Pittacus was forced to readmit them, and that this event marked the end of the third exile; Burn, op.cit., 234, somehow assumed that the subsidy had been offered to Pittacus, but this ignores the pointed contrast between the ἄμμ' of line 3 and the ὀ δέ of line 6. Bowra (*GLP*, 141) supposed that someone who was not Pittacus talked Alcaeus' companions out of receiving money which Alcaeus himself wished to take. Treu (*Alc.*, 171) makes the most thorough attempt to face all the difficulties and supposes the following scenario: an exiled Alcaeus has petitioned the Lydians for full military backing, but they have responded with a mere gift of money, which Pittacus then somehow cheated them out of. This supposition would allow for the tone of outrage that pervades the song, but not for that of triumph, and worse, it assumes that the 2000 staters somehow represented an inadequate and despicable sum.

[15] Nicolaus Damasc. 90F 65 Jacoby; Thuc. 4.52.2; see Mazzarino, op.cit., 74, note 2.

[16] Page (*S&A*, 232). This calculation has been challenged by L. Breglia, 'Gli stateri di Alceo', *Numis. e Ant.Cl. Quad. Ticenesi* (Lugano 1974) 7–12, who argues that the stater was only about 1/3 as valuable as Page had supposed. Breglia's figures, however, are all from the late seventh century, and the event under discussion should belong to the first or second decade of the sixth.

[17] To explain the Lydian interest, Page (*S&A*, 231) supposed that it was the policy of the Lydians to back oligarchical tyrannies in the Greek states; in the present instance, however, he had to assume that they discriminated, Aristotle-fashion, between tyrants who came to power by force (whom they liked) and those who arrived as dictators appointed by the people (whom they opposed), and this seems highly unlikely. Mazzarino (op.cit., 63, note 2) posits an ancient connection between the Cleanactids of Mytilene and the court of Lydia; this was presumably interrupted when Pittacus came to power, thus rendering Pittacus unpleasant to Lydia. On this supposition, however, it would surely have been more sensible for the Lydians to offer their subsidy directly to their Cleanactid friends in exile, and not to the faction of Alcaeus which was itself unfriendly, at least some of the time, to the Cleanactid interests (cf. 112V).

proportion to every imaginable reality, and consequently this figure, so strongly emphasised by the singer, must represent a falsehood or at least a gross exaggeration.

The parallel of Antimenidas' opponent, the man who was more than eight feet tall, comes to mind at once and with it the realisation that the two songs have other points in common. The perverse greeting is filled with friendship, the perverse prayer with enmity, but both are dealing with something that is much too big because both are satirising someone else's lie. Just as the giant originated in Antimenidas' boasts, so the two thousand staters have grown from something that the trickster of the present song has said, and this means that in prose, the singer's statement goes like this: 'He told us that the Lydians were offering a king's ransom, but we weren't taken in by a tale like that!' Someone tried to make Alcaeus and his friends believe in a fabulous purse that might be theirs, if they took a certain city, urging them on by telling them that the work would be easy. He thought he was sly, but he went too far, and Alcaeus now leads the would-be victims of this 'fox' in bitter laughter over his vulgar lack of finesse.

This is all that the song contains, and any speculation about its reference to the real world must base itself upon two poetic facts. First, the fox and the faction are at odds, and secondly, they are in the same place and able to communicate. This means that if the fox was Pittacus (which certainly seems probable),[18] the poem's event must be thought of as occurring after he went over to Myrsilus (to account for the enmity), and specifically after the death of Myrsilus but before the time of the second exile (to account for the presence of Alcaeus and his friends in Mytilene). This is a period in which the Lesbian aristocrats might have established some form of oligarchy, had they not been outmanoeuvred by a very clever politician who knew how to use their factional differences, and so it is one that suits the present song admirably. The man who is to be the next tyrant is trying to consolidate his shaky position, but since he has not yet been given the power to banish those who oppose him, he must get rid of his enemies piecemeal and in some other way. A call comes from Lydia for mercenaries to help in taking some strategic city,[19] and Pittacus

---

[18] In favour of identifying the fox with Pittacus, note the other animal references to him (296aV where he is a lion; 70V and 129V, where he is an unspecified beast who devours; perhaps also 306(9)1–8V). Note however Bowra, loc.cit., who makes the fox an unknown man; Gallavotti (*Storia*, 24ff.) thought the fox was Myrsilus, trying to get the nobles out of town at an earlier time, and this would seem to be a strong second possibility.

[19] The fact that the city to be taken need not be Mytilene is recognised by Page as a secondary possibility: 'If the assaulted city is not Mytilene, we might entertain the supposition among others that Pittacus, perhaps in command at Mytilene, diverted

grossly magnifies the terms, hoping that Alcaeus and his friends will be tempted by the amount and will go off to mend their fortunes, far from Mytilene. They, however, see through his ruse, refuse to go, and rejoice in their good sense, not knowing that this fox will soon be able to drive them out forcibly.

Even drinking songs became invidious when the inner unity of the symposium was uncertain and the city outside absolutely divided. One drank, not peaceably against honourable hardship and in the aid of love, but violently, against dishonourable betrayal, celebrating hatred. This second sort of drinking was urged by Alcaeus, at the time of the return from the first exile (332V):

Νῦν χρῆ μεθύcθην καί τινα πρὸc βίαν
πώνην, ἐπεὶ δὴ κάτθανε Μύρcιλοc

Now is the time to drink, to drink
outrageously, for Myrsilus is dead!

Among trusted friends one might stretch the rules of aristocratic moderation a little, asking 'Why wait for the lamp?' but when comrades broke the sympotic ties and joined other banquets, while factions plotted against one another, excess became an excuse for virulent abuse. Alcaeus attacks an enemy (who must have been identified as Pittacus at the beginning of the song) by calling him a congenital drunkard and boor (72V):

```
. . . . ] . [
    ἐν[. .].λα[.]. . . . .[                                         2
λάβρωc δὲ cυν cτεί[.]. .[. .]ϵιαπ. .
πίμπλειcιν ἀκράτω [. . . .]π' ἀμέρα.[
καὶ νύκτι παφλάcδει . . .αχθεν,
    ἔνθα νόμοc θάμ' ἐν.[.].[.].νην.                                6
```

Alcaeus' party, which might otherwise be employed in seditious activities whether at home or in exile, to an undertaking in which they were likely to be enfeebled or destroyed' (*S&A*, 233). He assumes, however, that in this case, too, the Lydian offer would have been genuine and would have been accepted. G. Pugliese Caratelli, 'Su la storia di Lesbo nel età di Alceo', *RFIC* 21 (1943) 20ff. suggested that the 'holy city' might be Sardis, then went on to propose the campaign referred to in Hdt. 1.154, which, however, is much too late unless one accepts Mazzarino's late dating for Pittacus. Gomme confessed in an aside, 'I have sometimes thought that the city . . . "which Lydians helped us, by a large subsidy, to attack" might be Sigeion' (*JHS* 77, 256, note 6), but he did not explain why, in this case, Alcaeus should be so scornful of the wiles of one who tried to persuade them to accept the money.

κῆνος δὲ τούτων οὐκ ἐπελάθετο
ὤνηρ ἐπεὶ δὴ πρῶτον ὀνέτροπε,
παίcαιc γὰρ ὀννώρινε νύκταc,
   τὼ δὲ πίθω πατάγεcκ' ὁ πύθμην.   10

—

cὺ δὴ τεαύταc ἐκγεγόνων ἔχη⟨ι⟩c
τὰν δόξαν οἴαν ἄνδρεc ἐλεύθεροι
ἔcλων ἔοντεc ἐκ τοκήων

. . .

greedily . . .
they fill their cups with unmixed [wine]
by day. At night their splashings . . .
   . . . where it is the custom . . .

That man did not forget such ways
when first he turned things upside down,
but roused each night to action
   and beat the sounding jar.

And you – a twig from such a stem –
can you expect the same repute
that freemen born of nobles claim?
   . . .

This song of retrospective defamation begins with ancestors, goes on to father, and then strikes at its present victim not so much for personal faults as for being the scion of a disreputable race.[20] The

---

[20] Among many uncertainties there are three major problems here: (1) can σύ in line 11 refer to the same person as κῆνος . . . ὤνηρ in 7–8? (2) To what does the τεαύταc in line 11 refer? (3) Whose actions are being described in the first stanza? To the first question, the answer is surely No. 'That man' who occupies a distanced, third-person, past position in the second stanza cannot be suddenly addressed as 'you' in the third, and consequently we must recognise two separate men in the two stanzas. (The reason for trying to identify them was the excessively political translation of ὀνέτροπε in line 8 as 'overthrew the government' and the consequent assumption that this man must be Pittacus; see Mazzarino, op.cit., 43, note 3 and Kamerbeek, op.cit., 170.) To the second question, some answer with Page that τεαύταc must refer to the mother of the man under attack (so Andrewes and Gomme); others have suggested alternative implicit antecedents that are easier to deal with, and though Hunt's γόνη and Gallavotti's χώρα have gained few supporters, many follow Wilamowitz and assume an oblique reference to the γενέα implicit in ἐκγεγόνων. (So, e.g., Diehl, Mazzarino, Edmonds, Treu; the present translation works on this assumption.) To the third question, those who follow Page on τεαύταc will answer that this preliminary section must concern the mother. Others assume that this stanza describes the activities either of the man of stanza two or the man addressed in stanza three: consequently most take its subject to be Hyrras, while Bowra and Mazzarino assume that it is Pittacus, here, as in the two following stanzas. There is, however, a third body of critics who would make this early passage describe a group of people, variously identified as the companions of the man of the second stanza, the *genea* later implied (so Theander), or the inhabitants of a particular region, i.e. Thrace (so Gallavotti). I have assumed that stanza one deals with Thracian members of the *genea* of the man attacked in stanza three, forebears likewise of the κῆνος ὤνηρ of the second stanza.

elder generation, with its daytime drinking of unmixed wine, is probably said to be following the custom (*nomos*, 6) of the Thracians, since they were antiquity's most notorious drunkards, and if so the upstart of the second stanza must surely be Hyrras, the Thracian father of Pittacus who somehow found his way into aristocratic Lesbian society (DL 1.74; Diod.Sic. 9.12; see above, p. 112, note 18). That infamous man (*kēnos . . . ōnēr*, 7–8) never did learn to be polished in his habits, and now his son, though sprung from men who don't know how to drink, would bend an elbow as an equal at the banquets of the nobility. He had been a comrade and a hero, the killer of Melanchrus and the commander at Sigeum, but now Alcaeus in effect calls him a low-class alien, and the charge is a serious one since the *hetaireia* was oath-bound to keep all *kakopatrids* from positions of power: they had sworn it at the altar of Apollo (67V). There is, nevertheless, a certain coolness and generality about these verses, for they seem to speak not just for the faction but for all men of breeding – for all Lesbians, perhaps even for all Hellenes – as they accuse their victim of having no manners, no presentable father, and no heritage of luxurious civilisation. For this reason they seem to come from a time long after Pittacus' first betrayal of the faction, and might well belong to the same moment as the song of the wily fox – that time just before the second exile when Pittacus was courting the support of men who were not landholders or members of any *hetaireia*, men to whom drinking was an ordinary act and not a semi-sacred rite.

The *hetaireia* that feels itself dissolving and drinks self-consciously is no proper audience for love-songs. Its special friendships are dictated by power, not pleasure, and they may be threatened by intriguing outsiders. There is, for example, a song addressed to a certain Mnamon (a song known only from citations found in a commentary, 305a.15ff.V), in which Alcaeus makes the symposium his witness to a plea, not for love, but for a political *entente*. 'Let there be no war between us,' he says, and he explains that he holds no grudge against this sought-after friend, even though he once played a part in some inexplicable 'return' of Myrsilus.[21] Members of Pittacus' set may try to force a quarrel between them, but Alcaeus scorns such interference and in closing calls directly upon the one he would influence, after the

---

[21] Nothing is known of this 'return' of Myrsilus, though it seems to be referred to again in col. ii 8 of this same papyrus. The word κάθοδος is used elsewhere to refer to Alcaeus' own return from exile at P.Oxy. 2506 fr. 98, 13 = 306Ae.13V, but who could have sent Myrsilus into exile, and when? Some have assumed that his tyranny must have been divided into two phases by a revolt in which the *hetaireia* of Alcaeus briefly took power and banished Myrsilus; see Barner, op.cit., 165–6 and O. Bauer, 'Sapphos Verbannung', *Gymn.* 70 (1963) 1ff. There is, however, no need to suppose that Myrsilus was already in power, nor even that he was the object of an official act of banishment; he may simply have been temporarily forced out of the city by the power of his enemies, at some time in the period of disorder that followed the assassination of Melanchrus.

fashion of erotic song. There is no way to tell whether Alcaeus is here courting a new friend whom he would win from another faction, or reclaiming an old one who has strayed, but the significant fact is that, in the ideal *hetaireia*, Mnamon could be neither of these. In the faction that Alcaeus loved to praise, friends could neither fall away nor be annexed from another group.[22]

An embarrassed commentator supplies phrases from a second distorted love-song that seems to show the disintegrating *hetaireia* as a place where actions and emotions can reach an extreme of sordidness. All we have, however, are the fragmentary remarks of the ancient scholar, made as he tries to account for an Alcaic line that says in effect, 'I did not kill (name lost) though Amardis says that I did' (306AbV).[23] The commentator wants to acquit the poet of this self-reported charge, and in Alcaeus' defence he offers citations from two other songs, one in which the poet hails the putative victim as *kalos* in a context of wreaths and celebrations,[24] and one in which he suggests that the same young man met his end in battle: 'You do no bad thing in our eyes by dying, struck down by the Allienoi.' Then the commentator goes back to the song that principally concerns him and provides a real quotation, allowing us to recognise it as a version of the lover's reproach. Alcaeus is directing erotic abuse at a faithless boy who has run away, saying: 'Then you abandoned me,[25] o worst of boys,[26] rejoicing in the calumny of Amardis! You (chose other) companions, (leaving me) indignant, for I am in no way to blame for the blood of (name of *kalos* boy from the other song) . . .'

Amardis has told a present boy that Alcaeus was responsible for the death of a boy of the past, and the present boy has decamped. Such is the fictional situation of an Alcaic song in which the singer reproaches his beloved and protests his own innocence – a protest which the commentator supports with the citation that mentions the first boy's death abroad.[27] The commentator is thus finally satisfied, but he has

---

[22] Exception would be the annexation of an entire clan-group, as for example, if an alliance were made between the Archeanactids and the Cleanactids, which presumably might be expressed as a friendship between the leader of the one group and the leader of the other. In the present case, however, the commentary makes it clear that there is no question of a great alliance, for the obscurity of Mnamon is emphasised by calling him 'a certain Mnamon' and by explaining that this is a proper name, though it does not look like one.

[23] For discussion of the commentary, see M. Treu, 'Neues über S.u.A. POxy 2506', *QU* 2 (1966) 20ff. and W. Barner, 'Zu den Alk. fr. von POxy 2506', *Hermes* 95 (1967) 1ff.

[24] See ll.12ff. and fr. 368V, where Menon is indirectly called χαρίεις.

[25] The word is ἀπέθυσας (24–5), and Hesychius has ἀποθύσσῃ ἀποπνεύσῃ ἀποζεύξῃ, ἀποσείσῃ. Treu assumes that the form comes from ἀποθύειν, but he offers no parallels that would support a figurative sense for this verb. The interpretation ἀποθύω, 'rushed away' is proposed by Page, *Oxy Pap.* 29, 43.

[26] With ὦ πόνηρε (1.25) compare 119,1V, another example of infra-sympotic abuse.

[27] Alia is identified (by Barner, *Hermes* 95, 11ff.) as modern Krygyl, at 39° 13N 29° 21E, a place in the Highlands south of Constantinople. There is no reason to suppose

nevertheless drawn our attention to three poems, two of which seem to depict incidents of a very ugly sort. If we take them literally,[28] we are forced to contemplate a situation (real or imaginary) in which a foreigner, one who is probably a flute-boy or a pimp, can suggest that a leader of the faction has killed a boy he once loved. This tale is of course identified as slander, but what sort of symposium whispers (or sings) gossip like this, and what sort of audience applauds a cruel salute to the death of one whose beauty the same singer had recently praised? Death among the Allienoi would be at best death for pay, but Alcaeus has twisted his phrase into a telling litotes, not saying 'Your death was fair' but rather 'In our eyes your death was not foul'. Even if we pretend that the person in question was not a member of the fraternity – was of another class, perhaps an alien like Amardis[29] – the Alcaic symposium no longer seems to be a gathering of generous and noble men who are the protégés of the saving Twins.

In moments when trust among comrades could not be taken for granted, straight personal abuse might seem to have been a natural sympotic mode, but there are in fact very few examples of direct inimical attack among Alcaeus' surviving songs. The real enemies were the traitors, men now beyond the discipline of dining-hall abuse, and consequently a song of denunciation had no direct function – it could serve only as a personal release for a singer, unbearably galled, or else as a general goad to the virtue of the company that remained. Not surprisingly, Alcaeus' attacks are of the latter sort. Like Archilochus, he can be crude (Pittacus, who seems to have been a little lame, is variously called Dragfoot, Crackfoot and Floorsweeper, as well as Potbelly and Paunchy, 429V), but unlike Archilochus he does not choose his targets according to the quirks of his own private rage. Instead, he lampoons or excoriates a victim for violation of the canons

---

that the people of this place were enemies of Mytilene (unless the Lesbians made a raid into this area in connection with the mysterious expedition against Erythrae referred to in 444V), and consequently it is usually assumed that the young man must have been serving as a mercenary, perhaps in the pay of Lydia. This in turn leads some to the conclusion that he, and consequently the whole faction, must have been abroad in exile at the time, which would date this and the Amardis song to the period of the third exile. This follows, however, only if the youth was a member of the aristocracy; if he were not, he might have served with a foreign army at any time. Treu (*QU*, 1966, 20ff.) wonderfully identifies the kalos-boy as Pittacus, and then supposes that the tyrant, having given up his rule after the ten year stint, accepted a command in the service of Lydia and died among the Allienoi in about 475 (at what would surely have been a very advanced age for a mercenary captain). He further supposes the Alcaic faction to have been still in exile at this date, and to have returned to Mytilene only in consequence of Pittacus' foreign death!

[28] Since all of these matters come up in an erotic context, it is possible that the 'blood' of the first boy, and even his service and death abroad, may render sexual adventures in military language, in which case Alcaeus has merely been the butt of scandalous innuendo and the author of a bit of sexual calumny.

[29] There were Amardoi near the Caspian; see Barner, loc.cit.

of class – that class of nobles whose ethical health he equated with the health of the society – and so the same aristocratic norms that were dramatised in the call for a Fury (129V) appear as explicit or implicit standards even when the mode is savagely satirical. In one song, for example (167V),[30] a passage of gross abuse in which a defector is called 'Skunk Cabbage' and perhaps also 'Goat' gives way to a conclusion in which the singer reminds his audience that they are sons of soldier-fathers who once fought against the Athenians. As such, they are called upon in a final sequence to launch their 'swift ships' into the sea of new patriotic activity, as the shrillness of insult is replaced by the deeper tones of hortatory song.

The same note of generalised and impersonal outrage is sounded in three fragments that attack Pittacus on the score of his marriage. In what seems to be the first of these (5V),[31] the alliance is evidently only projected by certain men who busy themselves about improper things (9–10) while the bridegroom hopes, once 'she' is sweetly his, to hold the sceptre of a king (11–14).[32] Opprobrium is limited to the single term 'lance-bearer', attached to the would-be groom, and this hardly seems to be a jibe at all, since Lesbian nobles might carry such an arm (cf. 179V). The term could, it is true, denote a member of an élite corps (cf. comment at 60V), and possibly Alcaeus uses it to insinuate that in the past Pittacus was no more than a bodyguard to Myrsilus. Even if this is the poet's meaning, however, the song appears to do very little injury to its ostensible victim. It suggests that things are out of order when a man trades a lance for a sceptre (especially when he does so by marital, not martial exploits) but it ends with a commonplace trope that gives the whole performance a tone of exemplary self-righteousness. 'Let evil come to me, whenever I make a marriage of that kind!' may be said in formal condemnation, but hardly in rage.[33]

The next fragment in this series (75V) links the Penthilid name with the tyrant who has just overturned the state (10–11), and seems to say that one disgrace has produced another. As a child, the singer

[30] See Barner, *Neuere Alk.-Pap.*, 162ff. It is usually assumed that this song was aimed at Pittacus, the most notorious oath-breaker in the Alcaic oeuvre. There were, however, surely others who defected as well, and in this particular song the reference to Phrynon would seem to militate against any effective defamation of Pittacus, since it would inevitably remind listeners of Pittacus' heroic role at Sigeum.

[31] The fragment does not explicitly refer to Pittacus, but the statement that the marriage will bring something royal to the groom makes the supposition all but sure.

[32] See Theander's reconstruction at 13–14: ἐλπεταί πο]τα καῦταν γλυκέως [σχέθων / σκᾶπτρον ὡς βα]σιλεὺς ἔχην 'De Alcaei poematis' *Aegyptus* 32 (1952) 182ff.

[33] Compare 67V, an attack on the score of oath-breaking where the target, probably Pittacus, is called nothing worse than 'not unintelligent', i.e. 'wily', and the poetic concern is all for the constitution of the city: 'He wasn't without calculation . . . when he kept watch at the altar of the son of Leto, that no one of the kakopatrids should become prominent.'

saw (or was too young to see) a shameful action on the part of the royal family,[34] and now he sees it reduplicated among these same men of error, who will have to bear its consequences.[35] The thought is obscure, but its key lies probably in the gossip that Aristotle repeats (*Pol.* 1311b) when he says that the old king Penthilus was overthrown because he had stolen the wife of a certain foreigner named Smerdis. If this is the ancient shame that has produced a new and more disgusting version of itself, the shape of the present song becomes clear. The old royal misalliance had merely caused a king to fall, but this new one has done much worse, for it has raised a tyrant to power and paradoxically created a government that favours the base-born.[36] Once again, the Penthilids are the ostensible targets of abuse, and once again (as far as one can tell) there is no invective, crude or otherwise. The pattern of cause and effect that is discovered is a bitter one, but its presentation gives the poem a wise, indeed an almost Aeschylean, sound that links it with the mythic songs rather than with those where the anger is raw.

The third fragment is only hypothetically connected with the marriage, since there are no proper names to fix its reference (296aV), but its subject and its oblique approach seem to connect it with the other two.[37] In it someone is scolded for having had the reckless notion that Love might prove placable (1–2). Evidently he acted on his idea, but success did not follow, and instead the city has been destroyed by the will of Cronian Zeus (3). There has been conflict and men have died (4–5), men whose loss means that no soldierly work can be attempted now (6).[38] What was splendid and noble has been debased (7),[39] and a certain one deserves to be taken like a lion and flayed (8). The first man's[40]

---

[34] Page (*S&A*, 152) assumes that the incident remembered from childhood must have been one that concerned Pittacus, but this is because he is attempting to establish the relative ages of Alcaeus and Pittacus and makes no attempt to find the sense of the song.

[35] See the ambitious reconstruction offered by Theander (ibid. 187) where Dracon is named as the immediate recipient of the song's abuse.

[36] It is impossible to say how the κακοπατριδ[of line 12 applies since its case can't be fixed, but probably it somehow describes the tendency of Pittacus or his government.

[37] For fullest discussion, see Barner, *Neuere Alk.-Pap.*, 42–52.

[38] For πόνος as a work of war, cf. 350,4V and 6,2V (in the ship metaphor); compare also the ἔργον of 140,15V.

[39] As a noun, ἔσλος denotes a man honoured by others as having rank at 360,2V; at 391V it indicates the common sense of high rank that can unify divided groups; at 6,14V and 72,13V it is the epithet of fathers who confer such rank upon their sons. Here the neuter plural seems to refer to institutions built upon inherited rank.

[40] Barner (ibid., 47) and others assume that the man with the curious idea is the same as the lion-man below, but the rhetoric of the song seems to distinguish them. If the]δη of 3 is, as Page supposes, part of ἐπειδή, then the sense seems to be 'he thought . . . but then look what happened', and this separation of the initial man's intention from the rest of the song seems to be borne out by the probable ἀλλα in line 2. Even if (as Hamm suggests) the reading of line 8 is ὁδ᾽ ἠς, this final reference need not be to the initial man since a closer antecedent probably stood in the lost intervening lines.

attempt to manipulate Eros[41] has brought not love but a destructive beast into the city, a showy royal animal whose pelt would be worth taking: this seems to be the (once more Aeschylean) shape of the song's conceit. The scorn of the early lines gives way to an angry grief that is disciplined by reference to Zeus and Hades, but then – at the idea that further action is impossible – civilised emotions are replaced by a primitive desire for blood. The banal phrases about the foul and the fine are interrupted by the vital and unexpected figure of the beast, but he appears, pelted and dangerous though he is, only to be reduced to hideous bloody meat in the fantasy of the closing syllables.[42] This lion evidently represents one who would behave like a king, and it seems highly likely that Alcaeus meant him as the Pittacus whose marriage made him an in-law of the deposed royal family.

If it is indeed the husband of Penthilus' daughter who ought to be skinned of his cruel pretensions, then the man who thought to use Eros as an ameliorating power in Mytilenean politics is someone (perhaps, though not necessarily, a Penthilid) who favoured the marriage on the grounds that it might appease Pittacus' ambition and so soften the factional strife. Or perhaps he only hoped for advantage for himself, this man with the extraordinary idea. If his interests were selfish, he would be all the more deserving of the song's initial attack, but whatever his motives, it is plain that Alcaeus uses him only as a foil. His all too mortal foolishness has robbed the Alcaic faction of lives and, worse, of future hopes, but it is merely contemptible by comparison with the violence of the beast who has entered the city to destroy the whole order of society.[43]

In the ideal symposium the friendly jibe, the scolding administered to the whole party, and the laughing vilification of self were expressions of a confident unity. By such rough means the group kept its members' courage up, but since they had no real doubts of their own martial virtues, their self-denigration had about it a certain happy complacency, as, for example, when Alcaeus unmasks his brother's boasts or confesses to his own lost shield. Among comrades of uncertain faith, on the other hand, where treason and despair were real, a singer would sometimes deal in genuine recrimination and also in genuine shame. There is one piece, indeed, that seems to be a point-blank denial of everything that had made Alcaeus proud when he performed the song of the Hall of Arms (140V). It begins with an attack upon Pittacus, whose lyre is to be heard at the licentious banquets of thieves

---

[41] Page (*S&A*, 299f.) assumed that the mention of *eros* meant that the initial man was somehow bound by love to Alcaeus; he then made this man into one who stayed behind and didn't go into exile with the rest, and finally identified him as Deinomenes.

[42] For a similar fantasy of hunting down the tyrant, see 306g,1–8V, where men are to spring upon the back of Pittacus: ἐνθορεῖν καὶ ἐνορμ[ῆσαι τοῖς τοῦ Φιττάκ[ο]υ νώτ[οις.

[43] Compare the end of 129V for a similar sudden unleashing of final hatred.

since his marriage with a Penthilid, but the charge, though full of contempt, is coolly and almost formally made (70, 3–5V). It is only a preface, and in the next stanza the poet reveals that the true victim of his attack is his own sympotic audience, to whom he addresses an angry and sarcastic[44] imperative that in effect accuses them of having forgotten their proper work (70V):

].[.].χ....[
π.[.]τωι τάδ' εἴπην ὀδ.υ..[
ἀθύρει πεδέχων cυμποcίω.[
βάρμοc, φιλώνων πεδ' ἀλεμ[άτων
εὐωχήμενοc αὔτοιcιν ἐπα[5
—
χῆνοc δὲ παώθειc 'Ατρεῖδα[ν] .[
δαπτέτω πόλιν ὡc καὶ πεδὰ Μυρcί[λ]ω[
θᾶc κ' ἄμμε βόλλητ' "Αρευc ἐπιτ.ύχε..[
τρόπην· ἐκ δὲ χόλω τῶδε λαθοίμεθ..[9
—
χαλάccομεν δὲ τὰc θυμοβόρω λύαc
ἐμφύλω τε μάχαc, τάν τιc 'Ολυμπίων
ἔνωρcε, δᾶμον μὲν εἰc ἀυάταν ἄγων
Φιττάκω⟨ι⟩ δὲ δίδοιc κῦδοc ἐπήρ[ατ]ον.   13

. . .

So be it. Let this bridegroom of the Atreids   6
devour the city (as he did
with Myrsilus) until Lord Ares shall
return us to our arms, but may we then forget

[44] The heavy sarcasm is not always recognised, with the result that some critics read a song in which Alcaeus sincerely urges his friends to give up their resistance and let the tyrant have his way. Treu (*Alk.*, 114) discovers a new wisdom and moderation in this advice, as Alcaeus expresses 'den Wunsch, dass einst die Zeit käme, wo man den Groll vergessen könnte und der Bruderkampf ein ende fände, in den ein Daimon des verblendete Volk getrieben hat'. Readings such as this are, however, made impossible by the verb δαπτέτω, for if the poet were urging collaboration and resignation, he might say, 'Let him rule', or 'Let him bring us some order', but he could not say 'Let him gorge himself upon the city', since this suggests the confiscation of aristocratic property. Certainly Alcaeus calls for an abandonment of stasis, but by this he means strife among the various anti-Pittacus factions, a strife that will be forgotten when Ares is once more ascendant among them and they remember to make war where they should – against the tyrant. (In 130b.iiV stasis should be maintained as war against a tyrant, presumably Myrsilus.) The proposition is that the *hetaireia* should forget its inner dissensions, and that the various clans should forget their struggles, all of them allowing Ares to turn them to their true work, the defence of Mytilene against enemies outside or within.

our present bile, relax our canker'd hatreds[45]
and give up this cousin-strife that some Olympian
has roused to bring disaster to our city
even as he offers lovely fame to Pittacus!

Myrsilus is dead and Pittacus is moving towards his final assertion of power. An aristocracy too anarchic to resist seems to sanction his depredations, and soon a 'crowd of cheering citizens' will make him 'tyrant of this evil-fated lily-livered city' (348V). At this point, however, the Alcaic faction is still in the city; they can still resist, and the singer hectors them as if this were the eve of battle and they a reluctant army that must be whipped into combat. They are men of Ares (their arms gleam for his pleasure, 140.3V, and they hold it a privilege to die in his service, 400V), and yet they are passive, weakened by an evil to which Alcaeus gives three magic names, as if he hoped to exorcise it. Rancour, dissension, and family quarrels devour the hearts of his friends, making them unfit for their work, and so the singer says with bitter irony, 'As long as you are in your present state you are right not to resist.'[46] Nevertheless, he means to cure them of this wasting, aristocratic disease, and to do so he must make them truly angry. In their condition mere scorn will not touch them sharply enough, and so he adds mock-praise for their opponent. Pittacus is a beast who devours the goods of the state (7); his rise means the doom of the noble Lesbian host (*damos*, 12), but the song perversely displays him as bridegroom and victor. Indeed, it almost offers the traditional *makarismos*, for it hails a man who is at the height of blessedness, one who dines among the descendants of Atreus (6), rejoices in the favour of heaven (11), and receives the imperishable glory that all worthy men long to possess (13). Such a vision of the enemy in possession of the blessings of victory is an insult to all those who hate Pittacus, and it is offered knowingly, that it may inspire rage in every listener. The present divisive bile (*cholos*, 9) is to be swallowed up in

[45] The modal sequence at 9ff. is difficult, and Wilamowitz (*NJA* 33, 236) proposed changing the optative λαθοίμεθα to a subjunctive, so that the whole would depend upon θᾶς κε: 'until Ares shall decide ... and until we forget ... and relax ...' This produces a song that says, 'Let him go ahead until some vague further time when we are changed ...', thus leaving all its weight upon the virtually unchecked imperative 'Let him devour!' Massa Positano (*PP* 1, 369f.) proposed keeping the optative but taking χαλάσσομεν as future: 'potremo dimenticarsi di quest' odio e quindi disisteremo ...' Page, however, shows (*S&A*, 235) that the sequence of optative and subjunctive is not impossible: 'This our anger may we utterly unlearn again; let us abate ...'

[46] Compare the opinion of Perrotta, who reads a song that is sarcastic and scornful from beginning to end, one that expresses total disillusionment by saying, 'Oh yes, let's give the lie to our anger and quit this civil war and let Pittacus have his glory ... that seems to be what you want to do!' Like Treu and others, he assumes that forgetting stasis means giving up the fight against Pittacus, but unlike them he belives that Alcaeus speaks of such a truce with disgust: 'egli parla perfino con rabbia sdegnosa della pace' ('Alceo', *A&R*, ser. 3, 4, 1936, 226).

a larger anger like that of a buried hero against a foreign invader. As usual, Alcaeus sings to the members of his own *hetaireia*, but it is hard not to think that this time he hoped that his words would reach the ears of all men of quality, whatever their factional alliances might be – *ottines esloi ummeōn te kai ammeōn* (391V).

When the faction seemed to have forgotten its work, a given member no longer felt a perfect identification with the group, and consequently it was possible to stand apart and abuse it with real scorn. In the same way this lack of identification meant that when a man was physically separated from the *hetaireia* he no longer felt the support of its invested faith. He was prey to a sense of alienation unthinkable in a member of the ideal group, and he could suffer a collapse of will and a loss of pride such as Alcaeus describes in a unique song – the only one in his corpus to treat a state of mind (130b). It is a dramatic monologue and its imaginary scene is a hiding place at some distance from Mytilene, where the singer is in exile and alone.[47] He addresses an absent friend, Agesilaïdas,[48] in the following way:

> ’Αγνοις..ϛβιότοις..ις ὁ τάλαις ἔγω
> ζώω μοῖραν ἔχων ἀγροϊωτίκαν
> ἰμέρρων ἀγόρας ἄκουσαι
> καρυ[ζο]μένας ὦ (’Α)γεϲιλαῖδα   4
> ⟨—⟩
> καὶ β[ό]λλας· τὰ πάτηρ καὶ πάτεροϲ πάτηρ
> κα⟨γ⟩γ[ε]γήρας’ ἔχοντες πεδὰ τωνδέων
> τὼν [ἀ]λλαλοκάκων πολίταν
> ἔγ[ω . ἀ]πὺ τούτων ἀπελήλαμαι   8
> ⟨—⟩

[47] It is generally supposed that the imaginary situation belongs to the time of the first exile. Kamerbeek, however, (op.cit., pt.2, 179) supposes that line 14 refers to wanderings and consequently indicates the second; it is hard to follow either his reading or his reasoning, but there is no internal evidence which makes the time of the first necessarily preferable to the time of the second. All that can be said for certain is that the singer is supposed to be still on Lesbos. Mazzarino (op.cit., 63, note 1) supposed that the apparently perfect form in line 6 meant that the father and grandfather of the singer must still be alive, and concluded that Alcaeus must have been under 30 when the song was composed. To get rid of the perfect, Page proposed κἀπὶ γῆρας as an alternative, with ἔζων at the beginning of the following line, though admitting this to be unlikely (*S&A*, 203–4). A. Luppino argued for a much later time, on the untenable grounds that the longing for the herald's cry meant that agora and council were not only distant but abolished by the tyrant; as for the father and grandfather, they were not specifically the poet's, but indicated forebears in general ('Sul carme di Alceo in esilio', *RFIC* 90, 1962, 34).

[48] Mazzarino, op.cit., 53, note 4 suggests taking Ὠγεσιλαῖδα as (ἐγὼ) ὁ Ἀγεσιλαῖδα = 'I, an Agesilaid', and consequently as an indication of the poet's family name, but there is nothing to recommend the notion.

φεύγων ἐϲχατίαιϲ’, ὠϲ δ’ Ὀνυμακλέηϲ
ἔγθα[δ’] οἶοϲ ἐοίκηϲα λυκαιμίαιϲ
·[   ]ον [π]όλεμον· ϲτάϲιν γὰρ
πρὸϲ κρ.[....]. οὐκ †ἄμεινον† ὀννέλην·   12
〈—〉
·].[...].[..]. μακάρων ἐϲ τέμ[ε]νοϲ θέων
ἐοι[.....] μϝ[λ]αίναϲ ἐπίβαιϲ χθόνοϲ
χλι.[.].[.].[.]ν ϲυνόδοιϲί μ’ αὔταιϲ
οἴκημι κ[ά]κων ἔκτοϲ ἔχων πόδαϲ,   16
〈—〉
ὄππαι Λ[εϲβί]αδεϲ κριννόμεναι φύαν
πώλεντ’ ἐλκεϲίπεπλοι, περὶ δὲ βρέμει
ἄχω θεϲπεϲία γυναίκων
ἴρα[ϲ ὀ]λολύγαϲ ἐνιαυϲίαϲ   20
〈—〉
        ].[ʼ].[.]. ἀπὺ πόλλων πότα δὴ θέοι
        ].[ʼ]ϲκ...ν Ὀλύμπιοι·
                     ]......
·γα[   ]...μεν.   24

                    ...I
live as wretchedly as any peasant,
though I long to hear the cry that sounds
assembly, O Agesilaïdas,

and the council's sitting. Rights
my father and his father held for life
among these same unruly[49] citizens
are lost to me, for I am driven out,

an exile in the brush, an Onomaklees!
Some time I lived alone in wolf-haunts
[where I dreamed of] war, for it is base
to quit the fight against [such enemies].

[Now] in a precinct of the blessed gods
. . . treading the dark earth . . .
. . . in their festivals; here
I make a home and keep away from harm

where long-robed island girls parade
their beauty and are judged, the grove
resounding with a sacred note as women raise
the loud perennial cry . . .

---

[49] The word is ἀλλαλοκάκοι: literally 'men who harm one another'. This activity in a citizen-body amounts to self-mutilation, the most unthinkable of actions to a Greek, and it expresses Alcaeus' judgment of noblemen who allow a tyranny inimical to their own privileges.

...gods
...Olympians

The song begins by describing exile negatively, as the absence of city and power and masculine company, and it ends by redescribing it in an opposite fashion – as the presence of temple and feminine gatherings. What is lost is imaged by a herald's cry that cannot be heard; what is at hand, by a cry of another sort – the women's shout of thanksgiving that echoes loud and clear. The two descriptions are not baldly juxtaposed, however, nor are they evaluated negatively and positively so as to produce the statement: 'Exile means loss, but see what a lovely gain!'[50] On the contrary; a modulation is made from one to the other by way of an intervening phase – that of the wolfish habitation – and it is plain that the poem is not making any crude choice (or establishing any narrative sequence) with its three localities.[51] Rather, they are offered as equal components in the self-portrait of an exile, and this fact is made plain by the schematic use of three verbs meaning 'I live.' In line 2, it is 'I live wretchedly, having a peasant's portion . . .'; in line 31, it is 'I live safely in the *temenos* . . .'; and in between, at line 25, 'I lived in solitude, like a wolf'. The three superimposed states of life are correlated with three sorts of company as well as three places, for in the first the exile longs for political assemblies, in the third he is present at religious assemblies, and in the second, bridging instance, he is in the company of beasts, while he reflects upon the abandonment of those factional meetings and conspiracies which ought to prosecute war.

There is evidently more than one way of looking at the exile's state, and the song begins with the suggestion that it might have its heroic aspect. The first words carry an intentional reminder of Achilles in his wrath, for they derive from the passage at *Il.* 1.488ff. where the hero's first withdrawal is described:

> Nor did he go to the soldiers' assembly that brings a man honour,
> nor did he go into battle, but wasted his heart with his grieving,
> holding apart, though he longed for the one and the other.

Achilles grieved for the loss of politics (*agora*) and war (*polemos*) and it is the same *agora* that Alcaeus' refugee longs for, the same *polemos*

---

[50] For a contrary opinion, see P. Chantraine, rev. of Gallavotti, *SeA, Rev. Phil.* 24 (1950) 76f., who finds a 'beau mouvement . . . il s'y plaint . . . mais il trouve la paix dans ce sanctuaire'; likewise W. J. W. Koster, 'Ad Alcaei carmen recens inventum', *Mnem.* 4 (1951) 9–29, 'quam secura quiete gaudens' and Treu (*Alk.*, 120), who reports that the exile's bitterness becomes joy and fulfilment because of his glimpse of beauty.

[51] Because the song does not behave like a piece of prose, some critics have despaired of it. Kirkwood (*EGM*, 72) baldly reported that it contained 'no concerted, organized sense', and even Fränkel saw it as typical of a certain wilful Alcaic spontaneity and inconsistency (*DuP*, 216; cf. 218).

that his wolf-like fugitive still thinks of. Nevertheless, the suggestion
that the singer might be another Achilles is undermined by the fact
that he has been forced into exile and it is made positively ridiculous
by the word *agroiōtikos* which, as we know from Sappho, expresses
everything that is rude and contemptible from an urban point of view.
With this epithet attached to his lot, the singer becomes an absurd
country bumpkin who presumes when he likens himself to Achilles.
He has not withdrawn in dignity to a rich tent where he dwells with
his Myrmidons; he has been driven from town and he hides alone in
backwoods wretchedness. The effect is satiric, and it prepares for
further self-denigration to come, for the exile's occupation of the shrine
is explicitly labelled as anti-heroic by the phrase 'keeping my feet out
of trouble' (line 16). The words indicate a weak and unmanly caution
and they are the forerunners of taunts frequently made in tragedy
against collaborators and opportunists (e.g. Oceanus at Aesch. *PV* 264,
cf. 344; Odysseus at Soph. *Phil.* 1260).[52] A posture of cowardly self-
preservation cannot be reconciled even with ordinary manliness, and
when it is assumed by one who has reminded us of Achilles, the effect
is disastrous. If this is an Achilles, it is certainly not the angry hero
of epic but instead the folk-tale child who was hidden by his mother
in a *gunaikeion*, among the girls of Lycomedes' court (Apollod. 3.13.8).

Nor is our sense that this languishing exile is the opposite of an
Achilles ameliorated by his transitional phase of wolfishness. Instead,
the wolf image serves in the same way that the Homeric echo does,
for it too measures the degree to which the singer has fallen away
from his ideal. The wolf as a rule figures the liminal and consequently
suggests the initiate, the scapegoat and the exile,[53] but the animal
also represents the bold aggressor, in comparison with the fox or the
dog who fawns and tries to live by its wits.[54] Consequently, when the
singer places himself in a wolf-thicket, he seems about to romanticise
himself by suggesting that he has become a fierce and solitary killer
whose raids are to be feared. Nevertheless there is here (just as in the
previous stanza) a touch of deflating satire, for Alcaeus adulterates
his animal comparison with another, naming someone who was evidently proverbial as a wild-man. He can claim only to be a beast-like

---

[52] Compare also E. *Hipp.* 1293, where Artemis recommends such skulking to one who
has sinned as Thesus has; E. *Hcld.* 109, where the base herald argues that it is a fine
thing to keep one's feet from trouble; Aesch. *Cho.*696, where Clytemnestra uses the
phrase to describe Orestes' behaviour before he decided to avenge his father. It is
especially interesting to note Pindar's remark, at *P.*4.287, that the most painful part of
an exile's condition is his enforced abstention from noble deeds: καλὰ γιγνώσκοντ᾽ ἀνάγκα
ἐκτὸς ἔχειν πόδα. It sounds as if Alcaeus' song lay behind this later phrase.

[53] See H. Jeanmaire, *Couroi et Courètes* (Lille 1939) 558ff.; L. Gernet, 'Dolon le loup',
Anthropologie de la Grèce Antique (Paris 1968) 189–208; R. Goossens, 'Notes sur
quelques papyrus littéraires', *CE* 19 (1944) 267; *RE* sv 'Lycabas'.

[54] Compare the 'wily fox' of 69V, and the fox-wolf sequence at *P.P.*2, 76ff.

misanthrope who skulks and fulminates, and when he arrives at the concept of war (26)[55] he suddenly abandons even this ground. With the anti-gnomic statement that it is *not* good to give up the fight against opponents like his[56] – however often one may have been told to bow to superior force[57] – the exile frankly labels his own inactivity as 'base', and once this admission is made the whole attempt to see himself as a bold and dangerous beast collapses. The exile begins on his third and final depiction of himself, and at once confesses that he is not a fearsome and aggressive creature in a habitat of matching savagery. Instead, he is the furthest thing from it – a man so quiet and insignificant that his presence does not even disturb that most fastidious of celebrations, the ritual contest that was held annually to find the prettiest girl on Lesbos.[58]

In his final manifestation, the singer is not growling in a thicket; he is not even suffering peasant hardships; instead he is resting among the sweet scents and sounds of a temple enclosure, exactly like some faint-hearted youngster who chooses to linger with the women when the trumpet sounds. He is a man who would wish to be a wolf if he cannot be a soldier, but exile has made him a coward in action, without giving him the nature of a coward. It has taken his function and his class and his pride from him, and he has lost not just the city of the herald's cry, not just the honours that his forefathers knew, but his ferocity and his masculine identity. He does not doubt his cause, but shame makes him doubt himself, and for this exile's shame Alcaeus has found three images: the rustic who would be a raging hero, the

[55] The present interpretation assumes that the sense of line 11 is not φεύγων τὸ]ν πόλεμον as so often proposed, but something more like Page's '[planning] war'. Stasis should not be given up, but should be transformed into war when it is a question, not just of jockeying for power, but of rescuing the city from those who would change its form of government.

[56] Reading οὐ κάλλιον in line 27 with Page. Earlier editors took ὀννέλην in this passage to mean 'take up the fight', and thus achieved a comfortable statement that it is unwise to struggle against those who are superior in strength, but A. Vogliano ('Per il nuovissimo Alceo', *Athen.*21, 1943, 125–6) pointed out that the correct meaning is precisely the opposite: ὀννέλην = 'give up the fight' (cf. P. Chantraine, op.cit., 80). In addition, Page insisted (*S&A*, 206) that the letter that follows κρ in line 12 cannot be an epsilon, and that κρέσσονας is thus impossible (as is κόρτερον misspelled as κρότερον) and consequently 'the MS evidence cannot be said to support the opinion that superiors were mentioned here'. Some have persevered in versions of the older readings, however: G. M. Bolling, 'Textual notes', *AJP* 82 (1961) 162 suggested πρὸς κρέσσονος, 'to kill our stasis at the bidding of a mightier man is not best'. A. Luppino, op.cit., 35, would have the poet judge not the present but the past, by saying 'best would be not to have laid down the stasis', but the simplest way to take the thought is 'to give up or abolish stasis against such enemies is *not* the best thing'.

[57] The old saw that Alcaeus here reverses can be found in Hesiod (*Erg.* 210): ἄφρων ὅς κ' ἐθέλῃ πρὸς κρείσσονας ἀντιφερίζειν. Compare also P.O.10.39–40 and N.10.72.

[58] Athenaeus (13.610 = Theophr. 112) mentions a *kallisteia* at the temple of Hera; cf. AP 9.189.1ff. and for similar rites, note Schol.A.*Il*.1.129; Hesych. sv Πυλαιΐδες; *RE* 10. 1674, 2ff.; 11.2122, 38ff.

bogey-man who would be wolf, and the nobleman who lies passive among women when he ought to be fighting in the midst of his fighting faction.[59]

---

[59] Usually the song is described as one of 'self-pity and resignation' (so Page, *S&A*, 208); cf. Kamerbeek, op.cit., pt.2, 161, 'mi-mélancholique, mi ironique ... amère résignation'; Luppino (op.cit., 38) thought that it became melodramatic, as the women's cries joined the poet's 'grido di dolore'. Closer to the present interpretation is that of Gallavotti, who reported that it was 'la sua natura stessa che grida di volersi lanciare nei cimenti e nella lotta della vita attiva' (*Storia*, 61). Kamerbeek (in spite of the sheep that he discovered in the οἶος of line 25) likewise perceived the sense of shame that is central here when he explained, 'Poetam bellicosum versantem in templo ubi virgines pulchritudinis certamen habere solent, se ipsum cum lupo sive versipelli deverso in ovile comparare non absurdum est' (op.cit., 155). He cites the wonderfully appropriate passage from Plutarch, *de exilio* 12. 604B: ἀλλὰ μὴν τῷ «οὐκ ἄρχομεν οὐδὲ βουλεύομεν οὐδ᾽ ἀγωνοθετοῦμεν» ἀντίθες τὸ «οὐ στασιάζομεν».

Art Songs

There is one last set of Alcaic songs in which the singer, though he still stands among them, looks beyond his immediate companions to address an audience made up of men in general. These songs treat subjects like the efficacy of prayer or the disproportion of cause to effect, but their scale is miniature, their manner peculiarly Alcaic, and so it is in these, the 'art songs', that the poet is at once most available to moderns and most distinctively himself. In addition, he is at his most tranquil, as he sings these songs, for he does not press upon particular listeners, urging pride or love or scorn or shame, nor does he attempt to influence his supernatural auditors.[1] Instead, he treats of open and immutable problems, observing the shapes that destiny can take and amusing himself by casting the largest conceivable questions into the tightest of forms. This fitting of great wisdom to a few words was of course a favourite ancient game, but Alcaeus' mode of play was a special one. He did not produce the gnomes and aphorisms that rolled from the mouths of sages and wiseacres, but found his truths (or rather, pointed to places where they might reside) much as the dancing chorus did, employing myth as his investigative implement. Images drawn from the old stories could make a poet's thought sensual, but this was not just a technique for enrichment. Choruses danced to reconstitute mythic scenes, that their passing celebrations might be touched with permanence, and in the same way Alcaeus composed songs in mythic ciphers so that his momentary speculations might become solid and resistant to forgetfulness.

Of course the idea that myth provided a norm for reality was a

---

[1] Some have complained of this tranquillity; see, e.g., A. Setti, 'Nota a un nuovo frammento di Alceo', *SIFC* 28 (1956) 526 note 1, where the critic laments the absence of 'l'immediata spontaneità e la 'occasionalità' che si credevano essenziali all'antica lirica greca'. Wilamowitz had earlier objected, about the song of Helen and Thetis, 'es klingt zu Horazisch' (*NJA*, 1914, 393–4). Lesky with more objectivity describes these songs as 'kleine Schmuckstücke . . . für zwanglosen Vortrag in seinem Kreise' (*Gesch. der gr. Lit.*, Bern, 1957/8, 130).

commonplace among men who habitually justified actions by pointing to their mythic parallels. The art songs, however, assume and impose another and deeper conviction, according to which the enduring parts of human experience are found where life and myth (or myth and myth) are congruent. Myth does not provide mere isolated excuses, it displays illuminating designs which, once perceived, can lend a sense of order to man's patternless existence, and the poet's work is the discovery of such designs. Any mythic instant, properly examined, will betray patterns that rule its entire narrative, and the lyric process thus becomes one of selection, restriction and emphasis, as the lush detail of epic is cut away, the inner dynamic disclosed. This method would be brought to magnificent perfection by Pindar and Bacchylides, but Alcaeus proves that it can be employed even in monody, and his early and economical practices seem to have had great influence upon his more expansive followers. The later poets could indulge themselves not only with the movement and multiplicity of costumed dancers, but also with the licence of the periodic style and the length of a spectacle that did not have to pretend to spontaneity. Alcaeus, by contrast, stood alone with his lyre and sang the short Lesbian stanzas that imposed brevity upon each performance, since their too-frequent repetition would have meant musical banality. The shortness of his song imposed speed and compression; it made lavish decoration impossible, and what is more, it discouraged all those transitional passages and even the linguistic signals that ordinarily indicated the progress of thought. At the same time, however, this rapid sequence of miniature stanzas was perfectly suited to a mental process that was paratactic, symmetrical and dependent upon a strong sense of structure. No preliminary explanations were necessary, since a settled meaning already invested each scene or character and all the singer had to do was use his recurrent melody to mould his elements into shapes that matched, while he let the speed of the song superimpose them one upon another. By these means a performance that lasted only a moment or so could display its thought in the form of a complex emblem whose truth was inarguable.

Odd scraps seem to prove that Alcaeus in various places made use of the figures of Heracles, Perseus and Endymion,[2] but Achilles was evidently his favourite, for three of the four mythic songs that survive

---

[2] For Heracles, see Schol. at Hes. *Theog.* 313 (=443V) who reports that Alcaeus treated Heracles' battle with the Hydra; for Perseus, see perhaps Inc. auct. 30V = 255 LP; for Endymion, 317V (see above, 136 note 31). Cf. also 306AiV, which seems to describe a mythic marriage (on this fragment see Barner, *Hermes* 95, 2 note 1); 7V may possibly tell the tale of Phalanthus, founder of Tarentum (cf. Paus. 10.13.10); also *P.Oxy.* 2506 fr. 147 may mention the murder of Phokos by Telamon.

use him as their central device.[3] One of these was so short (four two-line stanzas)[4] that the singer can hardly have begun before he came to the end, but nevertheless we find him using his finite instant of performance to seize upon another mythic instant whose consequences expand and multiply almost to infinity. Only the last three lines exist, but it is clear from them that in the missing five Alcaeus must have named Achilles, indicated the time when his Trojan anger was new, and caused him to invoke Thetis. Now, in the lines that we have, Alcaeus sends his song flying away from the earth's surface and up to the awesome spot where destiny is made, then stops it there with sudden finality. Achilles has summoned Thetis, Thetis has touched Zeus, and the future fate of two armies, as well as of Achilles, has been inexorably fixed (44V):

μ[.]ρ[. . . . .]νι κάκω περρ[

μάτε[ρ. . . . . . .]άϲδων ἐκάλη να[6

νύμφ[αν ἐνν]αλίαν· ἀ δὲ γόνων [ἀψαμένα Δίοϲ

ἰκέτευ[. . . . .]τω τέκεοϲ μᾶνιν [8

. . .

calling his mother by name, as Naiad, [supreme

Nymph of the Sea, and she, touching the knees of Zeus,
begged that the [fell] rage of her son [might prevail].[5]

The little song refers to a pair of actions that occupy (along with their immediate causes) the first book of the *Iliad*, while their eventual consequences fill up the following twenty-three.[6] With his eight-line ditty, Alcaeus might well have seemed a mosquito in a thunderstorm as he sang to such a grandiloquent accompaniment, but it is precisely its unthinkable compression that brings the present song to its truth. Its two appeals, in their epic description, are separated by many events and by more than a hundred-and-fifty stately dactylic lines, whereas here they are not only juxtaposed but actually mixed together by the prolonged phrase that brings Achilles' voice into the stanza of his mother's interview with Zeus. This phrase, in fact, contains consider-

---

[3] In addition, the singer makes a hymn-like definition of Achilles in 354V, calling him 'he who watches over Scythia', and the context gives some slight support to the idea that Achilles may have been described there as the lover of Iphigeneia (cf. *RE* i.223f.; Fleischer, *Myth.Lex.* 1.56ff.; Rohde, *Psyche*[2], 371, note 2; the Lesbians had interests in the Troad and certainly knew the tomb of Achilles there; see Schmid-Stählin, *Gesch.gr.Lit.* i.1, 413, note 2).

[4] A coronis marks line 8 as the end, and line 1 is taken as the beginning by all editors except Gallavotti.

[5] In l.6 reading Νά[ϊδ᾽ ὑπερτάτον with Page, and in l.8 [ὀλόαν] with Maas ap. Dl.[1]

[6] Achilles first calls upon Thetis at *Il.*1.351; she begins her address to Zeus at 502.

able instruction in the art of the art song, for it does much more than merely join two separate stanzas. Achilles' appeal mingles with that of Thetis, and as it does so it proves that there are not really two characters here, much less two distinct scenes; there is only a single successful action that is twice performed. Names are uncannily effective in prayer, prayer uncannily effective in fixing heaven's will, and Achilles has only to offer Thetis the primaeval watery epithets that remind her of her ancient power (he calls her only 'mother' in the parallel *Iliad* passage) and his desire, still unexpressed,[7] is at once fulfilled. Being perfectly made, this first petition finds an answer that is simultaneous with itself, and the immediacy of Thetis' response promises a like immediacy on the part of Zeus. The hero speaks, the machine of fate begins to move, and the listener seems to experience the old fairy-tale phrase, 'no sooner said than done'. And yet this very speed is terrible, bringing a pang that is a part of the poet's calculation, for no one's wish was ever granted just as he expected, and the honouring of Achilles' wrath would cost him all he cared for most. The song, in its naked brevity, thus announces that prayer is an avenue that can lead from choice to fate, but that it is dangerous, like all the other gifts of god, because it lends men powers that they cannot understand.[8]

A second more extensive song places the figures of Achilles and Paris so as to achieve a telling symmetry. The stanzas this time are of the four-line Sapphic sort, and the initial ones are lost, but nevertheless the four that survive display the Alcaic technique in its consummate form (283V):

καιν[.]ων.υγ[   ]ν[
   ωνενου.ππ.[   ]   2
—

---

[7] If the preceding lines had reproduced the speech of Achilles, lines 5–6 would represent a closing formula like the Homeric ὥς ἔφατ(ο), and this seems extremely unlikely since these complimentary names are proper to the beginning, not to the end of an address.

[8] The poem may have used its initial stanzas to touch upon the long toil at Troy, so as to show how Achilles' prayer gave the enemy, in an instant, the advantage they had been ten years seeking; this would produce an effect something like that at B.12.133ff., where the Trojan drive to the ships is made to follow immediately upon Achilles' withdrawal. There is no need to suppose that the song attached itself to any worldly occasion or present sympotic moment, but it is possible to imagine it as a song of supplication in which the singer says in effect: 'I call upon you, X, just as Achilles did upon Thetis, and may you be equally quick to respond.' Page (*S&A*, 282) suggested that it might have had a political application, the wrath of Achilles representing the wrath of Alcaeus against his enemies.

κ'Αλέναc ἐν cτήθ[ε]cιν [ἐ]πτ[όαιcε
θῦμον 'Αργείαc, Τροΐω⟨ι⟩ δ' [ἐ]π' ἄν[δρι
ἐκμάνειcα ξ[ε.]ναπάτα⟨ι⟩ 'πὶ π[όντον
    ἔcπετο νᾶϊ,   6

—

παῖδά τ' ἐν δόμ[ο]ιcι λίποιc[
κἄνδροc εὔcτρωτον [λ]έχοc .[
πεῖθ' ἔρω⟨ι⟩ θῦμο[ν   Λήδαc]
    παῖ]δα Δ[ίο]c τε   10
[—]

    ]πιε..μανι[
    κ]αcιγνήτων πόλεαc .[
    ].ἔχει Τρώων πεδίω⟨ι⟩ δά[μεντας
    ἕν]νεκα κήναc·   14
[—]

πόλ]λα δ' ἄρματ' ἐν κονίαιcι[
    ].εν, πό[λ]λοι δ' ἐλίκωπε[c
    ]οι..[ ]βοντο φόνω δ.[
    ]..[..]ευc·   18

     ... [Paris]. . .
startled the heart of Argive Helen,
fluttered it in her breast, and mad about
that host-cheating Trojan guest she took ship
    and followed him over the sea,

leaving behind her pretty child,
leaving her husband's sumptuous bed, for
[Cypris] had led her astray with lust,
    the daughter of Leda and Zeus.

   . . .
numerous brothers . . .[the dark earth keeps]
men who succumbed on the plain of Troy
    each for that woman's sake.

Plenty of chariots [broke] in the dust,
plenty of glancing youths [lay]
trampled . . . spilled blood
    making [Achilles glad.[9]

Two stanzas of cause are followed by two of effect as the poet observes the disproportion of errant beginnings to dreadful conse-

---

[9] On ll.8–10 see note 17 below; on l. 17, see note 11 below. In ll. 12–13 reading [μέλαινα / γα]ῖ' with Page, *CR* 4 (1954) 25, and in l. 18, δῖος 'Aχί[λλ]ευς with Vogliano.

quences.[10] Such is also the observation of both comedy and tragedy, but in this case we neither smile nor weep, for the song is so cunningly wrought that admiration drives out every other emotion and we are left with a truth that is as neutral and undeniable as fate itself. There is no time to lament, nor any impulse to do so, as the poem makes its light run from Sparta in one moment to Troy in another and proposes Paris' flirtation in the first spot as the immediate preliminary to Achilles' joy[11] in the second. It is outrageous that anonymous human lives should be shaped, or rather maimed, by patterns such as these, but the listener is not outraged. Instead he is invaded by an archaic sense of dazzled helplessness as the singer elegantly balances his disproportionate elements, even while he insists upon their grotesque unsuitability.[12]

In essence what the song does is create two separate devices, making them as different as possible while it yet sets them side by side and insists that they are the mirroring parts of a single design. The stanza that begins at line three displays one Spartan Helen, heart palpitating as she moves off, seemingly alone upon a single ship; the last stanza shows countless young Trojans, eyes no longer glancing[13] as they lie motionless among countless chariots that are likewise still. There is, in other words, a device for lust and a device for death, and their

[10] See the discussion of M. Treu, 'Die mythischen Balladen des Alkaios', *Antike Lyrik* (ed. Eisenhut, Darmstadt 1970) 53ff.

[11] For ἔχαιρε as the last word of line 17, see C. Gallavotti, 'Auctarium Oxy.' *Aeg.* 33 (1953) 161–2; his suggestion is accepted by Bowra, *GLP²*, 170, note 1. The word is at any rate a verb, one that sets Achilles apart from the fallen men, and one that commands the dative φόνῳ.

[12] This is not the opinion of most scholars. Page (*S&A*, 278): 'The tone of the narrative is clearly one of disapproval ... the story ... is portrayed as a great misfortune to the world, an illustration of the power of love for evil, of disaster as the wages of sin.' Bowra (*GLP²*, 170): 'In Helen's unfaithfulness Alcaeus sees the cause of a huge slaughter ... With his strong loyalties and hatred of treachery he was likely to draw such a moral from the old story.' Vogliano, *Il nuovo Alceo* (Rome 1952) 6, found a larger subject in the song, for he thought it expressed the poet's horror of war, but this idea was contested by A. Setti, 'Nota a un nuovo frammento di Alceo', *SIFC* 28 (1956) 519ff., who criticised the song as not strongly felt – a passionless and moralistic treatment of an old story in which the poet engaged in approval or disapproval of mythic personages. Barner (*Neuere Alk.-Pap.*, 219) calls the poem an accusation ('das Gedicht ist eine Anklage') and suggests that perhaps in its hostility to Helen it is a piece from a 'Dichterstreit' between Alcaeus and Sappho on the subject of Helen's culpability. Kirkwood (*EGM*, 91), speaks of the 'moral earnestness' of the piece and says, 'Paris is clearly a figure of evil.' Treu (*Alk.*, 131–2) likewise finds that the central concern of the song is to fix guilt upon Paris.

[13] The epithet ἐλίκωψ makes these young men beautiful, and so in formal terms worthy of Helen; it also creates a painful sense of the life that they have lost. Page cites Pfeiffer at Callim. fr. 299.1, and insists that the word means no more than 'dark-eyed', but any reference to the eye, unless it is specifically clouded or closed, is a reference to life, and it seems more likely that the ceaseless movement of the living eye is what is described here; cf. Barner, op.cit., 213, who suggests 'in der Blüte ihres Lebens' as the implication of the term.

contradiction is made as extreme as possible by the addition of further oppositions, one being female and the other male, one singular and the other plural, one active and the other passive. Restless desire at Sparta is followed by unrestful death on the plain at Troy, and meanwhile the poem shifts from the unique and specific to an emphatically multiple generality as one woman, heart, ship – all lively – produce many men, eyes, chariots – all dead.

What is the meaning of a causal sequence so random that it can begin with one pleasure-seeking woman and end with a multitude of corpses in a field? The tiny song openly poses the question that the vast complexities of epic had obscured, and offers two responses – one covert and structural, the other open and theological. First of all, it multiplies the two essential terms – Helen and the Trojan dead – and arranges what are finally six elements so as to make a kind of symmetry. The basic set is incompatible, and so the poet makes a ring around it, flanking its dread discrepancies with another pair of ciphers that are easier to reconcile, those of Paris[14] and Achilles. They are enemy opposites, Trojan and Greek, fop and warrior, and so they still represent two poles, but they are nevertheless conceptually identical since both are epic heroes. They suit one another as a pair of statues might, and consequently they lend an air of architectural stability to the unstable images that lie between.

In addition to this pair of added outer terms there is also an inner pair, to be found in the two central stanzas of the song, for here Helen's abandonment of one child[15] and one husband is set beside Paris' loss of twelve brothers, 'mastered' (*damentas*, 13) by death as a woman might be by love. The essential incompatibility remains, since the geographical division continues, with the Spartan side still feminine and active, the Trojans masculine and passive. Nevertheless, the numbers have been expanded on the one side and contracted on the other, so that instead of the absolute 'one' and 'many' we now have a roughly comparable 'two' and 'twelve'. A kind of transition has been made, at

---

[14] We do not know that Paris is the subject of ἐπτόαισε but we do know that he must have been established in some way in the lost first part of the song, as antecedent to the 'host-deceiving' Trojan of line 4. It is often supposed that it was Eros who 'startled' Helen's heart, but it is hard to see why, if the poet had initially given Eros this anthropomorphic form, he would then reduce him to a mere instrumental in line 9. Kypris startles the φρήν at AR 1.1232, but at E.*IA* 585–6 the exchange of glances between Helen and Paris causes the latter to be fluttered by love, and at Sappho 31.6V, it is the aspect or the situation of the beloved that agitates the lover's heart in her breast. The Euripides passage seems quite probably to derive in part from the present song, and consequently in this initial (elsewhere undescribed) encounter of Paris with Helen, Paris (or the beauty of Paris), would seem to be the most likely subject for the verb, especially if there is something pertaining to a horse in line 2.

[15] The abandoned Hermione was probably decorated with an epithet that made her either attractive or pathetic; Gallavotti suggested [ἐράνναν, Latte [ἄνηβον, Page [ἐρήμαν.

least in the realm of numbers, and at the same time the two sets have been given a common context of kinship which lends them a bit of sense, since brothers might understandably have to die in recompense for a host betrayed. These central terms complete the pattern and make it, as a pattern, perfectly satisfying. In addition, the potential shock of contact between Helen and the dead is both contained and absorbed, as the poet sings of a hero, of a woman, of family members; then of family members, corpses, and a hero again.

Symmetries of this sort create an illusion of meaning, and the speed of the whole performance is so great that the ultimate raging Aeacid seems to spring directly from the initial roguish guest. We are made to feel that the infamous Paris prepared the fame that Achilles would finally know, but nevertheless the poet has discovered a transcendant reality beyond this appearance, and he points to Aphrodite as the only true connection between Helen and the field at Troy. Helen, when she followed Paris, was quite out of her mind (*ekmaneisa*, 5), as anyone must be to prefer a 'host-cheating' stranger[16] to a husband's 'well-spread' bed. Unreason such as this is a form of possession, and the song locates the source of Helen's madness in the goddess who actively 'persuaded' the heart that Paris merely 'startled'.[17] Using lust as her instrument (*eroi*, 9), the Cyprian worked upon the fate-filled daughter of Leda and Zeus,[18] and this explanation is made just as the singer ends the Spartan section and begins upon his stanzas of Trojan consequences. The mention of Aphrodite lets the poem pass from Helen's chamber to the Trojan plain with its buried and its unburied dead, and it is she who finally makes the transition endurable, since corpses made by a goddess are easier to accept than corpses made by an impressionable queen. The two heroes seem to be partners in a war that finally surrounds Helen instead of emanating from her, but in reality Aphrodite is at its core, here in this tiny song, just as she was in the *Cypria*.

[16] The word ξενναπάτας may have been invented for this passage; it is next found in Ibycus S 151 SLG.

[17] There are in general two ways of restoring lines 8–10, both of which assume an operation of Aphrodite's at this point. The first is that of Maas, adopted by Bowra and Page, in which *thumos* is taken as subject: ὡ[ς ϝ᾿ὑπείκην / πείθ᾿ ἔρῳ θύμο[ς διὰ τὰν Διώνας / παῖ]δα Δ[ίο]ς τε. This makes elegant use of the dative ἔρῳ, but its employment of διά or ζά in this sense is not a common practice, and its attribution of persuasive power to the *thumos* is unusual. The alternative is to finish line 8 with [ἄλλα Κύπρις (Vogliano) or [ἀ θέος γὰρ (Latte), and to read θύμο[ν as the object of the persuasion, continuing with something like παράγοισα Λήδας]/παῖ]δα κτλ. This seems preferable to the first solution, since it avoids the awkward phrase with διά, uses *thumos* in a more archaic way, and emphasises Helen's divine paternity while associating the word 'child' with her. It may be noted that Page, who would have preferred to make Paris the subject, confessed himself unable to find a way of doing so (p.277); Treu, however, insisted that Paris must somehow have stood here.

[18] This effect of course will not be present for those who follow Maas, Bowra and Page in reading διὰ τὰν Διώνας παῖδα.

In a second poem about Helen, Alcaeus once again sings a very simple melody but raises questions of disturbing complexity by means of images that are bluntly juxtaposed. The four Sapphic stanzas that survive in this case seem to represent the whole of the piece, and once more they resume the full saga of the Trojan War, but this time, instead of a single analysis of cause and effect, the little song sketches two such systems and leaves its listener to explain their curious interconnection. Indeed, the search for explanations – for *logoi* – is seized upon by the poet as his point of departure (42V):[19]

ὠс λόγος κάκων ἀ[
Περράμω⟨ι⟩ καὶ παῖс[ι
ἐκ cέθεν πίκρον, π[
  ῎Ιλιον ἴραν.   4

―

οὐ τεαύταν Αἰακίδαι[c
πάντας ἐc γάμον μάχ[αρας καλέccαιc
ἄγετ' ἐκ Νή[ρ]ηοc ἔλων [μελάθρων
  πάρθενον ἄβραν   8

―

ἐc δόμον Χέρρωνοc· ἔλ[υcε δ'
ζῶμα παρθένω· φιλο[
Πήλεοc καὶ Νηρείδων ἀρίcτ[αc.
  ἐc δ' ἐνίαυτον   12

―

παῖδα γέννατ' αἰμιθέων [
ὄλβιον ξάνθαν ἐλάτη[ρα πώλων,
οἱ δ' ἀπώλοντ' ἀμφ' 'Ε[λέναι
  καὶ πόλιc αὔτων.   16

Men say that, [thanks to their evil deeds,]
grief came to Priam and to his sons –
bitterly, [Helen,] from you! – [when Zeus
    set fire to] sacred Ilium.

Not such a bride was she whom,
bidding the gods to his feast, the son
of Aeacus led forth from Nereus' halls –
    a delicate untouched girl –

[19] A few scholars have supposed that an initial stanza was lost, and that these are not the first words; so Wilamowitz *NJA* 33 (1914) 231; Q. Cataudella, *Intorno ai lirici Greci* (Rome 1972) 60–5 = *A&R* (1928) 81–5; H. Eisenberger, *Der Mythos in der aiolischen Lyrik* (1956) 61ff. The translation is based on Page's ἄ[χος ἔννεκ' ἔργων in l. 1, his [ί ποτ', 'Ωλεν', ἦλθεν in l. 2, his π[ύρι δ' ὤλεσε Ζεὺς in l. 3, his φιλό[τας δ' ἔθαλε in l. 10, the [φέριστον of Dl.¹ in l. 13, and Wilamowitz's Φρύγες τε at the end of l. 15.

into the centaur's cave. Chaste robes
he loosened and love [had its way
between this fair nymph and Peleus;
    then, when a year had gone,

she bore him a son, [strongest] of demi-gods,
driver of bays, the blessed charioteer. But
round about Helen, the [Phrygians] died
    and with them their city fell.

Why does Alcaeus place Thetis side by side with Helen? This is the usual critical question and it is answered all too often in a puerile way. The poet's intention, we are told, is to teach girls to be good girls, and so he has offered Thetis as a model to be imitated and Helen as one to be shunned![20] On the basis of this proposition a complacent critic will find the poem successful but trite (in that a naughty Helen suffers and a nice Thetis does not), while a slightly sharper scholar will report it as a failure even as a commonplace (since everyone knows that Thetis was neither happy with Peleus nor a model wife). The latter will at least be right in saying that the song in effect refuses to function as a cautionary tale, but the real truth is that it does not even do the first thing that scholars have generally asked it to do, since it does not, in fact, make its comparisons between a pair of female figures, whatever their fates or their natures. It is not two women, but two marriages that are here juxtaposed, and consequently we may as well ignore all of the standard judgments that have been made upon this song (most of them touched with disappointment if not downright distaste) [21] while we approach it afresh.

Here are four four-line stanzas almost innocent of verbal decoration, their narrative proceeding by a series of child-like statements that are joined paratactically. And here also are two brilliant and populous epic scenes. The implicit cast of characters is beyond count, since it

---

[20] See Page, *S&A*, 280. Just how this purpose is to be reconciled with an imagined recitation among friends 'sober and tipsy' I have not understood. Bowra, *GLP*[2], 169, concludes: 'The chief aim of the poem seems to be the emphasis which it gives to the good wife, Thetis, in antithesis to the faithless Helen.' Peter Smith, even though he finally finds the poem to be ironical (in a paper delivered to the APA, December 1975), speaks of the poet's 'distanced (and untraditionally critical) moral stance towards his epic subject', as well as of its 'celebration of virtue'. It should be noted, however, that one or two critics have been able to free themselves from the delusion that this is a 'moralising' poem; see Barner, op.cit., 220, and Cataudella, loc.cit.

[21] Wilamowitz (loc.cit.) found the song to be excessively artful and impersonal; A. W. Gomme ('Interpretations', *JHS* 77 (1957) 255ff.) objected because Alcaeus seemed to have forgotten that Greeks as well as Trojans died in the Trojan war; Page (loc.cit.) announced that the poem was redeemed only by a 'patriotic ring' in its praise of Achilles, and in general he rejoiced that such 'second-hand moralising' was 'almost unique here in Lesbian poetry'. Kirkwood approved the 'moral earnestness' that Page deplored, but discovered after all that the song was insufficiently profound (*EGM*, 90) and that the poet awkwardly forgot the tale of Thetis and failed to see the irony of Achilles the destroyer. Campbell (ad loc.) notes that Thetis is an 'odd choice'.

includes all the citizens of Troy and all the guests, mortal and divine, who attended the marriage of Peleus and Thetis. And in spite of its apparent simplicity the song is like a miniature wrought under a lens, for its organisation is almost as complex as its materials. It is made (like so much of archaic verse in general and like the song of Paris and Achilles in particular) of rings within rings, and it is put together like a puzzle where the placement of each element depends upon that of every other.

The outer, all-defining ring is created conceptually by the fall of Troy, for this is the subject of the first stanza and also of the last two lines of the final one. This circle of thought is made tight by a specific echo that has been arranged between the first and the fourth clausula, since the 'sacred Ilium' (*Ilion iran*) that is destroyed at line 4 falls again anonymously, as the city of the Phrygians, in the final line (*kai polis autōn*). The song thus finds its opportunity and its consummation in the fall of a Troy that loses its name, but just within this largest ring there is a second one, drawn now between the Helen[22] who is addressed in stanza one and the Helen who presides over the slaughter of the penultimate line. Inside this double circlet (Troy, Helen . . . Helen, Troy) an alternate subject is contained, defined by the clausulae of the two internal stanzas where a virginal bride and a gestational year are placed in responsion: *parthenon abran* and *es d' eniauton*. The song in this way enfolds the engendering and birth of Achilles within its Trojan disaster, as if this second but earlier set of events were somehow the core or the clue to the first. No explicit connection is made[23] but there is at least a bridge of wit, since the destructive fate[24] that appears in the first two lines of stanza one is said to have 'come forth from' Helen (*ek sethen*) as if by a process of birth, and in this way it is likened to the child who appears in the same lines of stanza four.[25] Of course, the bane is 'bitter' while the child is 'blessed', and what is more, Helen's offspring is actively destructive of children (*paisi*, 2; cf. the *paida* that opens line 13), but each in its way is the product and the measure of the marriage that brought it into being.

[22] In line 15 Helen's name is represented only by its initial letter, but it is generally recognised as having stood there. In line 2, Page's restoration [ποτ', Ἤλεν', ἦλθεν recommends itself since only with the name in this position can the ἐκ σέθεν of line 3 be anything but awkward; only with it here can we avoid the presumption of an initial lost stanza; only with it here is the right rhetorical rhythm set up so that the οὐ τεαύταν that opens the next stanza has a reference that is equal and clear.

[23] For the rhetorical pattern (X: far other was Y) that links the first and second stanzas, compare P. *N*.8.23ff., where the antistrophe speaks of the self-inflicted wound of Ajax, and the epode begins ἦ μὰν ἀνόμοιά γε . . . ἔλκεα. . .(28).

[24] Reading ἄχος with Page. Much less attractive are the τέλος of Wilamowitz and the γέρας of Cataudella.

[25] Hecuba dreamed she gave birth to a torch-bearing erinys (P.*Pa*. 8.29ff. and E. *Alex*; for which see R. A. Coles, *BICS* Supp. 32, 1974); cf. also the word-play of Catullus (64.92), by which Ariadne is made to 'conceive' a flame and 'give birth to' quarrels (198).

The performance begins and ends with Troy and Helen, but it gives the bulk of its lines – if that can be the proper expression for anything so light – to the wilds around Pelion and the wedding of Peleus. Every essential member of this ceremony is mentioned, and the whole celebration is used to provide a reverse description of the 'wedding' at Troy for which Zeus lit such lurid torches.[26] A virgin nymph here stands in the place of Helen; the most virtuous man of his time in the place of Paris; and a centaur in the place of Priam, since a simple cave has replaced the rich palace of Troy.[27] An apparently consenting Nereus is master of the house from which the bride comes, and so makes a perfect foil for the dishonoured Menelaus implicit in the nuptials that marked Helen's arrival at Troy. And finally the happy invited gods throng in to remind us of the angry divinity who punished the Trojan guest who became an unsanctioned groom. Each figure makes its commentary upon a corresponding one in the balancing scene, but we notice that Thetis, the second bride, is treated only obliquely[28] and is never even named, for Peleus is the focus of all poetic attention here. In the entire passage, he is the only figure to move, and he performs the threefold duties of the groom as he invites the guests, leads out the bride, and loosens her girdle that he may initiate the lawful act of love. Only when a year has passed and the final stanza has begun does Thetis appear as the author of any action, and even then the verb *gennato* is one that keeps the engendering father strongly present in her work of bringing her son to birth. Until the appearance of Achilles, it is thus Peleus who is pre-eminent, and his three deeds define this marriage as one that is divinely approved, legitimate in the secular sense, formally consummated, and finally confirmed by the fruitfulness of the passive bride.

The two brides thus offer only a superficial point of contact between two marriages, one of which is the embodiment of reverence for gods, custom and family, while the other is an episode in which a woman was taken, not publicly but by stealth, from a house that was not her

---

[26] Whether it is Zeus (as in Page's reconstruction, [ὤλεσε Ζεύς]) or Helen herself ([αἰθάλωσας], Wilam., [ἐξόλεσσας], Jurenka) who lights the fires of line 3, it is probable that Alcaeus meant to suggest the conventional association of Helen's wedding torches with the burning of Troy; cf. Achilles Tat. 1.8.35 and Verg. *Aen.* 6.518; and note the extension of the conceit at E. *Tro.* 309ff., where Cassandra would light her wedding torches from the fires of Troy.

[27] Chiron brings primitivism and rustic purity to this wedding, making the other by implication over-sophisticated and corrupt; he also stands as a promise of the kind of education Achilles will be given; cf. E.*IA* 1064ff. where he literally prophesies the hero's future, and compare Ovid *Met.* 11.217–65, where the Chiron role is given to Proteus.

[28] Thetis does not appear in the nominative case and as far as we can tell her only epithet is the ἄβραν of line 8; the lost word of line 9 more probably modifies the ζώνη than the girl, judging from the parallel phrases at P.*I.*8.44, Hes. 339MW. and *Od.* 11.245: λῦσε δὲ παρθενίην ζώνην.

father's but that of her husband.[29] The final difference, however, is shown in the issue of these two couplings, for the produce of one is life, that of the other, fire, death and a city's dissolution. This, at any rate, is the effect of the triumphant blast of epithets that greets Achilles in line fourteen, marking him as the poem's overt goal. The marriage at Pelion produces a vigorous, beast-mastering, god-like boy, and this image is at once brought into conjunction with the nameless and numberless corpses that are the creation of Paris and Helen. The boy and the dead are kept apart syntactically by the particle *de*, in line fifteen; they are also separated by the slight pause that will have marked the end of line fourteen, and in a sense they are divided by geography, too, since the young hero caps the song's Thessalian section, while the dead belong to Phrygia. For a moment they seem to stand at opposite poles in a clean, schematic world where piety and shamelessness are clearly separated by a sea.

And yet, though the poem formally proposes Achilles and the corpses as if they were mutually exclusive concepts, its fiction inevitably connects them, since Achilles was the killer of so many of these dead. And in fact Alcaeus insists upon this connection. His Achilles is born at the opening of line thirteen; five words later he drives forth in all his happy semi-divinity, and he is evoked with such force that no pause and no particle can check his élan. He is the only three-dimensional figure in the song, and he drives a team of ponies who have been given the only colour-word when they were specified as chestnut. The word *xanthos* belongs to the hero as well as his horses, and it gives a special brilliance to the final image of the son of Peleus and Thetis, but it is much more than a simple embellishment. Everyone knows that Xanthos was the name of one of the team that drew Achilles' chariot across the plain at Troy (*Il.* 16.149), and no one will forget that it was that same Xanthos who spoke out the names of the men who would kill him there (*Il.* 19.404–17).[30]

The chestnut ponies are thus the poet's device for sending his 'blessed' hero across the Aegean and on to the battle-field of the song's final lines.[31] In spite of the line end that marks the shift to Troy, the

---

[29] The convention of two marriages compared is perhaps best known in the form, Agamemnon-Clytemnestra/Odysseus-Penelope, as at *Od.* 11.441ff.; Pindar compares Peleus-Thetis/Cadmus-Harmonia, at *P.*3.86ff.; Plutarch compares Paris-Helen/Odysseus-Penelope, at *coniug. praecep.* 21; Catullus considers Peleus-Thetis/Thetis-Ariadne and adds a third implicit term, the 'union' of Achilles-Polyxena, in poem 64.

[30] According to Apollod. 3.13.5, the horses were Poseidon's gift to Peleus at his wedding, a reward for taking the bride that the gods could not deal with, and so in a sense a recognition of the son that Peleus would engender; cf. Schol. *Il.* 16.140.

[31] A similar leap from Achilles' birth to his death is taken by Pindar at *P.*3.100–103: ὅνπερ. . . τίκτεν ἐν Φθίᾳ Θέτις, ἐν πολέμῳ τόξοις ἀπὸ ψυχὰν λιπών, κτλ. Compare E. *IA* 1070, where Chiron predicts that it is Achilles who will set fire to Troy, and Cat. 64.337ff., where the Achilles to be born is first praised as athlete, then as Hector's opponent, then as a killer of many enemies and finally as one who will have a great funeral.

image of Achilles that was logically completed in line fourteen insists upon mixing with that of the dead Phrygians of line fifteen as we, under the poet's guidance, continue the poem beyond its artfully measured close. The first result of this imagistic merger is that Achilles joins Helen as the agent of those Trojan deaths; immediately, however, there comes the notion of the numerous Greeks who died along with their enemies, and this at once forces a recognition of the unsung end of the piece, as we remember that Achilles too must first suffer and then be added to these piled-up dead.[32] He, the Life that Thetis and Peleus made, joins Helen, the mother of the fate at Troy, as a source of Death, and then goes on to join the corpses that are heaped around her *(amph' Elenai)*, 15) as the song's sounds die away. His figure has taken the measure of the two marriages and has shown that, while they were wholly unequal by one calculation, they were yet almost identical in their ultimate, destructive conclusions.

The legitimate marriage has not been rewarded; instead, the harm that the unsanctioned one made has been implemented by the off-spring of the sanctioned union to which it is compared, and the song ends in violence. Is it, then, an early exercise in amoral cynicism? We would have to say so if (as most critics assert) the two causes that bring a single dread effect had been sanctimoniously judged, one as evil and the other as good. This, however, is not the case, for there are no words of evaluation here, nor are there any that suggest the ethics of human choice. The evil deeds of the first line refer to past Dardanian crimes,[33] and Helen is treated simply as the source from which Zeus draws their bitter punishment. The later convention of blaming her had not yet become popular (Stesichorus, just at this time, was apologising to Helen for an attack that was probably no more than a poetic fiction),[34] and Alcaeus' audience was no more likely to censure Helen automatically than were the elders of Homer's Troy. The rape of Helen was part of a divine plan, and in the case of Peleus' wedding, though the divine interest was in self-preservation rather than in the punishment of crime, the providential element was equally strong. A cataclysmic danger[35] inhabited the ancient goddess of the sea,[36] and when

---

[32] Alcaeus' audience would surely remember that at *Il.* 18.86–7 Achilles is brought to wish that his parents' marriage had never occurred: αἴθ᾽ ὄφελες σὺ μὲν αὖθι μετ᾽ ἀθανάτης ἁλίησιν / ναίειν, Πηλεὺς δὲ θνητὴν ἀγαγέσθαι ἄκοιτιν.

[33] This is reading Page's κάκων ἄ[χος ἕννεκ᾽ ἔργων . . . ἦλθεν which seems preferable to the various attempts to force a more specific sense on the line, e.g. Cataudella's, which assumes a previous stanza from which Paris may be taken, as subject for κάκων ἀ[πένεικε λέκτρων, the object being a γέρας that would stand in line 2.

[34] *PMG* 187–93; see J. A. Davison, 'De Helena Stesichori', *QU* 2 (1966) 80–90.

[35] Cf. P.*N*.4 and 5; *I*.8; Aesch. *PV* 768, etc.

[36] For Thetis as a cosmic power, see Alcman 5, col. ii *PMG*, and the discussions of M. West, 'Three Presocratic cosmogonies', *CQ* 13 (1963) 154ff.; 'Alcman and Pythagoras', *CQ* 17 (1967) 1ff.; J. P. Vernant, 'Thétis et le poème cosmogonique d'Alcmane', *Hommages à Marie Delcourt* (Brussels 1970) 38ff.; M. Detienne and J. P. Vernant, *Les Ruses de l'Intelligence* (Paris 1974) 136–66.

Zeus conferred her upon Peleus he forced her to waste the father-surpassing potential of her son in the mortal realm. The marriage, in other words, was Zeus' escape from a heavenly revolt that might otherwise have displaced him, and though there were two standard versions of the tale this fact was recognised in both of them. Some singers made Thetis a form-changing, dragon-like creature who had to be taken by force from the sea,[37] thus emphasising her kinship with the powers of chaos, while others made her as Olympian as possible, describing her as a handmaiden of Hera's who could be given away by her master like a piece of property.[38] The first group made open admission of the dubious good fortune of the groom who received such a bride, while the second did its best to make the marriage a signal honour for the mortal who had been chosen to face the son whom Zeus and Poseidon wished to avoid. No one, however, could ignore the threat that waited in Thetis' womb, and some sang of her attempts to make Achilles immortal,[39] while others described her marriage as the moment in which a dread conflict was transferred from heaven to earth in the fruitful form of a wedding gift.[40]

It is clear that Alcaeus' song draws upon the second, Homerised version of the marriage, for there is no hint of unwillingness, no tendency to turn herself into beast or fire, in his 'elegant maid'.[41] Furthermore, the masculine focus of the stanzas about Pelion seems to indicate that this tiny epyllion is not unrelated to the tale told in the Hesiodic Catalogue,[42] wherein Peleus eschews the sin of Paris, refuses the wife of his host and is rewarded by Zeus with the rule of

---

[37] Compare P.N.4 62ff. and Soph.fr. 161N²: ἔγημεν ὡς ἔγημεν ἀφθόγγους γάμους τῇ παντομόρφῳ Θέτιδι συμπλακείς ποτε. For vase-painting representations, see A. Schneider, *Der tragische Sagenkreis*, 78.

[38] This is the version of Il.24.60 and AR 4.790–809; see also Hes. *Cat.* frr. 210, 211 MW and *Kypria*, fr.2 Bethe. In this version, Thetis may refuse Zeus' advances, and be given away by him in anger; cf. Apollod. 3.13.5 who mentions this alternative version. For an analysis of the various forms that the story took, see R. Reitzenstein, 'Die Hochzeit des Peleus und Thetis', *Hermes* 35 (1900) 73ff., and A. Lesky, 'Peleus u. Thetis im frühen Epos', *SFIC* 27/8 (1956) 216ff. = *Gesamm. Schriften* (Bern 1966) 401–9.

[39] For Achilles in the fire, see AR 4.866–79; Apollod. 3.13.6. Statius, *Achil.* 1.133–4 and 269–70, had him dipped into Styx. Compare the action of Demeter with Demophon when she was a demoted and earthwandering goddess and likewise the potential source of a revolt against Zeus.

[40] Lesky (op.cit., 219) notes the view that it was the narrow escape of the Olympians that dictated the scale of the celebrations in connection with Thetis' marriage, and concludes that this notion belonged to a 'Themis-gedicht' that was older than the *Cypria*.

[41] For the phrase, compare Hes. fr. 339MW ἄβρη παρθένος; the normal Homeric epithets are ἀδμής or αἰδοίη. It is curious to note that Pindar, in a passage that contains both Thetis and her opposite, Hippolyta, applies the epithet ἄβρα to the latter, as if it suggested corruption (N.5.26).

[42] Hes. frr. 209–11MW; the tale is referred to by Pindar in *Nemea* 4 and 5; cf. Horace *Ode* 3.7.17.

Iolcus, and incidentally with a wife worthy of his chastity.[43] Never-theless, the emphasis upon the celebrations at the centaur's cave suggests that Alcaeus was above all conscious of the opening scenes of the *Cypria*, with its glorious description of the wedding where Apollo played his lyre, the Muses sang, Hera held the torch and Hermes and Ganymede served out the wine.[44] With just thirty words to spend, he could not begin to imitate his original in richness of detail, but he could in compensation surpass it in the terse clarity of his design, expressing the pattern that commanded such detail far more plainly than an extensive epic could. According to the poet of the *Cypria*, this one wedding night, with its mixture of mortal loves and immortal quarrels, engendered both the hero son of Peleus and the future es-capade of Paris, and so the entire war at Troy. The epic, however, had to pursue its garrulous way to Ida for the judgment, to Argos for the rape, and finally to Troy for Helen's reception there,[45] while its prodi-gal hexameters worked to obscure the sharp outlines of this god-im-posed destiny. Alcaeus, by contrast, takes four stanzas of crafty Lesbian verse and locks the two couples together, giving to both mar-riages the context of fire and slaughter which was the result of their curious interdependency.

It is as a complementary pair, then, and not as a pair of foils, that Alcaeus has set his two weddings side by side, and this is why their differences are noticed, only to be erased again. It is finally not sig-nificant that one resulted from a breach of hospitality while the other was a reward for its observance, and it is finally not even significant that one bred death and the other life. The truth that Alcaeus would express is that the festival at Pelion – the reverent wedding that he has set at the core of his song –[46] was in a sense the father of the other, irreverent one. Men say that Troy fell because of Helen and the kind of marriage she made, but they don't tell the whole story, for there was another marriage, of a wholly different sort, that was even more germane to the Trojan War. It is thus not the mortal Helens who give destiny its shape, but the gods – those same gods who may decide

---

[43] Pindar makes Peleus' distinguishing virtue perfectly clear: ξεινίου πατρὸς χόλον δείσαις. (*N*.5.33–4); cf. Ar.*Nub*.1063: καὶ τὴν Θέτιν γ᾽ ἔγημε διὰ τὸ σωφρονεῖν.

[44] For versions of the wedding before the *Cypria*, see the discussions of Reitzenstein, op.cit., 73ff. and Lesky, op.cit., 219. Homer makes Apollo perform (*Il*.24.63) and Pindar adds the Muses' song (*N*.5.23–4); Hermes is cupbearer at Sappho 141V, Ganymede at E.*IA* 1053; Hera carries the torch at AR 4.790–809. In later versions there were also prophesies about the future of Achilles spoken at the wedding; see *IA* 1064 and Cat.64. 337ff.

[45] That the Trojan reception was thought of as a marriage is proved by Proclus *Chrest.* i²: καὶ ἀποπλεύσας εἰς Ἴλιον γάμους τῆς Ἑλένης ἐπετέλεσεν.

[46] The marriage at Pelion is thus like the point of furthest time that a choral ode often reaches, there to discover an omen or a shaping incident; cf. e.g. the glimpse of olive trees in P.*O*.3.

to send a Thetis down among men, leaving them to deal with her son.[47]

In addition to these three art songs there is a long poem partially recovered from several papyrus fragments, in which the singer insists that Pittacus should be both stoned and hanged (298V).[48] Its immediate business is exhortation and abuse, but its call for action is followed by a demonstration that expands and transforms the piece, as an apparently static epic example proliferates into scenes of fullest vitality. Ajax is introduced as formal proof that the unpunished criminal is a danger to his community, but what happens is that his crime elbows the example out of the way and, for an instant, takes over the sung performance.

```
]cαντας αἰϲχυν[. . .]τατα μήνδικα
]ην δὲ περβάλον[τ' ἀν]άγκα⟨ι⟩
]χϵνι λαβολίω π.[. .]αν·                           3
   ] Ἀχαίοιϲ' ἦϲ πόλυ βέλτερον
   ].. ηντα κατέκτανον
]παρπλέοντες Αἴγαιϲ
   ]. ἔτυχον θαλάϲϲαϲ·                              7
]ϵν ναύω Πριάμω πάϊϲ
Ἀ]θανάαϲ πολυλάϊδοϲ
]απαππένα γενείω
δυϲμέ]νεεϲ δὲ πόλιν ἐπῆπον                          11
   ]υπ[..].αϲ Δαΐφοβον τ' ἅμα
   ]ον οἰμώγα δ' [ἀπ]ὺ τϵίχεοϲ
]ι παίδων ἀύτα
   ]ον πέδιον κατῆ_ιχε_ι·                           15
λ]_ύ_ι_ϲϲ_ι αν ἦλθ' ὀλόα_ι ν_ι ἔχων
   ].[].ναϲ_ι Πάλλα_ι δ_ι οϲ, ἀ θέω_ι ν_ι
_ι ϲι θε]οϲύλαιϲι πάντων
   ].·_ι τα μακάρων πέφυκε·                         19
```

[47] If one wished to speculate upon the immediate sympotic 'occasion', as did Jurenka ('Neue Lieder der Sappho u. des Alkaios', *WS* 36, 1914, 229) and Gomme (op.cit., 258), it would be best to reverse the suppositions of those two scholars (i.e. that someone had just sung a song in praise of Helen), and imagine instead a previous performance that had blamed her in the newfangled way that was perhaps just becoming fashionable.

[48] R. Merkelbach, 'Ein Alkaios-Papyrus', *ZPE* i (1967) 81ff., identified 298a+bLP (P.Oxy. 2303) with Pap.Col. 2021 (Page, *SLG*, 262); he also suggested that 135V represents a version of lines 19–21 of Pap.Col.2021, and discussed the fragments further in *ZPE* 2 (1968) 154 & 224. Further reconstructions and remarks may be found in H. Lloyd-Jones, 'The Cologne fragment of Alcaeus', *GRBS* 9 (1968) 125–39; C. Gallavotti, 'Alcei Carmen de Aiace', *ZPE* 9 (1969) 174 and 'Ricostruzione del nuovo carme d'Alceo', *QU* 8 (1969) 83–5; G. Tarditi, 'L'asebeia di Aiace e quello di Pittaco' *QU* 8 (1969) 86ff.

⌋ϲι δ' ἄμφο]ιν παρθενίκαν ἔλων
⌋παρεϲτάκο]ιϲαν ἀγάλματι
⌋ὀ Λ⌊ό⌋κροϲ οὐδ' ἔ]δειϲε
⌋·ϙϲ πολέμω δότϵ⌊ρ⌋ρ]αν   23
⌋ν· ἀ| δὲ δεῖνον ὐπ' ⌊ὄ⌋]φρυϲι
— ϲμ[⌋π⌊ε⌋|λ⌊ι⌋δγώθειϲα κὰτ οἴνοπα
— ἄιξ[ε⌋ πόντο⌊ν⌋, |ἐκ δ' ἀφάντοιϲ
—   ἐξαπ[ίν⌋αϲ ἐκύκα θυέλλαιϲ·   27

[. . . shaming those who do unjust deeds . . .]
[Best] fasten a noose around his neck
    and finish him with stones!

So the Achaeans better might
have killed [the man the gods drove mad;]
then they'd have found a [smoother] sea
    for turning Aegae's height.

Inside the temple, Priam's child
[held fast to] Athena, Giver of Spoils,
dependant, touching the idol's chin
    while foemen stormed the town.

[Priamid princes], Deïphobos too
they killed; lament [rose from] the wall
and voices of children [went out]
    to fill the plain of Troy.

[Ajax] came raging battle-mad
into the shrine of the chaste Athena,
she of all gods most harsh to men
    whose crime is sacrilege.

Laying two hands upon the girl
stationed beside the idol, the
Locrian [ravished] her, nor did he fear
    the child of Zeus, war's

[gorgon-eyed] patroness, but she
with dread bright glare, darted across
the purple sea and out of the darkness
    churned up sudden storms.[49]

(Some of the six stanzas that follow may be variants of the above; there is eventual mention of Pittacus, as 'son of Hyrras', at line 47.)

In imagination Alcaeus here seems to address all the noblemen of Mytilene, asking them to treat Pittacus as any community must treat

[49] The translation is based on restorations from various hands, as reported by R. Merkelbach, *ZPE* 1 (1967) 82ff.

one who has outraged the gods.[50] Stoning is the right punishment,
being communal, public and apotropaic,[51] and Alcaeus backs up his
recommendation with what amounts to a myth-based threat, for he
reminds his audience that the Greeks who drowned on the way back
from Troy did so because, like the Mytileneans of today, they failed to
punish an Ajax who likewise should have been stoned. The episode
from the tales of the Achaean return is frankly chosen for the lesson
that it bears, and the poet at first lends it a heavily gnomic cast by
identifying it only by the place-name, Aegae. His tone is almost riddling and certainly pedagogical, for, by making his listeners supply
the hero's missing proper name,[52] he forces them to join him and to
confirm his argument willingly, in their own minds.

In all logic this mythic demonstration is complete at the end of line
seven, and if Alcaeus' purpose had been merely to strengthen his
demand for a public attack upon Pittacus, he might well have rested
his case. That is not what he does, however, for instead of cutting his
Trojan example off he prolongs it and lets it change radically just at
this point. Gnomic argument is abandoned for pure lyric discourse as
the song for a few moments turns from the general idea of punishment
to dwell instead upon a very specific crime. Rhetoric gives way to
narrative and this shift is signalised by a total conceptual change, for
the singer leaps backwards in time, eastward in space, from Euboea
and the returning Greeks to Troy on the day of its fall. His leap is

---

[50] There is no agreement as to how to take the first preserved word, which seems to
be δρά]σαντας; Tarditi suggests that these may be men around Myrsilus who have
misbehaved under Pittacus' influence; Gallavotti converts the participle into a singular
form by writing δρα]σαντά σ' αἴσχυν[' αὖ]τα τὰ μῆνδικα, 'your acts of injustice shame
you, their doer'; Lloyd-Jones reads δρά]σαντας αἰσχύν[νοντα, and translates '(putting to
shame?) those who (had acted?) unjustly', which might conceivably describe a Pittacus
so outrageous that he outruns all ordinary criminals. The final word of line 2,
ἀν]άγκα(ι), offers another problem; it is taken by some editors as an impersonal verbal
expression commanding a missing infinitive, but it is glossed in the margin with an
accusative form, τὴν ἀγχούην οὕτως εἴρηκε δεσμά, τὴν ἀνά(γ)κην; see W. Luppe
ΑΝΑΓΚΑ im Kölner Alkaios', *ZPE* 33 (1979) 29–30.

[51] Compare 68V, where Alcaeus speaks of fathers worthy of stoning; Tarditi (op.cit.,
91) argues that the reference there is to the father of Myrsilus and the father of Pittacus,
but the sense might be more efficiently rendered as 'Pittacus' father, Hyrras, deserves
stoning and even the father of Hyrras, for that one (H.) is guilty of having engendered
a hateful and impious villain'. On stoning as a punishment, see R. Hirzel, 'Die Strafe
de Steinigung', *Abhandl. Leipz. Akad.* 27 (1909) 243–4, and on lapidation for a scapegoat
or demon, Fr. Schwenn, *Die Menschenopfer bei den Gr. u. Rom.*, Relig. V. u.V. 15, 3
(Giessen 1915) 39, and L. Gernet, *Anthropologie de la Grèce antique* (Paris 1968), 170.
According to tradition, the Greeks were set to stone Ajax (Paus. 10.31.2; cf. Proclus
Chrest. 261 = Séveryns *Texte et Apparat.* 1, p.x.) when he, with matchless *sang-froid*,
took his place at Athena's altar and escaped as a suppliant (Paus. 10.26.3; 1.15.3); see
the discussion of Lloyd-Jones, loc.cit. For what may be fragments of Sophocles' tragedy
about this Ajax, see pap. Oxy. 3151 (*Oxy.Pap.* 44, 1976, 1ff.).

[52] Ajax seems to be indicated only by a participle, in line 5, and from the marginal
θεοσύλην ὄντα Page reconstructed the beginning of the line as αἰ τὸν θεοβλ]αβέντα (apud
Merkelbach, *ZPE* 1).

also made from sea to land, from nature to architecture, and from storm to quiet order, and it is accomplished in the breathing space between the end of the second stanza and the beginning of the third. There is no transition or connection; we simply discover a Cassandra who has been summarily set down inside Athena's Trojan shrine.

Cassandra is quite alone, she is not described, and like the Ajax of the preceding lines she is not even named, though she has her patronymic. We are evidently meant to look only at her movements, not at her person, and her three lines are all used to make this daughter of Priam do just one thing, for they fix the ritual gesture that makes her sacrosanct.[53] The last line of her stanza sets the besieging army in motion outside, and then the sharply-lit moment is over, the episode done. In the pause that follows (between stanzas three and four) Troy falls, and at line twelve the men who were without are discovered within the walls, busy with killing, while the experience of defeat is resolved into two sounds. The fourth stanza thus serves as a kind of choral interlude in which a panoramic view is conveyed by a wail of women and a cry of orphans,[54] but when it is finished the song once more narrows its focus to a single figure within a single frame. Stanza five sets Ajax in motion and brings him from the mayhem outside into the closed temple that was established in stanza three. Cassandra is there, dedicated to the statue, but we know this only from the earlier passage, for she is not even mentioned as Ajax bursts into the place. Like Hector he is mad with a desire to destroy (cf. *Il.* 9.304–5), but unlike Hector he is not on the battlefield, nor is he seeking a masculine enemy. What he does seek no one knows, for his name and the fact that he rages are the only things told of him by a singer who places all of his emphasis upon the building where he finds himself, and the nature of its resident deity.

In the following stanza the raging hero seizes a victim who is still nameless and deprived of all personal aspect, a virginal creature represented only by the participle that places her beside the image of her goddess. A single word once took care of his action – a word given emphatic position at the beginning of its line, and for that reason lost on the damaged papyrus. It may have been 'dragged', 'seized', 'shamed', 'drew forth', 'outraged',[55] but fortunately the particular two syllables are not as crucial as they might seem, for it is not the act of rape but the act of sacrilege that the singer means to portray. The violence of the Locrian is the song's only concern at this point, but Alcaeus is not interested in its particular definition any more than he is in its mortal

---

[53] On the curious ἀπαππένα γενείω, see S. R. Slings, 'Some problems in Lesbian grammar', *Mnemosyne* 4.32 (1979) 243–67.

[54] For the conceit by which the conquered 'occupy' what they have lost, see *Il.*16.79; A. *Ag.* 454–5.

[55] ἔρυσσ᾽, Merk.; κάτελκ᾽ Colonna; αἴσχυν᾽ or αἴσχυν᾽ Ll.J.; ὔβρισσ᾽, Page; ἔξηλκ᾽, West.

victim. He has made Cassandra a puppet without a face because it is
Athena's presence that lends significance to the deed of Ajax, and the
essential statement is the one that follows: 'nor did he fear the child
of Zeus.'[56] This is the aspect of his crime that brought such extensive
punishment, and the fact that the mortal affront and the divine retaliation are parts of a continuum is expressed structurally with the
only inter-stanza enjambement to appear in the surviving parts of the
song.[57] The unfeared goddess of stanza six becomes the angry deity of
stanza seven and one last epithet is carried over to inaugurate the
section in which Athena becomes a moving, vengeful force.

The dynamics of the poem cause the cult image, a mere frozen
agalma at line 21, to be transformed by a mortal crime into an active
supernatural power who does, in the last four readable lines, what
divinity can do and what lyric can imitate. She breaks out of consecutive time and space, leaving chronology and narrative behind and
rushing into the future to establish the situation with which the
mythic section began. She flies to the western side of the Aegean, to
Cape Aegae, and there she waits with the same storm that was eu-
phemistically mentioned when the Ajax example was first introduced.
Blandly indicated by the smooth sea that the Achaeans did not find,
the storm of stanza two was supplied by each listener from the comfortable recesses of his own memory. It was then merely the notion of
a storm, but now a tempest that is neither gnomic nor exemplary is
imposed by the singer as a fully sensed disaster. Churned forth by the
aorist *ekuka* (27) and contained in the turbulent noun *thuellais*, it
stands in affective prominence as the last word of a clausula – a
realised lyric event worthy of its victim and also of its divine creator.

The whole of this miniature narrative has been marked by a pretence of artless objectivity, for the singer, like a true balladeer, seems
not to judge the deeds that he recounts.[58] In fact, however, Alcaeus
has no intention of duplicating the oversight of the Achaeans, and he
sees to it that his condemnation of Ajax, though it hides in the decoration and the structure of his song, shall yet be perfectly plain. As
verbal instruction, he offers only the words that embellish the goddess
Athena, but these, taken together, say everything that needs to be
said. Athena is *polulaïs* (10),[59] the goddess of plentiful spoils, and so

---

[56] West suggested reading τὰν βάρ]εος here instead of Merkelbach's παῖδα Δ]ίος, but
since Athena is Δίος θυγάτηρ at 206, 1 V and Zeus' κόρα at 310V, and since Cassandra
is 'child of Priam' above in line 8, the patronymic seems most appropriate here.

[57] Gallavotti (*ZPE* 4 and *QU* 8), however, joined stanzas three and four as well, with
his ἔπηπον / δόμον Λακαίν]ας. . .

[58] Compare the remarks of Max Treu, (op.cit., above, note 8, 58ff.) who notes the
unabashed repetition, vernacular lack of self-consciousness, and non-epic ability to omit
names and other details.

[59] At *Il.*10.460 Athena is Ληῖτις, and Pausanias describes an altar of Athena Laitis at
Olympia as one of the twelve established there by Heracles (5.14.5).

has jurisdiction not just over the defeated (as Cassandra knows) but also over the victors whose prizes depend upon her consent. Not only their prizes, but victory itself is within her gift, for she is *polemō doterra* (23),[60] the patroness of war (as Ajax refuses to know). She is also awesomely chaste (*agna*, 17),[61] pure as consecrated things are, and consequently the most dreadful of all the gods when an act of ritual uncleanness occurs. Whether Alcaeus calls her *deinotata*, *pikrotata* or *ainotata* we cannot know because of the lacuna in line nineteen, but her dread power is displayed in the last epithet that she receives, for she is apparently *gorgōpis* (24), one whose glance is filled with baneful and primitive magic. All of which means that what Ajax does is steal from the very goddess who might, according to her epithets, have granted him a captive girl. He affronts her by seizing something that is hers thrice over, being spoils, suppliant and virgin. He insults her by attacking her human replica, he makes her furious by smirching her consecrated place, and all this he does to one who is his own natural protector, a goddess who gives strength and allows conquest but who is, like himself, terrible in her ferocity.

Another sort of instruction is implicit in the two crisp gestures attributed to Cassandra and her ravisher and depicted in two temple tableaux that are, in their formality and their answering opposition, like two metopes for the neck of some early painted jar. Each quick scene is a study in arrested motion, and each makes use of one active figure and another that is perfectly still, so that we first see Cassandra touch a statue with reverence, then (after two divisive stanzas) we see Ajax touch Cassandra, irreverently. One of these movements is the stretching of a single hand to the chin of a protector in a manner controlled by ritual, while the other is the work of two hands that are beyond all control. The phrase 'with both hands' opens the line that opens the sixth stanza and so it dominates the instantaneous vision that follows, filling it with a violence that is almost grotesque. The two hands are emphasised with a rare Lesbian dual form and they are employed in a movement that is likewise rare, for a suppliant is raised with a single hand, a female captive taken with a single hand (the other holding the sword),[62] and even Minos, when he offered insult to Eriboea, did so with the touch of his single hand (B. 17.11). Ajax, however, seizes this girl with two, and his gesture is brutal and almost

---

[60] Compare the similar epithet, πολεμάδοκος, at 325V (in reference to a cult at Coroneia) and at 3V.

[61] Merkelbach read ἄγνας in l.17. Homer most frequently uses this epithet for the virginal Artemis; later it came to be applied to persons or things that had been sanctified or purified, but B. Gentili has argued ('La veneranda Saffo', *QU* 1966, 37ff.) that the essential quality signified was the power to inspire fear and veneration.

[62] The taking of captives can be seen to perfection on the relief pithos from Mykonos, published by M. Ervin, *Arch. Delt.* 18, 1 (1963) 37–75.

obscene, for (except in mortal combat)[63] two hands denote an exaggeration of lust and greed.[64] The poet thus uses the two manual gestures almost iconographically: Cassandra's one hand as a signal of discipline, custom and piety, Ajax's double grasp as a sign that he is lawless and defiant of society, as well as irreverent.

The movement of Ajax within the temple is in the abstract almost the same as the movement of Cassandra, though in ethical terms the two confront each other as opposites. In the same way, the wild rush of Ajax into the sacred place is conceptually very similar to the wild rush of Athena out of it and across the sea, though one of these actions is crime, the other its punishment, and it is upon this likeness that the ultimate sense of the fragment rests. The battle-lust of Ajax and the dread glare of Athena are given the same musical phrase (at 16 and 24), while the tune of the final storm (26–7) is made to echo that of the goddess' invariable response to those who despoil the gods (18–19). It looks as if there were at least eight more lines in which the disaster at sea was realised poetically,[65] but the pattern of the poet's

---

[63] Heracles seized Death with both hands, at E.*Alc.* 847 and 1142; similarly, the brand that blinds Cyclops is manipulated with both hands (E.*Cycl.* 630), and Alcaeus uses both as he tries to kill the Calydonian boar (Ovid *Met.* 8.397). Bacchylides makes *phthonos* into an enemy who belongs in this almost demonic class by insisting that its excesses must be repulsed with two hands (5.188).

[64] The two hands of lust are used by Nessus (S. *Trach.* 565), and would be used by the satyrs at *Cycl.* 169ff.; they characterise Apollo's taking of Creusa, according to her accusation (E.*Ion* 892) and are in play at the end of Archil. 478 *SLG.* For the one hand of a respectful lover, see e.g. Poseidon with Tyro at *Od.* 11.246. Rude violence is expressed in the two-handed gesture of the Greek woman who destroys the yoke of Atossa's dream (A.*Pers.* 194), in the murderous intentions at E.*Cycl.* 379, in Zeus' destruction of Asclepius at P.*P.*3.57, and in Hipponax's wish to have two right hands, that he might punch Bupalus in both eyes (120/21 W); a boxer naturally uses both his hands (Simon. 4/509 PMG). Excess seems to be the point at S.*OT* 1466 and 1510, where Oedipus would touch his daughters with his two hands and Creon reproves him, himself marking his own protection of them with a one-handed gesture. Even in phrases with ἀμφί the single hand is often to be found, where the embrace is loving and moderate (cf. e.g. Simon 38/543 PMG; E.*IT* 799); see Fränkel's note at A.*Agam.* 1559. Excess is also in question at E.*Alc.* 612, where Pheres' too-lavish gifts are brought in two hands, and excess taking the form of greed is expressed by Heracles' two-handed manner of seizing his cup at E.*Alc.* 756; cf. AR 1.472. (Two hands may however be used in willing acceptance of a gift or offering as on the Parthenon frieze, and at P.*P.*2.9 Artemis uses two to give the crown of victory. It should be noted also that the gesture of showing two open hands or arms spread wide apart has no negative significance, though it does have the same quality of emphasis, being used for mourning as at A.*Sept.* 856, E.*Phoen.* 1351; for farewell, e.g. *Il.*4.523; or for begging, e.g. *Il.*21.115.)

[65] It is clear that the stanza beginning with line 44 has returned to the immediate occasion, since line 47 refers to Hyrras, the father of Pittacus. The nature of the stanza that preceded this one (40–3) does not, however, announce itself, and the one above it (36–9) looks very much as if it were an alternate version of the seventh stanza (24–7), which is marked with an obelus in the margin at line 24. The two stanzas from 28–35 seem to be concerned still with the Achaean disaster, and Ajax is named at line 30, but if the papyrus is recording variants, these may simply be a slightly altered repetition of what we have, rather than an extension of it. On the question of the obelised line

judgment is fixed by these tempestuous winds. The divine vengeance and the human rage that provoked it have been given a perfect congruity and so we are left with a sense, not of tragedy, but of a supernatural justice that is appropriate, in spite of its promiscuity.[66]

The Pittacus song becomes, for these few instants, an Ajax song in which a mythic act of perversity is exposed as a naked scheme, and yet also musically reconstituted and thrust upon listeners as an event actually perceived. The piece is thus a consummate exercise in Alcaeus' pecular lyric art, but whether or not it was effective as a political weapon there is no way to know. It gives the criminality of Pittacus a blazon so superb that the would-be tyrant's actual crimes – however impious or bizarre – will have grown sordid and shabby by comparison, and this result may not have been foreign to the poet's intention. Nevertheless, he took a great risk with this Ajax song, for surely any victim must be unreasonably enhanced when he is made the object of such glorious abuse.

(or stanza), see R. L. Fowler, 'Reconstructing the Cologne Alcaeus', *ZPE* 33 (1979) 17–28; Fowler would keep both the seventh and the ninth stanzas, postponing Athena's rush westward until the trial and oath of Ajax had been described – a supposition that leaves the frowning goddess of l. 24 rather up in the air.

[66] It is important to notice that Alcaeus has imposed this pattern by making Athena, and not Poseidon, the creator of his storm; see M. Detienne, 'Le navire d'Athéna', *RHR* 4 (1970) 154ff., where it is pointed out that Athena's natural interest is in ships, not in the weather that destroys them.

PART III

Sappho

Circle

Sappho sang for an audience in some ways very much like the fraternity that Alcaeus fought with during the day and drank with at night. Her circle, like the *hetaireia*,[1] had a customary role to play in Lesbian society, and it too was aristocratic, musical, and constrained only by bonds of love and loyalty.[2] When Sappho performed for this group, she used the same metres, the same song-structures, and the same mixture of local dialect with epic speech that Alcaeus used, but her songs were nevertheless of a very different sort, for where his subject was the changing world, hers was the unchanging beauty that sometimes touched that world.

Alcaeus' masculine association pressed outwards upon the communal life of Mytilene; the group was formed for action and its songs were meant to maintain its readiness for aggressive public gestures. Sappho's group, by contrast, drew inwards, keeping its members back in quietude and touching the community only in ritual moments; its public gestures were restricted to the dance, and its songs were made to emphasise the esoteric quality of its closed experience. Alcaeus' listeners were adults who heard another adult as he confirmed convictions that they already held, but Sappho's audience was not yet mature. Some indeed were hardly more than children, and for them

---

[1] Sappho calls her friends ἔταιραι (160V), and at 30aV a beloved girl is *hetaira*; compare Erinna, 5.7D=AP 7.710,7, συνεταιρίς. See J. Trumpf, 'Über das Trinken in der poesie des Alkaios', *ZPE* 12 (1973) 139, who describes Sappho's group as being like the masculine *hetaireia* and like other 'halb-kultischen, halb-politisch-sozialen Organizationsformen'.

[2] It is the assumption of the present study that the group met in daily intimacy and informality, and that most of Sappho's songs were first performed before this assembly of pupils who were also friends and temporary wards. Something similar is asserted by Kirkwood (*EGM*, 267ff.), but others have given the Sapphic circle a much more institutional, ritual and semi-public quality. R. Merkelbach, 'Sappho und ihr Kreis', *Philol.* 101 (1957) 3ff., was one of the first to state this position, insisting that every Sapphic song was meant for a specific and public occasion, but F. Lasserre has gone even further, denying the Sapphic group even the semi-privacy of a feminine version of the symposium; see his 'Ornements érotiques dans la poésie lyrique archaïque', *Serta Turyniana* (Urbana 1974) 5–33.

Sappho's songs were both education and initiation as an older woman taught them what it was to be a girl, that they might better become women later on. The restlessness of the male group instilled an urgency into the songs of Alcaeus; he addressed men who were in principle bound together for life, and he looked to an immediate future in which his dreams would become concrete realities. Sappho, on the other hand, sang to a group that was at leisure and yet in a constant state of dissolution, and her tone was one of meditative irony as she explored this brief and shifting present in search of inherent, less tangible ideals.

It is reasonable to suppose that the circle of girls around Sappho was something like one of the *agelai* that annually gathered Spartan girls together, but the comparison must not be pushed too far.[3] In the Peloponnese, membership of such bands was compulsory, and the young ladies had a season that included athletic training as well as festival appearances and common board, before their marriages drew them apart, but life on Lesbos was lived more delicately and more privately than this.[4] Nothing suggests team sports for Sappho's girls, nor was their common experience a thing that the state required of every member of a certain class at a certain age. On the contrary, membership in the circle seems to have been voluntary, irregular, and to a degree even international. Girls came from other parts of Ionia, and some stayed a considerable length of time, for Sappho mentions having known one of them (now grown to loveliness) when she 'seemed a skimpy child, not ready to be loved' (94V).[5] Nevertheless, once enrolled, a girl enjoyed the same membership in an extra-communal band that she might have found in an initiation class, for this élitist circle was evidently licensed by the community, just as the older puberty groups had been. It had a place within the public order as a

---

[3] Cf. Pindar 112 (S): Λάκαινα . . . παρθένων ἀγέλα. The major ancient descriptions of the Spartan groups are Xen. *Resp. Lac.* 1.4; Plut. *Lyc.* 14.2 and 18.4; Theoc. 18. W. Schadewaldt (*Die Grossen der Weltgeschichte* i (Zurich 1970) 306–20, would make the Sapphic *thiasos* an actual initiation group, its every activity ritually dictated; a more reasonable statement of the idea can be found at Merkelbach, op. cit., 4ff. The Spartan *agelai* are described, perhaps with too much emphasis upon their retention of primitive initiatory functions, by A. Brelich, *Paides e Parthenoi* i (Rome 1969) 157ff.; see the criticisms of C. Sourvinou at *JHS* 91 (1971) 172–3. For girls' musical groups, see C. Calame, *Les Choeurs de jeunes filles en Grèce archaïque* (Rome 1977) i, esp. 367ff.

[4] The commentator of Pap.Col. 5860.6–8 (=*SLG* 261A) reported a statement from Kallias of Mytilene, a student of the works of Sappho and Alcaeus, to the effect that Sappho educated *at her leisure* the best not only of the local females but also of the Ionian girls, and surely ἐφ᾽ ἡσυχίας must mean that Sappho acted as a private citizen, not as a priestess or as the appointed leader of an initiation group. On this commentary, see M. Gronewald, 'Fragmente aus einem Sappho-Kommentar', *ZPE* 14 (1974) 114–18, and on the foreign membership, cf. Strabo 13.2.4 and Suda sv Σαπφώ.

[5] For *charis* as the quality of one who has reached the age of love, see G. Lanata, 'Sul linguaggio amoroso di Saffo', *QU* 2 (1966) 63ff.

discrete social organism where society's usual rules for a time did not prevail.[6]

Ordinarily a girl belonged to her family, but when she was with Sappho she was separated from her relatives; Anactoria came from Miletus, Telesippa and Gongyla from Colophon, and Euneika all the way from Salamis, according to the Suda. Ordinarily a girl was trained in weaving and taught to supervise the other home-manufactures that were necessary to the archaic household, but here in the Sapphic circle her education seems to have been in dance and song. And finally, where the ordinary girl was involved only in household cults, there was apparently here a calendar of ritual duty for girls who sometimes functioned almost as a sacred band or *thiasos*.[7] Certain fragments picture them as they offer incense in a rustic bower (2V) or stand about an altar while the moon shines full upon them (154V), and a few lines like 'Sweet Adonis is dead, O Cytherean! What shall we do?' (140V) represent the cult hymns that they sang (cf. 168V also for Adonis, and 17V for Hera). Within the circle, Aphrodite was an object of special devotion ('I told my dream to Aphrodite', 134V), as were 'the soft Graces and the lovely-haired Muses' (128V). Indeed, because Sappho once spoke of hers as a 'house where the Muses are served', it is sometimes supposed that it was in a sense a temple where the girls tended an actual shrine with Sappho as their priestess.[8] In fact, the fragment will bear no such interpretation, since its essential statement is only that this is a place of joy (150V):

> οὐ γὰρ θέμις ἐν μοισοπόλων ⟨δόμωι⟩
> θρῆνον ἔμμεν' ⟨. . . . . . .⟩ οὔ κ' ἄμμι πρέποι τάδε

In a house where the Muses are served
weeping is not allowed . . . this were unseemly for us.. . .

---

[6] Cf. K. J. Dover, *Greek Homosexuality* (London 1978) 181: 'The relations between participants in a female chorus or between teacher and pupils in music and poetry may thus have constituted an overt "sub-culture", or rather "counter-culture", in which women and girls received from their own sex what segregation and monogamy denied them from men.'

[7] At Sparta, the girls' groups seem to have shared the celebrations for Artemis Orthia and the Hyakinthia with other segments of the community, while the festivals of Dionysos Kolonatas, Helen, and Artemis at Karyai were exclusively their responsibility; see Brelich, op.cit., 160–6; and also Calame, op.cit., 327ff.

[8] Such was the contention of K. Latte, reviewing Fränkel *DuP*, *Gött. Gel. Anz*, 207 (1953) 30ff. =*Kl.Schr.* pp.713ff, and he is followed by B. Gentili, 'La veneranda Saffo', *QU* 2 (1966) 55, and G. Lanata, op.cit., who notes that Mousopolos was a Dionysiac cult title in Thebes in the second century B.C., referring apparently to craftsmen (as evidenced in *IG* vii 2484). It seems, however, more probable that Sappho's is a house of the Muses simply because it is a place of education and not because it has actually been dedicated to their cult; see *RE*, sv 'Mouseion', for the generalised connection of the Muses with all schools.

Nevertheless, though they do not seem to have been formally dedicated to any particular service, the group must at moments have conformed to the vision of Philostratus, the connoisseur, who saw them as a set of nubile girls with honied tongues who stood within a myrtle grove hymning Aphrodite, under the eye of a woman skilled in song and poetry (*Imagines*, 2.1).[9]

Mytilene seems to have contained other groups like Sappho's, and echoes of rivalry suggest that, for certain public rites, choruses from the various houses may have been pitted against one another.[10] The few fragments of Sapphic invective seem, at least, to reflect song-contests in which each school praised its own membership (much as the girls of Alcman's virgin chorus do) and then maliciously found fault with the appearance and performance of those who challenged them. Nothing can be known about the specialities of the other houses, but music and deportment must have been the principal boasts at Sappho's, for these are the points on which she attacks. In lines that perhaps pretend to address a truant pupil she speaks of the mistress of another establishment with the terrible authority of one whose own whim determines what fashion shall be (57V):[11]

τίς δ' ἀγροτῶτις θέλγει νόον . . .

ἀγροτῶτιν ἐπεμμένα στόλαν . . .

οὐκ ἐπισταμένα τὰ βράκε' ἔλκην ἐπὶ τῶν σφύρων;

[9] Cf. Latte, op.cit., 36=720, 'S. steht zu den Mädchen zunächst nicht anders als Alkman; sie ist Chormeisterin und verfasst ihnen die Liedern, die sie vortragen.' This would seem, however, to describe only one part of Sappho's work, since she also taught her girls how to compose, and how to perform singly, and (unlike Alcman) she seems to have presided over their physical and emotional lives as well as over their public appearances.

[10] Maximus of Tyre (18.9 Hob.) called Gorgo and Andromeda the ἀντίτεχνοι of Sappho, and compared them to Gorgias, Thrasymachus and Protagoras in their rivalry of Socrates. Contest of some sort amongst these rivals is suggested by the comparative form found at Aristaenet. *Ep.*1.10 p.142ff.: καὶ πρὸ τῆς παστάδος τὸν ὑμέναιον ᾖδον αἱ μουσικώτεραι τῶν παρθένων καὶ μειλιχόφωνοι. Note as well that Philostratus made reference to rival groups that composed cult hymns and love poetry (*VA* 1.30). If there were beauty contests as well, they may have been survivals from earlier initiation proofs of virtue, like the *euandria* of the men's groups at Athens; see Brelich, op.cit., 339, and note that a kind of intramural rivalry for beauty is suggested by S. 82V: εὐμορφοτέρα Μνασιδίκα τᾶς ἀπάλας Γυρίννως. On the notion that some of Sappho's songs were meant for choral performance, see M. West, 'Burning Sappho', *Maia* 22 (1970) 327; Calame, op.cit., 370ff.

[11] The rival is identified as Andromeda, the girl as the Atthis of fr.94V, by C. Theander, 'Atthis et Andromeda', *Eranos* 44 (1946) 62ff. On Sappho as an abusive poet, see Philodem. *de poem.* 2, fr.29 (p.252 Hausrath): καὶ Σαπφώ τινα ἰαμβικῶς ποιεῖ, which refers to the temper, not the metre of certain songs. To this attack upon a clumsiness that affects elegance, compare Rochester's more vicious example from 'Monster All-Pride',

With a red nose, splay foot and goggle eye,
A ploughman's booby mien, face all awry,
With stinking breath and every loathsome mark
This punchinello sets up for a spark.

Who is this lout who fascinates [you?
She trails the hem of her rustic robe. . .
without the least notion of how
        to lift it and let her ankle show!

Evidently one learned, chez Sappho, not only how to walk with elegance (cf. 16.17V of Anactoria's remembered walk), but also how to dress according to the latest mode, and there is one fragment, itself a shabby tatter, that plays knowingly upon the adolescent's narcissistic love of clothes. Taking as her point of departure a present scarcity of exotic ornaments, the singer says (98V),[12]

— coì δ' ἔγω Κλέι ποικίλαν [
— οὐκ ἔχω – πόθεν ἔccεται; – [
— μιτράν⟨αν⟩· ἀλλὰ τὼι Μυτιληνάωι [

I've no embroidered [turban] for you, Kleïs –
where could I have found one?

The alternative possibilities are then half-seriously listed:

..].θοc· ἀ γάρ μ' ἐγέννα[τ   1
[—]
c]φᾶc ἐπ' ἀλικίαc μέγ[αν
κ]όcμον αἴ τιc ἔχη φόβα⟨ι⟩c[
πορφύρωι κατελιξαμέ[να   4
⟨—⟩
ἔμμεναι μάλα τοῦτο .[
ἀλλα ξανθοτέρα⟨ι⟩c ἔχη[
τα⟨ὶ⟩c κόμα⟨ι⟩c δάϊδοc προφ[7
[—]
c]τεφάνοιcιν ἐπαρτία[ιc
ἀνθέων ἐριθαλέων· [
μ]ιτράναν δ' ἀρτίωc κλ[10
[—]
ποικίλαν ἀπὺ Cαρδίω[ν
...].αονίαc πόλ{ε}ιc [

My mother
used to bind her head
when she was young
with purple cord –

[12] For Kleïs, see below, p. 279. The third line continues, 'but with (or to or by or for) the man of Mytiline . . .' These three lines, 1–3 of fragment b, are marked in the papyrus as being misplaced; there is no way to tell for certain where they stood in the song, but with their proper name they seem most probably to belong to the beginning (next in probability would be the end); see W. Kullmann, reviewing Treu's *Sappho*, *Gymnasium* 63 (1956) 142, and West, op.cit., 319.

that was finery! –
and when hair burned
more bright than flame

wreaths were worn or crowns
that bloomed with buds.
More recently

Sardian bandeaux . . .

Unfortunately, the Lydian millinery that everybody wants is no longer to be had, perhaps because of sumptuary laws in Mytilene,[13] and the few leftover bits of foreign finery are no more than

[13] The song has been much discussed for its historical content but it is impossible to reach any concrete conclusion about its political reference since the piece is not complete and the Cleanactid exile is only tangential to its subject anyway. In addition, the reference itself is obscure because the nether portion of fragment b is badly damaged. Line 8 has been variously restored: Gallavotti suggested an unlikely address to Alcaeus, φύγας, Ἄλκα᾽, ἔχει πόλις; Vogliano read φύγας ἄμμιν ἔχει πόλις, Srebrny, φύγας ἀ πόλις ἄμμ᾽ ἔχει; Page suggests, φύγας ἀ πόλις ἄδ᾽ ἔχει. Evidently luxuries that cannot now be had (the ποικίλας of b6) are a reminder of the exile of the Cleanactids, but is it the things themselves, or their lack, that point to that event? Sappho might mean 'bits of finery remind me of the period that followed the Cleanactid flight, when we were in touch with the mainland and could buy imported goods', or she might mean 'bits of finery remind me of the days when the Cleanactids were in power – and so, negatively, by being no longer available, they remind me of the Cleanactid flight.' (It might be noted that Steffen understood not 'Cleanactid flight' but 'flight from the Cleanactids', though τὰς Κλεανακτίδα[ν φύγας could hardly have any such meaning.)

The Cleanactids may have been a clan whose close ties to Lydia brought flourishing commerce when the family came to power, or they may have been anti-commercial, so that imports entered Mytilene only after they had gone. Mazzarino (op.cit., 56ff.) convinced himself that Myrsilus was a Cleanactid and that the Cleanactids stood for trade; he therefore made the time of luxury the time of Myrsilus' tyranny, and argued that this song belongs to the period after Pittacus came to power (equating him with 'the man of Mytilene' of b3). He assumed, however, that Sappho, whom he took to be a pro-Cleanactid (cf. Burn, *Lyric Age of Greece*, 227, who thinks she came from a commercial family) is singing this song in exile, and this makes no sense, since in that case Pittacus' sumptuary laws could have had no effect on her.

Page (*S&A*, 97ff.) likewise read a song composed in exile, but he supposed it to belong to the earlier period when Myrsilus was in power (p.102). Like Mazzarino he identified Myrsilus as a Cleanactid, but unlike Mazzarino he made Sappho belong to an anti-Cleanactid family, and so he imagined a refugee singer in the act of contrasting two sets of luxury articles: those current in distant Mytilene (presumably fresh and fancy) and these which she has brought with her (rather worn and tawdry). This interpretation has its amusing side (Sappho and Kleïs are roughing it, like Alcaeus in his thicket, and wishing they were back in the city), but it is badly adjusted both to the external and to the internal evidence. In the first place, the Marmor Parium seems to associate Sappho's exile with the third exile of Alcaeus, i.e. with the time just before Pittacus was chosen *aisymnētēs*. And in the second, even granting Page's reconstruction of the situation, how could Sappho call distant articles that she does not have – articles that are current in the Cleanactid city – 'memorials of the exile of the sons of Cleanax'? Page tries to explain (p.102) by paraphrasing, 'they are reminders of the time when our enemies were in exile and we were in the city', which he then glosses in this way: 'the inaccessible shops in Mytilene' are ' "memorials of happier days" because they remind her of the time when the party in exile was not her own but her opponents". Which is to say that Cleanactid objects which Sappho does not have are somehow memorials of a time when the city did not have Cleanactids – which is unthinkable nonsense.

ταῦτα τὰς Κλεανακτιδα[
φύγας †..ͺϲαπολιϲεχειͳ
μνάματ'· .ἴδε γὰρ αἶνα διέρρυε[ν   9

the town's reminders of
the Cleanactid flight, souvenirs and faded dreadfully . . .

Sappho's girls seem to have spent hours in companionable consideration of matters such as these, for other scraps of verse record the
appeal of a fine Lydian shoe (39V), a soft linen robe (100V), and a
particoloured cloak (152V). One shawl, in fact, is so perfect (or else so
redolent of its owner's charms) that a cupid seems to flutter in it,
causing it to rouse a pang of sharp desire (22V; cf. 101, 62V).[14]
    Cult, deportment and dress were all apparently matters for study
among Sappho's girls, but music was at the core of their curriculum.
At other houses girls may have done no more than learn the songs of
the day, with whatever liturgical chant was called for by the women's
rituals, but at Sappho's, voice was a principal point of praise, music
a measure of absolute value.[15] The finest thing is 'more musical than
the lyre, more golden than gold' (156V). It follows that lack of music
was a cause for invidious attack, and Sappho once abused an unknown
woman with these words (55V):

    If an historical reconstruction must be made, it would probably be safest to suppose
that the time of ancient simplicity (the singer's mother's time) is to be imagined as
pre-Melanchrus, perhaps even as the *ancien régime* of the Penthilids. The more recent
epoch of imported luxuries will have occurred either under the tyranny of Myrsilus, or
else in the period just after that ruler's death when various aristocratic clans, Cleanactids among them, alternated in dominance (so Gallavotti, 'Rilievi storici sulla nuova
ode di Saffo', *SIFC* 18 (1942) 161–6). And the song's present time of frugality and
shabbiness (surely exaggerated) will be the moment of Pittacus' rise; the banishments
have begun, but Pittacus has not yet been granted supreme power, and Sappho's own
clan still remains in a city that is about to embrace the austerities of its great tyrant.
The trinkets and ribbons that have been preserved were the last to be bought, purchased,
perhaps, just at the moment when the Cleanactids left Mytilene; they are an appropriate
reminder of that family because, like the banished aristocrats, they have faded
dreadfully.
  [14] In 22V the singer seems to tease a companion about her excessive sensitivity to
the charms of the shawl, but the lines defy any close interpretation. See Wilamowitz,
Kl.Schr. i.387; Milne, 'Sappho's ode to Gongyla', *Hermes* 68 (1933) 475; E. Heitsch, 'Zum
Sapphotext', *Hermes* 95 (1967) 388. West, op.cit., 319 offers a fanciful reconstruction
according to which Abanthis sees a dress that belonged to Gongyla and is reminded of
how much she misses her, while Sappho rejoices because Aphrodite has often criticised
her for praying for new loves and not thinking enough of the old!
  [15] Nothing survives to suggest that the music of any other school gained a reputation;
by contrast, the names of three 'students' of Sappho's are preserved and these women
are presumably singers: Anagora, Euneika and Gongyla (Suda sv Σαπφώ). Philostratus,
at *VA* 1.30, mentions as well a certain Damophyla (Damophila?) who is said to have
composed hymns and love songs in the Sapphic manner.

κατθάνοισα δὲ κείσηι ⌣ οὐδέ ποτα μναμοσύνα cέθεν
ἔccετ᾽ οὐδὲ †ποκ᾽† ὕcτερον· οὐ γὰρ πεδέχηιc βρόδων
τῶν ἐκ Πιερίαc, ἀλλ᾽ ἀφάνηc κἀν ᾽Αίδα δόμωι
φοιτάcηιc πεδ᾽ ἀμαύρων νεκύων ἐκπεποταμένα.

when you are dead you will lie forgotten –
none will remember you. Pierian roses were never your share
and down in Hades you'll disappear with the thin
and undefined dead, to flutter and wander there!

The inference is plain: Sappho's pupils were not like this. They were not even just sweet-voiced girls (153V), but true musicians, disciples (*mathētriai* in the Suda) who had been given a whiff at least of the Pierian rose. If they did not, like their mistress, win undying fame, they would at least know the conventional modes and be able to amuse their future households with inventions of their own.

Sappho performed for her girls in order to amuse them ('These things I sing among my friends to bring them joy', 60V),[16] but she also sang as a means of teaching pupils who were expected to imitate her songs. Hymns, epithalamia and other pieces of occasional poetry served as models for performances that would be required of them presently, and even the love lyrics were didactic, since they taught the girls to know their own emotions and to objectify them in song. They, too, performed, courting one another to the tune of their lyres, comparing one another's looks ('she likened you to a shining goddess', 96.4; cf. 82, 23V) and judging one another's style ('she loved your songs the best', 96.5V). Indeed, within the *thiasos*, music seems to have been the natural mode of expression, and the intimacy of the group was such that there was no secret that could not be shared, no subject that could not be sung.

Soon the girls of these youthful groups would marry, and it was to this end that their elegant accomplishments were acquired. Their value was being increased, so that their fathers could boast more fulsomely to their prospective grooms, but they were not just polished for the market – they were prepared for marriage itself. Or at least this was the case at Sappho's house, for there everyone learned the contradictory double lesson of the bride: that virginity kept was glorious, while virginity lost in a wedding-bed was an even more splendid thing. One had to be both pure and desirable, and the balance was not easy to keep, for chastity was provocative (105aV),

---

[16] This apparently obvious fact is denied by those who insist upon a formal and institutional 'occasion' for every archaic poem; cf. e.g. W. Rösler, 'Ein Gedicht und sein Publikum', *Hermes* 103 (1975) 275ff.

οἶον τὸ γλυκύμαλον ἐρεύθεται ἄκρωι ἐπ' ὔςδωι,
ἄκρον ἐπ' ἀκροτάτωι, λελάθοντο δὲ μαλοδρόπηες·
οὐ μὰν ἐκλελάθοντ', ἀλλ' οὐκ ἐδύναντ' ἐπίκεςθαι

like a sweet apple that ripens on the branch
high in the crown of the tree. Forgotten by pickers?
Oh no, but far beyond their reach.

Reached too soon, it was wasted forever (105b),[17]

οἶαν τὰν ὑάκινθον ἐν ὤρεςι ποίμενες ἄνδρες
πόςςι κατacτείβοιςι, χάμαι δέ τε πόρφυρον ἄνθος . . .

just as the upland hyacinth is crushed
beneath shepherds' feet, purple blossom on the ground.

There was, however, a divine model to follow, and Sappho presented her girls with the picture of a childish Artemis who has come to heaven to insist in epic style that virginity must be her permanent state (44A).[18] Arriving at Olympus

]cανορες . . [
Φοίβωι χρυcοκό]μαι τὸν ἔτικτε Κόω . [
μίγεις(α)   Κρ]ονίδαι μεγαλωνύμω⟨ι⟩.
"Αρτεμις δὲ θέων] μέγαν ὄρκον ἀπώμοσε
        κεφά]λαν· ἄï πάρθενος ἔccομαι   5
]. ων ὀρέων κορύφαιc' ἔπι
]δε νεῦcον ἔμαν χάριν·
ἔνευ]ce θέων μακάρων πάτηρ·

---

[17] W. Schadewaldt, *Sappho* (Potsdam 1950) 47, would place these lines in a wedding song as a description of the deflowering of the bride, an interpretation forced on him by his determination to find a ritual cadre for every surviving Sapphic fragment. Fränkel recognises the figure as representing a less auspicious loss of virginity, but he likewise supposes it to come from a wedding song (*DuP*, 195). A. W. Gomme, on the other hand, argued that these fragments came from a 'narrative song, not from an epithalamium' ('Interpretations of Sappho and Alcaeus', *JHS* 77 (1957) 258ff.), but why should these be the only alternatives? See below, p. 269, note 110.

[18] Page (*S&A*, 261–4) attributes this fragment to Alcaeus on the metrical grounds that he and Lobel outlined at *CQ* 2 (1952) 1ff., while admitting that 'the priority of Alcaeus' claim rests on slight foundations' (p.261). He states that there is 'no evidence that Sappho wrote poems of this general type', but both the Lesbian poets made use of Aeolic dactyls, and Treu (*Sappho*⁴, Munich 1968, 161) cites Philostratus *VA* 1.30, where a Sapphic hymn to Artemis is mentioned. Callimachus' parallel hymn suggests that Artemis is here shown as an infant divinity, her prayer being a feat of precocious strength.

ἐλαφάβ]ολον ἀγροτέραν θέρι
      ].ϲιν ἐπωνύμιον μέγα·   10
    ]εροϲ οὐδάμα πίλναται·
    ].[.]...μαφόβε[..]ἔρω·

  ...along with
golden-haired Phoebus whom the daughter of Coeus bore,
mixing in love with notorious Cloud-Dwelling Zeus,
Artemis straightaway swore the great oath of the gods:
'Yea, by your head, I will ever a virgin remain, unwed,
a huntress who wanders deserted mountain peaks.
Come now and nod your consent just to please me!'
She spoke, and the Father of All did nod,
causing immortals and men to give reverent
names to the maid, calling her Deer-Stalker,
Queen of the Wilds, whom Eros could never come near.

Virginity was of supreme importance and yet Sappho's maids, unlike Artemis, were not to spend their lives in the wilds, but were to enter luxurious households as brides. Ideally they were to have enough understanding of Eros to bring their husbands pleasure, and consequently their education in purity had to be seconded by another that taught them the value of physical love. And here their lessons were in part practical, for whenever one of the company was married in the locality they, as her age-mates, accompanied the bride almost to her bed.[19] Sappho taught them just what to do, and among her fragments there are scraps of song meant for the wedding eve, for the wedding night, for the convoy of bride and groom to their couch, and for their ritual awakening on the following day by girls who had spent the night in serenading (30V, 43V).[20] It is not always possible to tell whether they were meant to be sung by one voice or many, but however they were performed these marriage songs speak for a crowd, suggesting two parties of romping youths, the bride's friends and the groom's. They also speak directly to the nature of the festivity, for they are full of the sexual teasing that always and everywhere keeps bad spirits away from wedding celebrations.[21] In a good marriage, the

---

[19] On epithalamia in general, see B. Snell, 'Sapphos Gedicht φαίνεταί μοι κῆνος' *Hermes* 66 (1931) 75ff. =*Ges.Schr.* (Göttingen, 1966) 82ff.; R. Muth 'Hymenaios und Epithalamion', *WS* 67 (1954) 5ff.; also *RE* IA.2371ff.; VIII 2129ff.; IX 130ff.

[20] See Lobel's comments on 30V, at *Oxy.Pap.* 21, 1231 6A, 23, and Gallavotti, 'Auctuarium Oxyrhynchium', *Aegyptus* 33 (1953) 162. Fr. 27V looks as if it were composed for a groom's voice, and if the ὅδος μέγαν εἰς Ὄλυμπον at l.12 refers to the sexual act, it constitutes a distant parallel to the metaphors of Archilochus in the Cologne fragment. On the other hand, the phrase may be meant literally, in which case it is a mythic wedding that is sung.

[21] On obscenity at weddings, see T. Nissen, 'Zu Alkm. fr. 95D', *Philol.* 91 (1936–7) 470ff., where it is remarked that this kind of language is used not only to attract fertility but also to confuse and repel evil spirits.

husband was potent, the wife fecund and chaste, and these are the themes of the Sapphic epithalamia, where grooms are praised for size (111V, 110V, 115V?)[22] and brides for the untouched sweetness that will arouse a man's desire (112; cf. 103BV and perhaps 23V).[23] The songs are so broken that it is hard to imagine what they may have been as wholes, but they seem to have been rather more rowdy and explicit than certain ancient descriptions would lead one to think. Possibly later antiquity attached Sappho's name to its own notions of connubial sensuality; possibly there were in fact other, softer, wedding songs of Sapphic composition, but wherever the truth lies it is charming to find a Byzantine scholar who wishes (while congratulating the Bishop of Constantinople for taking the Church as his Bride) that he could offer epithalamia, 'such as Sappho sang when she twined her songs with soft rhythms and fainting melodies, compared the grooms to prize-winning steeds, the virgin brides to heaps of roses, and made her voice more melting than the zither's note'.[24]

Ritual songs of this sort were a form of instruction in the corporal side of marriage, but Sappho characteristically proposed another and more idealised way of thinking about the coming change in her pupils' lives. She provided a mythic model for marriage, just as she did for virginity, in a long, neo-epic song[25] that offered a heroic example as

[22] This motif is often understood as being frankly obscene, as urged by G. S. Kirk, 'A fragment of Sappho reinterpreted', *CQ* 13 (1963) 51f. Such a sense is extremely appropriate, but in the case of 111V, at least, parallels at *h.Dem.* 188–9 and *h.Aphr.*, 173–4 (as well as at Psalm 24) suggest that this extraordinary stature belonged to the groom's whole body, making him like a divinity, so that the phrase is a form of *makarismos*. (This of course does not exclude a second, obscene sense.)

[23] If 23V is a wedding song, the point is probably that the bride is now like Helen, no longer like Hermione.

[24] Cod. Oxon. Barocc. gr. 131 fol. 224ᵛ – 227ᵛⁱ; see P. Wirth, 'Neue Spüren eines Sapphobruchstückes', *Hermes* 91 (1963) 115. To this compare Himerios, *Or.* 9.16 =218V: Σαπφοῦς ἦν ἄρα μήλῳ μὲν εἰκάσαι τὴν κόρην . . . τὸν νυμφίον τε Ἀχιλλεῖ παρομοιῶσαι.

[25] The Sapphic authorship of fr. 44 has frequently been questioned; Wilamowitz, *NJb* 33 (1914) 230, refused to accept it, and he was followed by Lobel, *Sm* (Oxford, 1925) lxvf., *Am* (Oxford 1927) xff.; see also Schadewaldt, *Sappho* (1950) 48: 'Es felht der Zauber ihrer Einfachheit.' Rose, *Handbook*⁵ (1956) 98, note 61 supposes that the poem may derive from some non-Lesbian member of the Sapphic circle. In support of Sapphic authorship are H. Jurenka, 'Neue Lieder', *WS* 36 (1914) 214–20; Fränkel, *DuP* 196; Page, *S&A*, 70 (where he is somewhat doubtful; earlier, at *CQ* 30 (1936) 10–15 he had been more certain); Bowra *GLP*² (1961) 227; Lesky, *Gesch.*³ (1971) 171; J. T. Kakridis, 'Zu S.44 LP' *WS* 79 (1966) 21ff. Treu wished to reject the song on the ground that it lacked 'Selbstaussage', but admitted that this could not be allowed as grounds for final doubt (*Sappho*, 197). Snell, op.cit., 73, note 3, took Sapphic authorship for granted, as do also S. Radt, 'Sapphica', *Mnem.* 23 (1970) 345, Rösler, op.cit., 275ff., E. M. Voigt, 'Zu Sappho 55a, 6 D', *Hermes* 89 (1961) 251ff. The ground for doubt has been the epic style of the piece, but it is churlish to suppose that Sappho, a professional singer, could not control more than one mode; note also the contention of M. West, 'Greek Poetry 2000–700 B.C.', *QC* 23 (1973) 191, and J. T. Hooker, *Language and Text of the Lesbian Poets* (Innsbruck 1977), 78, that Sappho would have had Aeolic epic as well as Homeric to draw upon.

a splendid analogy.[26] It was a sumptuous piece (the fragment that remains is still the longest that we have) and it may have been meant for public performance,[27] but it was certainly also meant for the ears of her student audience. At the beginning of the surviving section, a herald who has come running into Troy announces the arrival of a bride whose wedding will prefigure every other wedding day (44V):

⟨«   ⟩   3ᵃ
τάς τ’ ἄλλας ’Αcίαc .[.]δε.αν κλέοc ἄφθιτον·
"Εκτωρ καὶ cυνέταιρ[ο]ι ἄγοιc’ ἐλικώπιδα   5
Θήβαc ἐξ ἰέραc Πλακίαc τ’ ἀπ’ [ἀϊ]ν⟨ν⟩άω
ἄβραν ’Ανδρομάχαν ἐνὶ ναῦcιν ἐπ’ ἄλμυρον
πόντον· πόλλα δ’ [ἐλί]γματα χρύcια κάμματα
πορφύρ[α] καταΰτ[με]να, ποίκιλ’ ἀθύρματα,
ἀργύρα τ’ ἀνάρι͜θμα ⌊ποτή͜ρι͜α⌋ κάλέφαιc».   10

---

[26] Compare the remarks of B. Gentili, 'L'interpretazione dei lirici greci arcaica nella dimensione del nostro tempo', *QU* 8 (1969) 12: 'l'episodio mitico diviene l'esemplificazione di una norma, di un aforisma, o di un aforistico preambolo oppure in rapporto all'occasione e alla situazione del canto la vicenda esemplare di un'azione lodevole o nefasta.' Some have held that the sense of the present song must be ominous, since all know that Hector will die, but this is to misunderstand the proper use of such magical and exemplary scenes: Danae can figure divine rescue (as at Sim. 543 *PMG*) though all know that she will have years of suffering after her box washes ashore (likewise the daughters of Proetus, in Bacchylides' tenth ode); Pelops, receiving the gracious aid of Poseidon in Pindar's First Olympian, can be a conveyor of a like grace into a present occasion, though all know that his continuing life will contain exile and bloodshed; Heracles, planting the olive in the Third Olympian, can figure divine care for humanity, though all know he was a seducer, murderer, etc. Surely we are not to suppose that when Sappho herself likened a bridegroom to Achilles (as Himerios says she did, *Or.* 9.16) she meant to introduce an ominous idea of death, so why should Hector's name necessarily darken the present song?

[27] Jurenka (op.cit., 220) thought the poem was meant for performance at a wedding; Page (loc.cit) reports it as an epithalamium, as do Bowra (loc.cit), Merkelbach (op.cit., 16), Gentili (op.cit., 43), and Lasserre (op.cit., 20). Lesky (loc.cit.) denied this, calling the story ill-omened, and reporting the piece as expressive simply of the poet's delight in a mythic subject; he was followed by Kakridis (op.cit.), who argued that Hector's arrival necessarily implied the bringing of his dead body into the city, as described at *Il.* 24.265. Kirkwood (*EGM* 146) concurred, concluding, 'it is reasonable to call 44 a lyric narrative rather than an epithalamion'. Nevertheless, Rösler (op.cit.) revived the wedding theory, proposing to take the piece not as an epithalamium but as a processional song that accompanied a movement of the guests: 'Durch die Betonung der Rolle des mythischen Publikums ist das Publikum der aktuellen Hochzeit in die höhere Realität des Mythos miteinbezogen' (p.282). Whatever the performance situation, it may be said in answer to Kakridis that if the song does indeed mean to suggest a doublet scene to its listeners, that doublet is more probably the scene of the arrival of Paris with Helen, likewise by water, as described in the *Cypria* (Proclus, *Chrest.* I²). This second marriage is choreographically a much closer parallel, and it would offer in good archaic fashion a blameworthy alternate version of the subject of praise.

ὢc εἶπ'· ὀτραλέωc δ' ἀνόρουcε πάτ[η]ρ φίλοc·
φάμα δ' ἦλθε κατὰ πτόλιν εὐρύχορον φίλοιc.
αὔτικ' 'Ιλίαδαι cατίναι[c] ὐπ' ἐυτρόχοιc
ἄγον αἰμιόνοιc, ἐπ[έ]βαινε δὲ παῖc ὄχλοc
γυναίκων τ' ἄμα παρθενίκα[ν] τ..[..].cφύρων,   15
χῶριc δ' αὖ Περάμοιο θυγ[α]τρεc[
ἴππ[οιc] δ' ἄνδρεc ὔπαγον ὐπ' ἄρ[ματα
π[   ]εc ἠίθεοι, μεγάλω[c]τι δ[
δ[   ]. ἀνίοχοι φ[.....].[
π[']ξα.ο[20
<   desunt aliquot versus   >
                                    ἴ]κελοι θέοι[c
                                    ] ἄγνον ἀολ[λε
ἰὄρμαται[   ]νον ἐc "Ιλιο[ν
ἰαῦλοc δ' ἀδυ[μ]έληc.[   ]τ' ὀνεμίγνυ[το
ἰκαὶ ψ[ό]φο[c κ]ροτάλ.[ων   ]ωc δ' ἄρα πάρ[θενοι   25
ἰἄειδον μέλοc ἄγν.[ον, ἴκα]νε δ' ἐc αἴθ[ερα
ἰἄχω θεcπεcία γελ.[
ἰπάνται δ' ἦc κὰτ ὄδο.[ιc
ἰκράτηρεc| φίαλαί τ' ὀ.[...]υεδε[..]..εαχ[.].[
ἰμύρρα κα|ὶ καcία λίβ.ανόc τ' ὀνεμείχνυτο   30
ἰγύναικεc δ' ἐλέλυcδο.ν ὄcαι προγενέcτερα[ι
ἰπάντεc δ' ἄνδρεc ἐπ.ήρατον ἴαχον ὄρθιον
ἰπάον' ὀνκαλέοντεc, 'Εκάβολον εὐλύραν
ἰὔμνην δ' "Εκτορα κ' Α.νδρομάχαν θεο<ε>ικέλο[ιc.

'. . . among his men
Hector is bringing a bright-eyed maid
over the salty sea by ship, away from sacred Thebe
and Placia's eternally flowing streams —[28]
gentle Andromache! With them the wind sends
bracelets of gold and purple robes, elaborate
trinkets, cups beyond number of silver, and
ivory objects as well!' When this man had finished,
Hector's father urgently rose from his place;
word fled through the prosperous city, reaching his friends,
and citizens hastily harnessed their mules
to big-wheeled carts. In climbed the crowd,
women and fine-ankled girls first (though
the daughters of Priam drove separately),
while the men yoked their horses to chariots

---

[28] On the motif of the bride (or the warrior) who leaves a homeland characterised by
its river, see E. M. Voigt, op.cit., 251ff.

... all god-like ... mightily ...
... drivers ...
    (several lines missing)
       ...like to the gods.
The sweet-sounding flute and the lyre
mixed with the chatter of castanets ... girls
sounded the sacred song and its ritual strain
rose to the upper air ... All along the way ...
... cups and jars ...
cassia and frankincense mingled with myrrh
and matrons repeated the alleluia
while all of the men gave the glorious shout
of the far-shooting Lord of the Lyre
and everyone hymned that god-like pair
– Hector and Andromache!

The song ends here, with the names of the groom and the bride. The singer seems to hail their arrival and so to draw them and their stately joy into the moment of her own performance, and indeed the admirable marriage has been bathed in such a noble ideality – the tangible concreteness of the Homeric event has been so diffused – that the glamour of the mythic moment seems to offer itself to a present bit of time. All of which means that the effect of this piece is close to that of a dynamic choral ode,[29] but very far indeed from that of the ordinary bardic narrative, where events were non-transferable and fixed in their finite past. The language and the rhythms here are still heavily epic – they must be, for otherwise the tale would lose some of its transforming power – but the scene is nevertheless both isolated and generalised so as to produce an effect quite unlike that of any epic event.[30] The episode is, in fact, almost dreamlike, for it is rendered by details that are rich, insubstantial and not quite germane. Even the gifts (seen only in the vision that the herald's words enforce) are such

---

[29] Specifically, the song's termination just before the fulfilment of its event is like the practice of choral lyric; cf. e.g. B.18. Kirkwood supposes that Sappho picked up the idea of the lyric genre-scene from Stesichorus during her exile in Sicily (*EGM*, 146), but there is no need to suppose that such scenes were a strictly western invention; see above, pp. 69ff..

[30] Note the remark of Snell (op.cit., 73, note 3): 'Es wird also kein fortschreitendes Geschehen erzählt, sondern Zustände werden beschrieben, Bilder werden nebeneinander gestellt.' On the epic style but non-epic effect, Fränkel notes (*DuP*, 197f.): 'In dem Liede also in welchem Sappho dem epischen Stoff, dem epischen Stil und dem stichischen epischen Vers so nähesteht wie sonst nie in der uns erhaltenen Resten ihrer Dichtung, ist die homerische Form, trotz der vielen übernommenen Einzelheiten, am allergründlichsten zerstört.' Radt, op.cit., 345ff. attempts to modify the description of Sappho's piece as un-Homeric by pointing to likenesses between it and the wedding scene at *Il.*18.491–6, but it is surely significant that only in a passage of ekphrasis can a generality like that of Sappho's scene be found. Rösler, op.cit., 282, notes the non-Homeric, possibly Lesbian details of the vocabulary of 44V: σάτιναι, μύρρα, κασία, λίβανος, κρόταλα.

as wind can send,[31] for every concrete object here is set in motion as soon as it is named, and all are replaced by music. In consequence, a city that could be any city (its streets have no doorways, its women no embroidered robes, its flutes and lyres no decoration or history) becomes simply a container for generalised movement and ritualised sound.[32] A Trojan throng that could be any procession of relatives rushes to the harbour to meet its bridal pair, but once again it is the idea of a bride and groom, not the epic actuality, that is found at the song's end. All is preparation, here, for a marriage that doesn't occur, for as far as this performance goes, Hector and his bride are ever approaching but never here. Always just off shore, they float on the water like figures in a Venetian masque, mannikins resting on heaps of glittering stuffs, enhancing and postponing the thought of the marriage that will eventually come to all of Sappho's girls.

The need to marry well was evidently what brought the members of the Sapphic group together, but the marriages they made moved them apart again. The circle of course could continue, replenished with new girls, but the individuals who went away ceased in a sense to exist, for they could never come back, could never be girls again. One of their songs says just this (104V):[33]

Ἔσπερε πάντα φέρηις ὄσα φαίνολις ἐσκέδασ' Αὔως,
φέρηις ὄιν, φέρηις αἶγα, φέρηις ἄπυ μάτερι παῖδα

---

[31] G. Tarditi, 'Le vesti di Andromaca e i fazzoletti per Afrodite', *RFIC* 84 (1956) 237–9, supposes that καταῦτμενα means 'vaporous' and modifies ποίκιλ᾽ ἀθύρματα to describe the diaphanous stuffs of Andromache's trousseau, though ἀθύρματα is not usually a word for clothing. (The present translation supposes that ἀθύρματα resumes the first category of objects of personal adornment, as it is distinct from the second category, household objects.) Page, following Lobel, assumes that the reading can only be κατ᾽ αὔτμενα '(coming) with the wind', but he complains that it is 'weak in sense here, and lacks grammatical attachment to the sentence' (*S&A* 69, note 1). For this reason a number of others have read a single word, καταῦτμενα = 'perfumed'. This, however, removes the only suggestion of a verb from the sentence, which consequently ceases to be a sentence and becomes a pendant list of objects that rival and diminish Andromache as the cargo of this ship.

[32] A preparatory song of virgins is followed by the *ololugmos* of the women and then by the men's song celebrating the fulfilment of a rite, as if a sacrifice had been brought, made, and rejoiced over. On the *ololugmos* as marking the culmination of a sacred act, see Deubner, 'Ololyge und Verwandtes' *Abh. Berl.Akad.* (1941) 1, 1ff., and on the ritual quality of this musical sequence, see Gentili, op.cit., 43.

[33] Taking ἄπυ in l. 2 as an adverb, in opposition to an understood εἴσω in the other cases; see V. Pisani, 'Zu S.104 LP, 120D', ΜΝΗΜΗΣ ΧΑΡΙΝ *Gedenkschrift P. Kretschmer* ii (1957), 58ff.; also M. Treu, 'Die Struktur von Sappho fr. 48.3 u.120D', *RM* 107 (1964) 289ff. Like 114V and 107V, this song is playful and reminiscent of the ditties that accompany children's games; note especially its quadruple use of φέρηις (with shifts of meaning that cannot be conveyed by a single English word), and its pun on ἔσπερος and εἰσφέρειν.

Dusk, you restore all that the glittering dawn has dispersed, –
bringing the sheep, bringing the goats, – but you keep the
    bride from her mother.

In their new households they would no longer be Micca or Atthis or
Anactoria, but the wife of a certain one or the mother of another, and
their change of status would be as total and as irreversible as the loss
of virginity that was its cause and its sign. Thus, in a song for two
voices, one girl would take the part of the Bride, singing, 'Maidenhood,
maidenhood, how can you leave me?', and another would answer, as
Virginity, 'Never and never again to come near you!' (114V).[34] The
line between girlhood and matronhood was as sharp as that between
life and death, which is why interpreters of dreams considered that
weddings and funerals were interchangeable. It was a line that separated a realm of youth, physical freedom, affection, health and joy
from another of engrossing age, enclosure, sexual subjection, sickness
and grief, and so it is not wonderful that a certain sadness attached
to the crossing of it. 'Then shall I,' one Sapphic verse asks, 'throw
away my maidenhood so soon?' (107V). Marriage would mean physical
separation from present companions, an end to a certain sort of friendship, and perhaps even the beginning of as yet unknown enmities, as
the fragment that says, 'Leto and Niobe once were loving companions',
(142V) seems to hint. Against this inevitable future Sappho prepared
her girls practically by teaching them the music that would touch
their new lives with elegance and harmony. And to those who would
understand she gave more, for she showed them an unchanging beauty
that, glimpsed first in girlhood, could accompany them into their distant and altered lives.

From Sappho her pupils heard about mode, music and marriage as
well as about cult, but above all they heard about themselves, for they
were not just her audience of imitators, they were also the subjects of
her poetry. The names that she gave them may not have been their
real ones, the moments that she described may not have belonged to
their actual histories, but they could nevertheless recognise sung versions of themselves in her verse. They had the daily experience of
hearing themselves transposed into music,[35] and by taking her songs

[34] West, op.cit., 327 and note 54, suggests that the two lines might have been sung by
a single singer, but this denial of the obvious question and answer pattern of game
songs is necessary only if one means to insist (as West in fact does not) that all Sapphic
lyrics were strictly monodic. This call to *parthenia* may have been modelled after the
(choral) call to *hymen*, especially if this word meant 'maidenhead' at some early time;
see R. Muth, loc.cit. Fragments 114V and 107V may come from actual bridal songs, or
from songs sung within the circle but made after the fashion of the wedding
performances.
[35] We can imagine them listening, like Isaac Dinesen's Calypso to Miss Nat-og-Dag,
whose tale, 'correct or not, was to the heroine herself a symbol, a dressed up image of
what she had in reality gone through' ('The deluge at Norderney', *Seven Gothic Tales*).

with them when they left, they took a poetic vision of their life along – a vision of light and motion, music and perfume, all nurturing, and nurtured by, desire. This was what they were to recall, for Sappho taught them that their present experiences of love, enhanced by song and volatilised by memory, would let them recognise beauty later on, in all of its various forms. Love was thus both an initiation and a discipline, according to this teaching, but the passion from which a knowledge of beauty might derive was by no means presented as a longing for the unattainable. Quite the opposite: its object is flesh that is scented, soft and available, and though Sappho in the surviving fragments never describes its actual consumption, there is clearly nothing gauzy or insubstantial about the love that she means. She uses language so simple and general that individual episodes take on the plain abstraction of symbols, but nevertheless the desire that she praises is physically felt, and the couch appears as part of her décor (94V; 21V, cf. 46V) to indicate that its satisfaction is physical too. She offers her girls the memory of a time when music, ritual and fleshly passion mingled smoothly together and an almost mythical beauty resided in carnal love, for in her song-made world there is no dissonance between beauty that is spiritual and beauty that is animal.[36] This easy assumption that love can be both sexual and sublime is the illuminating principle of all the songs about the circle, and it derives directly from the particular kind of love that Sappho there sings, for love, in these songs, means love of girl for girl. Physical possession is here untouched by the notions of shame, corruption, birth and eventual death that mark the sexual actions of women with men,[37] and Sappho treats it not simply as a metaphor but as a means, as she sings of unspoiled contact with an ideal.

For Sappho's girls heterosexual love would be identical with marriage; it would be an act of submission imposed by family and society (cf. pl. *Symp.* 192b 1–2) that would guarantee a place in the communal fabric, providing of course that it fulfilled itself in the pain of giving birth. Such love would be finite, visceral and unique in its object, its caresses fixed by anatomy and its social aspect by the need to make children who were demonstrably their fathers' own. The duty of het-

---

[36] M. Meunier, *Sappho* (Paris 1932) 205, remarks: 'Sappho certes n'aima ni chanta ce qu'aima et chanta la vierge d'Avila. Mais leurs ardeurs furent également de brûlantes ardeurs et maintes fois l'expression de leurs transports pourrait se mettre en parallèle. L'une et l'autre reconnurent tout ce que nous avons d'infini dans le désir de la chair et dans l'élan de l'esprit.' Compare the more economical summation of Bachofen, *Myth, Religion and Mother Right* (tr. R. Manheim, Princeton, 1967) 205: 'Wherever she found physical beauty, Eros impelled her to create spiritual beauty as well.'

[37] Lanata, op.cit., 67, notes Sappho's constant association of Aphrodite with the Graces and concludes that the love she celebrates is free of that 'oscuro e implacabile furore che ad esempio connota Eros nei versi di Ibico'. See also p.73, note 43, where she equates the moderation of homosexual love with the moderation that was valued generally in archaic aristocratic societies.

erosexual love, well-performed, would give a measure of importance to each of the girls in her life to come, but it was not intended to rouse her senses, much less her imagination.[38] Desire, unless she chanced to feel it for her husband, would be destructive of the household, as Helen's model proved, and consequently beauty in its masculine form would have to go unrecognised. Heterosexual love would be copulation fearsomely defined by a set of absolute commands and proscriptions, and it would not, most probably, encourage visions of mystical loveliness.

The circle's present love of girl for girl, on the other hand, was a thing so different as to need another name. It was neither sanctioned nor prohibited by the community;[39] its purpose was not generation, and its practice was consequently not deformed by fears and tabus. This love had nothing institutional to offer but (as it is portrayed in Sappho's songs) it could give its devotees delight, choice, reciprocity and a heightened sense of self. Since the question of virginity was not involved, nothing was forbidden; there was no hierarchy of gesture fixed by the nearness to a single defended goal, and so there was no shame-built need for secrecy. One caress was as sweet as another, a wreath could be as provocative as an uncovered limb, and because pleasure was luxuriously sensual but never obscene it could be thought of as a form of worship and sung in all its aspects. Finally, because this love was open and non-reproductive, an easy promiscuity was the rule, allowing love to follow always, wherever beauty was perceived.

Among themselves Sappho and her pupils sang mostly of this second sort of love – she because it was her chosen subject and they because as yet they knew no other kind. The girls are portrayed by the fragments as a band of affectionate companions who respond to one another with longing and desire (*pothos* and *imeros* are two favourite words).[40] They pursue and provoke, but they also slake and satisfy (48V):[41]

[38] Cf. Plato *Symp.* 191d6–e2, where the heterosexual imitation of homosexual love is found not in marriage but in adultery.

[39] Homosexuality among girls was, however, at least tacitly licensed or tolerated since it could be openly expressed, and probably this was an outgrowth of the licensed sexual freedom of certain initiation groups; see Calame, op.cit., 420ff., Brelich, op.cit., 157ff., and Lasserre, op.cit., 10, note 13, commenting on Alcman fr. 34 *PMG*.

[40] See 22.11, 48.2, 94.23, 102.2V, for πόθος, and 36V for ποθέω; see 95.11, 96.16, 78.3 and 6V, for ἴμερος, which appears in verbal form at 1.27V, and as an adjective at 78.3 and 112.4V.

[41] Probably Theocritus was remembering the first line of this song when he began his Idyll 12:Ἦλυθες, ὦ φίλε κοῦρε. The continuation of the Sapphic line is in doubt, however, for the notion of doing well derives only from emendations (κεὖ Edm., εὖ δ᾽ Lobel, ἔσλ᾽ Turyn). The reading of l.2 is likewise undertain: Lobel printed ὂν δ᾽ἔψυξας, but Pfeiffer, reviewing *Sm* at *Gnomon* 2 (1926) 317, revived Wilamowitz's old objection to the idea of 'cooling' as unromantic, and also his solution, ἔφλυξας 'you caused my burning heart to ignite' (see 'Lesefrüchte', *Hermes* 59, 1924, 267). This mistaken attempt to keep burning Sappho aflame is sensibly dealt with by Lanata (op.cit., 67); she points to the

ἦλθες, †καὶ† ἐπόησας, ἔγω δέ σ' ἐμαιόμαν,
ὂν δ' ἔψυξας ἔμαν φρένα καιομέναν πόθωι

You came – you did well! for I was on fire;
you cooled my heart when it flamed with desire.

They change partners[42] with quips and taunts (130V; 133V; 71V, cf. 22V?), but they know the joy of sleeping at the breast of a tender friend (126V),[43] and they dislike solitude (168BV):[44]

Δέδυκε μὲν ἀ σελάννα
καὶ Πλήϊαδες· μέσαι δὲ
νύκτες, παρὰ δ' ἔρχετ' ὤρα,
ἔγω δὲ μόνα κατεύδω.

The moon has sunk,
the Pleiades are gone; the night's
half-finished – love's hour past –
and I sleep alone.

Separated from their chosen loves, they are sad – though not always so sad as to forget to be clever, judging by one alliterative lament that remains (146V):

μήτε μοι μέλι μήτε μέλισσα

This world of fastidious flirtation and appeasement is Sappho's poetical creation and she stands at its centre, observing, enhancing and participating. Perhaps her own passions, being mature, are more intellectual – perhaps more physical – but that is her affair.[45] The important fact is that she discerns in this early girl-love a strain of

---

imitation at Theognis 1273, where the singer says of a boy who served him sexually for a short time: ἄμμε δ' ἀνέψυξας μικρὸν χρόνον. It might also be relevant to note that the final element in Theocritus' echo shows a similar shift from hot to cool as a figure for the slaking of passion (*Id.*12.9, where the lover hastens towards the returned boy as a wayfarer hastens from scorching sun into the shade of a tree). Possibly the Sapphic song is a parody of the masculine *prosphonētikon*.

[42] The commentator at P.Oxy. 2292, considering the word σύνδυγος, attempted to chart the shifting pairs; see Gallavotti, *Aegyptus* 33 (1953) 159ff., and Merkelbach, op.cit., who imagines a form of marriage for the girls (as does also W. Rösler, op.cit., 275).

[43] On the straightforward eroticism of 126V, δαύοισ' ἀπάλας ἑταίρας ἐν στήθεσσιν, see Lanata, op.cit., 70.

[44] In defence of the genuineness of this fragment, doubted for reasons of dialect, see J. T. Hooker, *The Language and Text of the Lesbian Poets* (Innsbruck 1977) 36–8.

[45] A number of fragments treat the idea of being too old for something (58.13ff., with the figure of Tithonos; cf. 21, with its similar reference to aged flesh; 121V, which pretends to refuse a young male), but these need not have been sung by Sappho in her own voice.

imperishable beauty which is a vivid subject for meditation and for song. The girls will leave to live wedded lives built on another kind of love, but before they go she teaches them (in her own fancy at least) to recognise something from their adolescent sexuality as superlatively fine. In her creed, a delicate sumptuousness (*abrosuna*, 58.25V), accurately enjoyed, gives both an outward brilliance and an inner splendour to one's love of life.[46] She expects her pupils, because they have known this ennobling luxury of sweetness with her, to discover the bright and the fine wherever it abides, for her ultimate lesson is that true beauty is simple and the same, whatever its form. This is why the ancients compared her to Diotima (cf. Pl. *Symp.* 210b) and why she uses a tight set of descriptive words for whatever she would praise, calling flesh, flower, voice, landscape or sensation always 'luxurious', 'soft', 'sweet', 'tender', or 'beautiful'. Any single experience of beauty repeats, and prepares for, every other one: this was the wisdom that her girls could take with them to Lydia or to mainland Greece – the same wisdom that has reached men and women separated from Sappho by much more than a stretch of moonlit sea. A great scholar once tried to prove Sappho's 'normalcy' by arguing that, had she been a homosexual, her poems would have been disgusting to those who were not like her,[47] but the truth seems to be just the opposite. Sappho's songs enchant all mortality because, through images of girl-love, they make one believe for an instant in a beauty that is splendid and imperishable but ready to be touched and possessed.

---

[46] The notion is expressed in the final words of a song in which Tithonos figures old age (58.25–6V): ἰέγὼ δὲ φίλημμ' ἀβροσύναν|]τοῦτο καί μοι / τὸ λάιμπρον ἔρως ἀελίω καὶ τὸ κάιλον λέιλJογχE. The point seems to be that luxury is necessary to love, and the lines are cited by Athenaeus (15.687b) as showing that Sappho does not separate delight in life from virtue: φανερὸν ποιοῦσα πᾶσιν ὡς ἡ τοῦ ζῆν ἐπιθυμία τὸ λαμπρὸν καὶ τὸ καλὸν εἶχεν αὐτῇ. Even with this gloss, however, the fragment is extremely mysterious and Page says frankly (*S&A*, 130, note 1): 'I have no conception of the meaning of the last two lines.' Edmonds translated, 'But I love delicacy and the bright and the beautiful belong for me to the desire of the sunlight'; Kirkwood (*EGM*, 260) gives, 'love of the sun (i.e. love of life) has in it for me both the bright and the good'; Lanata (op.cit., 76) somehow contrives to make 'l'amore luminoso del sole e la bellezza' into parallel terms, and West does away with λέλογχε, translating: 'My liking is for what is graceful; (because of) this it is love that shows me even the brightness of the sun, and what to hold fair' (*Maia*, 22, 330). In spite of the difficulties in interpretation, however, it is clear that Sappho equated or at least connected ἀβροσύνα with enjoyment of life (Athenaeus' ἡ τοῦ ζῆν ἐπιθυμία and the fragment's ἔρως ἀελίω), and found in this elegant appetite for living both an external brilliance and also an internal and almost ethical beauty.

[47] Wilamowitz, *Sappho und Simonides* (Berlin 1913), 63–78.

Desire

In recent years, hosts of occasion-seekers have examined Sappho's poetry, some looking for incidents in the singer's sentimental life, others for public rites where she performed professionally, but all convinced that the significant truth about each song lies somewhere outside it, beyond or behind its lines. Critics who expect lyric song to be a burning page torn from a diary have satisfied their own demands by inventing scenarios of betrayal, anguish and jealousy for songs which, left to themselves, are balanced investigations of the nature of desire. And meanwhile, critics who believe that archaic song responds exclusively to communal needs have constructed ceremonies previously quite unknown – new rites for a society that had a plenitude already – and then have argued that these ceremonies dictated lines that only seem to be marked by passion or subjectivity. If, however, each song is approached as being itself its own significant truth, most of these speculations can be forgotten since, as self-defining works of art, the six major poems of Sappho prove to be neither revelations of an inner personal condition nor expressions of a community's vital institutional system. Cast in metre and performed to a musical accompaniment, these poems are by definition something other than mere records of experience. On the other hand, though they often express a sense that certain moments may be privately ritualised, none of them (with the exception of the epithalamia) declares itself as made for public, pompous use, for even the hymns seem to belong to an idiosyncratic, if not a metaphorical, schema of religious observance. All six make use of conventional song-shapes, figures and modes, including first-person expressions for the singer, but with these means they neither confess nor chant. What they do instead is meditate, using a lyric way of thinking to extract truths from experiences that are never seen as unique but are presented always as proofs of a circular, Sapphic law according to which beauty demands love and love, in turn, creates the beautiful.

The six best-preserved songs of Sappho have been selected at random by the chances of millennial survival and they represent various types of performance, being two exhortations, two prayers, an anecdote (something like the sympotic anecdotes of Archilochus and Alcaeus) and an extended gnome. Each of the six has its own inner conventions, and though all were presumably performed once at least by the poet herself, they show a wide variety of ostensible relations between maker, singer and song. All use first-person forms, but neither in combination nor separately do they constitute a depiction of self in any autobiographical sense. Only twice does the performer name herself (once in prayer and once in the anecdote, 1 and 94V), only twice does she assert herself by using *ego* in the nominative (in the gnome and the anecdote, 16 and 94V), and only once is she betrayed by her grammar even as being feminine (31.14V). This is the Sapphic singer at her most aggressive; in two other cases her presence is almost unperceived, being reduced to a mere elided pronoun (*m'* at 2.1) or to an oblique 'us' employed near the end of a song (96.21). There is no way to determine the order in which these six poems were composed, but the question is of no importance since the thought is both complete within each performance and also consistent among them all. They were meant to be remembered and imitated and sung over and over again, in whatever groupings one chose, for they were to form a melodic amalgam in the minds of their loyal listeners, a single expression of the mood and ethos of a tiny court where the poet was also the queen. Nevertheless, since the separate songs must be considered as wholes (even when they sadly are not), they must also be considered in some sequence or other, and so they are presented here, quite arbitrarily, so as to recapitulate the phases of an ideal Sapphic love. First comes a song of initial doubt, last one of final relinquishing, an order that has the accidental advantage of allowing one to begin with what is generally considered to be Sappho's most personal poem.

According to her own fiction, the singer of fragment 31 is preparing herself to approach someone who has aroused her desire and who consequently provokes her awestruck fear.[1] She addresses the girl as if she were present, as one will the object of obsessive thoughts, but the song takes the form of an inner monologue that occurs while the lover contemplates a scene that she herself has set, a kind of dream-test from which she draws the courage to proceed (31V).

---

[1] The song's minimal fiction produces only a lover who is afraid to approach her love, but probably it is safe to assume in addition that the love is new and that such an approach has not yet been made; see G. A. Privitera (*QU* 8, 1969, 37–80 = *La Rete di Afrodite*, Palermo 1974, 85–129), who supposes a time before the love has been confessed, while it is 'ancora segreto'.

Φαίνεταί μοι κῆνος ἴcοc θέοιcιν
ἔμμεν' ὤνηρ, ὄττιc ἐνάντιόc τοι
ἰcδάνει καὶ πλάcιον ἆδυ φωνεί-
    cac ὐπακούει   4

καὶ γελαίcαc ἰμέροεν, τό μ' ἦ μὰν
καρδίαν ἐν cτήθεcιν ἐπτόαιcεν·
ὠc γὰρ ⟨ἔc⟩ c' ἴδω βρόχε' ὤc με φώνη-
    c' οὐδὲν ἔτ' εἴκει,   8

ἀλλὰ †καμ† μὲν γλῶccα †ἔαγε†, λέπτον
δ' αὔτικα χρῶι πῦρ ὐπαδεδρόμακεν,
ὀππάτεccι δ' οὐδὲν ὄρημμ', ἐπιβρό-
    μειcι δ' ἄκουαι,   12

†ἔκαδε† μ' ἴδρωc κακχέεται, τρόμοc δὲ
παῖcαν ἄγρει, χλωροτ[έρα δὲ π]οίαc
ἔμμι, τεθ[νάκην δ' ὀ]λίγω 'πιδε[ύης
    φα[ίνομ' ἔμ' αὔτ[αι.   16

ἀλλὰ πὰν τόλματον, ἐπεὶ †καὶ πένητα†

To me he seems to match the gods,
that man who sits before your face
and listens to the close
    sweet murmur of your voice

and your warm laugh, things, I swear,
that shake my heart with fear.
One glimpse of you and speech
    is far beyond my power,

my tongue lies shattered while a thin
flame runs beneath my skin;
my eyes can't see and drums begin
    to throb inside my ear;

chill sweat possesses me; a fit
of trembling takes my every part and,
pale as summer grass, I seem to be
    in death's near company.

Still, the risk is to be run, since
. . . even the beggar . . .[2]

---

[2] There are still some who believe, like George Thomson (*CQ* 29, 1935, 37–8), that this poem ends with line 16 and is thus complete; viz. Bowra, *GLP*[2], 185–6 and Kirkwood, *EGM*, 257, note 36; for a full bibliography of the question see Saake, *Kunst*, p.35. Nevertheless, the only reason for rejecting 'Longinus' ' indications of a fifth stanza is the completion of a ring, between the *phainetai* of line 1 and the *phainomai* of line 16, and this is not evidence for completion of the song, since rings often encircle parts that are less than wholes; cf. M. Lefkowitz, 'Critical stereotypes', *GRBS* 14 (1973) 120, who notes that the echo of the two verbs signifies conclusion of a section, while reference to the narrator 'signifies transition to a new subject'. It must be said, however, that some of the arguments that attempt to prove continuation on the basis of Sappho's 'usual

This poem was imitated by Catullus and treated as exemplary by the author of the *Treatise on the Sublime*, and it has remained the most admired, or at least the most noticed, of all of Sappho's songs. Every reader seems to respond to its curious mixture of cool diction and fiery emotion (sometimes it is entitled 'Love's Pathology'), but nevertheless when scholars write out their interpretations, their products are astonishingly different. In one camp, those who listen for a cry of helpless pain from every Sapphic song have made this the record of a seizure of sickening jealousy[3] (or even of a fit of 'homosexual anxiety'),[4] somehow delivered on the spot. And in another camp, critics who look for a communal setting ask us to view this song as if it were a tea-tray or a pickle-dish presented to a bride, describing it as a public performance that apes passion in order to prepare a pretty compliment for wedding guests to savour, along with the dancing and the toasts and the other pleasures of a wedding day.[5]

---

practice' are just as weak (e.g. H. J. M. Milne, 'Musings', *SO* 13 (1934) 21ff. and 'The final stanza', *Hermes* 71 (1936) 126ff.; R. Lattimore, 'Sappho 2 and Catullus 51', *CP* 39 (1944) 184–7), since the complete poems to support them do not exist. At l. 13 I am reading κὰδ δέ μ᾽ ἴδρως ψῦχρος ἔχει with Page.

[3] Some exponents of the jealousy theory are G. Perrotta, *Saffo e Pindaro* (Bari 1935), 30ff.; W.Ferrari, 'Il Carme 51 di Catullo', *Ann. Sc. Norm. Pisa*, Ser.II.7 (1938) 59–72; A. Barigazzi, 'L'Ode di Saffo φαίνεταί μοι κῆνος e l'additamento di Catullo', *RIL* 75 (1942) 401–30); Page, *S&A*, 33, who speaks of 'a love in jealousy'. A variant interpretation is based upon envy rather than jealousy, and discovers a poem that primarily expresses love for the girl; so W. Schadewaldt, 'Zu Sappho', *Hermes* 71 (1936) 372, and *Welt u. Dichtung* (1950) 99–104, 110–12; A. Setti, 'Sul fr. 2 di Saffo', *SIFC* NS 16 (1939) 195–221; Bowra, *GLP*[2] (1961) 188; V. Bongi, 'Ancora su Catullo e Saffo', *Aegyptus* 26 (1942) 96–101; Kirkwood, *EGM* 122.

[4] See G. Devereux, 'The nature of Sappho's seizure in fr. 31', *CQ* NS 20 (1970) 17–31, where the central statement is, 'Even if there existed no explicit tradition concerning Sappho's lesbianism, her reaction to her male rival would represent for the psychiatrist prima facie evidence of her perversion' (p.21). (One of the most striking characteristics of the Devereux piece is the openly condemnatory attitude of its 'scientific' author towards homosexuality: e.g. 'the libido is contaminated', p.25.) The contentions of this article were effectively demolished by M. Marcovich, 'Sappho fr. 31', *CQ* 22 (1972) 19–32, where the symptoms are shown to be all conventional and literary, and the male 'rival' a merely hypothetical being. Much less successful is the work of Odysseus Tsagarakis, 'Some neglected aspects . . .' *RM* 122 (1979) 97–118, who tries, by means of parallels from Greek folk songs, to prove that Sappho's symptoms are necessarily heterosexual and that therefore what she expresses is envy, since she wishes she could be in the girl's place, *vis à vis* the man!

[5] The major early exponents of the wedding-song theory were B. Snell and R. Merkelbach, though Wilamowitz had suggested the idea in *SuS* (p.58). In an influential article, 'Sappho's Gedicht, φαίνεταί μοι κῆνος', *Hermes* 66 (1931) 71–90, Snell studied two separate conventions of epithalamia – the flattering comparison and the *makarismos* – and then argued that the phrase ἴσος θέοισιν must have been applied to a groom. His arguments were lucidly criticised by G. Wills, 'Sappho 31 and Catullus 51', *GRBS* 8 (1967) 179–80, and indeed Snell himself had already retreated from his most extreme position, admitting that there was no necessity for believing that the song was actually sung at a wedding, but still insisting that nevertheless the epithalamium form 'zu grunde liegt' (*Gesamm. Schriften*, Göttingen 1966, 97). Merkelbach, however, had meanwhile re-asserted the necessity of a wedding occasion, insisting that this song,

The case-history poem and the wedding-gift poem are both the inventions of men who look for a physical 'occasion' and who find it, in this case, in the man who seems to be present. He is the hated love-rival, according to the one group, the admired bridegroom,[6] according to the other, but to both he is a particular, present creature and his meeting with the girl is a flesh and blood fact to which Sappho gives simultaneous documentation in verse. There is, however, another way of viewing this initial masculine figure, and it is one that accords far better with the generalising tenor of the rest of the song. Sappho, after all, says explicitly that the physical symptoms she lists are not to be thought of as having marked one memorable moment: they are instead what happens 'each time I look at you'.[7] The wave of weakness the description of which fills the body of her song is thus typical; it is also

---

sung as a kind of farewell from her companions, would be no more strange than the documented bride's lament for her lost virginity (which, incidentally, we do *not* know to have been sung at a wedding); see 'S. u. ihr Kreis', *Philolog.* 101 (1957) 6ff. and 'Individualität u. Konvention', *Antike Lyrik* (ed. Eisenhut, Darmstadt 1970) 82–9. The compliment presumably offered to the bride was paraphrased by Fränkel (*DuP*, 200) as: 'her loveliness transforms itself into love, into the reality of Sappho's burning love for her'. It might be noted that if this were what is said, it would be exactly opposed to the sense of fr.16, where love transforms itself into loveliness. S. Mowinckel, *Relig.u. Kultus* (Göttingen 1953) 121, supposes that this is not a compliment but a lament expressing the sadness of the bride's companions at the parting her marriage must effect. Bowra (*GLP²*, 213ff.) used the sociological argument that only at a wedding could a man and a girl sit together, and F. Lasserre, 'Ornements érotiques dans la poésie lyrique archaïque', *Serta Turyniana* (Urbana 1974) 5–33, extends this occasional argument by insisting that only in the case of a wedding could Sappho have known beforehand that such a pairing would take place and so have been able to get her song ready. L. thus spells out the unspoken assumption of so many critics, the assumption of a perfect synchronisation between poetic situation and actual performance conditions; in his mind, Sappho stands up, points a finger at 'that man', and begins to sing as the fellow actually sits and the girl actually laughs. The most recent adherent is T. McEvilley, 'Sappho fr.31: the face behind the mask', *Phoenix* 32 (1978) 1–18, who more moderately assumes that the performance was in fact only for the girls, but that the form of the wedding song was followed in its composition. See also C. Segal, 'Eros and Incantation', *Arethusa* 7 (1974) 159 note 19, who straddles the fence: 'The ritual context allowed Sappho to express an intensity of emotion which normal intercourse and the normal modes of relation in society would render difficult. On the other hand we know too little of what convention on archaic Lesbos would or would not have permitted.' Aside from Wills, the major critics of the wedding-song theory are A.Setti, 'Sul fr. 2 di Saffo', *SIFC* 16 (1939) 194–221, and Page, *S&A*, 26–33; there is a summary of the discussion in G. Jachmann, 'Sappho u. Catull', *RM* 107 (1964) 3–16. More recently, G. A. Privitera (*QU* 8, 1969, 37–80 = *La Rete di Afrodite*, Palermo 1974, 85–129), Saake (*Kunst*, 36–7) and Kirkwood (*EGM*, 121–2) have all rejected the wedding-song hypothesis.

[6] It is often stated categorically that only at a wedding could a man and a girl sit close to one another, but the fact is that we have no information whatever about such social usages, and it might be noted that West, at the opposite pole, is willing to suppose that women might have been present at some archaic symposia (*Studies*, 17, note 26).

[7] The generalising and Homeric quality of the symptoms was pointed out long ago in a detailed study of parallels by A. Turyn, *Studia Sapphica*, Eos Supp. 6 (1929) 7ff.; see also Page, *S&A*, 28–30; Privitera, *Rete*, 114–18. The generalising nature of the whole poem is thoroughly established by Marcovich, op.cit., passim.

rhetorical, since it proves the terrifying nature of the vision that is its cause, and consequently it is natural to suppose that the man who so oddly appears and disappears is likewise typical and rhetorical.[8] He is certainly not a dramatic character, for the continuing song abandons the scene in which he is introduced, producing meditation instead of any kind of anecdote and never asking that this man be thought of again. He is not a groom or a lover or a father or a brother; he is a faceless hypothesis[9] whose successful bravado contrasts with the singer's own failure and incapacity.[10] Which is not to say that he is

[8] The ὅττις clause is of the classifying-causal sort, specifying the reason why this anonymous man is as he has been described: see S. Radt, 'Sapphica', *Mnemosyne* 23 (1970) 340: 'Jener Mann, der so ist, dass er ... der imstande ist ... Der Satz mit ὅττις dient nicht bloss dazu, den Mann näher zu bestimmen (dazu hätte ja auch ὅς gereicht) sondern auch um Sappho's Urteil über ihn zu begründen.' Page has, 'that man, whatever his name, who ...' (*S&A*, 20) and Wilamowitz (*SuS*, 58) paraphrased τοιοῦτός τις οἶος; cf. Setti, op.cit., 202 note 1; Privitera, *Rete*, 99–102; Wills, op.cit., 183, 'virtually equivalent to εἰ'. Note, however, L. Rydbeck, 'Sappho's φαίνεταί μοι, *Hermes* 97 (1969) 161–6, who maintains that in Lesbian usage ὅττις = ὅς.

[9] Smyth concluded, ad loc., 'κῆνος is therefore not a rival of Sappho's but a creation of her fancy'; likewise C. del Grande, 'Saffo. Ode, φαίνεταί μοι', *Euphrosyne* 2 (1959) 181ff. and M. Ragone, *Contributo alla Interpretazione di Saffo, fram.31 LP* (Naples 1968), 33–8 noted that Romagnoli had suggested that the girl might perhaps have departed, the sociable scene being the lover's imagined version of her present condition. Gallavotti likewise saw that the man was 'nominato a principio piu o meno genericamente', and yet he insisted that he was in fact a particular lover of the girl's seen on a particular occasion ('Esegesi e testo dell'Ode fr.2 di Saffo', *RIFC* 21, 1942, 113ff.). The same mixed notion of an actual man taken as a hypothetical case is present in the discussion of Radt (op.cit., 340–3), who begins by saying that the man is here as a figure of calm reason and sense over against Sappho's excitement and folly, but who ends by saying, 'Es ist natürlich recht gut möglich dass Sappho im Leben eifersuchtig auf den Mann war – in diesem Gedicht aber schildert sie nicht ihre Eifersucht, sondern nur ihre Liebe.' In the same fashion, Privitera begins by asserting the general nature of Sappho's condition and the generalising effect of ὅττις, noting (op.cit., 95), 'L'apertura e favolosa, sospesa come una visione', but nevertheless announces later that 'l'occasione e una occasione particolare' (p.105), though he has just said that this occasion melts into a general condition (p.104). More recently, Wills (op.cit.), Lefkowitz (op.cit.) Marcovich (op.cit.) and West (*Maia* 22, 1970, 311ff.) have all clearly supposed that both the man and the scene in which he plays are parts of a Sapphic hypothesis.

[10] See F. G. Welcker, *Sappho* (1816) 68. Wills, op.cit., finds it necessary to convert Sappho's statement about herself into a like hypothesis by reading τὸ δή κεν in line 5: 'what he does *would* destroy me ...' (p.182). Such a change is of course not necessary if τό is taken to refer to the girl's laughter and talk, or if the thought is proleptic, i.e. 'His actions, when I imagine doing them, strike terror in my heart, for a mere glance, etc.' The objections usually put forward against Welcker's understanding of the opening are two: first, that there is no word to express the idea of the man's strength or endurance (so C.F. Neue, *Sapphonis Mytil. Fragmenta*, Berlin 1827, 29), and secondly, that ἴσος θέοισιν does not mean *strong* as gods are, but rather *happy* like them (so F. Dornseiff in a review of Turyn's *Studia Sapphica* in *Deutsche Literaturzeitung* 51, 1930, 395–7). To the first of these it may be answered that the concept of endurance or daring is expressed in the τόλματον of line 17 which will make the lover like the companion; to the second it can be argued (as Wills does, op.cit., 175ff.) that Homeric comparisons with the gods certainly did emphasise strength. In addition, it may be said that Sappho, because she was using not only the 'he must be made of stone' topos but also the ὄλβιος ὅς formula, needed an expression that would allow of both strength and felicity, and therefore chose this necessarily ambiguous one.

without significance – quite the opposite, for 'that man', sitting as he does at the top of the song, serves as a kind of marker, fixing the goal both of the lover and of the poet. His position and his conditions are the ends towards which all moves.

The man who opens this song is thus no fossilised being who once played a role in Sappho's personal life or in the public life of Lesbos. He is instead an implement of Sappho's poetic wit, and on closer study he proves to be a hybrid creature made up of borrowings from two quite different sources. First of all, this intrepid companion owes a great deal to the ubiquitous figure who allows so many love-songs, both ancient and modern, to argue that 'anyone who can resist you must be made of stone'. To the extent that he serves in this capacity, his later double can be recognised in one of Pindar's songs (123S):

> The man who meets the liquid glance
> that gleams from Theoxenus' eye
> and fails to swell with passion must
> have tempered his dark heart (of steel
> or adamant) within a chilly flame,
> or else he is misprized of sloe-eyed Aphrodite –
> does her work for hire
> or, woman-like, pursues cool paths [of chastity].
> I, like wax in sun's high heat,
> melt in sacred honey-drops
> when I so much as look upon
> the slender limbs of boys,
> and here in Tenedos
> Peitho and Charis both have come to dwell
> with him – Agesilaus' son!

Probably Pindar is only pretending to sing a love-song in these fastidiously suggestive lines, but whatever his intention he provides an example of the trope of the impervious creature in its everyday use – that of advancing the case of a lover who would display his own warmth. Ostensibly brought into the song as a gnomic measure of the boy's charm, the man who remains unmoved serves in fact as a denigrated foil for the singer's own more human response and so, as he slanders this figure of frigidity, Pindar can give value to the genial susceptibility that he himself confesses. He praises the boy for his erotic power but he also praises himself for his own lust and this happy double exploitation of the unmoved man makes the peculiarity of Sappho's use of the same poetic trick especially plain. Pindar's point is that he enjoys his 'sufferings' and would not think of changing places with his non-deliquescent opposite, whereas Sappho's lover urges just such an exchange upon herself, in her final stanzas, and so in the end makes a poem with a very different tone. What the phantom

companion does terrifies her, she says,[11] but she must dare it all the
same, and consequently she and he, the too-much moved and the
unmoved, are given evaluations that reverse those of the normal love
song that Pindar parodies. She, the lover, is not surreptitiously praised
for happy human weakness, but officially humiliated with a description of painful physical decline, and meanwhile her foil figure is not
scorned, but honestly admired. To serve the trope he needed only to
be excessively resistant or hard, but this man of Sappho's is easy and
fortunate, as well as being safe – he is not at all like a stone or a
eunuch, but instead like a god.

By likening her impervious figure to a god, Sappho smoothly suggests not only that the girl is too much for any ordinary mortal but
also that she, too, is godlike in aspect. (The proof is almost Euclidean,
since she whom the equal of the gods treats with equality must stand
to the immortals just as he does.) The song's opening flattery is thus
devious as well as double, and it is achieved with a clever economy,
but nevertheless it might have been essentially commonplace, since
girls were routinely likened to divinities by the members of this
group.[12] In fact, however, these two superficial effects are overborne
by a third, more powerful one as Sappho, with the words *isos theoisin*[13]
smilingly announces that she means to enter one of the stock philosophical debates of her time. Men liked to ask one another what mortal
could claim to be like a god because the comparison, being dangerous,

---

[11] Like so many words in this song, τό, the subject of ἐπτόαισεν, is perfectly ambiguous
(see Privitera, *Rete*, 103, on this studied and pervasive ambiguity). It has been held to
represent: (1) the talk and laughter of the girl (Snell, *Hermes* 66, 78; F. Tietze, 'Catulls
51 Gedicht', *RM* 88 (1939) 348, note 4; Setti, op.cit., 212; Smyth, ad loc.; Radt, op.cit.,
342; Lefkowitz, op.cit., 120; Marcovich, op.cit., 21ff., where the phrase is translated,
'this is what made me fall in love with you)'; (2) the whole outward aspect of the girl
(Saake, *Kunst*, 26); (3) the fact that the man is close to the girl (Page, *S&A*, 22, and
other exponents of the song of jealousy); (4) the man's self-possession (Gallavotti, op.cit.,
113ff.), or the fact that he can listen unmoved (del Grande, op.cit., 184f.); (5) the whole
situation, i.e. that anyone could sit thus and listen (Perrotta, op.cit., 47, note 1; W.
Ferrari, *Ann.Sc.Norm.* Pisa 7, 1938, 63; Wills, op.cit., 173). In cases (1) and (2) the
aorist will refer to some previous moment when the singer did once listen or look
closely; in the others it will be inceptive (Chantraine's aorist of access of present
emotion, *Gr. Hom.* ii.187), and will discriminate between an essentially intellectual
fear and the essentially physical and perceptual failures next to be described.

[12] Sappho 96.4V; cf. 23.5V.

[13] There has been much discussion of the exact meaning of ἴσος θέοισιν; see above,
note 10. The various positions (emphasis upon happiness, emphasis upon strength,
emphasis upon beauty, etc.) are summarised by Privitera, *Rete*, 96–9, where it is argued
that Sappho meant the term to be open and ambiguous – not limited to a single aspect
of divinity but suggestive of all. In support of this, it might be noted that ἴσος in Euclid
does not mean narrow congruency but a broader equality of content or area; see S. L.
Radt, 'ἴσος bei Euclid', *Mnem.* 29 (1976) 80.

was very highly prized.[14] The oldest view was that only marriage[15] or victory at the games[16] could give a particular man an experience like that of divinity and therefore that only in these moments could he be hailed with epithets that properly belonged to the gods – *olbios, makar* or *eudaimōn*. Philosophers and poets, however, soon began to argue other cases in which a generic man or even a whole class of men might be so described, and their conclusions profilerated into various wise sayings and gnomes. The topic was already old when Solon gave Croesus a lecture on mortal blessedness (Hdt. 1.30), for Hesiod had claimed that the man whom the Muses loved was blessed (*Theog.* 96; cf. *h.Hom.* 30.7),[17] and Alcman's chorus of girls had praised the blessedness of one who spins out a tearless day (1.37 *PMG*). Theognis announced that friends, hunting and the love of boys (in the opposite order) made a man rich in bliss (1253-4);[18] Bacchylides reminded Hieron that the mortal to whom god grants a portion of honour, nicely mixed with wealth and luck, is the blessed one (5.50-1), whereas Pindar had a plainer thing to say, since for him the blessed man was he who had a lasting fame (*P.*5.46).[19] And meanwhile the mystery religions were making another sort of assertion by describing their initiates with this same vocabulary. The Homeric hymn to Demeter promised that those who had looked upon the sacred sights and knew the sacred secrets would be touched with bliss. (*h.Dem.* 480; cf. 486–

[14] The correct view about mortals is expressed at Theogn. 441 (=1162a), οὐδεὶς γὰρ πάντ᾽ ἐστὶ πανόλβιος; as a rule, blessedness could only be safely claimed for the heroic dead, as at Hes. *Theog.*, 954f. (of Heracles): ὄλβιος ὃς μέγα ἔργον ἐν ἀθανάτοισιν ἀνύσσας / ναίει ἀπήμαντος καὶ ἀγήραος ἤματα πάντα. For this reason, one who claimed to be equal to the gods was apt to be guilty of criminal presumption, and the kings of Persia are described so (ἰσόθεος Aesch. *Pers.* 80, 856; ἰσοδαίμων, 633; cf. the ἰσοθέου τυρ- / ραννίδος at E.*Tro.* 1169). On *makarismos* in general, see G. L. Dirichlet, *De veterum macarismis* (Giessen, 1914); E. Norden, *Agnostos Theos* (Leipzig, Berlin 1913), 99ff.; A. J. Festugière, *Eranos* 54 (1956), 78ff.; O. Regenbogen, *Das Human. Gymn.*41 (1930), 11ff.=*Kl.Schr.*, 113ff.; C. de Heer, Μάκαρ · εὐδαίμων · ὄλβιος · εὐτυχής (Amsterdam 1969).

[15] For *makarismos* at weddings, Hes.fr. 211.7MW, τρὶς μάκαρ Αἰακίδη καὶ τετράκις ὄλβιε Πηλεῦ; Sappho 112V, ὄλβιε γάμβρε; cf. P.P.3.89; E. *Alc.*918; *Andr.* 1218; *Phaeth.* fr. 781.27; *Hel.* 375; 639; *Tro.* 311f.; *IA* 1076–9; 1404; Ar. *Birds* 1722–5; *Peace* 1333; Theocr. 18.16; see B. Snell, *Hermes* 66, 73–4.

[16] For *makarismos* of victor, B. 3.10 ἅ τρισευδαίμων ἄνηρ; cf. P.P.5.20; P.10.22; P.9.4; *O.*1.11 (victor's hearth is μάκαιρα); *N.*9.3 (victor's house is ὄλβιος); *O.*13.1 (play between secular and agonistic senses of ὄλβιος).

[17] Cf. Hes. *Op.* 826, where knowledge of lucky and unlucky days, plus abstention from crimes against the gods, makes one *eudaimōn* and *olbios*; see also fr. 33(a) and 13, 211–17.

[18] Cf. Theog. 933, where the man is *olbios* who has both virtue and beauty; 1335, where success in love makes a man *olbios*, and 1173, where the salutation ἆ μάκαρ is given to the one who has innate traditional good sense (γνώμη).

[19] Cf. P.O.7.11, where the man of good repute is *olbios*, and compare Alcman 11D. For *makarismos* based upon intellectual powers, see Emped. fr. 132D; Anaxag. 59A30; *Menandri Monosticha*, fr. 465, p.60 Jaekel.

7), and Pindar would repeat this of their initiates, saying, 'Blessed is he who goes beneath the earth having seen these things . . .' (137S; cf. 131aS).[20]

This is the discussion that Sappho joins with her present song (it is the second source from which she borrowed the girl's masculine companion), for she manages to correct the sages and also to applaud the girl as she says, 'The one who is equal to the gods is the one who sits near *you!*'[21] According to her phrase, such a one is not merely divinely happy but is the match of the gods in every way and so he caps all the victors, bridegrooms and initiates put forward by the rest of the world as examples of ultimate felicity. More important, he works, like all the others of his kind, as a signpost that points to the source of whatever heavenly bliss is to be enjoyed on earth. Hesiod's blessed man had indicated music; Alcman's, quietude; the blessed of the mystery religions indicated revelation; he of the epinician poets, victory and fame; but this man's supreme state points to the girl beside him as the element through which divinity enters mortal life. And in consequence, the girl of Sappho's song does not just resemble a god – anyone could have said that – she resembles as well melody, peace, success, a vision of sacred truth and all the other concepts to which men had given highest value by means of the 'he is godlike who . . .' locution.

These are effects brought into the poem from outside by the man whom Sappho has posed beside the girl. Within the song, he serves to identify a numinous place close to that wonderful creature, a place where the force that emanates from her is felt through every sense, yet received as if it were the gift of immortality. Or so it seems (and seemingness is what matters here) to the lover who occupies another place where conditions are just the opposite. From this second spot the girl is merely glimpsed, not heard, and so her influence ought in all logic to be felt to a lesser degree, but in fact her power seems to bring death to the one who is here. The chasm between the two places is immeasurable, just as the girl's terrible power is, and Sappho says as much by thus fixing its defining terms at heaven and the tomb. With characteristic irony, however, she also locates these two spots within easy sight of one another, mapping her cosmic topography on an intimate scale and so creating a distance that is totally impassable,

---

[20] Cf. Soph. fr. 753 N3=837P; E. *Ba.*73ff.; fr. 910; Ar. *Clouds* 463; *Frogs* 1482; Orph.fr. 32 (3) 10; Theocr. 15.146; Apul. *Met.* 11.16.2. See in general, N.J. Richardson, *The Homeric Hymn to Demeter* (Oxford 1974) 313; Norden, *Agnostos Theos*, 100, note 1.

[21] That the formulas of *makarismos* were early open to parody is proved by Theognis 1013–16; 1375; Hippon. 43W. A late parody of Sappho's version appears at *AP*5.94: 'I call him blessed who looks upon you, thrice blessed who hears your voice, a demi-god who kisses your mouth – but a god, a god indeed! is the man whose bed receives you.'

yet also traversable by a short step or two. Of course, since the two places serve finally to describe the aura of the indescribable girl, she too is presented through them in a double form. From the place of death she seems a Siren whose voice is so sweet it cannot be safely heard, a lovely Medusa who can only be viewed askance, while at the place of bliss she is merely a happy equal to whose chatter and low laugh a companion would gladly listen.

The notion of the companion's godlike status thus prepares for the song's major conceit (and it is a conceit, for all its clinical appearance), according to which alienation from the beloved becomes a form of death.[22] It also prepares for the song's most daring effect, since it allows the singer to describe the effects of beauty (we may presume that the girl is beautiful at least to the lover's eye) by means of what is generally agreed to be ugly – sickness and physical infirmity.[23] True, the symptoms suggest shock rather than festering or disease; they are reminiscent of epic moments of surprise and fear, but nevertheless the parts of the lover's body are here depicted in a state of malfunction and consequently in a state that is by nature unlovely.

The lover, glancing at the girl, is likened by her reactions to some triply unfortunate Homeric creature who receives bad news, feels death coming on, and sees an awesome sight all at one time.[24] Her condition, however, is even worse than this, or at any rate more complex, and in order to describe it more perfectly Sappho has added some new details and fixed the phases of decline into a telling order. One of the new symptoms is a roaring in the ears, and this innovation points to the first principle in this Sapphic process, for with the introduction of the ear she can render the lover completely helpless as far

---

[22] Archilochus had already made of *pothos* a state like death wherein he lay ἄψυχος (193W; cf. 191W) and Alcman had likewise associated desire with death (*PMG* 2 fr.3 col.ii).

[23] It was precisely this indirection that excited the admiration of 'Longinus' and so preserved the song.

[24] The Homeric models are discussed by Turyn, op.cit., 44–5; Schadewaldt, *Hermes* 71, 372 note 1; Tietze, op.cit., 363–6; Wills, op.cit., 175; Saake, *Kunst*, 25–7; Privitera, *Rete*, 118. Trembling and heart palpitations are associated with fear at *Il*.3.34; 10.95; 20.44; 22.451 & 461; *Od*. 3.34; 18.340; 24.49; ct.18.75; with astonishment at Hes. *Erg.* 447; loss of voice (usually accompanied by tears) is associated with giving or receiving fearful news at *Il*.17.696; Od.4.705; Od.10.246 (cf. *Theog.* 167) and Dolon babbles in his cowardice (*Il*.10.324), though voice loss is also connected with recognition at *Od*.19.71–2. Sweat is an accompaniment of pain at *Il*.16.109, but of fear at Archil. 122.4W (if ὑγρόν is to be read here), and pallor is a sign of fear at *Il*.7.479, 13.279 & 284; 15.4; 17.733; *Od*.22.42. Loss of vision is, however, almost always associated with death in Homer (e.g. *Il*.5.696), though Andromache, fainting with fear, experiences this blindness (*Il*.22.466). Archil. connects it with love (191W). Peculiar to the Sapphic lines are the subtle flush of heat (cf. the burning desire of 48V), the *chilly* sweat, and the drumming in the ears. (In Psalm 38 the same combination of symptoms is associated with being in a state of sin.)

as communication goes; deaf, dumb and blind.[25] Ever the poet, however, she puts the tongue[26] first and gives it the most emphasis, thereby suggesting that talk and persuasion would be primary in the approach that the lover can't even dream of, just as the girl's laughing chatter represents intimacy achieved. Accompanying this threefold communicative failure of speech, sight and hearing, is another triad of corporeal sensations, and here again a new symptom appears. Invention was needed to make up the three, and so, to the traditional sweat and trembling of Homeric fright, the singer adds a flash of light flame, burning under the skin.[27] And finally, when this twice-triple decline seems to have arrived at death, one last sign is added – pallor, another epic response to fear – and though it is traditional, it causes a new aspect of the Sapphic design to become clear. Only the lover could sense the internal incapacity of tongue, eye and ear, and only she could feel the concomitant feverishness, but when the singer added sweat[28] and trembling she admitted to a greater objectivity, since these are outward shows that another might as easily recognise. Now, with her last touch of paleness, she confirms this shift from internal to external, and cleanly separates her song from the lover's subjective experience, making it look on from the outside as a neutral observer might. Singer-self must stand beside lover-self in order to say 'I'm

[25] Those who would read φώνας οὐδ' ἔν ἔτ' ἴκει at 7.8 and understand 'your voice no longer reaches me' (see Wills, op.cit.,), would destroy this effect; in defence of 'it is not possible to speak', see Page, *S&A*, 23–4. Even for a non-poet, to be voiceless is of sinister importance, since it is associated with being breathless and so with death; note also that a frequent spell laid against an enemy causes his tongue to be bound, or makes him ἄλαλος ἄφωνος ἄγλωσσος (see Kagarow, *Gr. Fluchtafeln*, Eos Supp.4, 1929, 30 and 32).

[26] Unnecessary difficulties have been made over the 'shattering' of this tongue; Page, for example, objects (*S&A*, 24): 'Sappho's tongue is not in fact *destroyed*' (but for that matter, does a fire, in fact, run under her skin?) and Devereux, whom one would have expected to be fascinated by this broken organ, takes up Cobet's πέπαγε because he has case histories in which tongues seem to be glued inside the mouth (op.cit., 23; cf. Milne, *SO* 13, 20). West (*Maia* 22, 311) sensibly notes that the tongue is crippled like a broken limb, and reads either <μ'> ἔαγε with Sitzler, or γλῶσσαν ἔαγα, 1st pers. s. perf. Radt (op.cit., 345) cites E. Heitsch (*RM* 105, 1902, 285) and R. Hiersche (*Glotta* 44, 1966, 1ff.) in vindication of Ϝέαγε; Marcovich, op.cit., 28, assumes that 'my tongue is broken' was a colloquialism. Perhaps one might compare Archil. 252W, where slack members are described as 'broken'.

[27] See Privitera, *Rete*, 109ff. for an analysis of this sequence based on presumed patterns of parallelism and opposition. It looks as if some scholiast also tried to analyse the list if, as Kamerbeek supposes ('Sapphica', *Mnem.* iv 9, 1956, 99) it was a marginal ἕκτον at line 13 that 'Longinus' reports with εκαδεμ.

[28] The 'cold' sweat of the translation comes from the text that Page restores at line 13 (κὰδ δέ μ' ἴδρως ψῦχρος ἔχει), which seems best since χέει is banal, while ψῦχρος is necessary to mark the sweat as morbid. The phrase 'cold sweat' should be heard in connection with the 'light fire' of line 10 since both expressions are slightly oxymoronic: fire is expected to rage, not to be weak, and sweat is expected to be warm, not cold. For an opposite opinion, see West (*Maia* 22, 312), who argues that the grammarian of An.Ox.1208 cannot possibly have found ψῦχρος in his text.

pale as death', and as soon as this split has occurred the objective situation (i.e. the girl) can also be viewed differently. Self-discipline becomes possible, even courage, and above all there is now room for irony.

Though it ostensibly reduces her to death, the song's dynamic order has brought the singing lover to identify herself with the lively world that watches her disintegration, and meanwhile each aspect of her failure of nerve has, by suggesting its opposite, served to define the true goal of lover and song: love in its phase of full success. Dumbness predicts sweet conversation, and blindness and deafness reflect that heightened use of eye and ear that a returned love encourages. Near to the beloved a lover burns, not listlessly but madly, with a fire that can deliciously be quenched (cf. 121V); there the lover sweats, not coldly but with warm pleasure; there limbs do not tremble but loosen and relax in perfect satisfaction, and there, instead of growing pale, one becomes more beautiful. There, after all, one is godlike, instead of being death's simulacrum.

And so, with what seems to be her last fictional breath, the lover turns upon herself with a new objectivity and begins an exhortation.[29] She might be Odysseus on the doorstep or Archilochus with his *thumos* as she rouses herself to essay a courageous act: 'It's all to be attempted, for even beggars . . .' The poem is broken here at the beginning of the fifth stanza, but this proverbial beggar is clearly an emblem of hope since even a poor man, as Theognis says, may suddenly grow rich (662–3).[30] And with this beggar comparison, the chasm between the

[29] Snell (*Hermes* 66, 89) notes this as the point at which the poet calls herself back to the poem's formal purposes, assuming the sense to be, 'but all this can be borne, since you will have a happy future as a married woman'. Others take it for granted that the singer maintains her lover's persona to the end, but fail to note the strong quality of reversal in this 'Sich-Zurückruf'; thus Gallavotti discovers a simple continuation of thought: 'e tutto questo io supporto alla tua presenza' or 'ma tutto mi e tollerabile in cambio della tua presenza' (*RIFC* 21, 1942, 122). Milne (*Hermes* 71, 126ff.) supposed that Sappho, once herself fortunate with this girl, now finds herself beggared while the groom is *olbios*; Schubart's interpretation is similar, for according to him a resigned Sappho simply compares her own beggary in love with the 'früchtlosen Mühsal des Tagelohners' (*Philologus* 97, 311). West (*Maia* 22, 313) attempts a restoration in the form of a kind of self-consolation: ἀλλὰ πὰν τόλματον ἐπεὶ [θέος τοι / καὶ πένητα [πλούσιον αὖψ' ἔθηκεν] [καὶ κάτηλεν αὖθι τὸν ἐξισώμενον μακάρεσσι]. The alternate meaning for the πὰν τόλματον of line 17 is active rather than passive: all can be dared (even though it is dangerous or extreme; cf. Soph. *Phil.* 633. Wills (op.cit. 190 note 46) cites *Il.* 19. 14–15, where the Myrmidons do not dare to look upon the divine glories of the shield (οὐδέ τις ἔτλη ἄντην εἰσιδέειν, ἀλλ᾽ ἔτρεσαν) and explains τόλματον as equivalent to 'can be ventured', concluding 'she means to enter that presence, to bear the obliterating proximity'. Cf. 121.2V where οὐ τλάσομ᾽ seems to mean 'I wouldn't dare', not 'I wouldn't be able to endure'.

[30] Unlike Sappho, Theognis is turning what had been a simple old saw of fortune's reversal to a bitter purpose, since he finishes by observing that according to this rule the base man ends up with honour. It is possible that a version of a similar gnome (πλοῦ[τ]ον θέοι δίδοισιν [το]ῖσι [θ]έ[λο]ψσιν) appeared in another Sapphic song; see M. Treu, 'Neues . . .' *QU* 2 (1966) 13ff.

lover and 'that man', between here and there, failure and success, incapacity and strength, grows suddenly much more commonplace and bridgeable. When the lover, kept at a distance, powerless and merely looking, is figured now as a beggar, then the accepted companion who is close, strong, and enjoying with all his senses, becomes merely a wealthy man, and since *olbios* or 'rich' was one of the formulaic words for one who was blessed, the shift in the figure is made verbally smooth. A dying lover can hardly urge herself to do what only a god can do, but a beggar-lover may properly try to change places with someone whose fortune belongs to the world. The new and mundane image thus brings the song efficiently back to earth and allows for a shift in the lover's mood, but nevertheless the first and more grandiose conceptualisation has shaped everything up to this point, and the song as a whole continues to profit from it. In this one moment of reversal the lover is both realist and idealist, but we are left with the sense that when she has risen, entered the girl's potent ambience, and exchanged poverty for wealth, she will (if she survives) become herself the equal of the Blessed Ones.

And she will survive, for even as it portrayed her demise the song has whispered of a possible revival. 'Paler than grass' is the one full-blown figure of speech in these lines and it consequently carries great emphasis – indeed, it strikes the non-Mediterranean ear rather too forcibly as northerners forget to imagine grass bleached by months of sun[31] and consequently take the lover to be green. Even for the Lesbian listener, however, to whom grass would suggest the straw colour associated with sickness and fear,[32] the comparison would have been striking for its singularity, and also because it caps the sequence of decline and introduces the notion of death. Her paleness proves the mortal seriousness of the lover's condition and yet, by thus insisting on grass as its gauge, the poet makes her strike a note of hope even at this grave pass. With the word 'grass' we are reminded that this human failure, this decline that has been so neatly observed, has its encouraging parallel in the familiar 'deaths' of meadow and field, where what grows pale today has once been green and will be so again.[33] The paleness of grass does not mark a final end but only the presence of a certain season and so the lover who is pale may by this

---

[31] At the other end of the classical age the fact that summer grass was meant in such expressions was spelled out by Longus when he wrote, in Daphnis and Chloe, χλωρό-τερον τὸ πρόσωπον ἦν πόας θερινῆς (1.17.4). Plutarch summarising Sappho's song says (*Amat.* 18, 763 iv.436 Bern): ἡ καλὴ Σαπφὼ λέγει . . . καταλαμβάνειν ὠχρότητα. . .

[32] Epic fear is itself χλωρός (*Il.*10.376; 7.479; 15.4; *Od.* 11.43; 22.2).

[33] Fresh spring grass carried erotic associations with youth and tenderness and so with Aphrodite (Hes. *Theog.* 194; *Il.*14.347); compare *P.P.*9.37; Archil. Pap. Col. The more general signification of inexhaustible hope is clear in the Biblical promise, 'Your descendants shall be many and your offspring as the grass of the earth' (Job.5.25).

analogy expect to be robust again, just as parched leaves may expect eventually to know a tender verdant time.

Another point to be remembered about this lover's 'death' is that it is specified as a case of seemingness, (*phainom' em' autai*, 16) and so is made exactly parallel to the companion's semblance of immortality (*phainetai moi*, 1). She seems to be next door to death, but she is not; if she succeeds in approaching the beloved, she will become like her opposite, not only alive but equal to the gods. Or rather – and here is the song's last wise irony – she will seem to be so, just like the man of her hypothesis. No one really becomes like a god – not the bride-groom or the victor or even the initiate; instead, they merely show forth (*phainesthai*) a god-like aspect in the moment of their success, as a sign that god has had a hand in their felicity. And the lover's beatitude, or so says Sappho, is exactly the same. The transforming strength conferred by love's success will be as illusory as this present phase of fearful preparation, but nevertheless it is to be sought, for, like initiation, love achieved provides a moment of contact with the eternal, and an introduction into a blessed company.

The objects of one's desire were real girls, balky and changeable, but Sappho taught that love would fulfil itself in spite of them, if a lover stood in a right relation to Aphrodite. Temporarily exiled from a place near the beloved, one might have to fight to return, but there was a heavenly ally at hand, ready to help if one called. Redress was not quite so easy as this sounds, however, for calling upon Aphrodite in the midst of erotic distress meant calling upon the force responsible for one's suffering; one had to believe that she was truly god and yet that she could be inclined by prayer, before one could begin. All of which is said in lyric form in the one song of Sappho's that is surely complete, the so-called hymn to Aphrodite (1V).[34] Built upon the im-plicit fiction of a beloved who has strayed,[35] the song pretends to be

---

[34] The poem is cited by Dionysius of Halicarnassus, *de comp*. 23 (173–9; Opusc.2, 1, 144f. Usener-Radermacher); fragments of lines 1–21 appear in P. Oxy. 2288.

[35] A few critics have believed that the song treats of a girl's defection from the Sapphic *thiasos*; see R. Merkelbach, op.cit., 101 (1957), 1–29 and A. Rivier, 'Observations sur Sappho 1.19 sq.', *REG* 80 (1967) 84–92. The majority, however, have recognised a fiction (often taken as fact) involving Sappho's love for a girl. Strictly speaking, the poetic situation is that Sappho is at prayer because she is balked in some unspecified love-project, but if we are meant to suppose that her present situation is parallel to those that produced her previous prayers, then lines 18–19, if we could read them, would provide more information. Unfortunately the book text and the papyrus are at variance over the beginning of line 19, and no one has yet produced a reading that is generally accepted. Saake, *Kunst*, 54–9 reports thirty-eight opinions; to these may be added R. van Bennekom, 'Sappho 1.18–19', *Mnem.* iv 25 (1972) τίνα δηὖτε Πείθων αἶσ' ἄγην ἐς σὰν κτλ. 'It is fated that Peitho should lead whom into your love?' V. Pisani, 'S. fgg. 1 u. 31', *Glotta* 50 (1972) 28–9, who reads μαῖς = Oscan 'mais' to get 'Wen soll ich überzeugen damit ich noch mehr (oder noch einmal) zu deiner Liebe führe?'; Kirkwood *EGM*, 109 and Sanchez Lasso de la Vega, *CFC* 6 (1974) 9–93, who postpone the direct

Sappho's call to the power who tortures her, while in fact it explores the changes that can be wrought by prayer, in a petitioner and in a divinity.

Ποι⌐κιλόθρο⌐ν' ἀθανάτ'Ἀφρόδιτα,
παῖ⌐ Δ⌐ίⓙος δολ⌐όπλοκε, λίccομαί cε,
μή μ'⌐ ἄcαιcι ⌐μηδ' ὀνίαιcι δάμνα,
  πότν⌐ια, θῦ⌐μον,   4
ἀλλ⌐ὰ τυίδ' ἔλ⌐θ', αἴ ποτα κἀτέρωτα
τὰ⌐c ἔμαc αὔ⌐δαc ἀίοιcα πήλοι
ἔκ⌐λυεc, πάτρο⌐c δὲ δόμον λίποιcα
  χ⌐ρύcιον ἦλθ⌐εc   8
ἄρ⌐μ' ὑπαcδε⌐ύξαιcα· κάλοι δέ c' ἆγον
ὤ⌐κεεc cτροῦ⌐θοι περὶ γᾶc μελαίναc
πύ⌐κνα δίν⌐νεντεc πτέρ' ἀπ' ὠράνω‿αἴθε-
  ρο⌐c διὰ μέccω·   12
αἶ⌐ψα δ' ἐξίκο⌐ντο· cὺ δ', ὦ μάκαιρα,
μειδιαί⌐cαιc' ἀθανάτωι προcώπωι
ἤ⌐ρε' ὄττ⌐ι δηὖτε πέπονθα κὤττι
  δη⌐ὖτε κ⌐άλ⌐η⌐μμι   16
κ⌐ὤττι ⌐μοι μάλιcτα θέλω γένεcθαι
μ⌐αινόλαι ⌐θύμωι· τίνα δηὖτε πείθω
.⌐.cάγην ⌐ἐc càν φιλότατα; τίc c', ὦ
  Ψά⌐πφ', ⌐ἀδίκηcι;   20

_____

speech to understand , 'Whom shall I (Sappho) persuade you (Aphrodite) to bring back again into the love that is yours (Aphrodite's)?' One might note also that the βαῖσ' that West (*Maia* 22,309 note 5) dismissed as 'forced', returns as βᾶσ(α) in K. Stanley, 'The role of Aphrodite', *GRBS* 17 (1976) 314.

In spite of the confusion there seem to be a few predominant probabilities. The direct speech ought to begin with τίνα, because this clause is not coordinated with those that precede; the δηὖτε should not be tampered with because it is one of a series of three, like the three ὄττι; if the second letter in 1.19 is ψ, then ἄψ is the correct beginning for the line; ἄγην is probably right because it is the *mot juste*, correct for marriage, for magic, and for a military action; finally, any reading with Peitho is probably wrong because Peitho was not at this time a name for Aphrodite (Sappho elsewhere made her Aphrodite's daughter, see the commentary, 90.7–8V) and mention of a second divine agency would be too complicated for this prayer situation. If ἄγην could be taken as passive, as Lobel once suggested, the simplest reading would be ἄψ σ(οι) ἄγην 'Whom shall I persuade to be led by you back into your love?' If it must be active, then one may read Ϝαν with Lobel and get, 'Whom shall I persuade to lead you back into her love', which, however, gives the girl all the advantage of the aggressive ἄγην. As long as ἄψ is kept, the fiction will be one of an interrupted success in love; if the ψ that seems to stand on the papyrus is given up, then possibilities like εἰσάγειν = 'enter' (E. Heitsch, 'Zum Sapphotext', *Hermes* 95, 1967, 390–2) open up (though this particular verb is elsewhere intransitive only in its participial form), and with them the possibility that the poetic situation is one of a love affair at its beginning.

καₗὶ γₗὰρ αἰ φεύγει, ταχέωc διώξει,
αἰ δὲ δῶρα μὴ δέκετ᾽, ἀλλὰ δώcει,
αἰ δὲ μὴ φίλει, ταχέωc φιλήcει
   κωὐκ ἐθέλοιcα.   24

ἔλθε μοι καὶ νῦν, χαλέπαν δὲ λῦcον
ἐκ μερίμναν, ὄccα δέ μοι τέλεccαι
θῦμοc ἰμέρρει, τέλεcον, cὺ δ᾽ αὔτα
   cύμμαχοc ἔccο.   28

Blossom-clad deathless Aphrodite,
snare-weaving child of Zeus, hear me:
Do not, my lady, tame my heart to
   listlessness and despair!

Come to me just as you used to do
when, sensing my distant cries you
heard me, departed your father's halls and
   yoked up your team

fast to your golden car. Fine swift
sparrows took flight on beating wings
drawing your carriage to swarthy earth,
   down through the airs between;

then you were here, and you, my queen,
smiled your eternal smile, asked what
was it had troubled me this time, what
   caused me to call once more?

What could it be that I wished for
in my unruly heart? 'Whom shall I persuade
back again into your love, Sappho?
   Who does you wrong today?

If she hides now, she will soon seek;
if she scorns gifts, she soon will give;
if she despises, yet will she love
   even reluctantly!'

Come again, now, release me from
this inescapable care! Grant
all that my heart desires and stand
   as comrade-at-arms with me!

The song is light, and at first hearing it seems to use the language
and rhetoric of cult simply as a conceit. The solemn conventions of
prayer are set to the melodies of popular song, so that the metre itself
seems to comment saucily upon the matter. Worse yet, a final military
image is martialled in such a way as to make the whole performance
appear to poke fun at masculine battle-prayers, as words proper to an
Orestes about to kill or an Eteocles under attack are liltingly sung by

this feminine voice.[36] Such playfulness is perfectly appropriate, since in narrow truth this is not a prayer at all but a piece that represents the poet-lover at her prayers, a song in which Sappho has arranged to amuse her girls by compounding a confession of weakness with what amounts to an amorous boast. Nevertheless, this is not just a Lesbian version of the satirist's habitual mixture of parody, self-denigration and self-assertion. It does not attempt to create either scorn or admiration for any person or institution, but conveys instead an ultimate emotion of confident joy that forgets both the singer and her performance to focus upon the divinity who has been summoned and praised. And so in the end, though it is not an implement of cult, neither is this a purely secular song; instead it is a thing rare among the Greeks, the poetic expression of a personal religious faith. It is not offered directly to the sacred ear by a singer at an altar, and yet it is only technically a parody, for the poet is addressing a goddess whom she genuinely adores, knowing that Aphrodite will surely hear this 'prayer' and be pleased by its music, its wit and its decent observation of convention, whenever and wherever it is performed.[37]

The song mimics prayer because Aphrodite is always somewhere, listening, but it does so also for the sake of its mortal audience. Sappho would instruct the girls of her group in the ways of their favourite goddess, and she knows that with a dramatic petition she can create an illusion and thus impose an experience of this divinity upon every one of them. She might have made a statement: 'Whenever I pray to Aphrodite, she appears and says . . .' Or she might have composed an anecdotal song: 'Once, when I prayed, Aphrodite came and said . . .' In either case, the goddess' coming would have been an event held up at a certain distance for her listeners' consideration, provocative of an intellectual response. When, however, instead of describing her worship of the goddess, she acts it out, she is able to invest even the tale of past epiphanies with a present immediacy. The old message of affection spoken by the goddess to her devotee is not part of the scene that is being mimed, but somehow the song persuades anyone who listens that he has not only overhead Sappho at prayer but has also – quite illogically – heard Aphrodite's voice as well. A trick is thus played upon the listener, and the fact that it works is proved by the strange, mild hilarity that this song almost inevitably produces. Just *how* it works is a mystery, but surely its success is due in part to the fact that this singer who pretends to be not a singer but a suppliant is very nice in her observance of the old magical rules for bringing a demonic power into the world.

---

[36] Aesch. *Choeph.* 2; 18–19; 497–8, where Zeus is to send Dike as *summachos*; *Septem*, 266; cf. Archil. 108W.

[37] So must Herbert have believed, of 'Discipline'; Vaughan, of 'The Request'; Alice Meynell, of 'Veni Creator', etc.

The traditional 'cletic' hymn had a tripartite structure.[38] First the god was seized upon, wherever he was, by an effective manipulation of his names, his favourite haunts, and his characteristic powers. Next he was impressed and pleased by a reminder of past deeds, the petitioner's or his own. Finally, when he had been thus favourably prepared, he was made to listen to a direct appeal. In the first of these phases, the invocation, a knowledge of names, titles, parentage, powers, cult epithets, and divine geography was important, for with erudition of this sort one could catch the god in a specific form and bring him on to the scene with the attributes most needed in the present case.[39] In the second section, the *hypomnēsia*, the worshipper reminded the god of why his aid would be appropriate, proudly pointing out his own past offerings,[40] or else making his claim on the basis of the god's former deeds,[41] which could be even more effective. A god might, after all, choose to forget hecatombs and fat thigh pieces that had been given him, but he could never repudiate his own exploits; his actions were eternal and irreversible, and he could not make them senseless by refusing to repeat them. Reference to the god's deeds was thus more sophisticated and more deeply constraining, but whichever approach one took, this section was properly couched in conditional expressions ('If ever you had this of me, or did this for me . . .') that were inherited from incantations that had exercised a frank coercion upon demonic powers.[42] Something that manifestly had been done was

[38] See E. Norden, op.cit., 143–76; 177–207; H. Meyer, *Hymnische Stilelemente in der frühgr. Dichtung* (Würzburg: diss. Köln, 1933); H. Kleinknecht, *Die Gebetsparodie in der Antike* (Stuttgart-Berlin, 1937), 1, note 4 (for bibliography) and especially A. Cameron, 'Sappho's prayer to Aphrodite', *HTR* 32 (1939) 1–17. The different parts of the prayer could in practice be kept discrete or mixed together, and any one of them might be expanded.

[39] On the magic of names, see G. Meyer, 'Ein Beitrag z. Geschichte der διπλᾶ ὀνόματα', *Philol. Suppl.* 16.3 (1923) 48f. The maker of a prayer might even suggest a route for the god to take, and this inspired the topos of the god's own description of his departure and means of transport, as at Aesch. PV. 127ff., 286ff.; E.*El.*1241; *Androm.* 1232. This convention is parodied at Callim. *h.*3.183.191.

[40] Like Chryses to Apollo, 'If ever you tasted the smoke of fat thigh pieces . . .' (*Il.*1.40), or Pelops to Poseidon, 'If ever you knew through me the joy of love fulfilled . . .' (*P.O.*1.75–6). This sort of reminder could also turn into a challenge, as with Croesus' angry πού θεῶν ἔστιν χάρις; (B.3.38).

[41] Like Diomedes to Athena, 'If ever you stood favourably by me or by my father in fearsome battle . . .' (*Il.*5.116); compare Diomedes again at *Il.*10.284; cf. *Il.*15.372; S. *OT* 52–3. Another form of duress is the claim to kinship, as at *Od.*9.529 and B.16.52ff. In magical prayers there are reminders like that of Sappho, of old promises: see *Pap. gr.mag.* i,313; 320; iv, 451.

[42] '. . . exemplary narrative derived from a primitive form of spell . . . had a potency in bringing about the performance of future actions', F. Dornseiff, 'Literarische Verwendungen des Beispiels', *Vorträge der Bibl. Warburg* (1924–5) 206. Compare T. Krischer, 'Sapphos Ode an Aphrodite', *Hermes* 96 (1968) 9, of the reminding section: 'sie soll – das ist ihr ursprunglicher Sinn – die Gottheit zur Erfüllung der Bitte magisch zwingen.' This way of thinking is not exclusively archaic, as is proved by a passage from one of Donne's sermons: 'by prayer we incline him, we bend him, but by praise we

used as a bait to draw the old dynamism into the present, and then the petitioner could move on to his final section, the entreaty itself. This was usually expressed in a series of swift imperatives: 'Hear!' 'Come!' or 'Appear!' and then 'Give!' or 'Bring to pass . . .!'[43] Here again the pattern of expression was derived from older, more magical calls upon demonic servants, and this explains the terse, commanding tone and the insistence that the power addressed should act 'swiftly' or 'now'.[44]

Sappho's lyric prayer is plainly divided into these same three parts, and its extended reminding section (five stanzas that fall between one of invocation and one of appeal) makes it something like the great show-piece hymns that were composed for contests. Within each part, everything is formally just as it should be; even the phraseology follows the patterns set by cult,[45] and the listener is thus unable to resist the sense that this melodic appeal is actually going to work. Meanwhile, however, each 'correct' detail has also been made to fit into the song's own poetic scheme – its double portrait of a devotee and a divinity who are momentarily conjoined by the act of prayer.

The invocation is made with a patronymic and three epithets, (one of which establishes a characteristic power) and all are woven so tightly together that they occupy only a line and a half. It is a graceful but minimal gesture towards a formal call, and yet within its brevity every chosen syllable has its soft significance, and the ensemble ends by conjuring up a divinity very carefully defined as the particular one that Sappho would like to see, the one whose aid she seeks. To begin with the patronymic: 'child of Zeus' might seem unavoidable, but since Aphrodite had two possible mythic fathers, it constitutes a major choice at the outset. Sappho does not want a visit from the grand and terrifying Hesiodic Aphrodite who had Ouranos for her father, the Giants and Erinyes for her brothers and sisters, and a birth from sperm and foam (Hes. *Theog.*188–202).[46] The Aphrodite who is to come instead is an Olympian girl-goddess, that same child of Dione who

---

bind him; our thanks for former benefits is a producing of a speciality, by which he hath contracted with us for more . . . Prayer is as our petition but Praise is as our Evidence; in that we beg, in this we plead. God hath no law upon himselfe, but yet God himselfe proceeds by precedent: And Whensoever we present to him with thanksgiving, what he hath done, he does the same, and more again' (Sermon preached at St. Paul's, on Psalm 90:14). In magical hymns the hypomnesia tends to be as well a legitimisation of the suppliant; see H. Riesenfeld, 'Remarques sur les hymnes magiques', *Eranos* 44 (1946) 153–60.

[43] The standard cries were κλῦθι, ἐλθέ, προφάνηθι, δός, τελειώσατε; see Meyer, op.cit., 7–14; Cameron, op.cit., 5; and E. G. Kagarow, op.cit., 30 for more primitive parallels.

[44] Compare the familiar Anglican 'Oh Lord, make haste to help us!'

[45] See H. Meyer, op.cit., 51–2. No place from which the goddess is to start is specified here in the invocation, but this failure is made up for in stanzas two and three.

[46] Compare Aesch. *Suppl.* 1034ff. The Aphrodite that Sappho thus does not address is the one who was most like Ishtar in her explicit sexuality; see Farnell, *Cults* ii 657.

could be sent shrieking from a mortal battle to take refuge in her mother's lap (*Il*.5.370).[47] Such a divinity is appropriately called 'death-less', as Sappho calls her here, for by an odd custom this epithet in the singular was generally kept for beings about whose immortality there might be some doubt.[48] So described, the Aphrodite to come is delicately lightened and reduced by being made like some Thetis or Hebe or Circe who was deathless, to be sure, but not awesomely divine.[49]

Even more interesting are the two epithets that Sappho invented especially for this occasion.[50] The first of these, *poikilothronos*, has been placed as the very first word of the song and therefore must attract the attention both of the goddess and of the audience. In this position it fixes a tone and even announces an intention for the song to follow, and so its meaning must be thoroughly plumbed. Its first element, *poikilo-*, denotes anything that is richly decorated and wrought with complexity: both intelligence and skill are needed to produce its pattern of ordered variety. Jewels, tapestries, chariots and fawnskins[51] could all be called by this term, but so could a mind of elaborate wit.[52] Subtlety, complication and changefulness are necess-arily implied, and every sort of heaviness is rejected with this word. Where it is applied, all will be arabesque and nothing will proceed in a straight line. The suggestion of the first half of this initial word is thus that a richly devious poem is about to be addressed to a richly devious divinity, but the epithet is compound, so that this elaboration is contained by an object of some sort. And here Sappho, exercising her own subtle wit, chooses to be ambiguous, for the second element

[47] For this child of Zeus and Dione, cf. E. *Helen* 1098; Theoc. 17.36; 15.106; 7.116, and see Farnell *Cults* ii 621 and Roscher, sv 'Aphrodite' 405.

[48] See Page, *S&A*, 5. The one Homeric phrase that uses this epithet of Zeus (*Il*.2.741=14.434=21.2=24.693) was thought by the ancients to be a curiosity, if not an error. It was, however, possible to specify the bodily parts of a god as ἀθάνατος; see West, ad *Theog*.524.

[49] G. A. Privitera, op.cit., 58, insists against all reason that these epithets define Aphrodite as 'distant', but this is because the notion of distance is necessary to his view of the song's 'polarity'.

[50] The first, ποικιλόθρονος, occurs only here; the second, δολόπλοκος, is found also at Sim.541.9 *PMG*; Theognis 1386; fr. adesp. 949 *PMG*, all probably borrowings from Sappho. See also the -πλοκω at fr. adesp.919.7–8 *PMG*.

[51] Skins might seem to escape from the category of things that show skill in the making, but G. M. Bolling, 'Poikilos and Throna', *AJP* 79 (1958) 275–82, notes that at *Il*.19.228, where a fawn is ποικίλον ἑλλόν, the animal is depicted on a brooch, and at *Il*.10.30, where Menelaus equips himself with παρδαλέη. . .ποικίλη, the skin has been stretched upon a shield. On ποικίλος of patterned stuffs, see A. J. B. Wace, 'Weaving or embroidery', *AJA* 52 (1948) 51–5.

[52] Odysseus was ποικιλομήτης (*Il*.11.482; *Od*.3.163; 13.293); Zeus is so at *h.Ap*.322, and Hermes at *h.Merc*.155. The foxy Pittacus is ποικιλόφρων at Alc.69.7V, as is Odys-seus at E.*Hec*. 131. As a curiosity it may be noted that R. Neuberger-Donath, 'S. fr.1.1', *WS* 3 (1969) 15–17 proposed that we read ποικιλόφρον instead of ποικιλόθρον' in the present passage.

of her compound could derive either from *thronos*, 'chair', or from *throna*, '(magical) flowers or herbs'.[53] If she means the first, Aphrodite is to be imagined as seated on a carved or inlaid throne, and if she means the second, the goddess is to be pictured as dressed as she was in the *Cypria* (fr.6),[54] in stuffs that are blossom-patterned or blossom-dyed, and crowned with sweet-smelling flowers. Since both meanings occur in Homer the choice depends upon the immediate context, and since for an instant there is no context here, there is likewise an instant when both meanings operate together to give us a throned and floreate divinity. The developing course of the song, however, soon causes the listener to think primarily of an Aphrodite who wears or carries flowers, for the light, girlish divinity who is Dione's daughter and who likes to be told that she is deathless, easily makes herself attractive but less easily takes a high seat, and as the weaver of tricks she has the cunning fingers required for needlework or plaiting blossoms into chains. Sporting flowers, she will be the embodiment of the elaborate and seductive female beauty that is a prime form of trickery (as the tale of the bedizened and flower-crowned Pandora showed),[55] and she can also make visible, as her attribute, the magical plants that were used in her erotic charms.

An Aphrodite addressed as 'elaborate-throned' would have to divest herself of her epithet almost as soon as it had been bestowed, since it is not a description that could follow her into the scene of epiphany. Flowers, on the other hand, are almost required by that central scene,

---

[53] Homer has similar compounds that apparently refer to chairs (εὔθρονος, χρυσόθρονος) but these are not exact parallels, and Homer also supplies the phrase θρόνα ποικίλα (*Il.*22.441) to describe a flower pattern woven into the stuff of a peplos. According to the schol. at Theoc. 2.59, Homer used θρόνα of roses, simples, and stuffs, and the Hellenistic poet there employs it to describe plants needed for a love spell. Lycophron (674) and Nicander (*Ther.* 493.936) also used it of herbs with magical properties like the ability to break bones or put dragons to sleep, but Hesychius, sv τρόνα, gives the principal meanings as ἀγάλματα ἢ ῥάμματα ἀνθινά. The traditional view has been that Sappho here refers to a throne of state such as gods occupy in sculpture and vase painting, though Page (*S&A*, 5) complained that the idea contained in the compound 'elaborate-throned' was 'not at all common in literature'. The suggestion that flowers were intended was first made by G. Wustmann *RM* 23 (1868) and was repeated by Aly, *RE* sv 'Sappho' 2375; it has been revived by L. Lawler, 'On certain Homeric epithets', *PQ* 27 (1948) 80–4; E. Risch, 'Zusammenfass. Literaturbericht', *Glotta* 33 (1954) 193; Bolling, op.cit., and M. C. J. Putnam, 'Throna and Sappho I', *CJ* 56 (1960) 79ff. Note also G. Lieberg, *Puella Divina* (Amsterdam 1962) 22ff., who would interpret Bacchilides' ἀγλαόθρονος (17.124) as 'bright with flowers' so that the girls in their wreaths repeat the wreath of Amphitrite, which seems reasonable since these Athenian girls on their way to Crete certainly have no room for thrones in their luggage; compare the concurring opinion of R. Merkelbach 'ἀγλαόθρονος' *ZPE* 11 (1973) 160. In support of the idea that Sappho here means 'elaborate as to her flowers' it may be noted that she associates the word ποικίλος with earth's decoration of flowers at 168V. Resistance to the idea may be found in Privitera, op.cit., 27ff. and Stanley, op.cit., 310, note 26.

[54] Cited by Athen.15.682DF

[55] At Hes.*Erg*.73–5 Peitho and the Charites give wrought jewelry, the Horae give a flowery crown, to a Pandora who is, at *Theog*. 589, a δόλος αἰπύς.

since they are the chief ingredients in the sort of amorous magic that Aphrodite there promises to work. Homer's Aphrodite wore, just beneath her breasts, an elaborate amulet-belt (a *keston himanta poikilon, Il.*14.215 and 220),[56] in which she kept the simples and philtres of love and desire, along with the sly amorous tricks that undermine one's reason, and this present Aphrodite will have to be mistress of the same equipment if she is to do Sappho's work. Herbs and garlands and flowery embroideries are appropriately worn when she comes on this visit and, unlike a throne, they can be kept with her to the poem's end. The fancy *peplos* that the Charites had worked for her was not quite the thing for the field at Troy (*Il.*5.338), but it can flutter bravely on this Lesbian battle-ground.

With her second specially contrived epithet, *doloplokos*, Sappho specifies the power that she would like Aphrodite to bring with her for exercise in the present moment: she wants a goddess who can trick and deceive and even set a trap if necessary. A *dolos* is ordinarily used against an enemy, but it is the opposite of simple violence and it is properly shaped with a certain finesse; it is associated with secrecy and cunning, and it calls for a touch of wit.[57] A hole dug for someone to fall into is a low form of *dolos*, an ambush of chosen men is better (*Il.*6.187), and a wolf-disguise is *dolos* in perfection (*Il.*10). With the second half of this compound (*-plokos*, taken from the verb 'to weave'), Sappho seems to achieve one of her characteristic mixtures of the concrete with the abstract, but probably the sense of a physical net is dormant in the notion of the trick.[58] However that may be, the compound as a whole makes of Aphrodite the author of fabricated tricks or snares that are suitably the work of a woman, though one might also think of the cunning hunter or fisherman. And anyone who knew the Lay of Demodocus (and all of Sappho's listeners surely did) would probably think also of another woven snare, one that was not contrived by Aphrodite, but against her. She herself had once been captured in a web both strong and delicate, a binding snare (a *dolos-desmos*) that was Hephaestus' trick (*Od.*8.274–6).

Normally this brief invocation would be followed by the reminding

[56] See Campbell Bonner, 'κεστὸς ἱμάς and the saltire of Aphrodite', *AJP* 70 (1949) 1–6.

[57] For examples of δόλος in Homer, see *Il.*6.187; 7.142; and of course 10 passim; *Od.*1.296; 4.92, 529; 9.406; and note Athena's congratulations to Odysseus at 13.291ff.; Hes. *Theog.* 175. Note also the frequent compounds connecting δόλος with the mind: δολομήτης (*Il.*1.540, *h.Herm.*405); δολόμητις (*Od.*1.300; 3.198, 250, 308; 4.525; 11.422); δολοφραδής (*h.Herm.*282); δολοφρονέων (*Od.*18.51; 21.274; *Il.*3.405; 14.197, 300; 19.106). It is important to note the moral ambiguity of δόλος; as an alternative to simple βία it can be of positive value, but since it must be done λάθρᾳ, it inevitably has a negative quality as well; it is the appropriate means for any act of vengeance because of its secrecy.

[58] Privitera, op.cit., 40, pretends that the concept of the net is almost explicit in the present compound, but his argument is strained.

section of the prayer, but Sappho chooses to deviate ever so slightly from the cletic norm by interposing a glimpse of her suffering self just here. Technically what she does is split the appeal into two pieces, so that a prefatory plea can be made at this point, before the appeal's formal consummation in the four imperatives of the final stanza. She uses this early, minor appeal to offer herself as an example of Aphrodite's baneful power (a matter more safely left unmentioned in the actual invocation), but, more important, she uses it also to arrange for one of the changes that is to occur in the course of her song. She, the petitioner, is to be altered by the act of prayer, and this means that she must be shown now, as she is when she begins, as well as later, as she is when the full prayer has been intoned. This preliminary appeal thus represents Before, in what will be a Before and After study, and not surprisingly it is negative and apotropaic, expressing fear of an unpleasant aspect of the goddess that Sappho would as soon not see. It reflects the petitioner's damaged faith, but it also illustrates some further powers of the divine pharmacist whom she addresses, while of course it offers as well a description of love with no health in it. 'Do not subdue me with sickness' is a fearful way of saying 'Make me well again', but it also allows for a specification of present misery, and the lover's symptoms this time reflect, not the awe of anticipation, but the despair and disgust that come when desire has been baffled.[59] The two words *asaisi* and *oniasi* suggest a low discomfort and discouragement,[60] but there is evidently frenzy in this condition, too, for the earlier calls, at least, have all been made from a 'maddened heart'.[61] This lowered petitioner knows all too well that it is Aphrodite's nature to subdue, and she recognises the fact with her *mē* . . .

[59] The plurals suggest recurrent, repetitive sensations; see S. L. Radt, *Mnem.* iv 23 (1970) 337f.

[60] At Hes. *Theog.* 611, ἀνία is the aggravation of living with a bad wife (the word is modified by ἀλίαστος); at Theognis 76 (modified by ἀνήκεστος) it is the disgust and despair felt by one who is the victim of bad faith in what is probably an erotic context. The later meaning of ἄση seems to be the nausea or disgust that comes with surfeit, and at E.*Med.* 245 the context is frankly sexual, since the word describes the sensations of a man tired of his bed-partner. In its earlier occurrences, however, ἄση and its derivatives have instead a sense of defeat or frustration; at Anac.347.8 *PMG* it is a reaction to the fallen lock; at Theog. 593 the ἀσῶν feels the opposite of joy and behaves without courage, giving in to bad fortune (cf. Alc.335.2V); again at Theog. 989, he is βαρυνόμενος, and his state is one that should be hidden from friends (probably, then, despair over an erotic disaster), and if the lines at 991 were meant to follow this fragment, ἄση is here associated with ἀνία as in Sappho. Even at [Theocritus] 25.240, ἀσώμενος does not denote surfeit but describes Heracles' sense of futility when he cannot wound his enemy.

[61] K. Stanley, op.cit., 318 perceives a criticism of Sappho in Aphrodite's mention of her 'maddened heart' but the frenzy of love was an erotic commonplace; cf. Sappho 48V, and see G. Lanata, 'Sul linguaggio amoroso di Saffo', *QU* 2 (1966) 63ff. Aphrodite, though she finds Sappho's foolishness amusing, can hardly think it reprehensible (particularly not if, as W. Wyatt has argued, 'Sappho and Aphrodite', *CP* 69, 1974, 213–14, Sappho means to suggest that her name derived from ἀφροσύνη; this however, seems dubious).

damna.[62] She addresses a Mistress (*potnia*) who can master both men and gods, as Homer's Hera had said (*Il.*14.198–9).[63] The Homeric Aphrodite, however, had used the joys of love and desire as her means of mastery, whereas Sappho has been brought to her knees by humiliating frustration, and this is the situation that she would remedy.

The reminding section comes next, and it is here that the poem's own trickery begins, its purpose being to bring a past miracle into the present and to persuade the audience that they are witnessing it. In its opening words the passage betrays no special intention: 'Come, if ever you come . . .' merely repeats the formula by which one catches a god in the snare of his own past actions. From this point on, however, the poet seems to work with her eye fixed rather more firmly upon her human listeners than upon the divinity she hymns. Ordinarily, when a petitioner makes reference to past benefactions, he does so in terms as vague as possible, which is only common sense, since he does not want to offer any point that might be challenged or denied. Sappho, by contrast, decides to be concrete. Every detail in her account provides a potential loophole for a reluctant divinity, but she doesn't seem to care, for her evident purpose now is to put her listeners directly in touch with these past epiphanies. This is why the many visits are rolled into one, and why that one composite event is related from its start. Certain critics have objected to the scene of the departure from Olympus (calling it an unsuitable digression!),[64] but it is this stanza, for all its valentine quaintness, that bridges the gap between myth and reality. It shows Aphrodite doing, in the past and in heaven, exactly what she must be doing in this very moment – her ear catching a strain of Sapphic song – and consequently it is the immanent, actual goddess of the present that the song seems to place in the light con-

---

[62] The verb is used of mastering animals, inferiors and women, often taking on the special meaning of sexual mastery, as in the Homeric phrase παρθένος ἀδμής (e.g. *Od.*6.109; 228; cf. Aesch.*Supp.* 144–50; S.*OC* 1056; E.*Med.* 623, where the princess is ἡ νεόδμητος κόρη, cf. 1366). Theognis' frequent usage proves that it was applicable to homosexual mastery as well (e.g. 1344; 1350), and Sappho uses it elsewhere of desire (πόθῳ δάμεισα 102.2V).

[63] Compare *h.Aphr.* 3 (καί τ' ἐδαμάσσατο φῦλα καταθνητῶν ἀνθρώπων / οἰωνούς τε διπετέας καὶ θηρία πάντα) and Theognis 1388 (δαμναῖς δ' ἀνθρώπων πυκινὰς φρένας) where, however, the influence of Sappho's hymn can be felt.

[64] Page, *S&A* 18: 'Here at the height of her suffering, she devotes a quarter of her poem to . . . a flight of fancy, with much detail irrelevant to her present theme.' In a somewhat similar vein, Fränkel (*DuP*³, 200ff.=177 Engl.) judged that this must be a mere pretence of prayer and a false report of previous epiphanies because the scene of departure contained details that Sappho could not have seen (by which token the Homeric hymns would likewise be mere pretences, of course), and West prolonged this literalist reading by saying (*Maia* 22, 308): 'A real prayer could not have contained a description of previous epiphanies that the goddess must know to be fictitious and fanciful'. There is, however, nothing in the departure description that makes the song unsuitable for Aphrodite's ears, for just as West's goddess 'must know' what West knows, so Sappho's will know what she knows, which is, at the very least, that such a journey is one of the many epiphany journeys that Aphrodite regularly takes.

veyance (a curricle beside the chariot that Hera would have driven) that sparrows in the past so often drew, and must be drawing now down into the moment of this very performance.

What Sappho actually describes is an infinite number of old epiphanies, but she makes us feel that Aphrodite has alighted in our own finite present in answer to this witnessed prayer. 'Suddenly you arrived, you smiled, you asked,' she reports in the aorist, but since the visit is presented as the cap to all previous ones, it is subsumed into the very latest coming, the one momentarily being called for, and this the more easily because the goddess who arrives (in the past) is so exactly she to whom Sappho has just now called (in the present). The sparrows' wings have proved that she has the levity of Dione's child, and she enters Sappho's world familiarly, almost as one garlanded comrade to another, so that her worshipper need feel no least *frisson* of fear.[65] Fresh from Olympus though she is, she does not use the august tone that we might expect from a visiting divinity, nor has she any need to disguise herself as she did, for example, with Anchises. Her radiance is evidently not of the blinding sort just now, and when she parts her 'deathless' lips after her smile, she speaks with the speech of closest intimacy – almost with the speech of comedy. 'What's the trouble? Who's jilted you now?' she asks, like someone from Aristophanes or Menander,[66] but also very much like her own Homeric mother, when she herself was hurt (*Il.*5.373).[67]

This charming goddess treats Sappho with a familiar affection,[68] almost as if there were kinship betwen them, but she is also the weaver of spells, and when she comes to make her promise (stanza six), her colloquial diction takes on an overtone of sorcery. She almost chants her short, incantatory phrases and she uses formulae that are to be found again and again in the magical papyri. Witches knew spells against a lover who had gone, charms that contained phrases like, 'If he now rests, let him not rest; if he now drinks, let him not drink; if he now loves, let him not love...' – the variations could

---

[65] Even the confident Odysseus hastily murmurs an apotropaic phrase when Athena appears ('May you not come with any evil prepared for me', *Od.*13.228), and others were more strongly affected by the presence of divinity (cf.*P.P.*425; *P.*8.59; Aesch. *PV* 114, 127; E. *Androm.*1226; *Ion* 1549ff.). On the fear proper to an epiphany, see Cameron, op.cit., 6.

[66] For τί πέπονθας cf. Ar. *Vesp.*995; Men.*Georg.* 84; for τίς ἀδικεῖ σε E.*IA* 382; Pl. *Protag.* 310d; *Phaed.* 252c, and Ar.*Eq.*730, which parodies this epiphany by making Demos suddenly appear with a series of short questions capped by: τίς, ὦ Παφλαγών, ἀδικεῖ σε; The closest overall parallel is found in the habitually loving and protective speech of Pentheus to his grandfather, reported at E.*Ba.*1320ff.: τίς ἀδικεῖ, τίς σ' ἀτιμάζει, γέρον; / τίς σὴν ταράσσει καρδίαν, λυπηρὸς ὤν; / λέγ', ὡς κολάζω τὸν ἀδικοῦντά σ', ὦ πάτερ.

[67] *Il.*5.373: τίς νύ σε τοιάδ' ἔρεξε, φίλον τέκος; Athena can use much the same tone with Odysseus, as at *Od.*13.293: σχέτλιε, κτλ.

[68] Page (*S&A*, 13) succeeded in hearing a tone of 'reproof and impatience' in her speech, however, and Stanley, op.cit., 318f. perceives 'criticism'.

extend as far as the lover had money to pay.[69] The magician would also predict immediate effects, just as Sappho's goddess does (*tacheōs*, 21), and he or she would promise results that would come, even if the victim should resist, just as Aphrodite does (*kōuk etheloisa*, 24).[70] Symmetrical reversals, wrought with speed and ease, were what the magicians dealt in,[71] but the reversal that Aphrodite promises here is to the witches' work as white magic is to black. Her words, in fact, are almost exactly those of the fairy-king Oberon, when he promises Helena that Demetrius will return:

Fare thee well, nymph: ere he do leave this grove
Thou shalt fly him, and he shall seek thy love!

(*A Midsummer Night's Dream*, ii.1)

Tricks and charms there will be, but the pleasure of her client is to be ensured without any pain for the victim of this amorous sorcery when the flighty girl is brought back into the game of love, with its gifts, its flights, and its victories.[72]

The fugitive will be caught and returned to Sappho's love; her reluctance will be transformed into eagerness, no matter how unwilling she may now seem to be. Towards her, Aphrodite will act as weaver of snares, but towards Sappho she will meanwhile behave as a true child of Zeus. Her magic, after all, is a heightened form of persuasion

[69] *Pap.gr.mag.* iv 1511. C. Segal, 'Eros and Incantation', *Arethusa* 7 (1974) 139–60, attempts to discover elements of magical chant throughout the song.

[70] Cameron, op.cit., 9, cites the frequent magical ἤδη ἤδη ταχὺ ταχύ; T. Krischer, 'Sapphos Ode an Aphrodite', *Hermes* 96 (1968) 5 adds passages where swift action denotes supernatural power (e.g. Hes.*Theog.* 98–103; *Erga*, 5–7; *Od.*16.197). For the motif of action upon an unwilling subject as proof of power, see *Pap.Mag. gr.* i.125; iv 2934 and also Aesch.*Ag.*190–1 and the discussion of Turyn, *Stud.Sapph.*, 28.

[71] See Cameron, op.cit., 8 and 'Sappho and Aphrodite again', *HTR* 57 (1964) 237–9.

[72] Page (*S&A*, 14–15) argued that the anonymous girl is to suffer exactly what Sappho suffers now, and took this to mean that Sappho is to reject and cease to love her,' fleeing in earnest as the girl pursues. In support of this soon-to-be unwilling Sappho, he proposed to read κῶυ σε θέλοισαν in line 24 (after Knox, *SIFC* 15, 1939, 194, note 3), though there is no excuse for emending the text at this point since-there are epic precedents for the augmented form, as noted by Turyn (*Stud.Sapph.*, 28, to which might be added *Il.*6.164–5, of sexual unwillingness). By Page's reading, what Sappho prays for and what the love-goddess promises her is an end to her love, which is in total contradiction with the final stanza, since one about to quit the field hardly needs a *summachos*. Approved by A. Luppino ('In margine all'ode di Saffo ad Afrodite', *PP* 11, 1956, 359–63 and by G. Pascucci ('Ad Sapph.I.24L.P.' *A&R* NS 2, 1957, 223–9), Page's understanding of the poem has been contested by Cameron (*HTR* 57, 237–9) and refuted by G. Koniaris ('On Sappho fr.1', *Philol.*109, 1965, 30–8), who cites passages in which erotic pursuit does not necessitate flight by the other party. (Unfortunately Koniaris goes on to argue that the ironic lightness that Page would allow to the poem is contradictory to the tone of all the rest of Sappho's work; see 31, 35). West (*Maia* 22, 323) has added citations from Theognis (352; 1094; 1287; 1299; 1355) to show that the topos of pursuit and flight was common to love poetry; to these one might add the more general B.1.175, where pursuit of one who flees figures what is sweet.

(as Sappho slyly reminds us)[73] and it will be used in the interest of a special erotic justice which Aphrodite, like a little sister to Athena, here defends. A beloved who refuses to take the *charis* that is offered breaks the law of love, spoiling the proper balance that is *dikē*, and thus becoming guilty of injustice, or *adikia*.[74] Flight, too, is 'illegal', since the beloved who flees from an accepted lover flouts the cosmic law proclaiming that no one, man or god, can escape from Aphrodite's power (*h. Aphr*.34).[75] This is the jurisprudence of the mature lover who must deal with ever-unruly youth,[76] and it is well-expressed by Theognis (though not without a touch of obscenity) in its masculine form (1283ff.):

> Boy, be not unjust! I still have hopes
> of pleasing you, so kindly listen to me:
> you'll not escape by playing tricks –
> you've won, your victory's behind,
> but don't forget that I can wound you
> even as you turn your back to flee!

As soon as the goddess of the past finishes her promise of magical, erotic justice, Sappho calls out to her from the poetic present, and her final stanza of formal appeal shows that the central reminding section has worked in several ways. Aphrodite is now caught in the trap of her own undeniable past activities; she must be kind again, which means that the petitioner may now sue for her own release. What she

---

[73] Persuasive tricks were among Aphrodite's gifts to Hera in *Il*.14, and the goddess Peitho regularly worked with her and the Charites in the preparation of young people for love; note Hes. *Erg*. 73 and Ibycus 288. That her own power of persuasion was more than rhetorical is demonstrated by her success in bringing the unwilling Helen to Paris' bed in *Il*.3. Peitho later became one of Aphrodite's cult names; called in this way she was the giver of success in love (see Farnell, *Cults* ii, 665 and K. Keil, 'Griechische Inschriften', *Philol.Suppl*.2, 579–71) and it is to this aspect of her power that Sappho refers with the verb πείθω which appears in line 18.

[74] Note that at E.*Med*.158 Zeus himself is to support a lover betrayed: Ζεύς σοι τάδε συνδικήσει. Cameron (*HTR* 32, 10f.) discussed the religio-secular prototypes for the appeal of a victim of erotic injustice to a ruler or god, noting that this is a regular conceit (Hipp.115W; Epicharm. 286; P.*Phaedr*.252c); see also Privitera, op.cit., 75ff.; M. G. Bonnano, 'Osservazione sul tema della 'giusta' reciprocità amorosa di Saffo ai comici', *QU* 16 (1973) 110ff. B. Gentili, 'Il 'Letto Insaziato' di Medea e il tema dell' adikia', *St.Cl.e Or*., Pisa, 21 (1972) 60–72, assumes that by 'injustice' Sappho referred to a breach of contractual *dikē* (not just the *dikē* of reciprocal *charis*), and this seemed to support his notion that the girls of Sappho's *thiasos* formed homosexual marriages with fixed and public oaths. A. Rivier, *REG* 80 (1967) 84–92, doubled the number of contracts by supposing that a girl swore her public fidelity to the *thiasos* and also her private fidelity to her lover. He believed that the present poem concerned a beloved girl who had defected to another house and whom Sappho would now reinstate (reading Page's τάγην in line 19) in the group, as well as in their love affair.

[75] Compare Theognis 1389: οὐδέ τις ἔστιν / οὕτως ἴφθιμος καὶ σοφὸς ὥστε φυγεῖν.

[76] As Theognis knowingly remarked, τῶν δε καλῶν παίδων οὗτις ἔτ᾽ οὐκ ἀδικῶν (1282, with Welcker's reading; West suggests οὗτις ἔτεισ᾽ ἀδίκων or ἀδικῶν); cf. Anacreon's καλὸν εἶναι τῷ Ἔρωτι τὰ δίκαια (402b *PMG*).

actually asks, however, is much more, for the old plea of 'Do not subdue me!' becomes first 'Set me free!', and then 'Bring to pass everything that I want!', and finally 'Join me as my ally!' This lover had been bound and bewitched by her own obsessive thoughts (25)[77] through Aphrodite's agency, but nevertheless she now expects that same goddess not only to free her, but also to understand her innermost desires, and to fulfil them with the same magical effectiveness (26–7).[78] And having found the courage to make this demand, she who began her prayer in grovelling erotic nausea rises like some doughty warrior and claims the god who mastered her as her field-companion. She seems to feel rather like a god herself, as she sings these final syllables, and no wonder, for the countless past promises of which she has reminded Aphrodite (*dēute . . . dēute . . . dēute*, 15, 16, 18)[79] have reminded the singer of the equally countless number of past successes that she, with heavenly aid, has enjoyed. Revived by such recollections, she knows that she cannot fail, and her confidence produces her final image of Aphrodite's nature. She is not just the *sundikos* that she promised to be, but a *summachos*[80] as well – an ally

---

[77] For μέριμνα of obsessive erotic thoughts, cares, ambitions, cf. Theog. 1323; at 1385, it is said that Aphrodite can grant a *lusis*, as she does here, from ἄχθεα χαλεπά.

[78] There is a childishness about this demand for complete fulfilment of 'all that my heart desires' that corresponds well with the indulgence of Aphrodite's attitude. Nevertheless, the phrase is also magically and ritually correct; cf. the call to Hecate: ἔλθετε καὶ τελειώσατέ μοι τὴν πραγματείαν ταύτην (Kagarow, *Gr.Fluchtafeln*, 30). For some reason West (*Maia* 22, 308) contends that such vagueness proves the prayer to be not genuine; on the contrary, it is only politic to leave a god a little room for discretion (cf. e.g. *Od.*14.54; 17.355), and in this particular case the vagueness expresses a presumption of accord between the petitioner and a goddess who perfectly knows these undescribed aims (cf. with sinister effect, the prayers of Clytemnestra at *A.Ag.*973 and *S.El.*637ff.).

[79] For the use of δηὖτε in erotic poems, as an ironic reminder that love comes again and again, compare Sappho 130V, Ἔρος δηὖτέ μ᾽ ὁ λυσιμέλης δόνει; Alcm.59a; Ibycus 287; Anac. 358, 376, 394, 400, 413, 428 *PMG*. On its meaning here, see Snell, *Entdeckung*, pp. 95, 100, 111; Schadewalt, *Sappho*, 90; Gentili, op.cit., 61f. Page believed that this repeated expression indicated indignation and impatience on Aphrodite's part (*S&A*, 13); Privitera (op.cit., 75) argued that it is part of of her ultimate lesson on the rhythm of pleasure and pain. Nevertheless, since in Sappho's schema each call brings a promise of aid, a reminder of how many calls there have been in the past must be a reminder likewise of how many successful campaigns have been fought in the past. An important fact about Sapphic love is that it repeats itself endlessly, as it must for anyone who is an ἐραστής of all that is beautiful.

[80] For gods as *summachoi*, aside from the Aeschylean passages already mentioned (note 3), cf. Archil.108W; Hdt. 8.64 Aesch. *Supp.*342, 395; *S.OT* 274; *E.Supp.*630. The word is completely masculine in its connotations, but Bowra (*GLP²*, 202) reminds us that Aphrodite was conventionally ἄμαχος, which would make her the best *summachos* in the world. For the notion of an erotic 'battle' see Giuliana Lanata, 'Archiloco 69D', *QU* 6 (1968) 33ff., who notes S. *Antig.* 81, 800; *Tr.* 441–2; E.fr.433 N², to which might be added E.*Hipp.*527, where Eros goes to war; note also B. Marzullo, 'Il primo Partenio di Alcmane', *Philol.*108 (1964) 203 note 2, and C. Pavese, 'Alcmane, il Partenio del Louvre', *QU* 4 (1967) 126, who gives this sense to μάχεσθαι and ἀμύναι in Alcman's *Partheneion*.

and almost an equal for the lover whose faith is strong enough for prayer to her own subduer.

Learned men have argued over whether this song records what they call a 'genuine mystical experience',[81] but the question of whether or not Sappho ever spoke face to face with Aphrodite is one that should not have been raised. What epiphanies she saw are her affair, not ours, for it is the critic's business to discover, not what was shown to Sappho, but what she has shown forth in her song. In this case, the poet's meaning is itself an epiphany, for her performance is a demonstration that says: This is love; this is prayer; this is Aphrodite. She knew that Aphrodite was a wise and smiling power with whom a wise and smiling lover might share a kind of intimacy, and she let this knowledge shape and fill her song, not saying but showing that prayer to a divine enemy such as this might be transformed into conversation with a heavenly friend. Her followers, by this demonstration, are instructed in certain conventional forms,[82] and they learn as well the largest lesson of faith, for one must believe of any god one worships that what is cruel is kind as well. There is, however, an emphasis in this doctrine of loving prayer that is peculiarly Sapphic, and that is its implicit reliance upon the power of memory. The only way to turn towards a god who seems to turn away from you is by remembering him when he was well-disposed, and Sappho proves that this same necessary act of remembering can itself become an operative form of praise. That, however, is only an extension of the magical principle of the *hypomnēsia*, and Sappho has a second, more unexpected thing to show about memory. It makes the goddess show her friendly face, but it also quite independently causes the lover to change from despair to confidence, and the result is that this prayer, even as it waits for its divine response, works its own fulfilment by means of memory. Memory leads the petitioner to a new view of the present situation, for memory places the present love among many more like itself and thereby suggests that all of these separate affairs are, like Aphrodite's separate appearances, only one in reality. Memory thus leads this lover out of the immediate and specific and into the ideal and the

---

[81] Bowra, *GLP*, 193f.: 'Neither the epic nor Archilochus describe visions of this character, and the inevitable conclusion is that Sappho really believed that she had seen Aphrodite and that this poem, with all its accuracy and truth to nature, is after all a religious poem concerned with an experience which can only be called mystical.' Cameron's first article (*HTR* 32, 1–17) demonstrates the conventional elements of the song, presumably as a corrective to this view, but in its attempts to assess the genuine religiosity of the song it falls back on arguments like those of Page, assuming that religious belief can only be expressed with 'emotional urgency' and therefore that 'prettiness and . . . playfulness' cannot mark the expression of such a belief.

[82] This will be a secular version of the instruction one might receive, as part of an initiation, in how to call a god to his aid; see F. Pfister, *RE* sv 'Epiphanie', who discusses Diod. 5.49.5; 4.43.1; 4.48.1; Schol.Ar.*Pax* 277; Schol.AR *Arg*.i.917.

general, and this is a phenomenon that Sappho will elaborate in several of her other best preserved performances.

The Aphrodite hymn is signed with Sappho's name and filled with Sappho's sense of private alliance with her god, but there is a second prayer that has a wholly different tone. In it, divine aid is imaged in eucharistic instead of military terms, and in it a nameless worshipper who could be anyone at any time voices a general rather than a particular need, calling on the goddess on behalf of an unspecified group (2V):

```
. . ανοθεν κατιου[c|-                                               1ª
†δευρυμμεχρητεcιπ[.]ρ[     ]|.† ναῦον                                1
ἄγνον ὄππ[αι    ]| χάριεν μὲν ἄλcοc
μαλί[αν],| βῶμοι δ' ἔ⟨ν⟩ι θυμιάμε-
νοι [λι]|βανώτω⟨ι⟩·                                                  4
ἐν δ' ὕδωρ ψῦχρο ͜ν ͜ | κελάδει δι' ὔcδων
μαλίνων,| βρόδοιcι δὲ παῖc ὁ χῶροc
ἐcκί|αcτ', αἰθυccομένων δὲ φύλλων|
    κῶμα †καταιριον·                                                 8
ἐν δὲ λείμων| ἰππόβοτοc τέθαλε
†τωτ...(.)ριν|νοιc† ἄνθεcιν, αἰ ⟨δ'⟩ ἄηται
μέλλι|χα πν[έο]ιcιν [
    [          ]                                                     12
ἔνθα δὴ cὺ †cυ.αν†| ἔλοιcα Κύπρι
χρυcίαιcιν ἐν κυ|λίκεccιν ἄβρωc
⟨ὀ⟩μ⟨με⟩μεί|χμενον θαλίαιcι| νέκταρ
    οἰνοχόειcα                                                       16
```

Come, [if to Cretans you came,]
for here in this sacred haunt
apple trees crowd in a gracious grove, shrines
    are perfumed with smoke.

Here the cool water sings its song
deep in the apple-boughs;
all is rose-shadowed and restless leaves
    drop sleep like a spell.

Here is a meadow fit for horse,
thriving with [early] bloom; sweet
breezes are blowing their honied breath
    . . .

Take up a [crown] then, Cyprian:
pour, for our cups of gold,
suave mixture of nectar with festive joy –
    be thou our bearer of wine!

The words seem to express, even to induce, the soft trance that numinous natural beauty can impose and their magic is increased by the chance of their preservation, for they come directly from the hand of a Hellenistic Egyptian who had made them his talisman. Except for a few citations in ancient grammar books,[83] the prayer had disappeared and it would have been lost forever had not a large Ptolemaic potsherd turned up, about forty years ago, covered with Lesbian verse.[84] Someone[85] had been so much struck by the song that he wished to have it always available, and he had penned out its words on the convex surface of a bit of broken vase about the size of a man's palm. When it was found in 1937, the *ostrakon* had lost its upper right corner, its surface was rough, and its ink was badly faded. In addition, the spelling of its copy was aberrant and the dialect distorted, but nevertheless the pocket-sized piece of clay still gave out something of Sappho's music, and the first publication, by Medea Norsa, was greeted with an inebriate reverence that would have satisfied Ronald Firbank himself.

[83] Hermogenes, περὶ ἰδεῶν 2, 4, 331–2, ed. Rabe, cites lines 5–6 and 7–8 in his discussion of literary styles and the pleasure they convey. These were fragments 4 and 5 in Bergk⁴, fragment 5 in Diehl. In addition, Athenaeus (11, 463c–e) had cited a version of lines 13–16, and individual words had been mentioned for their Aeolisms by various others.

[84] First published by Medea Norsa, 'Versi di Saffo in un ostrakon del sec. II aC,' *Annali della Scuola Normale Superiore di Pisa*, Lett. e Stor. e Fil., Ser. 2, 6 (1937) 1–2, 8ff. with photograph. See also Norsa, *La scrittura letteraria greca dal sec. IV aC all' VIII dC* (Florence 1939), 11–12, and 'Dal primo libro di Saffo', *PSI* 13, 1300 (Florence, 1953), 48. There is a slightly better photograph published by K. Matthiessen, 'Das Gedicht Sapphos auf der Scherbe', *Gymnasium* 64 (1957) 554ff. and Tafel XVII. The hand is usually identified as belonging to the second century B.C. but Page (*S&A*, 35) assigns it to the third. The sherd is in the Biblioteca Laurenziana in Florence, but it has deteriorated to such a degree that it is even less legible than the photographs, according to Dino Pieraccioni, 'Recenti edizioni de Saffò ed Alcaeo', *Maia* 8 (1956) 56–71.

[85] There is disagreement about the identity of this scribe because of the evident contradiction between the high quality of his writing and the low quality of his spelling and rendering of dialect forms. Some believe that he was a schoolboy of extraordinary skill in penmanship who wrote from dictation and understood nothing; see A. Setti, 'Il frammento Saffico dell'ostrakon fiorentino', *SIFC* 19 (1943) 125ff.; V. Martin, 'La poésie lyrique et la poésie dramatique dans les découvertes papyrologiques', *MH* 4 (1947) 74–100, esp. 81; G. Lanata, 'L'ostrakon Fiorentino con versi di Saffo', *SIFC* 31 (1959) 64–90. Others, following Gallavotti, 'L'Ode Saffica dell'ostracon fiorentino', *SIFC* 18 (1942) 187, understand this to be the work of 'un egiziano colto che poco sapeva di ortografia ma che molto si compiacque degli splendidi versi'; E. Siegmann, 'Anmerkungen zum Sappho-Ostrakon', *Hermes* 76 (1941) 417–22, remarks 'Es ist nicht die Hand eines Schulers oder Berufsschreibers, sondern die feinzügige Schrift eines Mannes der sich die Notiz liebhabermässig zu genanntem Zweck machte', (p.418). Page (*S&A*, 35, n.1) limits himself to the pronouncement that this is 'certainly not . . . a schoolboy hand'. All in all, the second supposition seems the more probable, since it is easier to suppose a practical man unfamiliar with Lesbian poetry but struck with this example, than a Ptolemaic schoolroom where Sapphic poems are dictated to ignorant boys who write with practised ease.

The *ostrakon* song was easily recognised as a Sapphic prayer to Aphrodite, but it was obviously not intended for use on formal public occasions. Instead of beginning with patronymics, titles, powers and residences, in order to attract the attention of its divinity, this plea begins with a familiar call[86] and as it continues it leaves out as well

---

[86] That is to say, the first stanza that we have begins in this way; most scholars would insist that this is not the beginning of the song, but the evidence is exceedingly hard to evaluate. There are letters at the top of the sherd, preceding its first whole stanza, which look something like ορρανοθενκατιου, and these are usually interpreted as representing the last line of a preceding stanza. Theiler and Von der Mühll have even reconstructed the whole in the following way:

[Παῖ Διώνας Κυπρογένηα σέμνα
παρκάλημμί σ᾽εἰς ἐράταν ἑόρταν,
ἔλθε δ᾽ὠκέως ὀράνω κ]αράνο-
θεν κατίοι[σα

('Das Sapphogedicht auf der Scherbe', *MH* 3, 1946, 22–5). However, since the *ostrakon* preserves its original size (except for the loss of the upper right-hand corner after the time of its inscription), the reading of its uppermost words as the close of a preliminary section of the song involves the supposition that the writer was using a series of sherds and continuing his material from one to the next. This is a practice that can in fact be occasionally observed in the recording of long Homeric passages (see Setti, op.cit.), but one that seems highly improbable in the case of a short poem. A further objection arises from the more recently broken corner, since, if it was inscribed (as every other bit of space is) the words we have could not of course be considered as the final ones of the preceding stanza. Furthermore, the most obvious supplement, ὠ]ράνοθεν, won't scan; A. Turyn, 'The Sapphic ostrakon', *TAPA* 73 (1942) 308ff. first proposed κα]ράνοθεν; others (Treu, Matthiessen, Körte, Saake) suppose that words have been left out between ὠ]ράνοθεν and the final participle. If the first words do not represent the close of a previous stanza, what else might they be? Gallavotti, op.cit., 190ff. made the ingenious suggestion that they had not been written first but last, added when the scribe realised that he had omitted the close of the third stanza of his sequence. Of course they are as difficult to handle as the close of this stanza as they are the close of an initial one, but the problems of space are solved (since the assumption is that this was not part of the continuing inscription, and consequently the sherd may be supposed to have been left blank in the missing right-hand corner). Gallavotti went on to restore lines 10ff. as αἰ δ᾽ἀήται / μέλλιχα πνέοισιν υ– υρανο- / θεν κατιοίσαι and Pieraccioni, op.cit., 63ff. suggests that Turyn's κα]ράνοθεν might be employed here (though breezes don't ordinarily blow down from the tops of mountains). Colonna, *L'Antica Lirica Greca* (1963) prints the song in Gallavotti's way, as complete in four stanzas.
    Another solution is to dismiss the sherd's first line as not belonging to the Sapphic song at all, but coming from another poem that is not even Lesbian (the participle indeed shows a non-Aeolic form); this is the suggestion of R. Pfeiffer, 'Vier Sappho-Strophen auf einem ptolemaischen Ostrakon', *Philolog.* 92 (1937), 117ff., who is followed by T. McEvilley, 'Sappho, fr.2', *Phoenix* 26 (1972), 323ff. Such an arrangement, however, could only result if the writer had not only been using a series of sherds, but had been recording a random sequence upon them – something like an anthology – and this seems hardly tenable.
    A third possibility was proposed by E. Siegmann, op.cit., 161ff., and taken up by West, *Maia* 22 (1970) 315ff.: the difficult words at the top of the sherd may be a kind of summary, an 'aide-mémoire', paraphrasing a first stanza which the writer does not record, perhaps because he already has it by heart. Deriving from this is a fourth possibility, for the words might also serve as a kind of title or identification of the poem

all demonstration of past aid and proof of present need.[87] There are no arguments from old gifts given or old favours received, there is no fiction according to which the suppliant sues for specific support, nor is the urgent pressure of danger or distress applied to the divinity.

---

as a song 'for Aphrodite as she comes down from heaven'. In either case their non-Lesbian aspect, the metrical impossibility of ω]ράνοθεν, and the possibility of there having been more writing in the upper right corner are all taken care of. In addition, if the words represent a title, we no longer have to assume a missing first stanza, and can agree with the proposal of A. Rivier, 'Sur un vers-clé de Sappho', *MH* 5 (1948) 227–39, that the poem actually began with the line usually reported as line 5. In rejection of either of the last two solutions it is usually said that the song cannot possibly begin without naming its goddess in a formal invocation, but since this is evidently not a true cult hymn, but rather a song that mimics the *hymnos kletikos*, a beginning with Δεῦρυ is not after all unimaginable. For other prayers beginning in this way, cf. S.127V, Δεῦρο δηῦτε Μοῖσαι and 128V, Δεῦτέ νυν ἄβραι Χάριτες κτλ. cf. S53V; Alc. 33a, Alc. 34V and Hipp.3aW (where the δεῦρο is in the second line).

[87] There is, however, an encapsulated hypomnesia if the first line really contains the words αἰ Κρήτεσσί περ which are the basis of the translation offered. This reading derives from a suggestion made by F. Lasserre, 'Un nouveau fragment d'Archiloque', *MH* 5 (1948) 15: αἰ Κρήτεσ <σ>ιν [ἔ]β[ας ἔ]ναυ<λ>ον; Rivier (op.cit., 227ff.) altered this to αἰ Κρήτεσ<σ>ί π[οτ' ἔλθ' ἔ]ναυ<λ>ον and was supported by Matthiessen (op.cit., 554ff.); Lanata, op.cit., 66, proposed αἰ Κρήτεσ<σ>ί π[ερ and she is followed by Kirkwood, *EGM* p. 114. 'Come, if to Cretans you came' would presumably make reference to a famous epiphany in Crete, or else to a Cretan cult whose votaries were reputedly visited by the goddess. The only evidence for any special cult of Aphrodite in Crete is the statement of Diodorus Siculus (5.77) that she was one of the divinities whom the Cretans claimed as originally theirs; Hesychius, sv 'Antheia' locates a cult of Aphrodite Antheia at Knossos.

Lasserre's version put the present shrine into the 'if ever' clause and so placed it and Sappho in Crete: cf. Setti's ἐς Κρήτας πρ[οφάνατε ναῦον and Turyn's Κρήτας πρ[οσίκοι]ο ναῦον. W. Theiler and P. Von der Mühll, 'Das Gedicht auf der Scherbe', *MH* 3 (1946), 22ff. and V. Martin, op.cit., p. 81 reverse this transplantation and bring Cretans to Lesbos as founders of a 'Cretan' shrine (ε<ὶ> Κρῆτές π[ο]τ' [ἔσαντ]ο ναῦον). The versions of Rivier and Lanata, however, allow for a separation between singer and Cretans by putting the latter in another time and place.

Those who read line 1 with Lobel, as containing ἐκ Κρήτας find a reference to a favourite place rather than to previous epiphanies. Some of these even make this Cretan place the apple-grove; so C. Theander, 'Zum neuesten Sappho-Fund', *Philol.* 101 (1937) 468, ἐκ Κρήτας προλίποισ' ἔναυλον and B. Lavagnini, 'Ancora sull'ode di Saffo', *Annali della Scuola Norm. Sup. di Pisa, Lett. Stor. Fil.*, Ser.2, 11 (1942), 8–19. Others (Page, Saake and many more) leave the place unspecified and construe κατίοισα or δεῦρυ . . . ἐπὶ τόνδε ναῦον or ἔναυλον, though κατίοισα is odd for a journey from Crete to Lesbos and ἐπὶ τόνδε is prosy at best. M. Galiano attempts to avoid these difficulties by reading ἐκ Κρήτας προσίκοιο ναῦον, 'Algo mas todavia sobre el ostrakon Saffico', *An.de Fil.Cl.* (Buenos Aires) 5 (1952), 81–90.

Yet others deny the existence of the kappa of line 1 and follow Schubart's suggestions of εἰς ῥήτας ('on the appointed day') or ἐς 'Ρείας ('to Rhea's shrine'); see 'Bemerkungen zu Sappho', *Hermes* 73 (1938) 297ff., and 'Zu mehreren Gedichten der Sappho', *Philologus* 98 (1948), 312. M. West, op.cit., 317, suggests ἐς βρήτας ἐπόνελθε ναῦον, 'come again on this appointed day, as you have before', the ἐπόνελθε presumably acting as a kind of hypomnesia. Against this line of interpretation are the facts that the kappa has been generally read, and that the imitation of this song made by Gregory Nazianzen also mentiones Crete; see Q. Cataudella, 'Saffò Fr.5–6 Diehl', *Atene e Roma* 42 (1940) 199ff. For a useful, schematised breakdown of all the early readings of line 1, see Matthiessen, op.cit., p.556.

Instead, the prayer of the potsherd calls for its epiphany in soft words of confidence, as if Aphrodite might come down for her own pleasure, tempted by beauty and joy. The song seems to say, 'Come! How could you resist such a spot?', and it is its concentration upon place that is its central oddity as prayer, but also its central charm as poetry. Other prayers mention localities from which their gods are formally asked to come, but this one uses three of its four stanzas to create instead the place that will receive its heavenly visitor. This topographical emphasis is not quite so strange as it might be, however, for the enchanted grove to which Aphrodite is called proves to be a kind of Archimboldo portrait in which the goddess's best-known attributes and parts are rendered by bits of landscape.[88] It thus serves (much as a mythic episode might serve in a longer hymn) to specify and re-inforce the aspect of the divinity that the worshipper would meet. Gardens, apples, perfumes, roses, field-flowers and horses remind Aphrodite of herself, as she is worshipped in her various cults.[89]

The Sapphic singer is at pains to prove that Aphrodite will find only herself in this place, and in addition she deploys all her art to purge the spot of any residual earthliness, as she prepares for the goddess' coming. Consequently there are no changing seasons here, for roses and apples mix summer's beginning with summer's end,[90] and in the

---

[88] In a sense, then, this description of the grove is comparable to the conventional aretalogy of a hymn, since it is a description of the god offered to the god for his pleasure; see Saake, *Kunst*, 97, who treats the poem somewhat as Eitrem did the Hymn to Hermes, finding in it systematic references to details of Cretan Aphrodite cult.

[89] For the general connection between Aphrodite and gardens and meadows, see Langlotz, *Aphrodite in den Gärten* (Heidelberg 1954); H. Motte, *Prairies et Jardins de la Grèce Antique*, Acad. Royale de Belg., Mem. de la Cl. des Lettres, 2ᵉSer.61 (1973) 121ff. For gardens in cult Paus.1.19.2 (Athens); Strabo 14, 683–4; Pliny *HN* 5.130 (Cyprus); *P.P.*5.24 (Cyrene); Farnell, *Cults* ii, 642 (Paphos); for roses, Paus. 6.24.7; Bion 1.66; E.*Med.*840; Schol.Lyc.831; Geop.11.17.3; cf. Philost. *Epist.*1; Clement on *Perv. Ven.*33 (and note Aphrodite's rose-crown as wedding gift to Amphitrite, B.17.118); see also Preller, Bd.I.358, paragraphs 282–4 for apples, Farnell, *Cults* ii 643 (Magnesia), 676 (Sikyon), Theoc.5.88 (with roses) and 10.34 (see Gow ad 10.34), and see also refs. at note 102 below; for field flowers, Hes.*Theog.* 194–5; Bion 1.66 (anemone); Farnell *Cults* ii 680 (poppy); for horses, Anacreon, fr.1 *PMG* 346 (and see B. Gentili, *Anacreonte*, Rome, 1958, 184ff.), Schol.*Il.*2.820; Preller, Bd.I, 351, note 1, 373, note 5; *RE* sv 'Hippomanes', esp. 1879ff.; for perfume, *Od.*8.362; *h.Aphr.* 61–2 (and see M. Détienne, *Les Jardins d'Adonis*, Paris 1972, 118ff.); sleep, Hesych. sv Aphrodite (Mandragoritis); Farnell, *Cults* ii, 680 (Sikyon, 'the goddess who lulls the senses and gives sweet sleep').

[90] Contrast the garden described by Longus (*Daphnis and Chloe*, 2), where the characteristic products of each season are carefully discriminated. Nevertheless, this is usually called a spring poem (so Theiler and Von der Mühll, op.cit., 25 and West, op.cit., 317), presumably because of the word ἠρίνοισ<ιν> (which is often restored in line 10. Other epithets are equally possible (see the summary at Matthiessen, op.cit., 561), but this one is almost formulaic (cf. *Il.*2.89; *Erg.*75; *Theog.* 279; *h.Dem.*401) and it may very well have qualified the field-flowers of stanza three; it cannot, however, alter the fact that roses thick enough to cast a shadow belong to early summer (see Ingrid Waern, 'Flora Sapphica', *Eranos* 70 (1972) 1–11), and that apples belong to summer's end. It might be argued that, though fruit is the first association with apple

same way there is no fixed time of day, since warmth and coolness, light and shade, sound and silence all exist simultaneously. The only motion here takes place in air, curiously mingling up with down as smoke rises, sleep falls, breezes lift and nectar drips into cups, while other seemingly opposite concepts meet and mix in a similar way. The rich colour of a rose becomes shadow's dark absence of hue, and the singing water from the ground somehow joins with the leaves above, in trees where sleep, not fruit, falls from shimmering boughs.[91] No image retains its solidity, for the first stanza's material grove and altars give way to the perfumed smoke of its clausula; the tangible water and branches of the second stanza are transformed into the drowsy numbness of its final line, and (as far as one can tell) the fields and flowers of the third are subsumed into a breeze.

The laws of matter evidently do not obtain in this sacred spot where Aphrodite will join her petitioner. Substance here tends to give way to insubstantiality, and the place is set off from the rest of the world in other ways as well by a singer who begins at the dark core of this magic space and moves in an orderly way out into its bright periphery.[92] The first stanza fixes an inner spot – the grove itself – and sets the true centre of all by establishing altars there. The second moves out from these altars but remains within the grove as it adds water, in the form of a fountain or brook, to the amenities of the inner place. Then the third stanza – the last one to be spent on description – passes out beyond the apple-grove and draws around it an encircling field that knows sunshine and animal life.[93] The sequence of the stanzas

---

trees, these were meant to be thought of as in blossom, were it not for the fact that the flowering season is in February, which is not a good time to escape the heat in a cool glade and fall asleep under a tree. Similarly, it is often said that the 'time' of the poem is evening; this was the contention of Schubart, ('Bemerkungen', *Hermes* 73 (1938) 300), who argues that roses couldn't cast shadows except in the slanting sun and that therefore (dawn somehow forgotten) this must be a moment when the sun is setting. Fränkel (*DuP*, 204) reported this as a 'stille Abendstunde', and for doing so is accused of northern romanticism by S. Radt ('Sapphica', *Mnemosyne* 23, 1970, 337–47). Radt in turn insists upon a moment at midday, while Theiler and Von der Mühll (op.cit., 25) believe that the poem concerns a night-long festival. These contradictory opinions all reflect the fact that the poem does not describe a specific temporal moment in the day any more than it does a calendar season or a geographical location.

[91] See the discussion of Max Treu, *Von Homer zur Lyrik*, Zetemata 12 (Munich 1955), 211, where the fairy-tale quality of this unexpected mixture is emphasised: Treu compares the Dream-Tree of lullaby, and hails this as a breach in Sappho's usual faithfulness to nature, though he does cite the somewhat comparable partnership between winds and sorrows at fr.37.3V.

[92] The formal syntax sets trees, altars, water and meadow all within the largest sacred area, the ναῦος ἄγνος; within this definition the repeated apple trees at lines 3 and 6 establish a kind of ring that holds everything inside it inside the grove, while it leaves the meadow outside the grove but still a part of the whole.

[93] It should be noted, however, that there are no horses in this poem – only whatever subliminal suggestions as are made by the adjective ἱππόβοτος, which explicitly only makes this the sort of field where horses may grow fat, i.e. one that is rich in grass.

means that the cool still inner shrine with its shadows, roses and sanctified altars, is lapped about by the brilliant warmth of an untended pasture where field flowers grow. Apparently it is separated from the world, yet linked to it as well, by this outer zone that is at once wilder and more profane.[94]

Obviously this apple grove is something other than the scene of a jolly picnic,[95] for here one does not sleep, one lies entranced – here one drinks nectar rather than wine.[96] The place is likewise too unnaturally abstract to be a mere physical shrine where public rituals were actually performed.[97] Even to our modern ears some further

---

[94] Possibly with an awareness of this Sapphic song, Anacreon later composed a piece that makes use of two similar places (P.Oxy.2321=346 fr.1*PMG*). In his song, however, the two are set against each other as opposites rather than being seen as a whole, for he is making a playful attack upon a girl whom he accuses of having become a prostitute. She, who is supposed to be being nurtured demurely in one spot (possibly a place of lilies, possibly ruled by Aidōs), proves actually to have escaped to another of hyacinths, where Cypris tethers her horses and lets them graze. The escape, of course, is a figure for the end of the girl's virginity, and the strong discrimination between the two places is obviously determined by the poem's special purpose of blame. S. R. Slings, 'Anacreon's two meadows', *ZPE* 30 (1978), 38, takes it as certain that the first place contained lilies and was described as a veritable 'meadow of Artemis', but it should be noted that Peitho could as easily be the nursemaid of line 5, as she is at Ibycus 266 *PMG* (cf. Hes. *Theog*.349). Slings likewise insists that the tethered horses of line 9 are 'slaves' of erotic pleasure and so somehow victims of a negative evaluation, but they are probably simply emblems of pleasure, horses at leisure to graze with as much freedom as tamed horses could ever know in a place where fences were not in use.

Within the same convention, Theognis, 1249ff., uses the horse directly as a figure for the young person who has discovered sex. Unlike Anacreon, however, he repeats Sappho's easy mixture of grove with meadow, identifying the hybrid spot as a place where love follows inclination; by way of contrast he proposes the stall as a place where love sells itself:

You, boy, are just like a barley-stuffed horse – having
  eaten your fill, back you come galloping into my pasture again,
full of desire for a rider who's noble, a meadow that's sweet,
  coolness of springs and the shadowy, leaf-dappled glade.

[95] West, op.cit., 317: 'Sappho and her companions are enjoying a picnic.'

[96] Sappho's grove is wonderfully like the place where Venus took Adonis, when, in the *Faery Queen* (iii.1.28ff.), she

Entyst the Boy, as well that art she knew,
And wooed him her Paramoure to be:
Now making girlonds of each flowr that grew,
To crowne his golden locks with honour dew
Now leading him into a secret shade
From his Beauperes, and from bright heavens view,
Where him to sleepe she gently would perswade,
Or bathe him in a fountaine by some covert glade . . .
And ever with sweet Nectar she did sprinkle him.

[97] The apple-grove is generally taken to be a specific spot actually frequented by the Sapphic group, a place either on Crete or on Lesbos. Some critics, however, have understood it differently; Turyn, op.cit., 308ff. thought that it was a Cretan shrine that Sappho imagined in mystical terms; R. Merkelbach, op.cit., 28, suggested that an actual

meaning seems to invest each local detail, and this is because Sappho has given this dark grove surrounded by bright grass the attributes of a demonic place. In its outer reaches it is like the paradise that the initiated dead enjoyed,[98] and we are reminded especially of the meadow of Pindar's threnody (114B=129S), where the fortunate ones sport under the sun among roses, perfumes and golden fruit, with horses and music and games for their entertainment. At its darker centre, however, Sappho's grove is closer to those gardens where nymphs were to be found, for they loved wild places that were cool and dark and grassy (*Od.*6.123) and water was central to all of their playgrounds (AR *Arg.*3.882).[99] And finally, in its entirety Sappho's sacred spot within a flowery border is strongly reminiscent of the antique landscape of female sexuality. Calypso had her dark cave (*Od.*5.63ff.) with its streams of fresh water, encircled by meadows that were soft with violets – Odysseus, to escape, had to retreat to barren sand – and the same system of imagery caused Archilochus to speak of the grassy garden outside the gate of his mistress's maidenhead (Pap.Col. 7511). Pindar's Apollo likewise talks of culling the sweet grass from Cyrene's bed (P.*P.*9.36–7; cf. the figure at AR *Arg.*3.898–9), and it has often been noticed that throughout antiquity significant erotic encounters were thought of as taking place in just such blossoming fields as these.[100]

Its timelessness, its golden cups, and its horse-feeding meadows all give an intimation of immortality to Sappho's grove, but shadow and sleep do not belong to the fields of bliss, and anyway, since this is explicitly Aphrodite's place, its normal associations are with love and life. The occupants of this grove are therefore to be thought of either as virginal nymphs in some secret and protected haunt, or else as young creatures already engaged in amorous adventures – but which? The song calls for Aphrodite's visit, but since in the one case she would come to perfect an erotic potential, in the other to confirm an erotic

---

temenos was being described as if it were a Nymphengarten; Saake, loc.cit., proposes the grove as a representation of Aphrodite's cults; McEvilley, op.cit., 331, believes that the scene depicts the state of Sappho's spirit, her 'readiness in the heart' for a mystical meeting with Aphrodite.

[98] See Turyn, op.cit., who cites Ar. *Frogs* 448f.; Ps.Plato, *Axioch.* 317c (Dieterich, *Nekyia* 31 and 121); Orph.fr. 32a5 and 9 Kern; Virg.*Aen.*6.637; Lucian, *VH* 2.5ff. The same elements often appear in medieval paradise scenes; cf. e.g. Bernard of Cluny's Jerusalem the Golden.

[99] Note that Demetrius, *de Comp.*, 106, listed νυμφαῖοι κῆποι among Sappho's subjects. On the homes of the nymphs, see also Pausanias 10.32 on the Corycian cave, and the essay by P. Saintyves 'Les grottes dans les cultes magico-réligieux et dans la symbolique primitive', in J. Trabucco, *Porphyre. L'Antre des nymphes* (Paris 1918).

[100] See Motte, op.cit., 210; J. M. Bremer, 'The meadow of love', *Mnem.*28.3 (1975), 268ff., and the discussion of W. Bühler, *Die Europa des Moschos*. Hermes Einzelschr. 13 (Wiesbaden 1960), 75.

actuality, its whole meaning depends upon the nature of this place. Is the apple grove suggestive of a Nymphengarten, or is it closer in its associations to Calypso's cave?

It might seem that the twice-emphasised[101] presence of Aphrodite's fruit, the apple,[102] would settle this question at once, but in fact the apple was associated both with virginity and with its loss. It reified ripeness for love, but it could represent that ripeness either as ready for enjoyment, or as just now enjoyed, and it was this ambiguity that made it a frequent emblem for marriage. Gaia had caused an apple tree to grow in the gardens of the Hesperides, to commemorate Zeus' first mastery of Hera there (Pherecydes, *FGH* 3F16),[103] and golden apples were consequently a favourite wedding gift among the gods. This divine apple of fulfilment had its secular doublet in the apple that was eaten, according to Plutarch, as a part of the Solonian wedding ceremony.[104] By an easy extension, however, the apple could also represent the virginity that a bride brought to her marriage, and this quality was applauded when the wedding guests threw apples after her as she left with the groom. Indeed, the suitors were good enough to do this even for Helen, as she went off with Menelaus (Stes. 187 *PMG*). Sappho uses the same notion of the apple of maidenhood when she praises a girl as being 'like the sweet apple that ripens on the bough. . .' (105V).[105] As represented by the apple, virginity was always very much *en jeu* and love could be sought by throwing this fruit of Aphrodite at the beloved, or even at his dog (as Galatea does, in Theocritus' Idyll 6). The symbolism of this rustic act of provocation is

---

[101] Gallavotti (*SIFC* 18, 1942, 179) found the repetition so emphatic as to be 'brutta ed inutile', so he decided to read an adverb, μαλίαν (Hesych.sv εὔφημον, ἥσυχον, πραεῖαν) in the second instance, in this way arriving at the banal phrase 'cool water springs gently through the leaves'.

[102] For the apple of love, see Hes.fr.85 MW; Ar. *Clouds* 997 and Schol.; Theoc.2.120, 3.10, 6.7, 10.34, 11.10; *AP* 5.80; Ovid *Tr.*3.10. 73; Verg. *Ecl.*3.64; Luc. *Dial. Mer.*12.2; Aristaen. 1.10; Anton. Lib. 1; Heliod. 3.3.8; Hesych., sv μήλῳ βαλεῖν. In addition to the discussions of Gow at Theoc. *Id.*3.40 and 5.88, see B. O. Foster, 'The symbolism of the apple', *HSCP* 10 (1899) 39ff.; H. Gardoz, 'La requisition de l'amour et le symbolisme de la pomme', *Ann. de l'école prat. des Hautes Etudes* (1902), 5–33; E. S. McCartney, 'How the apple became the token of love', *TAPA* 56 (1925), 70–81; J. Trumpf, 'Kydonische Äpfel', *Hermes* 88 (1960), 14–22: M. Lugauer, *Untersuchung z. Symbolik des Apfels in der Antike* (Erlangen 1967); I. Chirassi, *Elementi di culture precereali* (Rome 1968) 73–90.

[103] Also Eratosth. *Catast.* 3; Hyg. *Astron.* 2; Athen. 3.83c (quoting Asclepiades of Myrlea); Serv. *ad Aen.* 4.484. Note that Euripides made springs of ambrosia also appear beside this inaugural couch of Zeus (*Hipp.* 748).

[104] Pl. *Coniug. Praecept.* 1, 138D; cf. *Quaest. Rom.* 65. 279F.

[105] Compare the modern Greek song from Pyrgos that urges an end to virginity:

Σὰ μῆλο ποὺ 'ναι στὴ μηλιὰ τὸ παραγινομένο
ἔτσ᾽ εἶναι καὶ τ᾽ ἀνύπαντρο σὰν ἔρχετ᾽ ὁ καιρός του.

spelled out in an epigram from the Anthology which does much to explain Atalanta's fate (5.79):[106]

> I'm tossing you an apple – if you love me
> keep it, and give me your virginity!

The apple trees in Sappho's grove thus suggest that this was a place where youthful ripeness was to be found, but they do not tell us whether it was flaunted, sought after, defended or lost in such a spot.

Water, shadow and breezes all suggest the nymphs, and if it were certain that Sappho, as some editors have supposed,[107] called Aphrodite into a grotto (*enaulos*) instead of a shrine (*naos*), the problem would be solved, for it was in this kind of cavern that Hesiod's nymphs chose to live (*Theog.* 129). Even without such an echo, however, the Sapphic apple-grove seems to be almost identical with that 'perfect garden of the virgins' where Ibycus saw Cydonian apple trees watered by a stream and standing among shady blossoming vines (286 *PMG*). Nor is the open outer meadow inappropriate, since Nausicaa's girls, playing in the open by the sea, could still be compared to nymphs who thronged about the goddess Artemis (*Od.*6.123–4). True, the anachronistic voice of Euripides' Hippolytus asserts that Aphrodite has no proper place in a 'meadow of purity' – that such a spot belongs exclusively to the virgin Artemis (E.*Hipp.*73–82) – but his views were entirely his own. There is no trace in the seventh and sixth centuries of the exaggerated nostalgia for the asexuality of youth that made him reject Aphrodite and likewise caused Deianeira to yearn for that happy pasture where, as a pre-adolescent, she had 'grazed' in perfect ignorance of sex (S.*Tr.* 144–7).[108] Since it was Aphrodite who, with her

---

[106] Hes., fr.42, 43 Rz., proves that the apple belonged to the early versions of the Atalanta myth; cf. Theoc. *Id.*3.40 and Gow ad loc. The apples used by Melanion-Hippomenes were the gift of Aphrodite and were usually said to have come from the Hesperides, though the Schol. at Theoc. *Id.*2. 120 says that Aphrodite begged them from Dionysus, citing for this version Diodorus, 'the Corinthian poet', and Philetas of Cos. See Robert, *Hermes* 22, 'Archaeol. Nachlese', 445, for a vase of Polygnotus with Aphrodite and Eros offering apples to a young athlete about to compete with a naked girl.

[107] Pfeiffer, op.cit., 117–25, read ἔναυλον for the sherd's .ναυγον; he has been followed by Theander, op.cit., 465–9, Rivier, op.cit., 227ff., Lanata, op.cit., 71 and Kirkwood, *EGM*, 115. Schubart and Lobel read ναῦον (*Hermes* 73 (1938) 297–303, with *Beitrag* by Lobel), as does Page (*S&A*, 36). The word ἔναυλος appears – but always in the plural – at Hes.*Theog.*129; *h.Aphr.* 74 and 174; E.*Hel.*1107; *HF* 371; *Ba.*122; see the discussion of Pertusi, 'Euripide e Saffò', *PP* 8 (1953) 377.

[108] To these exclusive choices of the asexual Nymphengarten over the meadow of love one might perhaps compare the close of Theocritus' *Idyll* 7. There a group of young men rest in a sacred spot where there is a magical spring and where trees interlace to make shade. Leaves murmur, water sings, and the mesmerising song of the cicadas occupies the branches as pears and apples roll softly on the grass beside the reclining forms of the companions. It is notable that in this spot wine becomes nectar mixed by nymphs, not by Aphrodite, for, judging from the songs that have preceded, this garden is one that is reached by following the paths of friendship and renouncing the pursuit of sexuality.

gift of *charis*, differentiated the youth from the child, she was for all ordinary Hellenes a goddess who might easily and correctly enter the groves that belonged to the nymphs.[109] Her coming there was simply the sign that the season of sexuality was to begin, and so Ibycus discovered her with Peitho, at work among the rosebuds, nurturing the ready beauty of a favourite of theirs and his. Alcaeus in the same way marked the fact that Damoanactidas had become an erotic object by saying that Cypris had found him among the olive trees and had caused the gates of spring to open for him there (296bV). The notion that the virginity of the Nymphengarten was very much the love-goddess's affair, since it existed only to be lost, is reflected also in various writers of late antiquity. Catullus, for example, brings Hymen from a nymph's cave and sees a bride as a hyacinth plucked from a rich flower-bed (61.85.90);[110] Porphyry calls Homer's nymphs generative spirits (*de Antro* 12), and Longus makes Eros romp through the virgin's garden crying suggestively, 'Look out! See if I haven't left a branch broken, a piece of fruit tasted, a flower trampled or a clear spring muddied somewhere!' (*Daphnis and Chloe*, 2).

All of these similarities suggest that Sappho's apple-grove might well represent a virgins' garden, in which case the song as a whole would celebrate the coming of age of girls who were now potentially ready (like Damoanactidas) for sexual experience. Aphrodite's cup of nectar would act, under these circumstances, as a kind of preparation as it welcomed new members either to the class of those who were

---

[109] Aphrodite was put in the company of the nymphs in the *Cypria* (Athen.682F) and she was called Nymphia in a cult near Troezen (Farnell, *Cults* ii 657); her assistant, Peitho, was named first among the nurturing nymphs by Hesiod (*Theog.*349), for these nymphs were givers of fertility (*Theog.*347), an idea repeated by the Schol. at P.P.4. 106a: οὔτε γάμος οὐδεὶς ἄνευ Νυμφῶν συντελεῖται. This same easy communion causes nymphs and Graces to share in the honours of nurture, and so Pindar gives the Graces a garden like that of the nymphs at *O.*9.27; cf. Χαρίτων θρέμμα at Ar.*Eccl.*974 and the Muse's description of the nurture of the young Rhesus at E.*Rhes.*928–30. On a fourth-century vase by the Meidias painter (BM E224) Eros picks the apples of the Hesperides for a very young Heracles; see F. Brommer, 'Herakles und die Hesperiden auf Vasen-bildern', *Jb.*57 (1942) 105–23; *Heracles* (Münster 1953), pl.30. For a general discussion, see Bremer, op.cit., *passim*, who insists that the garden or meadow of youth was never *inviolabilis*, always *violanda*.

[110] Compare Sappho 105bV: 'like the hyacinth in the mountains that shepherds trample upon, its purple flower on the ground.' Some have thought because of Catullus, that these lines refer to a bride; Bowra (*GLP*², 224) believed that a girl no better than she should be was being described, and Merkelbach (loc.cit.) supposed that the hyacinth represented a girl who was not properly sheltered in the Sapphic circle and so was brutally deflowered before her time (see above, p. 217 note 17). The lines are not necessarily Sapphic, but if they do belong with 105a, they probably contain the idea of virginity lost, as a foil to the apple that has remained untouched at the top of the tree, and in this case the mountain hyacinth will be kin to Anacreon's hyacinth that marked the meadows of Aphrodite (346/1 *PMG*).

marriageable[111] or else, more privately, to the group who might be approached by lovers from within the circle. Notions such as these are in no sense alien to the little that we know of Lesbos in the early sixth century, and yet, as soon as the full sensory effect of this song is felt, an initiatory reading of this sort becomes flatly unthinkable. Nymphs are better placed among olives, and a garden of virgins ought to have a sense of spring time about it (witness the vine-blossoms and rose-buds of Ibycus, and Alcaeus' gates of spring),[112] but these are only superficial objections beside a third that encompasses the whole, making it impossible that this prayer should be heard as part of a coming-of-age performance. The stumbling block is this. If a poet (or anyone else) posits one of life's phases as a place, then he will necessarily see the shift from that phase into the next as a form of motion and specifically as motion that includes departure from the predicated place (compare the open gate of Alcaeus 296bV and the 'escape' from the Anacreontic place of nurture, 346 fr.1 *PMG*).

When Aphrodite enters Sappho's glade it evidently will not be to urge an escape from a virginal spot into an outer place where sex is. Instead, she will come to a place that is already full of herself, and she will confirm her followers in their continuing enjoyment of the spot. This must, therefore, be in some sense a garden of love, but it is at once more tranquil and more sensual than those flower-strewn fields that saw the rapes of Persephone, Europa, and Creusa and so many other ladies of mythology. Here the magic stillness is untroubled by any such adventures, for there is neither sign nor symbol of any mortal approach. Indeed, the quiet is so perfect here that one is reminded of that garden of ideally regulated love (a dream engendered among the corruptions of Medea's Corinth) where, under the eye of a rose-crowned Aphrodite, the Erotes conversed with Sophia (E.*Med.* 835ff.). It cannot, however, be moderation or restraint that secures the serenity of Sappho's glade, for here in the moist swooning centre of a meadow of pleasure every sense is aroused. Sexuality is open here, but there is neither fear nor violence, for this is a place where no outsider comes, where only beauty ravishes, and where embraces work no change upon the virgin state. It is not, however, just a pretty spot where transports of a Wordsworthian sort are ecstatically shared. Love is physical here, as it must be to be worthy of Aphrodite's notice, and though the song describes no act (instead, it substitutes a god-given drink for the waters of its dark spring), we are made to feel that desire and satisfaction work hand in hand in this sacred grove. Sappho

---

[111] Merkelbach (loc.cit.) believes that Sappho is describing an actual *temenos* of Aphrodite but representing it as a Nymphengarten because her girls are about to become brides.

[112] Nymphs were friends of springtime and sent pleasing soft weather; *Orph.hymn* 48; Porphyry, *de antro* 8.

has chosen to make the occupants of the spot invisible at first (even at the end they amount to no more than the hands that must be presumed as supports for cups), but their pleasure is overwhelmingly present as perfume, apple-boughs and purling stream combine to produce a strange sleep which, like everything else in the grove, belongs to Aphrodite. The coma that is the achievement of the first two stanzas is no careless doze or simple afternoon nap, but a deep and lethargic trance that suddenly enwraps one like death, or like love when it knows satisfaction.[113]

The coma that drips from apple-leaves in a sense peoples Sappho's glade, since trance demands the entranced just as sleep demands a sleeper. In addition, it confirms the supernatural and amorous suggestions of the place, for coma is induced either by a god or else by magic,[114] and it usually stuns its subject with a pleasure that has an erotic aspect. Athena causes Penelope to fall into just this state while magical enhancements are added to her beauty, that the suitors may be thoroughly aroused (*Od.*18.201), and a Hellenistic writer shows

[113] In its epic appearances, κῶμα acts by means of the verb καλύπτειν (*Il.*14.359; *Od.*18.201; Hes.*Theog.*798) which also serves for the action of the cloud of death or for that of eros (*Il.*3.442); see P. Wiesmann, 'Was heisst κῶμα?' *MH* 29 (1972) 1–11, and for the general similarities between sleep, death and eros, consult E. Vermeule, *Aspects of Death* (Berkeley 1979), 145ff., where all are seen as examples of the 'change of experience'. The actual Sapphic verb is however in question, since the book text provides the non-Lesbian καταρρεῖ and the sherd seems to show either καγριον or καταιριον. In the absence of an object, the verb ought to be intransitive, and this is why Schubart (op.cit., 299, where the meaning is given as 'drowsiness departs'!), Lanata, op.cit., 80, and Kirkwood, *EGM*, 114, all adopt κατέρρει. Page denounced this as a verb 'not known to have existed and certainly not written here' (*S&A*, 38), but Treu (*HzL*, 211, note 1) pointed to Erinna fr.402,25H (σιγᾶι δ᾽ ἐν νεκύεσσιν· τὸ δὲ σκότος ὄσσε κατέρρει) where the meaning (= κάλυψεν) is appropriate but where the verb is unexpectedly transitive. Page himself proposed καταίρει, 'descends', though in Lesbian the form is ἀέρρω, aor. ἀέρραι, and the usage always transitive (see E. Risch, 'Der göttliche Schlaf bei Sappho', *MH* 19 (1962) 197ff.). The third major possibility, κατάγρει, is not only a known Lesbian form (cf. Alc.48.9V; 124.4V) but appears in another Sapphic fragment, perhaps with ὕπνος as its subject (149V: ὄτα πάννυχος ἄσφι κατάγρει, where the object would seem to be ὄππατα or φρένας). If the object of this verb could be suppressed when it was obvious, then κῶμα κατάγρει might mean that this trance takes hold of anyone who is present; cf. J. C. Kamerbeek, 'Sapphica', *Mnem.*9 (1956) 60, who would take the understood object to be τὸν χῶρον, 'the whole place'.

[114] Hesychius defines coma as καταφορὰ ὕπνου βαθέος but it was never an ordinary sleep; the Dioscuri spent their alternate days of mortality in such a trance (Alcm. 7.2 *PMG*), and Ares was immobilised in the same way by Apollo's lyre (P.*P.*1.2) his coma being explained as magical by the scholiast. These more than natural aspects of coma are emphasised by Wiesmann, op.cit., who ends by defining the sleep as a kind of θαῦμα, a numbness that comes in the presence of the supernatural; he notes the connection with a magical action (θέλγειν) that is made in three Platonic epigrams (*AP* 9.826; 9.827 and 16.13). E. Heitsch, 'Sappho 2, 8 und 31, 9 LP', *RM* 105 (1962) 285, describes coma as 'nicht die natürliche Müdigkeit sondern die Macht die – wie das Gedicht selbst – unmerklich in den Bann zieht, so das der Eintretende seiner selbst vergisst und aufgenommen wird dort, wohin auch die Göttin kommen wird.'

Eros himself lying in a coma of sensual lethargy.[115] Best-known of all, however, is the coma with which Hypnos disabled Zeus, after Hera had tricked him into the act of love, in Book 14 of the *Iliad* (359–60). Apparently Sappho's song was meant to revive memories of this very passage, in fact, for there are other points of contact between her Lesbian glade and the spot where the divine couple made Homeric love. Hera had used Aphrodite's nectar to make herself even more god-like before she sought her husband out, and she had found him on Mount Ida, in what became a perfect meadow of love (*Il*.14.347ff.):[116]

> Under their warm embrace the earth sent up new grass,
> vaporous lilies, crocus and soft, crowded bloom of hyacinth
> lifted them up, and there the two divinities lay
> lapped in a lovely cloud of gold, as dew fell softly down.

The apple-trees suggest that the Sapphic grove is a place where virginity is ready and the coma is proof of a love that pursues its ends actively, bringing consummation and its swooning drowsiness. If any doubt could remain about the erotic nature of this lovely place, it would be dissipated at once by a passage from Ovid's *Heroides*. There, in the Fifteenth Letter, the Sappho of late antiquity – a heterosexual poetess who leapt to her death from the Leucadian cliff because she was spurned by a beautiful young man[117] – writes to her faithless lover.[118] She tells him how she woke from a dream of their lovemaking and ran into the woods to visit again the glade where they used to couch (134ff.), and to us the spot is immediately recognisable. A sacred spring is there, under sheltering boughs (157ff.), and there Ovid makes Sappho find the outlines of her own and Phaon's bodies, still marked upon the grass.[119] She calls upon the breeze (177) to carry her words to her lover but, instead of a love-goddess bearing reviving nectar, she

---

[115] A satyr is urged to walk lightly, μὴ τάχα κοῦρον κινήσῃς ἀπαλῷ κώματι θελγόμενον (*AP* 9.826; cf. 827); Pan and Priapus similarly picture Daphnis in the same state (Theoc. *Epig*.3.6 = *AP* 9.338).

[116] This passage came into the mind of Hermogenes as the natural companion to Sappho's lines about the grove, though his point was that the Homeric passage gives 'sweetness' to pleasures that are 'innocent' (Περὶ ἰδεῶν 2, 4).

[117] For the history of the Sapphic biography, see H. Rudiger, *Sappho. Ihr Ruf und Ruhm bei der Nachwelt* (Leipzig 1933), 4ff.; M. Lefkowitz, *Lives* 36-7, 61–4. Wilamowitz offered his own interpretation of the Phaon story, as a part of his defence of Sappho's 'pure womanhood', making it a metaphor for her love of the unattainable (*Gött.Gel.Anz*. 1896, 623ff.=*SuS*, 63–78); for a very different treatment, see Détienne, op.cit., 133ff. and G. Nagy, 'Phaethon, Sappho's Phaon, and the White Rock of Leukas', *HSCP* 77 (1973) 137–78, and note also the symbolic use of the Leucadian leap, as a figure for initiation in the Basilica at Porta Maggiore (see discussion of J. Houbaux, 'Le Plongeon Rituel', *Mus.Belge* 27, 1923, 1–81).

[118] On this letter, see H. Dörrie, *P. Ovidius Naso. Der Brief der Sappho an Phaon*. Zetemata 58 (Munich 1974).

[119] Does Ovid perhaps even pun on the Sapphic κῶμα, with his phrase, *et multa texit opaca coma*, at 144?

meets with a cool spirit who teaches her how to make an end of her unhappy love in death. All this bitterness felt in a place of happy memories is Ovidian, but the baroque contrast between setting and sensation is enriched by genuinely Sapphic echoes, as the Roman poet makes a cruel parody of the *ostrakon* prayer. If they were to take full measure of his cleverness, his audience too would have had to know the original but, whether or not they did so, he at any rate was familiar with it and, what is more, he clearly knew it as a poem of sexual fulfilment.

The coma that slips from apple-boughs is thus to be taken as the trance of desire allayed. Zeus knew such a trance among the magical flowers of Ida, and Sappho's phrases stun her listeners' senses into a like confusion, bringing paradoxical visions of smoky petals, singing coolness, whispering shade and flowers that breathe in the wind. But if this is the case, then how are we to take the nectar that is the explicit and final object of the prayer? Those who believe that an actual ceremony is described assume that 'nectar' is Sappho's way of referring to a sacerdotal drink that is physically swallowed by celebrants, but even if we could be sure of an external ritual occasion, we would still need to know the function of this metaphor within the song's own poetic system, and all the more so, of course, if the entire rite is metaphorical.

Nectar came ordinarily from a fountain in the garden of the Hesperides (Alcman fr.100B *PMG*) and some thought that the Pleiades brought a daily supply from there to the gods; at any rate, they carried it to the newborn Zeus on Crete (*Od*.12.62). Among the immortals on Olympus Hebe poured it out like wine (*Il*.4.3), but nectar was used in that company for more than quenching thirst. Originally indistinguishable from ambrosia, it conferred an immortality that was necessarily related to beauty, and so Hera used nectar to make herself more god-like and thus more beautiful, before she tempted Zeus into the act that left him in a coma (*Il*.14.171–2). If enough of it were given to a mortal he became like a god (*P.O*.1.62–3); it could heal a living body[120] or keep a corpse from putrefaction (*Il*.19.379), and Eidothea was even able to turn the mortal stench of seals into a celestial perfume by applying the twin substance, ambrosia, to their furry pelts (*Od*.4.445). Perhaps most interesting in the present context is a case cited by

---

[120] In the cases of Demophon (*h.Dem*.237 and Richardson ad loc.) and Achilles (ARA 4.869) the process was a double one as mortality was purged by fire, immortality induced with nectar. At Verg., *Aen*.12.419 Venus succeeds in healing the wounded Aeneas with water into which nectar and ambrosia have been sprinkled; in Bion, fr.1 (Gow), on the other hand, Apollo fails to revive the dead Hyacinth, though he anoints him with nectar and ambrosia (compare the similar attempts at Ovid *Met*.4.249ff. and 10.737). On nectar and death, see Vermeule, op.cit., 127, who points to the common syllable that links nectar and *nekros* (citing P. Thieme, 'Nektar', in R. Schmitt, *Indogermanische Dichtersprache*, 1968, 102ff.).

Hesiod (*Theog*.798), where oath-breaking divinities are put into an evil trance (*kakon kōma*) by being deprived of nectar and ambrosia. After they have lain on their beds, breathless and voiceless, for a year, they are brought out of this state, and since it is nine more years before they may attend banquets, this is presumably done with a simple cup of reviving nectar.

Beauty, vitality and incorruptibility are thus the normal nectarine properties, but Sappho's nectar is nevertheless often taken to be nothing more than the taste of amorous completion. Sometimes Hellenistic and Roman passages are cited wherein a lover's kiss is compared with the divine liquid;[121] sometimes a specifically sexual meaning is assumed;[122] sometimes again a vague sentimental paraphrase is offered – 'le don bienheureux de l'amour'.[123] In each case, however, it is assumed that this ultimate cup does no more than supply a second image for the experience already represented by the sweet coma, as if Sappho were given to redundancy. She is not, and here she makes it plain that these are distinct and separate notions, necessarily sequential, and each of decisive significance to her song. Far from being confounded (as, say, the smoke and the apple trees are) or superimposed (as water is upon the vision of the grove), the two are clearly held apart: in imagination by the intervening meadow, in performance-time by the singing of a stanza. The coma is the result of, or the last phase of, the sensual arousal that takes place in Aphrodite's grove, but it is not the subject of petition here. Quite the opposite, for it is shown to be one of the given elements in the mortal, topographically conceived situation from which the petition grows. The nectar, on the other hand, must be called for; it is tasted after, not before, the onset of exhausted lethargy, and it is explicitly a new and problematic element that may or may not arrive. Coma is what the goddess (if she comes) will find; nectar is what she will bring.

The sequence of stanzas imposes a sequence upon the 'events' that are described, so that as the song is experienced the trance is felt first, and then Aphrodite is begged to come and pour out her drink. The receipt of the nectar is thus discriminated from the sense of satisfaction – indeed it is set against it, almost as a kind of antidote[124] – and this means that the late notions of nectar as kiss or climax are quite incongruous here. The archaic associations with revival, bliss and a

---

[121] *AP* 5.305; Alciphron 4.11; Catullus 99.2; Horace *Carm*.1.13, 15.

[122] Motte, op.cit., 129ff., 239 note 15. Note denial, at Treu, *HzL* 210.

[123] Rivier, op.cit., 238; cf. Theiler and Von der Mühll, op.cit., 25: 'Dass am Feste die Süssigkeit der Liebe nicht fehle, dass die thaliai eratai werden ... das ist es, was die Dichterin in ihren zarten Sprache erbetet.'

[124] This mystical drink is to a degree paralleled by the drink of cool water that is so important in Orphic afterlife scenes, where it works a revival of the soul through memory; see B. Gladigow, 'Zum Makarismos des Weisen', *Hermes* 95 (1967) 404ff. For Sappho, too, memory puts one in touch with what is eternal.

beauty that will not decay are, on the other hand, perfectly suitable, and once they are allowed, the rhetoric of the song is clear. Its pattern is after all that of a typical prayer, as the power that has taken strength away is sued for its restoration in a better form. Aphrodite, with a ritual gesture, is to end the lifelessness that her grove has induced, allowing worship to take the place of trance. The earlier shifts from substance into insubstantiality are controlled and capped now by a substance that is divine, as the song allows itself to be led back into an altered reality by a goddess who goes to work among the ritual implements.[125] Aphrodite is to mix nectar, the matter of the gods, into the immaterial festivity of her followers,[126] but it is curious to note that even here the singer orders the divine gestures so that they will harmonise with the rest of the song and continue to replace physical images with concepts that can only exist in the mind. The goddess is to pour her proffered drink into golden cups, but the first element to be mentioned is the most substantial one, the metallic vessels.[127] Next comes the mortal but insubstantial festivity, and lastly the immortal and ideal liquid, so that the finite gives way progressively to the infinite as this longed-for miracle is described.[128]

The Sapphic apple grove contains reminders of the garden of youth, mixed with elements from the meadow of love and even from the fields of blessedness,[129] because the subject here is sexual pleasure, whatever its timing or form. Similarly, nectar follows coma here because this is a place where such pleasure is dedicated to its divine creatrix and

---

[125] Compare the endings of two Orphic Hymns: Βαῖνε γεγηθὼς / ἐς τελετὴν ἁγίαν πολυποίκιλον ὀργιοφάνταις (6.10–11) and ἔλθετ᾽ ἐπ᾽ εὐίερου τελετῆς (7.12). In later time these calls for participation in the rite may have been invitations to the divinity to enter into the cult statue with the effect of *ellampsis*; see P. Boyancé, *Le Culte des Muses* (Paris 1937) 56ff.

[126] Compare two less daring phrases, Pindar's εὐθαλεῖ συνέμειξε τύχᾳ (*P*.9.72) and Sophocles' οὕτω συγκεκραμένην (*Aj*. 895), and see the discussion of Treu, *HzL*, 211.

[127] Gold may serve here, as it does in Pindar, as an emblem of divinity, but it nevertheless provides a much more solid image than either joy or nectar does.

[128] This effect may have been somewhat blunted if the song did not in fact end as it seems to do with the final stanza of the sherd. Its true end is in question because Athenaeus followed his citation of line 16 with the phrase τούτοισι τοῖς ἑταίροις ἐμοῖς γε καὶ σοῖς (11.463e), and in spite of their non-Lesbian masculine forms these words were included as part of a succeeding stanza by Norsa, the first editor of the sherd. (N. had to suppose that the prayer was a composition intended for male Cretan recitation.) It is now generally supposed that the phrase, as it stands, is Athenaeus' work, but whether it reflects the sense of some lost stanza from the original (so Page, *S&A*, 39; West, op.cit., 317, note 25), or whether it is a free invention by which the later writer attached the song to his own imaginary festal moment (see Pfeiffer, op.cit., 22; Theander, op.cit., 465; Lanata, op.cit., 87; Gallavotti, op.cit., 180; Treu, *Sappho*⁴, 1968, 26–7; McEvilley, op.cit., 323, Saake, *Kunst*, 100–1), no one can be perfectly certain.

[129] For other such mixtures, compare the generally idealised spots at Plato, *Phaedr*.258e6; Horace *Carm*.2.6, 2.23; Plut. *Amat*.766b, where the spot is both erotic and mystical, since it is where the souls of lovers await rebirth, having gone εἰς τοὺς Σελήνης καὶ Ἀφροδίτης λειμῶνας.

consecrated by her. In this spot, which is any spot made sacred by Aphrodite's influence,[130] the favours of the goddess are accepted and then offered back to her, and consequently the prayer that belongs to the place begs for the transmutation of finite satisfaction into something a goddess may receive – a change like that of frankincense into perfumed smoke. As ever, it is the divinity herself who must work the mystic process, and so what the singer says to her is this: 'Aphrodite, because of you we follow sexuality to swooning powerlessness. Rouse us now; confirm the immortal nature of our amorous delight, and help us to return it to you, in the form of praise!'[131] Perhaps the rite is actual, perhaps it is metaphorical; perhaps the singer speaks for a large number, perhaps only for self and partner – no one knows because it doesn't matter. The prayer is voiced for all lovers who would have their enchanted acceptance of Aphrodite's grace refashioned into an act of worship that will reciprocate the divine generosity. And of course it carries its own response within itself, since the plea that Sappho shapes is a form of praise – praise of sensual pleasure and praise of the goddess who invented it.

The song of the *ostrakon* implicitly makes physical love a divine gift that must, like all gifts, be both received and somehow returned, and meanwhile the performance is itself explicitly a return of the sort it prescribes. By reciting these words to the goddess, a devotee might transform any and every act of love into a proper offering: equipped with these short stanzas, he might meet Aphrodite anywhere. In a sense, then, the Sapphic song is something like the petitions that were inscribed on golden leaves and buried with the dead, as a reminder of what to say to Persephone.[132] Those metallic words, addressed to the goddess of the underworld, allowed one to live like a god after one had died, whereas the words of the *ostrakon*, repeated to the Cyprian at the proper time, would let one make love like a god right here in this world, and perform an act of worship at the same time. No wonder, then, that someone copied them on to a piece of clay and kept them like a charm!

---

[130] For the meaning of ἁγνός, see J. Rudhardt, *Notions fondamentales de la pensée religieuse* (Geneva 1958), 39ff.; D. Gerber, 'The gifts of Aphrodite (B.17.10)', *Phoenix* 19 (1965) 212ff.; B. Gentili, 'La veneranda Saffo', *QU* 2 (1966) 37ff.; W. Burkert, *Gr.Religion* (Stuttgart, Berlin, Köln, Mainz, 1977) 405–6. The quality of inspiring reverence through power seems to be what is referred to in archaic usages of this word: here the epithet emphasises the exclusive sacredness of the place that is forbidden to those outside the cult or outside the Sapphic circle, according to Gentili, op.cit., 42.

[131] The transition from private to public, from lazy trance to the convivial gestures of sacred service, is parallel to that of frag.96; see below, pp. 300ff.

[132] For the oldest of these (c.400 B.C.), see G. Pugliese Carratelli, 'Testi e monumenti', *PP* 29 (1974) 108–26, and G. Zuntz, 'Die Goldlamelle von Hipponion', *WS* 89 NS 10 (1976) 129–51. It is interesting to note that the formula for a Christian prayer was copied on to another potsherd; see Tait, *Gr. Ostrak.*, no.415.

Memory

Desire is Aphrodite's gift, and so is its fulfilment, which means that love achieved is like an initiation that brings momentary contact with a divine principle. At the same time, however, desire is by nature inconstant, and its best fulfilments are by necessity short-lived, especially in this adolescent and perpetually disintegrating group. Aphrodite thus describes a perfect contradiction – an experience at once eternal and ephemeral, divine and destructible. Such is the conclusion of the three songs already studied, and it is one that has been reached by most poets of love. No other, however, has sensed as faithfully as Sappho does the real presence of a god in all of love's passages. For her, Aphrodite is no figure in a painted ceiling, no projection or personification of mortal needs or wants, but a being whose power is truly other, more than magical, at work within nature and beyond it as well. From such a divinity she looks for something more than a fancy paradox; such a goddess, rightly approached, will offer an antidote to the sharp brevity of sensual experience, and to Sappho at least this mysterious and enduring benefaction comes in the form of memory – a disciplined memory that renders the transience of beauty incorruptible. Without, of course, ever lecturing, she explores the connections between impermanence and permanence, between beloved flesh and remembered loveliness, in three more almost perfect songs. In one of them the act of recollection is assessed, in another its discipline is urged, and in the last the vision to which memory can lead is reflected in an image of changeless luminosity.

There is no word for memory in the song about Anactoria (16V), and it is only at its close that we recognise the fictional situation as one in which the singer has been suddenly overcome by the recollection of a girl who has gone. Memory reminds her of all that she can no longer see, and she finds that her one desire is for an actual glimpse of the absent one. This somewhat surprising discovery leads her to meditate, in her performance, upon the question of what it is that one sees and why one values certain sights. Where does beauty reside?

Ο]ἰ μὲν ἰππήων ϲτρότον, οἰ δὲ πέϲδων,
οἰ δὲ νάων φαῖϲ' ἐπ[ὶ] γᾶν μέλαι[ν]αν
ἔ]μμεναι κάλλιϲτον, ἔγω δὲ κῆν' ὄτ-
    τω τιϲ ἔραται·   4
[—]
πά]γχυ δ' εὔμαρεϲ ϲύνετον πόηϲαι
π]άντι τ[ο]ῦτ', ἀ γὰρ πόλυ περϲκέθοιϲα
κάλλοϲ [ἀνθ]ρώπων Ἐλένα [τὸ]ν ἄνδρα
    τὸν [αρ]ιϲτον   8
[—]
καλλ[ίποι]ϲ' ἔβα 'ϲ Τροΐαν πλέοι[ϲα
κωὐδ[ὲ πα]ῖδοϲ οὐδὲ φίλων το[κ]ήων
πά[μπαν] ἐμνάϲθ⟨η⟩, ἀλλὰ παράγαγ' αὔταν
    `   ]ϲαν   12
[—]
    ]αμπτον γὰρ [
    ]...κούφωϲτ[   ]οη.[.]γ
..]με νῦν Ἀνακτορί[αϲ ὀ]νέμναι-
    ϲ' οὐ] παρεοίϲαϲ,   16
[—]
τᾶ]ϲ ⟨κ⟩ε βολλοίμαν ἔρατόν τε βᾶμα
κἀμάρυχμα λάμπρον ἴδην προϲώπω
ἢ τὰ Λύδων ἄρματα κἀν ὄπλοιϲι
    πεϲδομ]άχενταϲ.   20

Some say a company of horse, some
name soldiers, and some would call a fleet
the fairest thing on earth; I say
    it is the thing one loves.

This truth is plain and can be proved
to all: herself the perfect gauge
of what we know as fair, fair Helen
    left the best of men

and sailed away to Troy, not thinking
of her child, forgetting both
her cherished parents, gladly led
    upon a crooked course

[by Kypris? by Eros? . . .]
. . . easily . . .
which brings my thought to Anactoria
    for she as well is gone

and her beloved step, her teasing
brilliant glance, are sights I'd rather see
than all the cars of Lydia
    or men in panoply.

The apparent simplicity of this song at first seems to shame the clouds of exegesis that have gathered around it. It is short, it is evidently complete,[1] and it is strongly reminiscent of another familiar Sapphic shred that likewise seems to be ingenuous in its praise of a pretty girl (132V):[2]

"Εϲτι μοι κάλα πάιϲ χρυϲίοιϲιν ἀνθέμοιϲιν
ἐμφέρη⟨ν⟩ ἔχοιϲα μόρφαν Κλέιϲ ⟨ ⟩ ἀγαπάτα,
ἀντὶ τᾶϲ ἔγωύδὲ Λυδίαν παῖϲαν οὐδ' ἐράνναν . . .

I have a girl-child fair as flowers of gold,
Kleïs my much beloved, and for her
I wouldn't take the whole of Lydia, nor . . .

Behind its apparent candour, however, the song of Anactoria hides a number of complex thoughts, and even the lines about Kleïs are deeper than they seem. Playing with the problem of evaluation, the singer there takes Kleïs like a commodity into an imaginary market-place where all that is most precious can be found, but only to announce that she will make no exchange. She is just like the merchants who would offer her kingdoms and gold, for she too values the girl above all, and so the fantasy of the refused exchange allows her to say that, whereas men ordinarily treasure different things differently (and so can do business together), in this one case all are agreed: Kleïs is beyond compare, and cannot be bargained for.[3]

The case of Anactoria is, in spite of superficial likenesses, very different from this. To begin with, this second poetical market deals only in visions; it is not a place where girls are (or are not) traded for kingdoms but one where the sight of one thing is offered against the sight of another. Further, it is not just the market that is imaginary and balked in this second case, but also the singer's possession of her commodity, since she does not in fact have this sight that she would refuse to trade. And finally, trade in this place is unthinkable anyway, not (as with Kleïs) because there is too much agreement as to value,

---

[1] That the poem is complete is the general consensus; note, however, H. Eisenberger, 'Ein Beitrag zur Interp. von S's fg. 16LP', *Philol.*103 (1959) 130–5, where a sixth stanza is postulated. West (*Maia* 22, 318) reports the ending at line 20 as 'not certain'.

[2] This song is almost always described as meant for Sappho's daughter, but the reasons for identifying Kleïs in this way derive from traditions that are not necessarily authoritative, and the possibility remains that παῖϲ here means what it would in masculine society; elsewhere in the Sapphic corpus it means 'girl' ten times, 'child of x' five times. Kleïs seems to be mentioned with Sappho's mother in 98bV, and later antiquity gave this name both to the poet's mother and to her child; see *P.Oxy.* 1800, i.14 (=252V) and the Suda sv 'Sappho' (=253V).

[3] On the relation of the invention of money to the practice of fixing hierarchies of value, compare Arist.*Nic.Eth.*5.5.9–12 and see E. Will, 'De l'aspect éthique des origines grecques de la monnaie', *Rev. Hist.*212 (1954) 209–231.

but rather because there is no agreement at all about the relative worth of the merchandise. Here each possessor thinks his own item the finest and so no one will offer the trades that the singer fantastically rejects in her final stanza. She and the world are at odds on the value of a glance at Anactoria, and from this difference she has made a song that, for all its elegant lightness, treats of weighty matters. It assures us that, to her lover, Anactoria is supremely beautiful, but it asks at the same time whether qualities like beauty are real, and whether they inhere vividly in the object or live and die outside, in minds that do or do not perceive and remember them.

Deprived of all poetic content and reduced to its prosy non-equivalent, the song says just this: 'Not everyone would agree with me, but to my mind Anactoria as I recall her is more beautiful than all the great military shows that others applaud as superlative.' The comparison with Lydian armaments allows Sappho to display her usual wit,[4] as she boldly sets the undulating step[5] of a single absent friend beside the grand deployments of the martial world, and pits the remembered sparkle of a girl's eye against the sheen of countless waves and shields and windfilled sails. The praise is frankly disproportionate,[6] and it is offered smilingly to listeners who are expected to admire the splendour of these massive images even as they smile back at a singer who so justly measures the disproportion of her own partiality. On this, the ironic level of the performance, the singer seems to stand away from herself, even to join the rest of the world, as she exclaims, 'Look what love does – I don't even see what other people see!' Nevertheless, this same singer will finally insist that what she sees is the only thing that matters. The world counts and compares and disputes about its wares in hand, and yet in the end all its wise modes of evaluation are ridiculous because men perceive with a chaotic subjectivity. In all logic, of course, this argument ought to apply to her own discriminations as well as to those of others, but to this objection the song has two responses. The first is that love's subjectivity, being god-given, is entirely different from all other kinds, and the second is that logic in any case is only another worthless show that men admire. Some of them build formal demonstrations, some cite proofs from myth, but Sappho's truth derives from Aphrodite, and from Anactoria.

Where beauty is in question, the practices of conventional sagacity

---

[4] A contrary opinion may be found at Page, *S&A*, 57, where this stanza is described as either 'a little fanciful or a little dull'.

[5] The word βᾶμα might refer to Anactoria's manner of dancing; cf. *AP* 9.189: Λεσβίδες ἀβρὰ ποδῶν βῆμαθ᾽ ἑλισσόμεναι and see H. Jurenka, 'Neue Lieder der S.u.Alk.', *WS* 36 (1914) 201–43. Note that this remembered 'step' is qualified as ἔρατον, to repeat the ἔραται of l.4: because her recollected movements are loved, they are beautiful.

[6] See W. Schadewaldt, 'Das Schönste', *Antike Lyrik*, ed. Eisenhut (Darmstadt, 1970) 80–1, who remarks upon the 'innocent irony' bringing an emotion of tenderness into contact with 'das ganze männliche Brimborium'.

are useless: This the singer slyly suggests by disguising herself (like some Portia or Rosina) and aping the modes of masculine disputation in an initial stanza that creates confusion where clarity is expected to appear. She begins with an extended example of one of the most popular forms of demonstration, the priamel,[7] and then goes on to make her entire song into a kind of anthology of the topos, twisted this way and that. The device, in her time, was much in use, and had developed many learned and highly-mannered forms, but to begin with the making of such brief, evaluating lists seems to have been a branch of the old, convivial riddling game. A speaker was challenged to name the best, the first, the strongest, the sweetest item in a given category, and he responded with an ordered sequence that showed off his command of erudite information. Eros would thus be named, after other divine contenders, as the fairest of the gods (cf. *Theog.* 120); Hesperos, after other luminaries, as brightest of the stars (cf. *Il.*22.318), and Troilus, after many competitors, as handsomest of all the Greek and Trojan heroes (cf. Ibycus 282 *PMG*). The final term had to be given a special epithet in order to fix and enhance its value,[8] but even so these first comparative lists could be made by almost any dolt, and so they were replaced in sophisticated circles by a sharper game. With this, the true priamel, a witty man could distinguish himself, for by breaking out of the category or shifting the grounds of evaluation he might establish an unexpected item in the final seat of superiority. Violation of category might, for example, produce 'Ajax was strong, Achilles was strong, but wine is strongest of all, for it could conquer both'. Shift of value could create, 'Air is pure and water is pure, but gold is best because it brings a man happiness.'

Made according to these looser and more fanciful rules, the priamel ceased to be merely a game and became an inducement to thought, for it dissolved fixed sets of ideas (or introduced the values of one set into another) and so produced new notions instead of merely repeating

[7] The priamel is usually defined as a chain-saying with parallel members and a pointed closing (see Fränkel, *WuF*, 68); G. Wills, 'The Sapphic "Umwertung aller Werte"', *AJP* 88 (1967) 434, calls it a 'climactic catalogue'. On this archaic form of demonstration, see F. Dornseiff, *Die archaische Mythenerzählung* (Berlin-Leipzig 1933) 13, where the medieval term 'priamel = praeambulum' is first applied to such 'prefaces'; further collections and discussions may be found in W. Kröhling, 'Die Priamel', *Greifs. Beitr.* 3, Lit.u.Stilforsch. 11 (1935) 9ff.; W.A.A. van Otterlo, 'Beitrag zur Kenntnis der gr. Priamel'. *Mnem.* 8 (1940) 148–53; E. L. Bundy, *Studia Pindarica* (Berkeley 1962), 4–10; U. Schmid, *Die Priamel der Werte in Gr. Literatur* (Wiesbaden 1964), reviewed by G. Binder, *Gnomon* 37 (1965) 441ff.; T. Krischer, 'Priamel', *Grazer Beitr.* 2 (1974) 79–91; R. G. M. Nisbet and M. Hubbard, *A Commentary on Horace: Odes Book I* (Oxford 1970) 1–3. On the more general search for the superlative, see B. Snell, *Dicht. u. Gesell.*, 103, with bibliography there.

[8] It is amusing to note a late version of the simple list that exemplifies this requirement; at *AP* 9.571 eight poets are named (Pindar, Simonides, Stesichorus, Ibycus, Alcman, Bacchylides, Anacreon and Alcaeus) and then capped by Sappho, who is described as not ninth among men, but a tenth Muse.

opinions that were commonplace. The search for superlatives encouraged abstract speculation about the nature of qualities such as strength or purity, and even about the nature of the superlative itself, and in consequence the priamel soon recommended itself to men whose minds took a philosophic turn. Since it also permitted an accumulation of magnificent concepts and images, the priamel likewise became a favourite device of the archaic poets, and they quickly found out all its possibilities.[9] It was, after all, a priamel that allowed one of them, Xenophanes, to conclude an extended list of athletic glories with the sublime but seemingly well-grounded boast: '. . . but every sort of prowess / shown by man or beast is bested by my poetry!' (2W).

Thinking about the things that others valued, and amused by the idea of praising a girl with this pompous masculine form of demonstration,[10] Sappho found a special set of priamels ready to her hand. The seventh century had evidently debated much over the finest form of military equipment,[11] islanders holding out for fleet, main-landers for foot and Lydians for horse, and this argument had spawned many little lists. There were serious formulae like the political, 'Fleet, foot, horse – all are without value unless they be commanded by a great king', or, with an ethical conclusion, ' . . . unless they be moved by virtue or courage.' (In the Psalms, this becomes, 'Some boast of chariots and some of horses, but we boast of the name of the Lord our god', 20.7). There were as well sympotic versions, in which a singer capped the system in a lighter way by placing drink in the position of ultimate power, by rejecting all martial exertion and calling for a *kalos pais*, or by asserting that the power of a beautiful woman was greater than that of lances and shields, victorious over iron or fire (Anacreontea 24, Edmonds).[12] A set of such capping terms, themselves arranged as a kind of priamel of superlatives, is to be found in a story from the apocryphal First Book of Esdras. There, three young men of the Persian guard decide to compete as makers of the wisest sentence in the

---

[9] In general, priamels are either cumulative or rejecting. In the first class the basic pattern is: x, y, and z are good but A is best (e.g. P.O.1; 106S; B.3.85–92; *AP* 6.169). In the second, the pattern is: take away x, y and z and just give me A (e.g. Archil.19W cf.114W, with only one rejected item; [Theoc.] 8.53–56; Callim. *Aitia* 3, fr. 75.44–9). In a subtler form, the latter can produce: x, y and z are valueless unless they have the quality A (e.g. Tyrtaeus 12.9; E.*Med*.542; Pl.*Laws* 2.660e2–661c5). Either form, of course, could be offered seriously or with a breath of parody.

[10] Note the contention of P. du Bois, 'Sappho and Helen', *Arethusa* (Spring 1978) 93, that the priamel was especially suitable here because women themselves were articles of trade and therefore subject to a literal masculine evaluation in the archaic marriage market.

[11] Reflections of this debate (to which one might compare the Herodotean debate over the best form of government), can be seen at Alcm.1.92–95 *PMG*; P.*I*.5.4–6 and fr.221S; Aesch. *Pers*.18.

[12] This would seem to be a conflation of two simpler priamels, one in which Woman capped a hierarchy of the elements, another in which she topped a list of weapons.

world, and the three scraps of writing that are deposited under the pillow of Darius read, 'Wine is strongest', 'The king is strongest', and finally, 'Women are strongest, but above all things Truth beareth away the victory.'

The anecdote from the Book of Esdras is late, prosy and popular, but it resumes the process that Sappho uses, for she too collects and crosses lists and systems so as to make of her song a total priamel. Primitive lists had already placed one or another sort of equipment at the top of a hierarchy of strength, and primitive lists had likewise already placed Helen at the peak of mortal beauty; in addition, sophisticated men had already created priamels that crossed these two, placing beauty above every sort of armament since the war at Troy had been fought for Helen's face. Now Sappho, with Anactoria up her sleeve, returns to the list of armaments, holds Helen in reserve, and meanwhile fixes the quality to be sought this time as beauty, rather than strength. She pretends to respond to the question, 'What is the most beautiful sight that one can look upon?' but she also pretends that the generally accepted beauties are all military, and so her answer begins with the list, 'foot, fleet, horse . . .' before its final element is produced. If her ultimate purpose were simple praise of Anactoria, we might expect the name of the girl as the capping term (in the position of the sympotic *kalos pais*). Alternatively, something like the pastoral, 'but sweetest is to sit with you' (cf. Theoc. 8.53–6) might have been her conclusion. Satisfied love could also be proposed as the cap of a list of pleasures (cf. *AP* 5.169), and likewise it could be offered as the super-cap in a priamel of life's superlatives, as is proved by Theognis when he announces (255ff.), 'Justice is fairest; wealth is most useful; but the greatest of pleasures is to be successful with the one you love.'[13] Sappho, however, plays her game differently. She does not propose a particular name at this point, nor does she choose a grand concept like Truth or Love. She does not violate her category of sights one can look upon, nor does she shift the value that is being sought in the superlative – it remains the Beautiful. What she does do, however, is move, in her last definition, from the outer objects on view to the inner disposition of the viewer, and in so doing she transforms the value that she seeks. The spectacular look of the three material displays simply dissolves when this fourth term is proposed, for Sappho, by turning aside to look for beauty's source, almost does away with its container. Matter is external to this quality and grandeur has no

---

[13] This priamel of caps is almost identical with the one inscribed on the Leto temple at Delos: 'The most beautiful is the most just; the most sacred is health; the sweetest is possession of what one loves' (cited by Schadewaldt, op.cit., 75); cf. Soph.fr. 329N=356R and see E. Fränkel ad *Agam*.899–902 (*Agam*.ii 407).

relevance at all, since anything or anyone that anybody loves is invested by beauty in its superlative form.[14]

The cap to Sappho's priamel is ostentatiously open and ubiquitous ('that thing, whatever it be, that one loves'),[15] and the neutrality of the phrase seems to mark it as a covering principle. This fourth term is evidently not a parallel or alternative to the others, but is instead an analysis that includes and resolves their differences, and consequently each of the previous opinions now appears to be correct, though naively formulated. A horse, if it be what one loves, is supremely beautiful, and likewise a ship or a company of men, for each loving viewer is constantly making his own superlative.[16] There is no more argument, but in a sense there is no more beauty, either – only what each man admires – [17] and so the demonstration of stanza one concludes, like so many exercises of wisdom, in the near destruction of the thing it would define.

Either this search for best beauty was foolish from the start, or else, since beauty comes from love, we must begin again, find love at its strongest or best and then in its object discover the fairest sight on earth.[18] These are the only logical conclusions to be drawn from Sappho's too-philosophical priamel, but her listeners have time only for

---

[14] To this discovery of the ultimate source of the superlative quality, compare Pindar's similar priamel on the subject of priamels at the opening of *I*.5: 'Theia, many-named mother of Helios, it is because of you that men prize gold as strong beyond all things; because of you, ships contest upon the sea; for your rewards, horses yoked to chariots move in marvellous swift courses and he gains lovely glory, whose head the crowns bind after victory of hands or feet . . .' Paraphrased, this says: Other men, by means of other priamels, have discovered superlative values in gold, ships, horses, victory, etc., but I see the true principle that shapes all these values and it resides in Theia, the touch of the divine.

[15] Wills, op.cit., 434ff. would interpret this phrase to mean not 'whatsoever one loves', but rather 'that by which one loves', i.e. the principle according to which one evaluates. At the other extreme are the many who simply forget the force of the neuter κῆνο and translate 'whomsoever one loves', or, worse, 'the one you love'.

[16] That armaments could be the object of love is proved by Odysseus' proto-priamel at *Od*.14.222–28: 'I didn't like farming; I didn't like family life, though lovely children are its fruit; what I loved always were oared ships and battles, polished spears and arrows, all instruments of death and everything that fills an enemy with fear.' The phrase (technically modifying the ships) is φίλαι ἦσαν (224).

[17] A number of scholars have argued that this is Sappho's final statement and that it is meant to go uncorrected, so as to dominate the whole song. According to Fränkel (*DuP*², 212; cf. *WuF*², 91), Eisenberger (op.cit., 131–2), and V. Steffen (*Ant.lir.gr.*, Warsaw 1955, 109), she means that there is no superlative beauty and that each man measures in his own way. According to Dornseiff (op.cit., 79) and Schmid (op.cit., 53ff.) she defends herself for thinking differently from the world at large, and Kröhling (op.cit., 10f.) believes that she apologises for loving a girl whom others think plain! According to Wills (op.cit., 441) what Sappho announces is that logic must destroy all objective values.

[18] That this is Sappho's true meaning is the view of G. A. Privitera, 'Su una nuova interpretazione di S.fr. 16LP', *QU* 4 (1967) 182–7; cf. E. M. Stern, 'S.fr.16LP', *Mnem.* 23 (1970) 348–61. Both of these scholars would make of the present poem a kind of Aphrodite hymn, a song that praises that goddess as the source of beauty; Stern,

a vague sense of discontent at the end of the song's first stanza. The singer recognises their confusion, however, and teases them about it by insisting, scholar-like, on the validity of what she has just said. She chooses a phrase reminiscent of the pomposity of an epinician singer,[19] and promises to convince not just the instructed but everyone that her conclusion is perfectly correct. To do so, she makes use of a second favourite form of demonstration, the example drawn from myth. 'If you can't', she seems to say, 'follow my speculative argument, perhaps you will appreciate another that is more practical'. With beauty as her topic there was no avoiding Helen, anyway, and at first glance the epic demonstration seems to serve the abstraction of the priamel quite appropriately. Helen had topped many a list of beauties,[20] and Helen had been used to show beauty's supremacy over other forms of power, since she had set all three kinds of armament in motion. The singer can thus turn to her easily, asserting that, since beautiful Helen was moved by something that had power over her, that something must have been beauty in its superlative form. And what was it that set her in motion? It was the one she loved!

Paris moved Helen the beautiful, ergo Paris must be the fairest thing on earth. The argument slyly inserts an illegal proposition by assuming that the beautiful is what moves one, but it is so swiftly and so cleverly set forth that at first it fools the listener. On closer study, however, it betrays not only this but other weaknessses as well. True, it replaces a publicly handsome Helen with a publicly handsome Paris as the winner of a world-wide beauty contest, but this result does less than nothing to prove that *whatever* one loves is supremely beautiful. For that you need a Bottom in his ass's head, not a pretty prince from Troy. The flick of an epithet might at least have made this Paris a

---

however, by making the goddess the source of both erotic and non-erotic beauty destroys the poem's carefully constructed system of exclusions and returns the beauty of the beloved to the class of what is measurable and may therefore exist in a quantifiably superlative form.

[19] Compare the φρονέοντι συνετὰ γαρύω at B.3.85; cf.P.105aS. This epinician heaviness is also noted by G. Koniaris, 'On Sappho Fr.16(LP)', *Hermes* 95 (1967) 260; cf. Fränkel *DuP²*, 212, and *WuF²*, 260.

[20] Compare Sappho's own 35V, where Helen's beauty tops that of Hermione and is the test against which all beauty is to be measured. Here in 16V Helen, 'surpassing all' in beauty, represents a superlative that has been calculated statistically, in the world's way, by priamels and by a consensus of those who merely admired her. Her beauty is thus exactly parallel to that of ships or horses; it is something that can be discussed and assessed – something wholly different from the Aphrodite-given beauty of an Anactoria. So also Wills, op.cit., 440, who calls Helen's victory in beauty and Menelaus' superlative epithet 'the agreed estimates of society'. For the opposite opinion, see Privitera (op.cit., 184) who believes that Helen (because of her connection with Aphrodite) is another image of the kind of beauty that Sappho finds in Anactoria: 'L'espressione, "colei che di molto superò per beltà ogni creatura" equivale a "colei che molto fu amata da Afrodite su ogni altera creatura".' Stern (op.cit., 335, note 4) criticises this with a terse: 'es steht einfach nicht da.'

law-breaker, a blasphemer, or a deceiver of his host,[21] so that he would have some moral unloveliness that Helen's love might beautify. Sappho, however, chooses to present him without a single blemish. In fact, though he is the focal point of her current proof and the realisation of her previous proposition, she leaves him also without a face and as far as we can tell never even pronounces his name.[22] He, with his ostentatious beauty, is just the sort of figure that the learned world would produce to clinch an argument, but Sappho is about to abandon her professional tone, having her own kind of beauty to sing and her own way of finding it. She needs, for her purposes, not Paris but the opposite elements that the Trojan tale provides and so, where logic calls for emphasis upon what Helen followed when she went away, Sappho sings instead of what she left behind.

The song has passed from the too open theorising of its first stanza to the too confining example of Paris in its second, and it is ready now (like Helen) to take a crooked course towards its own superlative, Anactoria. There will, however, be very little point in saying that Anactoria is beautiful, if the sense of the priamel continues to operate, for that demonstration seemed to say that beauty could be imposed in its very best form upon any item whatsoever, whether horse or ship or man or girl, simply by the longing preference of a dazzled eye. Such a conclusion makes beauty into a commonplace delusion – 'to the child, even an ape is beautiful!' – and as decoration for a poem in praise of a lovely girl it is almost grotesque.[23] If the priamel is not somehow corrected or controlled, the lover will have to class herself with armchair military experts and amateurs of every other sort as she reviews her memory of Anactoria. Her perceptions and judgments, like theirs, will be confessedly directed by her avid predilection and the superlative beauty that is embodied (or rather, disembodied) in the recollection that the girl has left behind will be no different from the splendour of sound horseflesh to an equestrian, or of a well-made wheel to a charioteer.

The cap, 'whatever anyone loves', makes the priamel, but it could break the song for Anactoria, and Sappho, since she formed the phrase herself, knows its cynical potential. This is why, having produced a tale to prove her general proposition, she nevertheless tells it in a way

---

[21] Cf. the ξ[ε.]ναπάτα<ι> at Alc. 283.5V, and the ξειναπάταν Πάριν at Ibycus 282.10 *PMG*.

[22] The name might conceivably have appeared somewhere in lines 13–14, but either Kypris or Eros is usually restored here; for summaries of the older suggestions, see C. Theander, 'Studia Sapphica', *Eranos* 32 (1934) 70, note 5, and 71; also R. Hampe, 'Paris oder Helena?' *MH* 8 (1951) 141ff. The arguments of Kamerbeek, 'Sapphica', *Mnem.* Ser.4.9 (1956) 99, have generally prevailed, however, causing Aphrodite's presence to be recognised.

[23] Hence Kröhling's supposition that Anactoria was in fact an unattractive girl; see above, note 17.

that will constrict the openness of her own initial conclusion. She overlooks Paris, for he figures the dangerous concept 'whatever', and concentrates instead upon the Helen who represents 'anyone who loves', causing her to eliminate all desire for things, indeed all non-sexual love, from the continuing discussion.[24] This Helen is no longer Aphrodite's bribe, the traditionally passive object of desire, but she is still Aphrodite's creature and she loves in Aphrodite's way, as she shows by acting out a second priamel which serves now to correct the first. The category is creature-love this time, and within this exclusive class Helen makes a negative list, rejecting love-of-husband (himself the best of his kind),[25] love-of-child, and love-of-aged-parents, to follow her Trojan amour.[26] Her choice cleanly discriminates *eros* from three kinds of *philia* or, considered in another way, it places unsanctioned desire above three forms of sanctioned tenderness.[27] It is inspired by Aphrodite[28] and it exemplifies the one sort of love that the singer is concerned with in this song – the one love that can discover true beauty in its superlative form.

Helen does not do away with the generality that was first enunci-ated, but her presence (or rather, her departure) allows the singer to claim that her own views are exempt from the hopeless subjectivity that *kēn' otto tis eratai*, 'whatever anyone loves', seems to establish as the universal rule. That original 'philosophical' conclusion is still correct for the world in general, for its love is dictated by its own conventions and necessities, not by Aphrodite. The love of things that the world knows is man-made and so it creates a grab-bag of man-

[24] Koniaris (op.cit., 257ff.) argues that this exclusion was already evident in the ἔραται of the priamel, and he is supported by S. Radt, 'Sapphica', *Mnem.* 23 (1970) 338. The verb does not, however, have an exclusively sexual meaning at this time, as Archil.19W proves, and these arguments would make the specifying effect of the Helen example redundant.

[25] The first in Helen's list of rejected items is 'husband' and it is notable that this husband stood as the cap of some other list, just as Helen herself did, for he is qualified as ἄνδρα τὸν [πανάρ]ιστον. (Who was the best of husbands? Why Menelaus, the most uxorious of men!) It is also to be noted that this abandoned husband stands in immediate responsion with his opposite, the κῆνο of stanza one.

[26] Compare Catullus 64.116ff., where Ariadne turns from father, sisters, and mother to follow Theseus, whom she 'values most' (*praeoptarit*). The existence of evaluated lists of the kinds of human love is suggested by Antigone's well-known hierarchy of her kin at S. *Ant.* 897–912.

[27] Many scholars have regretted Sappho's failure to condemn Helen, and one has even found 'a pragmatically sympathetic evaluation' of Helen's conduct (West, *Maia* 22, 318), but there is in fact neither praise nor blame for Helen, whose action is recorded simply because it will advance this phase of the poem's argument. Moralising treatments of her escapade were of course popular in later times, and it is amusing to see how the chorus of Euripides' *Cyclops* (182ff.) makes use of Sappho to parody these.

[28] Probably the name Κύπρις stood at the beginning of line 13, emphasised by en-jambement and by first position in the new stanza (so Theander, Schubart, Kamerbeek, *et al.*) Eros might possibly have been named instead, but Aphrodite was so directly concerned in the episode as it was related in the *Cypria* that her presence would be felt, even without her name.

made beauties – animal, vegetable and mineral – that are equally 'the best'. Erotic love, on the other hand, the love that Sappho means, is sent by a goddess in defiance of the world, and this means that the beauty it discovers is not simply lent by the lover's eye. It is the gift of the same divinity,[29] and as such is an absolute and immutable quality. Men in general may look for superlative beauty in objects, measuring and testing it against numbers and weights and how many people follow it, but Sappho will recognise that superlative only in the aspect of a creature whom one may love sexually. Indeed, according to this song there is even one further limitation, for the singer here finds the best beauty of all not in the presence, but in the remembered aspect of such a one.[30]

[29] Compare the consummate beauty that Aphrodite confers upon the bride at S.112V; cf. Hes.*Scut*.5ff.; Theoc. 17.36–9. In general, see G. Lieberg, *Puella divina*, 21, and Privitera, op.cit., 182–7.

[30] Sappho has of course been thinking of her all along, but the lover of the song's self-portrait pretends to stumble upon the girl in the course of her meditation and so it is natural to ask what it is, within the poem's closed frame, that reminds her of Anactoria. The question is parallel to that of fr.31 (What is it that makes the lover's heart pound?), and the answer here, as there, is a composite one. The following five elements (arranged in order of decreasing specificity and immediacy) seem to contribute to this recollection:

(1) Helen's light motion as she went, which is like the remembered βᾶμα of Anactoria.
(2) Paris' beauty in Helen's eyes, which is like Anactoria's, in the lover's eyes.
(3) Aphrodite's power over Helen, which is like her power over the lover in the case of Anactoria.
(4) Helen's beauty in the world's eyes, for Anactoria too has this, as well as the special beauty of the beloved.
(5) The whole problem of what is fairest, because Anactoria is the true cap of the opening list.

Merkelbach, in the course of his report of this as a spiteful song of blame (*Philol*.101 (1957) 13ff.), argued that Helen's pursuit of Paris is the reminder, because Anactoria has likewise followed false beauty (a husband, this time) and gone off to Lydia, abandoning a Sappho who (like Menelaus) is actually the better man. This reading has unaccountably been revived in recent years. See also C. W. Macleod, 'Two comparisons in Sappho', *ZPE* 15 (1974) 218. Another suggestion as to the reminding element makes use of the old supposition that ll.13–14 contained general reflections upon the foolishness of the human or the feminine heart (see Wilamowitz, *NJb*.33 (1914) 227; Agar, *CR* 28 (1914) 189–90; Theander, *Eranos* 32 (1934) 71; Bowra, *Hermes* 70 (1935) 240; Schadewaldt, op.cit., 74; criticised by Schubart, 'Bemerkungen zu Sappho', *Hermes* 73 (1938) 297ff.). West (*Maia* 22, 318) paraphrases the movement from Helen to Anactoria thus: 'For though the heart be proud and strong, love easily makes it its servant. Which puts me in mind of Anactoria . . .' This, however, is surely too gnomic in an already gnomic song; it seems better to assume that in these lines the poet pursued her specific evocation of the departure of Helen, somewhat as Aeschylus does in the Helen Ode of the *Agam*., where there may indeed be a conscious imitation of the present song (note *Agam*.403. . .6, λιποῦσα . . . βέβακεν in comparison with Sappho's καλλίποισ᾽ ἔβα, and the fact that Aeschylus' Helen leaves a heritage of armies and fleets to her abandoned fellow-citizens). If this comparison is valid, then the κούφως of line 14 will describe the manner of Helen's exit, just as Aeschylus' phrase, ῥίμφα διὰ πυλᾶν does, at *Agam*. 406–7, and it will also lead directly to the idea of Anactoria's characteristic motion in line 17.

The beauty that is lent by men's admiring eyes is subjective, but it is statistically measurable, its superlative occurrence a matter of consensus. Such beauty will be calculated by arithmetic and will necessarily show a greater total in the prance of hundreds of eight-legged chariot-teams than in the progress of a single two-legged girl. The beauty that is Aphrodite's gift is, on the other hand, always infinite; it cannot be computed but only preferred and so, with the final magniloquent comparisons, the singer lightly rejects what men call reason,[31] when it attempts to approach the phenomenon that interests her. Some may argue by priamel, some may cite mythic examples, but she will find out her own truth, by way of Anactoria. Or, reading the sequence in a slightly different way: men choose love of things; Helen picked a man to love, but the singer will choose Sapphic love, the love of a girl who is gone. She thus chooses the one over the many, the private over the public, and the sensuality of women over the science of men, and her song implies other choices, too. When Helen chooses Paris over hearth and family, she relegates moderation and *aidos*, the two best kinds of female moral beauty, to positions of inferiority,[32] and when the singer chooses Anactoria over breastplates, plumes and sails, she works a parallel reduction upon the masculine fairness of glory and reputation. Between the two of them they thus proclaim the aesthetic supremacy[33] of erotic values over every one of the accepted moral ones.

Because of Aphrodite's power, the best beauty invests the object of desire and it is more beautiful than any moral comeliness, but this does not mean that the best action is to depart, like Helen, in pursuit of fairest flesh. The myth, after all, is only a second preface to the central matter of the song, for it too is capped and corrected by the final vision of an Anactoria who moves among images of ships and men. It is Anactoria, not Paris, who is the ultimate cipher for beauty, her absence adding a last touch to the song's definition of beauty's superlative form. And likewise it is the singer, not Helen, who figures the lover in whose memory this fairest sight appears. The girl is gone, and not even in her poetic fancy does the singer try to follow her;[34]

---

[31] West (*Maia*, 22, 320) reports that Sappho 'defends herself for not prizing visual beauty the most highly'. I would say rather that she flaunts her refusal to follow the world in its methods of considering beauty.

[32] Helen also rejects the spouse and children that were, traditionally, possessions a warrior was expected to value more than his life; cf. e.g., *Il.*15.662; 21.587; Tyrt.10.13W.

[33] Schadewaldt (op.cit., 75) claims that Sappho's supreme evaluation of love and its beauty is not restricted to the realm of the aesthetic, but that she means, by τὸ κάλλιστον, 'das Höchste, Beste, Wirklichste auf Erden'. In fact, however, her implication is more limited, for the Helen example does not suggest that love is more valuable than honour, etc., but only that the beauty that the lover perceives in the beloved is more beautiful than that which the virtuous person perceives in virtue, etc.

[34] *Pace* Eisenberger, (op.cit., 135), who thinks that a final prayer may have begged for the return of Anactoria.

instead she renders the absent one even more intangible by recalling only her most fugitive parts – the dancing step and glancing eye that were beyond possession, even when the flesh was near. The Helen example has served to show that love, in this song, means physical desire, but Anactoria is here (or rather, she is not) to prove that the beauty to be discovered by such love is as insubstantial and sublime as virtue and glory are said to be. It is an absolute that exists neither in the beloved's flesh nor in the eye of the lover, a measureless value that the singer only pretends to measure, a Fairest Sight that is unseen but yet perceived, asensually, by a lover's memory.[35]

Recollection brings an understanding of beauty at its best, but there is nothing sentimental or backward-looking about the Sapphic doctrine of memory, and its practitioners are not to be thought of as listlessly fingering old souvenirs. What Sappho taught was a disciplined mental process which, by reconstructing past actions in a certain way, kept one fit for the best that the present might propose. Or such, at least, is the tenor of a song in anecdotal form that describes a scene of parting (94V):

τεθνάκην δ' ἀδόλως θέλω·
ἄ με ψισδομένα κατελίμπανεν   2
⟨—⟩
πόλλα καὶ τόδ' ἔειπέ [μοι·
ὤιμ' ὡς δεῖνα πεπ[όνθ]αμεν,
Ψάπφ', ἦ μάν σ' ἀέκοισ' ἀπυλιμπάνω.   5

τὰν δ' ἔγω τάδ' ἀμειβόμαν·
χαίροισ' ἔρχεο κἄμεθεν
μέμναισ', οἶσθα γὰρ ὤς ⟨σ⟩ε πεδήπομεν·   8

αἰ δὲ μή, ἀλλά σ' ἔγω θέλω
ὄμναισαι [...(.)].[..(.)].ϛαι
ὀς[– 10 –] καὶ κάλ' ἐπάσχομεν·   11

πό[λλοις γὰρ στεφάν]οις ἴων
καὶ βρ[όδων ...]κίων τ' ὔμοι
κα..[– 7 –] πὰρ ἔμοι π⟨ε⟩ρεθήκα⟨ο⟩   14

---

[35] For Sappho, love produces vision; this is the opposite of Gorgias' argument (which is probably influenced by this song) at *Helen*, 15–19, for there vision produces love, evicting habitual character and thus proving that appearance *is* reality, since it works upon men's minds and actions.

καὶ πό͵λλαις ὐπα͵θύμιδαc
πλέκ͵ταιc ἀμφ' ἀ͵πάλαι δέραι
ἀνθέων ἐ[– 6 –] πεποημέναιc.   17
⟨—⟩
καὶ π.....[   ]. μύρωι
βρενθείωι .[   ]ρυ[..]ν
ἐξαλ⟨ε⟩ίψαο κα[ὶ ͵βαc͵]ιλήίωι   20
⟨—⟩
καὶ cτρώμν[αν ἐ]πὶ μολθάκαν
ἀπάλαν παρ[   ]ογων
ἐξίηc πόθο[ν   ].νίδων   23
⟨—⟩
κωΰτε τιc[οὔ]τε τι
ἴρον οὐδ' ὐ[   ]
ἔπλετ' ὄππ[οθεν ἄμ]μεc ἀπέcκομεν,   26
⟨—⟩
οὐκ ἄλcοc .[   ].ροc
                    ]ψοφοc
                    ]...οιδιαι   29

'I candidly want to die!'
     She wept as she went away

murmuring this as well:
'Sappho what dreadful pain we feel!
     I leave you against my will.'

I said in answer: 'Go,
rejoice, and remember me; you know
     how we have loved you here –

or do you forget? If so
let me remind you of the fair
     [pleasures] that we have suffer'd:

how often you crowned your head
with violets, rose, crocus, and thyme
     while I was beside you!

Often again you twisted chains
heavy with bloom to hang about
     your delicate throat,

and often [you poured] the rich
myrrh . . . costly perfume . . .
     down over your [breast],

sinking upon your soft-spread
couch . . . to find
     release from desire.

Never did . . .
temple . . . nor . . . occurred
    unless we were there;

no sacred grove . . . [no chorus?]
rattle [of castanets?]. . .[36]

. . .

'Go rejoicing[37] as you remember', is what the Sappho of this brief
scene urges, and then she marks out the path that her friend's thought
should follow. The continuing song is thus a kind of icon or a *memorandum* which could serve all of the girls as the object of their later
meditations as they looked back on the Sapphic life. Nevertheless,
before we consider the kind of memory that is recommended here, we
will have to settle a preliminary question since, by the received reading, Sappho herself announces that the process of recollection, though
all very well as a consolation to be offered to another, is useless in her
own case. She is inconsolable, according to most critics, and she con-
fides to her audience that she would like to die in the first surviving
line of her song.[38]
    Because of this interpretation, the fragment has come to be known

[36] The translation supposes that l. 18 began πόλλωι; see Page *S&A*, 78–9.

[37] Page, *S&A*, 77, reported that χαίροισ᾽ cannot mean what it seems to because
rejoicing 'would be out of place here'; he gave the word its neutral, Attic, fifth-century
sense, and made this a phrase of dismissal, such as, he felt, would not be out of place.
Nevertheless, in every other Sapphic occurrence the word has what Page calls its 'old
meaning', and the wedding wishes are particularly telling (116 and 117V); see also
22.14V and 96.5V, where there is clearly happy pleasure in the word, and notice too
155V, where the irony of the sentiment (which is there, according to Maximus of Tyre)
depends on an overt meaning that is strongly joyful.

[38] The fragment was first edited by W. Schubart, 'Neue Bruchstücke der S.und des
A.', *SB Berl.*ph.hist.Kl.1902, 195ff. There the first of its lines was understood to belong
to the girl of the reported scene, but T. Reinach, taking up a suggestion of Henri Weil's,
attributed it to Sappho in his report, 'Nouveaux fragments de Sappho', *REG* 15 (1902)
60ff., esp.65, and the same was done by G. Fraccaroli (*Boll.di Fil.Cl.*8 [1901/2] 252ff.)
and H. Jurenka (*Zeitschr.öst.Gymn.*53 [1902] 290ff.). Wilamowitz concurred (*SuS*, 50)
and scholars generally have followed, agreeing with W. Schadewaldt that the attribution of the wish to die to the Sapphic singer could no longer be in any doubt at all ('Zu
Sappho', *Hermes* 71, 1936, 364). Nevertheless, Gallavotti revived Schubart's way of
reporting in his *Lira Ellenica* (Milan 1955) 107, though not in his *Saffo e Alceo*² (Naples
1956) ii 123; in 1957 A. W. Gomme argued for it in his 'Interpretations of some poems
of Alkaios and Sappho', *JHS* 77 (1957) 255–6, and a number of subsequent editors
agreed (see C. del Grande, *Phorminx*, Naples 1959, 24; G. Monaco, *Charites* (Palerm
1960) 112; D. A. Campbell, *Greek Lyric Poetry* (London 1967) 47 and 278f.; note also
that in Snell's *Frühgr.Lyriker* iii (Berlin 1976) the translation casts the line into the
girl's speech). Gomme's arguments were extended by J. Danielewicz, 'Experience and
its artistic aspect in Sappho's subjective lyrics', *EOS* 58 (1969–70) 168; F. Cairns,
Generic Composition, 50ff.; and A.P. Burnett, 'Desire and memory', *CP* 74 (1979) 16–27.
Others have admitted the possibility of the line's belonging to the girl, but have chosen
to continue in the way of Reinach; see D. Gerber, *Euterpe* (Amsterdam 1970) 175;
Kirkwood, *EGM*, 263; J. G. Howie, 'Sappho fr.94 (LP)' *Papers of the Liverpool Latin
Seminar* 2 (1979) 301–3.

as 'The Confession',[39] quite as if this were an objective description, as 'The Ostrakon' is of the poem on the sherd. We hear of 'sheer and absolute sorrow' or 'abandoned hysteria'[40] as the emotions that it conveys, and we are asked to imagine a singer who, having been calm during the event she describes, now gives tongue to her desperate state. 'Oh yes, I was wise enough then,' she is supposed to say, 'but what is wisdom – look at me now! I want to die'. It is curious that she should have given seven of the surviving ten stanzas of her performance to pleasures richly evoked, if her true impulse was to confess her ardent pain, but nevertheless this is what she has done, according to most of those who have studied the fragment: it is the song of one who cannot follow her own counsels and who admits to the perfection of despair.[41]

But is it the singing Sappho who wishes to die? Nothing about the text proves that its first line was delivered by the poet in her own persona, and there are good internal reasons for asserting that it was not. To begin with, it is only a freak of chance that makes this the first line to be found on the papyrus, and the stanza form shows that it is the second of its stanza, while it may be the fifth, the eighth, the eleventh, etc., of the original song. The line did not, in other words, have the initial oracular prominence in the unbroken song that it enjoys in the scrap that remains, nor did it have its present ambiguity, for the preliminary context will have made its connection with the pendant narrative perfectly evident. Having lost these preceding indications, we must consider the line only on the basis of what follows, and the first thing to be noted is that in bare logic the wish to die might have come from any of three mouths. This is, after all, a song made like the idylls of Archilochus, for it is an anecdote told in dramatic form with the singer-narrator cast as one of its characters. The piece in consequence has two planes of poetic reality: one in which the present singer addresses her audience ('and I answered her and said . . .') and one in which her past characters address each other (' "Sappho, I swear I don't want to go" '). In itself the first line is not clearly marked as belonging to either of these planes, and consequently it might in theory belong to the present Sappho-singer, to the past Sappho-lover, or to the girl of the past who was going away. Actually, the content of the line is wholly irreconcilable with the tranquil tone that the Sappho-lover uses in the anecdote, and for this reason the second of these possibilities is not to be thought of further.[42] The girl, however, remains, and since a present wish to die on the part of the

---

[39] Saake, *Kunst*, 187ff. and *Studien*, 85ff.

[40] Bowra, *GLP²* 197 and R. Bagg, 'Love, ceremony and daydream', *Arion* 3 (296) 47.

[41] For the various ways that the song has been interpreted, see Burnett, op.cit., 16–20.

[42] Cf. E. Degani and E. Burzacchini, *Lirici Greci* (Florence 1977) 156ff.

singer creates a poem that devalues its own emotional effects as well as its own specific counsels, the girl's candidacy is *a priori* strong.

Who wants to die – is it the Sappho who stands singing to her circle, or the imaginary girl who is saying goodbye? The expression contains only three words, but perhaps there is something in its content or even in its style that can provide a clue. Such a wish, we know, could be employed conventionally by any poet who wished to mark the thing without which one couldn't go on – the thing that makes life desirable. Homer makes Achilles say *autika tethnaiēn*, 'would I might die straightaway' (*Il.*18.98) when he can no longer be of service to Patroclus; Mimnermus echoes *tethnaiēn* (fr.1.2D) when the Aphrodite days are past, and Anacreon too, probably for amorous reasons, prays for death's release (411a *PMG*). Sappho also, in another fragment, recounted a scene between herself and someone who was probably Hermes, in the course of which she had asked to be taken down to Acheron, saying, ' "Master, . . . a longing for death has taken hold of me" ' (95V).[43] That may have been a song about the loss of Gongyla, but whatever its content, Sappho's phrase there shows that the artful wish for death was a poetic practice that she allowed herself. Paradoxically, however, this parallel actually weakens the case for supposing the first line of our fragment to be a confession made by the Sapphic singer, for the words addressed to Hermes are in no sense a moan of anguish that exists on the surface of their song. They belong instead to the anecdote, and they come from a dramatic speech presented in direct discourse, which means that if the two songs were formally alike, we might be led to suppose that the wish for death in fragment 94 is likewise part of the fiction and not a communication made directly to the audience.

The wish to die is a poetic commonplace with amorous overtones and one that we know Sappho made use of elsewhere, but these facts cannot fix its attribution in the present poem.[44] There is, however, a point of style, even in the three words of the ambiguous line, that goes a long way towards settling the question, and it is one that is illuminated by the Sapphic wish to visit Acheron. When she addresses Hermes, Sappho (a fictional Sappho) uses a phrase that is unadorned: *katthanēn d'imeros tis echei me*, 'a longing for death takes hold of me' (95.11V).[45] She does not assure the god that she means what she says,

---

[43] On this fragment, see D. Boedeker, 'Sappho and Acheron', *Arktouros. Hellenic Studies presented to Bernard Knox* (Berlin 1979) 40–52.

[44] Cairns has argued (loc.cit.) that this song belongs to the same genre as the later *propemptika*, which would certainly mean that a wish for death would be misplaced in the singer's mouth. However, though Cairns is surely right to insist upon the sophistication of the piece, he seems to stretch a point in his identification of its type since this song, as far as we can tell, entirely ignores the motif of the journey and in no way looks forward to the girl's coming fortunes or adventures.

[45] Though there was wit in her choice of the word ἵμερος.

and her plainness there draws our attention to the urgent adverb *adolōs* that appears in the wish of fragment 94. The word is usually translated as 'honestly' or 'truly' but it was uncommon enough to have kept its privative sense, and it means literally 'without trickery'. Whoever uses the word thus lays explicit claim to an absence of guile and by doing so brings that very notion into play, since he implies that his listener suspects some crookedness. The word also has associations with Aphrodite, or at any rate with the Aphrodite that the Sapphic circle knew, for Sappho elsewhere calls that goddess *doloplokos* (1.2V), 'she who weaves snares'. Aphrodite is thought of as playing tricks because she entraps mankind, pretending to favour lovers but often causing them pain and inspiring the objects of their love to similar tricks, in imitation of her own.[46] The speech of love is full of snares of exaggeration or placation – it is that 'beguiling speech that steals reason away' that Aphrodite kept in her elaborate kirtle (*Il.*14.217) – and because it is tricky, love's speech is likewise full of protestations of sincerity. The lover insists with 'honestly' or 'I really mean it' because he knows that the straightness of his words is open to suspicion. In the present case, then, the one who uses the word *adolōs* speaks like a lover in direct colloquy with a beloved, but not like a singer making a revelation to her audience. A poem does not expect suspicion from the posterity that will finally receive it, nor does Sappho need to claim guilelessness as she sings to her group.[47] A beloved girl, on the other hand, might well be portrayed as protesting with exactly this sort of consciousness as she assures her mistress of her unhappiness. The word *adolōs* thus points to the youthful lover as the creature who says (by the singer's report), 'No fooling, I want to die', with the same melodramatic effusiveness that marks her when she swears (*ē man*) that she is forced to go.[48]

With the wish to die contained within the anecdote, Sappho's song is relieved of the dissonances that the critics' distraught singer had brought into it. That singer is now as calm as the Sappho-lover, and it is perfectly clear that the girl's despair is superficial, almost flirtatious, and also that it is here to be reasoned away. It provokes the doctrine of memory, for it is in fact no more than a poetical device which allows the song to approach its true matter with an air of conversational intimacy. The Sappho-singer means to teach a lesson, but she will relieve it of any heaviness by putting it into the Sappho-lover's mouth. Her intention, however, is plainly announced

---

[46] Cf. Archil. 184W, where woman is δολοφρονέουσα.

[47] Consequently, if the singer did say ἀδόλως in her own persona, the word would touch her whole performance with irony by suggesting that she had uttered the same wish many times before; this remains a remote possibility.

[48] On the girl's informal, popular style (and its contrast with the style of the Sappho-lover), see Howie, op.cit., 306–10.

in the sequence 'Remember . . . you know . . . or if you don't, I shall remind you . . .' that binds the second and third stanzas together, and meanwhile the purpose of her dogmatism is expressed in the witty revision of the verb *pathein* that transforms the girl's 'what dreadful things we have suffered' into the Sappho-lover's 'what lovely things we have felt.'

Remembering correctly will transform distress into pleasure, but evidently this involves some shift in the objects upon which the mind is to exercise itself, for the lover who begins by saying 'Remember me' in an instant offers to revive the girl's knowledge of how the whole group had gathered adoringly about her.[49] Evidently it is the full emotional ambience of the circle that the girl significantly 'knows' with a knowledge that should allow her to rejoice. Judging by her present grief, however, one would think she had already forgotten it – so says the Sappho-lover, and with this playful excuse she merges with the singer, and the song discovers a new plane of reality. The stanzas that follow are technically still a part of the direct speech of the anecdote, but the scenes they evoke belong strictly neither to the performance-present nor to the anecdote-past. They are summoned from a deeper and more general past and by the poet's art they become both visionary and immediate.

Sappho offers to remind the girl of facets of love that are not dreadful but fine, suggesting that such things, remembered, can turn grief to joy and outlive separation. Then she reviews a series of pleasures in such a way that even those who have never experienced them seem to remember. One image follows another with apparent carelessness, as if the singer's only purpose were to stun the senses with random glimpses of erotic luxury, but nevertheless there is a perceptible order in the sequence, and from it 'sense' of another and surprising sort arises. According to these instructions, the girl, in remembering the life of the circle, is to remember not her lover and not the others, but herself; however, of herself she is to remember neither her own person nor any single moment of her own history. Instead, she is asked to recall a schema of generalised experience organised around external objects – a series of four gestures (oriented towards four implements) that she and her friends have made over and over again. These formal motions led in the past to the satisfaction of desire and, recalled in this way, even the experience of sexual release is subsumed into a system of regularised, almost ritualised activity.

The first gesture that Sappho revives for the remembering girl is that of wreathing herself, for this was the way that one asked the

---

[49] The verb μεθέπεσθαι should mean 'follow' or possibly 'frequent', and the 'cherish' that is reported by *LSJ* depends exclusively upon attempts to translate this passage; see the remarks of Page, *S&A* 77. The probability of an erotic overtone is convincingly argued by G. Lanata, 'Sul linguaggio amoroso di Saffo', *QU* 2 (1966) 65.

Graces for their grant of erotic attractiveness. Sappho elsewhere (81V) urges Dika to 'put an enchanting crown upon your curls', explaining that the wreathed Charites 'shun the ungarlanded', which means of course that they favour those who wear crowns. A flower chaplet was provocative in itself (*eratos*, 81.4V), but more than this it was a sign that one was ready to please.[50] It was reminiscent of the crown that Aphrodite wore (of roses, at E.*Med*.840); indeed, a wanton Eros might sport among its blossoms (Alcman 58 *PMG*), and this is why the Horae put a wreath of spring flowers in Pandora's hair (Hes.*Erga* 73–5; cf. *Theog*.576–7). With it they marked the fact that she was of an age to love and that her mission was seduction.

The second gesture, the placing of a shoulder-garland, is again a re-enactment of one of Aphrodite's coquetries, though her necklaces were made of gold (*h.Aphr.* 88).[51] Such a garland entranced its wearer with its odours, but it also drew the attention of others to a tender, vulnerable throat, and the girl in memory will put it 'around her delicate neck' (16).[52] In addition, the flower-necklace enhanced the breasts that it shadowed, breasts which are the focus of the next remembered gesture, the application of perfumes. Both Alcaeus and Anacreon speak of myrrh poured upon the breast,[53] but here there is a second richer unguent as well, and one is reminded of Archilochus' salute to the girl whose perfumed hair and breasts were enough to raise a greybeard's lust (48W; cf.205W and Semon.16W, evidently of a prostitute). Scented unguents and salves were major ingredients in any recipe for provocation, which is why Hera begged perfumes from Aphrodite's *kistē* when she meant to numb Zeus' wits with sex (*Il*.14.171–72). It is also why Aphrodite herself applied scent before she visited Anchises' hut (*h.Aphr*.61–2), why she took a pot of myrrh along for her appearance at the Judgment (Soph. *Krisis* fr.361P and note), and why she gave a phial of the same sweet salve to Phaon, who used it to drive the ladies of Mytilene wild (Ael.*VH* 12–18). In *Lysistrata*, oil of myrrh is a telling weapon in the women's arsenal,

---

[50] On the notion that the Charites bestow a *charis* that marks one as ready for love, see Lanata's discussion of fr.49V, op.cit. 63ff.

[51] At *h.Aphr*.6.10–11, Aphrodite makes all the immortals want her for their wife by thus bedecking herself.

[52] With this ἀπάλη δειρή compare the ἀβρὸς αὐχήν of the shorn boy of Anac.347 *PMG*. On ἀπάλος, see M. Treu, *Von Homer zur Lyrik*[2] (Munich 1968) 178–83, who notes a change from the subjective Homeric meaning to the affective, erotic, Sapphic use. It is quite probable that these garlands were specified as creators of desire, since the easiest completion of line 17 is ἀνθέων ἐρ[άτων (Schubart, Zuntz and others).

[53] Alcaeus 362.3V; Anac.363 *PMG*. At a symposium perfumes were applied chiefly to the head, but where drinking was not the chief occupation they were rubbed into the flesh; see Athen. 691f–692, citing Philonides, *On perfumes and wreaths*. Commenting on the Sapphic passage, Zuntz says, '*Ego pectoris quoque mentionem in v.18 vel v.19 fuisse coll.Athen. 674c et 678d sqq. divinaverim*' ('De Sapphus Carminibus ē3, ē4, ē5', *Mnemosyne* ser. 3, 7 (1939) 87).

along with diaphanous frocks and foolish little shoes (Ar.*Lys*.946), and there is a girl in middle comedy who has a different scent for each different part of her well-groomed body (Antiphanes, *Thōrikioi, CAF* 2.53).[54]

The Sappho-lover has proposed to reminisce about 'how we treated you', but the continuing song works in fact to remind the girl of how she behaved and how she courted love when she lived in the circle and had Sappho as her friend. She is told of a time when the ritual of provocation was her repeated rule, and then in stanza eight she is taught to remember the satisfaction that was one of its elements.[55] Having recalled the triple preparation, she is to think next of the fulfilment of her desire, as it was acted out on couches where she found release from amorous longings.[56] The singer has made sure, however, that the couch of this eighth stanza should be occupied only by the weightlessness of a creature powerfully sensed but wholly insubstantial, for the hair on which the crowns rest, the throat encircled by garlands, and the flesh on which the unguents shine are known by implication rather than by description. The gesturer is only a presence called up by the gestures, and consequently it is not the body of a girl (large or small, dark or light) that seems to lie here, it is a kind of phantom made of the touch of petals, the odour of perfume, and the sheen of soft skin. What is more, this figment almost seems to be alone on its soft cot for as her partner the poem has proposed only the almost invisible pronominal companion of her garlanding, the *emoi* of line 14.[57] The event is to be thought of as having occurred many many times, but it is evidently to be recalled almost as a dream

[54] Compare the royal bride who anoints her flesh with myrrh in the *Tereus* of Alexandrides (Kock ii 156), and the woman in Alcaeus' *Palaestra* (Kock i 761) who sends a substitute in to her lover, well-perfumed.

[55] The sequence is something like what C. M. Dawson perceived in Mimnermus 2, 'the briefest of short stories: κρυπταδίη φιλότης, a quiet stolen kiss or embrace; then μείλιχα δῶρα, further concrete inducements; and finally εὐνή, the consummation'; see 'Random thoughts on occasional poems', *YCLS* 19 (1966) 49.

[56] Attempts have been made to treat this πόθος as non-erotic; see, e.g., J. M. Edmonds, *Lyra Graeca*² i (Cambridge, Mass., 1928) 243, who thought the condition was hunger and that it was satisfied by eating one's fill; Bowra, *GLP*², 191, who proposed a longing for absent friends; or C. Theander, 'Studia Sapphica', *Eranos* 34 (1936) 59ff., who suggested homesickness. It is however generally recognised that lines like καὶ ποθήω καὶ μάομαι (36V) and ὄν δ' ἔψυξας ἔμαν φρένα καιομέναν πόθωι (48V) establish the erotic meaning of Sappho's πόθος, and also that the Homeric phrase ἐξίης πόθον means to escape by way of satisfaction; see Page, *S&A*, 79–80; Zuntz, op.cit., 89–90; and Lanata, op.cit., 10. It might be noticed that this erotic longing is specified as 'the desire that girls feel', if νεα]νίδων is correctly restored at 23. The line would then mean (in Zuntz's translation: '*Explebas desiderium id, vel tale, quale puellae sentire solent*'.

[57] That Sappho is here at all is denied by many and surprisingly by F. Lasserre, who admits the sexual satisfaction denoted by ἐξίης πόθον, but still insists, 'Il ne s'agit pas d'un amour de Sappho' ('Ornaments érotiques', *Serta Turyniana* (Urbana 1974) 24, n.35). Certainly the present song does not necessarily place the historical Sappho in this couch, but it does put its fictional Sappho-lover there.

would be, for the song has removed it from history, from narrative, and from all contact with the mundane world of either fact or fiction. These couches are neither indoors nor out; they have neither carpet nor grass beneath them since they don't have to support lovers of any weight. Instead, Sappho's art has here done what she would train her listeners' minds to do, drawing from the actuality of the couches not an image, but an idea of softness[58] which can appropriately receive the idea she has made of the girl's seductiveness and its success.

This is not the end of the Sapphic lesson, however, for the remains of two more stanzas prove that the song was designed so as to produce a final burst of festive activity. The lines are badly damaged, but the words 'temple' and 'grove' are here, and probably also 'chorus' and a term for a musical sound, either natural or artfully produced (*psophos*, 28).[59] More important, the rhetorical shape of the passage is clear, for the repeated negatives (*kōute* ... *oute* ... *oud'* ... *ouk* 24, 25, 27) testify to a statement that went: 'Not this, nor this, nor this occurred when we were absent, nor did ...' And so it is clear that the final stanzas reminded the girl (in litotes, for variation) of the many sacred duties that the lovers had fulfilled together. The song's pilgrimage of pleasure thus did not reach its goal at the couch but continued into a further phase of experience that was enjoyed by the circle in its entirety. For the listener, it is as if the dimly seen lovers had risen from their cot almost as soon as they reached it and danced away into a populous complex of worship, or indeed as if their lovemaking had been a part of some larger pageant of prescribed observances. The idea that one may celebrate the eternal through sensual experience is thus enforced by the progress of a poem that blends the private joys of physical love with the public pleasures of a community of celebrants.

'Remember our life together as if it were an endless ritual' – this is what the Sappho-lover says to the one girl of the anecdote and what the Sappho-singer says to the many of her audience. It is plain that reality is to be reformulated, but all the same this advice has caused some literal-minded critics to ask whether in fact the *thiasos* actually performed the rites that moved from couch to chorus, and to propose, at times, some rather entertaining answers.[60] Their speculations are useless, however, and their question bluntly contrary to the spirit of this song, since finite actuality is exactly what Sappho teaches us not to dwell upon. The memory that she recommends is an organising and

---

[58] For the erotic associations of μαλθακός, cf. 46V and see J. M. Bremer, 'Meadow of love', *Mnem.* ser.4, 28 (1975) 268f.

[59] For ψόφος in nature, cf. P.*Pa*.6.8; in music, cf.E.*Ba*.687; *Cycl*.443f.

[60] See e.g. Saake, *Kunst*, 200, where it is argued that all the activities here described are part of an actual cult celebration for the Muses. A more moderate (though less precise) position is taken by T. McEvilley, 'Sapphic imagery and frag.96', *Hermes* 101 (1973) 268: 'Fragment 94 does not present exactly a rite nor exactly a party, but a private occasion which involved the symbolic objects common to both.'

classifying one, and it must be accompanied by a complementary process of forgetting, as particular moments are dissociated from their particular contexts and rearranged with others of their kind. No single act of wreathing could ever be duplicated in every one of its details, but when all are assimiliated to one another and then grouped with like classes in the thrice repeated, ' many ... many ... many ...', a sense not only of habit, but of potential renewal is created. Placing a wreath is no longer a discrete experience, nor is sinking upon a couch, and in consequence love itself, having been generalised as a part of this all-embracing system, is both eternal and open to repetition. When this girl is gone someone else will take her place in the *thiasos* and presumably in Sappho's preference, but the song proves that her own experience (correctly recalled) is indestructible. Memory preserves, and the conceit of the ritual confers a permanence, for a rite holds within itself all of its past and all of its future performances and is never rendered futile by one particular completion. The girl will remember that by her own gestures she fixed her love in this pattern – making it beautiful, making it a part of the continuing Sapphic cult of Aphrodite, making it an action that could not possibly excite either grief or regret.

Many of the same ideas are expressed in another song that takes, this time, the form of an exhortation delivered directly to a friend named Atthis whose beloved has gone away (96V):

] cαρδ.[..]

πόλ]λακι τυίδε [.]ων ἔχοιcα   2

[—]

ὠcπ.[...]..ώομεν, .[...]..χ[..]

   cε †θεαcικελαν ἀρι-

      γνωτα†, cᾶι δὲ μάλιcτ' ἔχαιρε μόλπαι·   5

⟨—⟩

νῦν δὲ Λύδαιcιν ἐμπρέπεται γυναί-

   κεccιν ὤc ποτ' ἀελίω

      δύντοc ἀ βροδοδάκτυλοc ⟨cελάννα⟩   8

⟨—⟩

πάντα περ⟨ρ⟩έχοιc' ἄcτρα· φάοc δ' ἐπί-

   cχει θάλαccαν ἐπ' ἀλμύραν

      ἴcωc καὶ πολυανθέμοιc ἀρούραιc·   11

—

ἀ δ' ⟨ἐ⟩έρcα κάλα κέχυται, τεθά-

   λαιcι δὲ βρόδα κἄπαλ' ἄν-

      θρυcκα καὶ μελίλωτοc ἀνθεμώδηc·   14

⟨—⟩

πόλλα δὲ ζαφοίταις' ἀγάνας ἐπι-
  μνάσθεις' ῎Ατθιδος ἰμέρωι
    λέπταν ποι φρένα κ[.]ρ...βόρηται·   17
⟨→⟩
κῆθι δ' ἔλθην ἀμμ.[..]...ισα τόδ' οὐ
  νωντα[..]υστρνυμ[..(.)] πόλυς
    γαρύει [..(.)]αλογ[.....(.)]το μέσσον·   20

ε]ὔμαρ[ες μ]ὲν οὐ.α.μι θέαισι μόρφαν ἐπή[ρατ]ον ἐξίσω-
    σθαι συ[..]ρος ἔχη⟨ι⟩σθα[...].νίδηον   23

[   ]το[...(.)]ρατι-
  μαλ[   ].ερος
    καὶ δ[.]μ[   ]ος ᾽Αφροδίτα   26

καμ[   ] νέκταρ ἔχευ' ἀπὺ
  χρυσίας [   ]γαν
    ...(.)]απουρ[   ] χέρσι Πείθω   29

. . .
. . . at Sardis she guides
  her constant fancies towards

[us and our life when she thought you]
like to a goddess undisguised, and
  loved your songs the best.

Now, among Lydians, she is first,
just as the rosy moon, sun gone,
  takes easy precedence,

dimming the stars. Moonlight prevails
equally over the bitter sea
  or ploughland filled with flowers;

dew in its sweetness descends, rose
and delicate clover and dill then
  expand in honied bloom.

She cannot rest; memory brings
yearning for Atthis, and chagrin
  eats at her fragile heart.

[Sometimes she calls] to us to come
[. . . but we cannot hear . . .]
  speaks [. . . the sea between.]

Not one of us is fair enough
to equal a fair divinity
  but you . . .

(At least five more stanzas follow, containing the words 'Aphrodite . . .
poured nectar from a golden . . . in the hands of Peitho (?) . . . the
Geraistion . . .')

These verses come from yet another song of love and pomp, for here
a completed evocation of emotion is placed in direct contact with a
moment portrayed in full ceremonial dress. How much is lost at the
song's beginning and end we cannot know,[61] but the surviving section
shows seven stanzas built so as to produce a sharp sense of pain,
followed by at least six in which the nearness of Aphrodite and Peitho,
like the employment of golden vessels and sacred nectar, recalls the
rite of the apple-grove.[62] A girl who is not here suffers, but her particular passive grief is replaced, as the song proceeds, by a general
ritual, or pseudo-ritual, activity, and this is a truth that must not be
forgotten even as we submit to the bewitching perfections of the passage that survives – a passage that creates images of both anguish
and peace.

The psychic question here is the same as it was in fragment 94:
What is to be done with a love that continues, when the time for its
satisfaction is past? And here, more than anywhere, the Sapphic song
presents itself as a piece of instruction as the singer takes a token
pupil[63] in hand and leads her step by step, from memory through
imagination and on to the contemplation of an aspect of passion that
can continue to mix with her continuing life. The fiction that serves
this lesson is simplicity itself:[64] a girl[65] who once adored the pupil

---

[61] The pap. text is most thoroughly studied by G. Zuntz, op.cit., 93–108.

[62] Compare also Ibycus 288 *PMG* and see the remarks of Treu, HzL, 204.

[63] The number of fragments addressed to Atthis suggests not so much a complicated
love life for the girl as a fondness, on Sappho's part, for her name.

[64] Nevertheless, many critics have found a tangle of emotions beneath this simplicity.
One school believes that Sappho expresses her *own* longing for the absent girl; it has
even been supposed that she is jealous of Atthis, a hard-hearted girl for whom the
distant one pines when she ought to pine for the broken-hearted singer. Schubart first
spoke of the 'Sehnsucht' of Sappho (*SB* Berl., 1902, 204), and Schadewalt takes it as a
demonstrated fact: 'Hier lässt S. ihrem eigenen Sehnen die visionär gespürte und
geschaute Sehnsucht jener Andern entgegenstreben' ('Zu Sappho', *Hermes* 71, 1936,
372–3). Wilamowitz (*SuS*, 54) agreed with this interpretation, arguing that since the
girl in Sardis was now wife and 'hoffentlich' mother, she of course would not be crying
out with unsatisfied desire; therefore Sappho must have portrayed her own emotion
through her. Another school believes that Sappho is in fact in love with Atthis and
courts her now with a song of consolation that is really meant to persuade her to turn
towards the singer as the lost girl's replacement. See Snell, *Gesammelte Schriften*
(Göttingen 1966) 91, note 6, and Saake, *Kunst*, 177–8, where Sappho's purpose is 'eben
um diese Zuneigung für sich, Sappho selbst, zu werben.' West *(Maia* 22 (1970) 319ff.)
complicates matters even further by supposing a cast of four interested parties: Sappho,
Arignota (to whom the song is addressed), the girl in Lydia, and Atthis (whom the
absent girl now longs for, though once she loved Arignota).

[65] If ἀριγνώτα (nom.) is read in ll.4–5 the absent girl will be named Arignota, and so
she is reported by the elder critics (beginning with Wilamowitz, *SuS* 53; see also
Kamerbeek, *Mnem.* 9 (1956) 100). Page read ἀριγνώται, modifying θέαι, calling the

Atthis has gone away to Lydia and is cut off now from her beloved and from all of her friends, just as the mainland is cut off from the island of Lesbos. Perhaps she has gone to be married,[66] in which case she is thought of as older than Atthis, but Sappho does not care to tell us this. In fact, she tells *us* nothing, for according to the poem's convention, she is now singing just to Atthis, and this is the second truth that must be kept in mind as the song is heard.

Sappho addresses only her single companion – so she pretends, and this pretence keeps the picture of poet and listener hung always like a scrim between us and the substance of her song. Nevertheless, this girl who is nominally present, this listening Atthis, is hardly more than a device to give the poem immediacy, and the second girl is no more vivid than she, though the surviving section of the song is ostensibly hers. She is gone, she once loved, she is beautiful and she grieves: these things we know about her, but she remains transparent, almost indiscernible, and she is overshadowed by a brilliant simile. All of which means that in a sense what Sappho treats here is the love of an absent shade for a present poetic convention, and indeed the whole piece has a kind of moon-struck abstraction about it, for it establishes a world of surreal simplicity. In its geography, a She who is There is divided from a We who are Here by an intervening track of traversable sea,[67] but this map can also be read as showing a Now

---

proper name 'otherwise unknown', (*S&A*, 89), though B. Marzullo, 'Arignota l'amica di Saffo', *Maia* 5 (1952) 85–92, noted a disciple of Pythagoras (Porph. *Vita* 4; Suda, sv), a fourth-century author of a work on the mysteries (Nilsson *GGRel*.ii 97), and a nickname at A.*Eq*.1278. As an adjective, ἀρίγνωτος occurs seven times in Homer (Il.13.72; 15.490; *Od*. 4.207; 6.106 and 300; 17.265, 375), once in Anacreon (*PMG* 347), twice in Pindar (*P*.4.95; *N*.5.12), and four times in Bacchylides (5.29; 17.57; 10.37; 9.64), almost always designating the peculiar quality that makes known the presence of divinity. (Anacreon uses it to refer to a mortal woman apparently notorious in a purely secular way, and at P.*N*.5.12, the meaning seems to be merely 'famous'). West (op.cit. 319, note 31) complained that θέα ἀριγνώτα was an 'oddly compressed expression', an 'uncharacteristic modification of the formulaic "like a goddess" ', but he did not note that the alternative which leaves the goddess unqualified is extremely flat in this context. (West also takes ''Αριγνώτα as a vocative, making her not the absent girl but the addressee and a rival to another girl named Atthis for the absent one's love.) Since the act of likening to a goddess is central to this song, it seems more probable that Sappho chose to emphasise it here by saying that Atthis was likened to a divinity *in the beauty of a full epiphany*. It also seems quite possible that she had in mind the passage from the *Odyssey* in which the lovely Nausicaa, already likened to Artemis, comes 'like one whose divinity is easily recognised' (*Od*.6.101–9). See further the discussions at Treu, *Sappho* (1963) 215 and Saake, *Kunst*, 163ff.

[66] A. Turyn, *Studia Sapphica* (*EOS* Supp.6, 1929) 59, thought that the word γυναί-κεσσιν at 7–8 proved that the girl had gone to be married and of course this is the most obvious explanation for the girl's present existence in Sardis. I cannot, however, follow T. MacEvilley, 'Sapphic imagery', *Hermes* 101 (1973) 259–78, who finds the present song filled in every one of its parts by the idea of marriage.

[67] Whether this dividing sea is actually mentioned outside the simile (10) is uncertain, but the]αλον[of line 20 is usually reported as δίαλον or δι' ἄλος and taken, in connection with the subsequent τὸ μέσσον, to specify the stretch of water that acts as a barrier between the girl and her friends.

that means pain and cries of grief,[68] divided from a Then that meant songs and joy by a stretch of time that is untraversable. Strangely enough, the singer and her companion belong locally to the joyful past and not to the painful present (as the song defines these areas) and their ultimate task is to bring their own emotions into harmony with their situation.

Sappho and Atthis are working together on this, the Lesbian side, ostensibly trying to efface distance, time and the sense of loss, and their first operation is to imagine an estranged beloved who is likewise imagining, or rather remembering, over there in Lydia. The minds of Sappho and Atthis thus create a mind for the girl and all engage in a mutual mental activity that begins to mingle there with here and joyful past with present pain. Music proves to be the first line of connection as Sappho, herself singing here and now, reminds Atthis (through the other girl's conjectured memory) of old songs of hers that still sound in the other's ear, though she is now in another company. The statement 'She remembers your songs', will cause Atthis to remember them too, and so in its first surviving lines this song sounds much like fragment 94. We soon realise, however, that its tenor is quite different, for Atthis is not departing. She stays and is led into a state of exaltation, in preparation for a final ritual, and consequently the objects proposed for her meditation are divested of all that is physical.

Atthis is not urged to remember shared actions of love; instead she is to imagine another who so remembers, and yet she is not to think of that other as a fleshly creature – she is not to recall the other's hair or perfume or even her motion as she walks. Instead she is to imagine her thought, and that imagined thought is to be of a dematerialising sort, for the absent girl is not to be supposed to dwell upon the physical

---

[68] The distant girl's present cry is implicit, though not as dramatic as Wilamowitz made it when he proposed to read (*SuS*, 54): κῆθι δ' ἐλθὴν ἄμμ᾽ [ὀξὺ βοᾶι· τὰ δ᾽ οὐ / νῶν τ᾽ ἄ[π]υστα νὺξ πολύω[ς] / γαρύ[ει δι᾽] ἄλος 'Laut ruft sie, wir sollten dorthin kommen. Das vernehmen wir beide nicht; nicht erzählt es uns die Nacht, die mit ihren tausend Ohren alles hört über das Meer herüber; aber. . .' Because of this version, Treu (*HzL* 204) makes the girl break into a loud cry of 'Kommt hierher!' at the beginning of stanza seven, but with the text as read by Zuntz, l.18 ends . . . ισα τόδ᾽ οὐ. The verb that controls the infinitive ἔλθην may thus be one of wishing or desiring and not necessarily of calling. Nevertheless, the presence of γαρύει in l.20 (whether its subject is still the girl, or whether it is something else, representing or negating her) still strongly suggests that what we have to do with is some form of speech. It is instructive to consider West's attempt to replace the all too compelling version of Wilamowitz with something cooler and more accurate (op.cit., 319): κῆθι δ' ἔλθην ἄμμ᾽ [ἔλπις ἴσα· τὸ δ᾽οὐ / νῶν γ᾽ ἄ[κο]υστον· ὔμην πόλυς / γαρύει[. . .]αλουπ[. . . ὄ]ν τὸ μέσον. 'And equally she hopes that we may go there. But you and I cannot hear this; the wedding cry rings loud between.' The construction ἔλπις plus acc. and infinitive is no more satisfactory than is this use of ἴσα (equal to what?), nor does ὔμην γαρύει resemble anything Sapphic, but ἄκουστον seems a good possibility in l.19, and if it is right it confirms the older notion that something more vocal than a hope is attributed to the girl.

charms of Atthis. Instead, what she remembers is the praise that she herself once gave to those charms. (It is not even really the music of Atthis that she remembers, but instead her own delight, as she used to listen to it.) In the past she had lovingly idealised phenomena that her eye and ear perceived – she had thought her friend 'divine'[69] – and what she thinks of now is her own past idealisation. Except of course that it isn't the distant girl who remembers these evanescent things; this volatilising memory of an old illusion doesn't belong to her at all, for it is only what the singer asks Atthis to suppose.[70] It is thus an imagined version of another's recollection of a visionary experience that Sappho would now place in her pupil's mind!

From her communion with the imagined mind of the other girl, Atthis learns that love-in-separation is a return to the idealising part of the self that originally recognised beauty in the physical beloved. With this lesson learned, she is ready to consider the objective, external aspect of the lost beloved, and in the following operation she is taught to re-enact (and incidentally to repay) the initial recognition in a new way. Just as she herself was likened to a goddess, in the time that she was visible to her friend, so the song now leads her to liken the beauty of that friend, though it has become invisible, to the beauty of an eternal divinity. The lost girl is compared to a superb and tranquil moon, and as soon as this act is accomplished, her unseen beauty becomes a present force that can be contemplated, for the moon is brought directly into the song.[71] It appears and spreads its light abroad, so that all the separated, equalised, subjectified elements – then and now, there and here, pain and joy, girl and Atthis – sink for an instant into one timeless dewy song-space that is submissive to its beams.

This moon that briefly brings all to a common stillness has received

[69] For the convention behind this sort of comparison with a god, see G. Lieberg, *Puella divina: die Gestalt der göttlichen Geliebten* (Amsterdam 1962) 13–34. Some critics have supposed that this likening to a goddess was a 'makaristiche Motiv' linking this song with fragment 31 and with the wedding songs (see Saake, *Kunst* 166–7, *Studien* 80), and MacEvilley, op.cit., argues that the present poem apes the form of the wedding song because there had been a kind of marriage between the two girls, one that has now been replaced by a more conventional marriage in Lydia.

[70] Note the ποι at line 17, which will operate to remind the listener that Sappho's imagination is at work (unless, perhaps, this word represents an actual Ϝοι; see below, note 90).

[71] The only earlier comparison of anyone with the moon is at *h.Aphr.* 89, where Aphrodite is adorned, ὡς δὲ σελήνη. The moon moves out of its simile and into the primary matter of the song as smoothly as if it were simply mounting the sky, but critics who like tidy definitions usually mark the simile as ending in the middle of line 9, at ἄστρα; everything after this point is then labelled either as description of actual nature or as a symbolic representation of some sort (see Turyn, *Stud. Sapph.*, 59–65; Fränkel, *WuF*, 49; 72–6; *DuP*, 209; Schadewaldt, *Hermes* 71 (1936) 372). Saake, however, recognises the essential unity of the whole moon section, from line 6 to line 14 (*Kunst*, 170f.).

a great deal of critical attention. There are of course those who have seen it as one more piece of frivolous Sapphic decoration, but most scholars have viewed it as central to the song, and it has inspired rhetorical definitions, romantic descriptions of Aegean landscape, and a few disquisitions upon the moon as a universal symbol. It has been called *ekphrasis*, runaway simile, digression, foil, hymeneal compari-son[72] and intentional irrelevancy,[73] and in addition we have been told that from it 'die wirkliche Nacht' steps forth,[74] though whether this means that the girl's are night-wanderings or that Sappho's is a night-meeting with Atthis, critics cannot agree.[75] For some, this even becomes a song performed at night and a combination of this actu-alised darkness with the sea that may or may not be mentioned in line 20 has inspired others to envisage a darkened seascape and then to cite parallel scenes from Homer where night and sea mean despair and desolation.[76] More attentive critics have however noticed that this is no ordinary monthly moon and remembering that night is never mentioned, they have looked for effects that are less literal. Some of them find that this spreading light represents, not actual nature but Sappho's pure longing,[77] either for the distant girl or for the Atthis at her side; some find that the light is sanctifying, and that it describes a space like the sacred area within a *temenos*;[78] still others discover a strong sexual symbolism in it, and hear in the moon-filled stanzas a powerful reference to a past union (or else a *mariage manqué*) between an Atthis-Sun and a Moon-Girl who is now gone.[79]

---

[72] McEvilley, op.cit., 262 'by virtue of the simile Atthis and the departed girl are seen for the moment as potential bride and groom'. He believes that the simile is borrowed from actual wedding songs.

[73] C. Carey, 'S.fr.96LP', *CQ* NS (1978) 366–71 argues that such images are typical of archaic poetry and that they work so that 'all emotion is drained from the poem' (368).

[74] W. Schadewaldt, 'Zu Sappho', *Hermes* 71 (1936) 372. For him, this is a 'Nachtlied'.

[75] Saake, *Kunst*, 172, has it both ways: Sappho and Atthis are under the moon while the Lydian lady is wandering in a moonlit flowery field.

[76] Turyn, op.cit., 62 who puts the distant girl at the edge of the sea: '*puellam illam in maris littore maestam mente turbata.*'

[77] J. Trumpf, 'Kydonische Äpfel', *Hermes* 88 (1960) 22: 'Ein Ausdruck ihrer eigenen Ergriffenheit.'

[78] W. Schadewaldt, *Sappho*, 121ff.

[79] See McEvilley, op.cit., followed by C. W. Macleod, 'Two comparisons', *ZPE* 15 (1974) 217, where it is assumed that the girl's present, legitimate marriage is being contrasted to a past union with Atthis. Since the union of Sun and Moon usually served antiquity as a figure for impossibility (cf. e.g. Pliny *HN* 2.221–2; Plut. *de Isid.et Os.* 367D–E, and see W. H. Roscher, *Über Selene und Verwandtes*, 76–84), those who wish to entertain ideas such as these would do well to avoid the notion of a Lesbian 'marriage' between two girls, and to hear instead a reference to a past connection that was precisely *not* an imitation of a heterosexual union. They might also be advised to refer to *Theog.*371 (cf. E.*Phoen.*175), where sun and moon are anomalously presented as sisters, though in a Hermetic fragment they appear as brothers instead (Nock-Festugière, *Corpus Herm.*iv, Paris 1964, 23, 34, 11). All the care in the world, however, cannot hide the fact that Sappho nowhere suggests that Atthis be thought of as the sun.

If we return to the lines of the fragment, the minimal truth appears to be this. The moon is introduced, with stars, in stanza three as part of a conventional simile for the surpassing beauty of the absent one – a beauty that Sappho's instructive song offers to the mind of Atthis for recognition and consideration. This moon then rises above its simile (and also above the stars) to shine out alone in stanza four as a simple poetic fact with consequences that are described in stanza five, also as poetic facts that are within the direct cognisance of the song.[80] The light of this realised moon stretches across the pause between stanzas five and six (since the listener cannot know that the subject will be changed), but in line fifteen it meets the girl from which it first derived, and at this point it disappears. Moonlight thus for an instant takes on a 'reality' equal to that of the girl in Lydia, with whom it ceases to be identical, but it is no more physically present than she is. The song does not point to an actual luminary, nor even to a bit of scenery from its fiction; nor does it say, as is so often supposed, 'Look at the visible moon – at this moment it touches you both, and brings you together again!' Sappho is never banal, and in this case she does not insult the separation that she sings about with any such prettified resolution. On the contrary, her lesson is as free of sentiment as it is of cheap consolation as she tells her young friend: 'Look upon the invisible loveliness of her who loved you: it is a moon that you may contemplate.'

This moon of absent beauty, as Sappho presents it, reaches the earth (and Atthis) in two forms – first with its spreading and general light, and secondly with its dripping and tangible dew. The epithet 'rosy-fingered' gives it at the outset the form of a youthful female divinity, but the adjective also points to beams of moonlight that stretch out to touch the landscape.[81] The light of this moon is not mere passive

---

[80] It is amusing to find the same development in Virginia Woolf's *Mrs. Dalloway* (p. 62, Harcourt Brace ed.) where a moon is introduced as a simile for grief and then allowed to invade the reportage of the actual fictional situation: 'Of course I did, thought Peter; it almost broke my heart too, he thought; and was overcome with his own grief, which rose like a moon looked at from a terrace, ghastly beautiful with light from the sunken day. I was more unhappy than I've ever been since, he thought. And as if in truth he were sitting there on the terrace he edged a little towards Clarissa; put his hand out; raised it; let it fall. There above them it hung, that moon.'

[81] Note that Sappho elsewhere makes the Charites 'rosy-armed' (LP53). Page characteristically objected to βροδοδάκτυλος of the moon (*S&A*, 90) and Fränkel as typically embraced it ('from Lesbos we see the moon, still ruddy from the mist of the horizon, ascending above the Lydian coast . . .', *DuP* (Engl.) 184). E. Heitsch, 'Zum Sappho-Text', *Hermes* 95 (1967) 392 argues that the epithet does not carry any notion of actual colour since Hesiod could apply it to the presumably greenish Nereids; that its connotations are simply those of youth and divinity. Saake (*Kunst*, 168) proposes a close association with Dawn which will give this moon a psychic coloration full of expectancy (the 'Nicht-Mehr' mixed with the 'Noch-Nicht'). To return to the obvious, one might point out that the reciprocity fixed here, between the 'rosiness' of the moon's beams and the roses (13) that receive their dews would seem to justify the epithet (if justification were needed) and also to maintain its sense of colour.

illumination, however. It 'takes' what it touches (even 'conquers' or 'occupies') with a verb that is almost militant,[82] and Sappho insists that the realm that it controls is a double one – not just land, but estranging, dividing sea as well. As for the dew that derives from this Sapphic moon, it causes plants to flower and perfumes to be released in seasonless fields everywhere. The two stanzas of the moon's predominance culminate in this image of dewy full-blown blossoms under moonlight – roses under the touch of the rosy-fingered one – and it is right to remember that, according to ancient belief, it was the moon that brought plants to their perfection, and it was by moonlight that flowers were gathered for beneficent magic and for medicines.[83]

The moon's light and the moon's moisture were thought of as the source of all that was cool, fresh, round and soft,[84] in contrast to the heat, salt and hardness produced by the sun.[85] The moon was feminine,[86] and it controlled not just fecundity but ripeness in general; not just menstruation but all the bodily liquids and humidities.[87] Dew sent by the moon[88] nourished all fruits and flowers, and plants that were peculiarly moon-influenced were used in women's pharmaceuticals.[89] Nevertheless, this fostering luminary stood in a reciprocal relation to the earth to which its damps were sent, for it fed itself in turn upon the exhalations that rose from clear lakes and springs.[90] This then is the moon that Atthis is to contemplate: she is to see it as having drawn up to its own distance the beauty of the girl in Lydia, but she is also to sense how it proliferates in beauties everywhere, and

---

[82] ἐπίσχει (10); cf. the militant Aphrodite of frag.1.

[83] A. Delatte, *Herbarius. Recherches sur le cérémonial usité chez les anciens pour la cueillette des simples et des plantes magiques* (Acad.Roy.de Belg., Cl.des Lettres, Mem. liv.4.1961), 6 and 43ff.

[84] Athen.276e; cf. Theophrastus, *Hist.plant.*5.1.3, where the moon softens even wood.

[85] Pliny *HN* 2.223: 'As the opposite of the sun, the moon is feminine and gentle; it releases the humidity of the night and draws it up again, attracting it without destroying. Proofs of which are: in moonlight the corpses of wild animals rot; the moon draws the languor of sleepers into their heads; the moon melts ice and loosens everything beneath her humid breath. In this way the principle of alternation is set up, assuring a constant sufficiency in fortune's change as some stars draw things together, others loosen them. Fresh sweet water is the food of the moon; salt that of the sun.'

[86] Alcman 57; Aristotle, *HA* 582a34b3; Pliny *HN* 2.223 (above); Plut.*de facie*, 939F; Proclus ad *Tim.* 61; see K. Reinhardt, *Kosmos und Sympathie* (Munich 1926) 329, 340, 349.

[87] *SVF* iv index p.127 sv 'ali lunam aquis'; see Reinhardt, op.cit., 176, note 1; C. Préaux, *La Lune dans la pensée grècque* (Acad.Roy.Belg., Mem.de la Cl.des Lettres, 2ᵉ Ser.61.4, 1973) 132–5.

[88] At Alcman 57 dew is child of Zeus and Selene (the passage is cited at Plut.*de facie* 940A); cf. *quaest.conv.* 659B, *quaest.nat.* 918A; Lucan *VH* 1.20; Pliny *HN* 2.221–2; see W. H. Roscher, op.cit., 49–55.

[89] Roscher, op.cit., 55–7; Préaux, op.cit., 89.

[90] Préaux, op.cit., 116.

how it cools, conquers, ripens and heals.[91]

The typical Sapphic substitution of idea for actuality, original for replica and whole for part is manifest in this moon as is also the persistent sexuality of the Sapphic ideal. Through its moon, the song teaches a hypothetical Atthis and an actual audience to look upon a beauty that perpetually nourishes and enhances all who can understand it. For them, the instructed, the idea of divine female beauty can bring a hush of peace and fulfilment, preparing them for ritual activity, but in spite of its spreading equality, its unction cannot reach those who are imperfect in the Sapphic philosophy. The moonlight fails, for example, to reach the girl in Lydia, as the singer makes plain by abandoning the quiet field of dew-filled flowers in order to offer a second and paradoxical glimpse of the departed one. This girl's own remembered loveliness, subsumed into its source, is causing growth, but she is not remembering now, she is desiring, and by doing so she is destroying herself.[92] The moon is tranquil and silent but she is in

---

[91] Compare the lines of Raleigh, from *The Phoenix Nest* (1593):

Praisd be Dianas faire and harmles light,
Praisd be the dewes, wherwith she moists the ground;
Praisd be hir beames, the glorie of the night,
Praisd be hir powre, by which all powres abound.
. . .
In heauen Queene she is among the spheares,
In ay she Mistres like makes all things pure,
Eternitie in hir oft chaunge she beares,
She beautie is, by hir the faire endure.
. . .
A knowledge pure it is hir worth to kno,
With Circes let them dwell that thinke not so.

[92] The older way of reading lines 15–17 was to cut them, taking ζαφοίταισ(ι) as the finite verb in an initial sentence that ended either with ἰμέρῳ or with φρένα, and then reading a final sentence built around the verb βόρηται. Page, however, showed that there are no grounds for believing in a Lesbian 3rd s.-αισι ending (*S&A*, 91) and the division was in any case unattractive, since it meant either adding a connective particle (as Wilamowitz did: κῆρ<δ'>ἄσα<ι> βόρηται), or else doing without one. Sense is achieved when the girl who is the subject of the two participles is made the subject of the single finite verb, but a major problem is then posed by the sequence of letters in 1.17 which Zuntz (op.cit., 95ff.) read as K.ΡΑΣΑ. Ever since Schubart's second report ('Bemerkungen zu Sappho', *Philolog*.97, 1948, 311ff.) the word κᾶρ has been generally recognised as standing here, either in the nominative (or acc.) and followed by ἄσαι (or ἄσα), or else in the dative, as κ[ἄ]ρι σα(ι) (see Page, *S&A*, 92): its meaning is usually taken to be 'heart', though Zuntz and Page would have it mean 'fate', on the grounds that Sappho uses either καρδία or θῦμος for 'heart'.

A number of combinations of meaning and case appear to be possible, but no one has yet manoeuvred them so as to produce a wholly satisfactory result. Page's dative yields the statement 'her tender heart is consumed because of your fate', which is manifestly impossible since Atthis' merely staying where she was could not possibly be called her κᾶρ, which ought to indicate a fate equal to death. On the other hand, if the girl is the subject of βόρηται, then all the readings with nominatives (Schubart's κ[ἄ]ρ ἄσα βόρηται, Wilamowitz's as above, and Zuntz's φρένα κᾶρ ἄσαι βόρηται) must be ruled out, leaving only the acc. And the acc. is not manageable since βόρηται seems to be intransitive and

restless motion, dissatisfied, perhaps even crying aloud. The lunar vision thus dissolves to show a pair of lovers who seem to be more sharply separated than before, since the nameless girl is in physical distress now, wandering painfully over there, while Atthis, here, in the final phase of the song, takes an honoured part in a rite that Aphrodite sponsors.

The contrast between the conditions of the two girls is so extreme as to seem almost invidious, and a few sentimental critics have found it to be more than they could bear. In the belief that a healthy poem ought to leave both lovers in a state of frustration and grief, they remove the festal stanzas (assigning them to a separate performance) and report the song as ending in line 20 with a cry that's lost at sea.[93]

---

an accusative of respect is already supplied by the preceding φρένα. Kamerbeek, following a suggestion of Lobel's did away with κᾶρ altogether by reading ἰμέρῳ λέπταν ποι φρένα κ[α]ρ[τέρωι] – 'she is devoured in respect to her fragile heart by a powerful longing' – but this is not easy to accept as Sapphic because of the contrived and rhetorical postponement of the epithet ('Sapphica', *Mnem*.9 (1956) 100f.). Another solution is proposed by C. Calame ('S.fr.96, 15–17', *QU* 4 (1967) 101ff.), who would return to a nominative form, on the basis of Homeric analogies wherein a person represented by nominative participles is replaced by a part of himself as actual subject of verb. Calame argues that the pattern represented by ὅδε. . . πεποιθώς. . . γοῦνα φέρει (*Il*.6.510f.) and μεμαὼς . . . ἕλεν μένος (*Il*.5.135f.) might justify ζαφοίταισα . . . κᾶρ βόρηται, especially if the ποι of l.17 is corrected to Ϝοι. C. also notes that Schubart first read Κ.ΡΑΣΑ as ΚΑΡΔΙΑ, and so his report of the final phrase is ἰμέρῳ λέπταν Ϝοι φρένα καρδία βόρηται. His translation ('sous l'effet d' ἴμερος elle sent son coeur s'alourdir et agir comme un poids sur la fine membrane qui l'entoure') reflects the older interpretation of βόρηται as coming from βαρέομαι, but Page notes that elsewhere Sappho has βαρ – in her 'heavy' words.

An alternative to Calame's reading might be to leave ἴμερῳ in the previous phrase and to read λέπταν Ϝοι φρένα κᾶρ ἄσαι βόρηται ('remembering Atthis with longing, her heart is devoured as to its fragile container by a sickening distress'). In this case ἴμερος would work upon the mind while ἄσα attacked the visceral parts of the girl. Either way, the poet will have intentionally juxtaposed the words φρήν and κᾶρ (or καρδία) in order to convey a specific psychophysical state in which one is sharply aware of unusual sensations in the chest. For similar distinctions or interactions between the two, cf.*Od*.20.10ff., πολλὰ δὲ μερμήριξε κατὰ φρένα καὶ κατὰ θυμόν; Archil. 191W; Aesch.*PV* 881; B.1.161ff. where wealth swells up the φρήν, while reverent actions cheer the κέαρ. (On Aeschylus' use of φρήν, θυμός and κάρδια, see D. Sansone, *Aeschylean Metaphors for Intellectual Activity*, Hermes Einzelschr. 1975). It may be noted that at 48V it is the φρήν that is fired by a mad desire which the coming of the beloved extinguishes in satisfaction. And as to this 'eating' of the heart, cf. Theognis 1324, where Aphrodite is begged to scatter the lover's μερίμνας θυμοβόρους; cf. also Hes.*Erga* 799. One might cite also later compounds like δηξίθυμος (Helen at *Agam*.743 is δηξίθυμον ἔρωτος ἄνθος); see West ad *Erga* 66 (where he would read γυιοβόρους) and ad 799.

[93] The argument for ending the song at line 20 was ostensibly based on Milne's principle of the Sapphic ring-composition, since stanzas six and seven return to the idea of the distant girl and her longings which was introduced at line 2. Since, however, one cannot know what preceded the first of the surviving stanzas, and since inner as well as outer rings are possible, the argument is extremely weak and in fact most recent scholars have assumed that the song continues. The song is cut at 20 by Edmonds, *Lyra Gr*.² (1928) 246; Theander, 'Studia Sapphica II' *Eranos* 34 (1936) 66ff.; Lavagnini, *Aglaia* (Torino 1938) 143; Schadewaldt, *Sappho*, 120; K. Thomamüller, *Ade, rosenfingriger Mond!* Forum Linguisticum ii (Frankfurt 1974) 103; Zuntz (loc.cit.) would cut it after line 23.

Cut in this way, the song takes on a most familiar shape and sound: it is dominated by a heartbroken girl at Sardis, it spends its moon to show that tranquillity can be found only in the sky, and it dies away in its last lines with an anguished wail. Indeed, a setting by Mahler or Richard Strauss would be more appropriate to it than the accompaniment of an archaic lyre, and this is only one of several good reasons for refusing to consider this tearful, truncated song. To begin with, the act of surgery that creates it is not recommended by anything in the text, nor is it supported by any marginal sign. Worse yet, it divides poetic elements that seem to have been conceived as units, for the poured-out nectar of stanza ten repeats the dew that pours down in stanza five; the goddesses of comparison in line 21 reflect their prototype of line 4,[94] and the Aphrodite of the close gives a new face to the moon of the central passage.[95] No one has the right to disrupt these interdependencies[96] – not when the only thing to be gained is the union of two girls in a common romantic agony. The interrelated ideas of immortal beauty, dew-fed blossoms, love's nectar, and girls like goddesses, announce themselves as motifs that bind all the surviving stanzas together, and this means that for Sappho, the song was finished only when visionary moon, distant suffering and present ritual had all been juxtaposed – only when the one girl's private pain had given way to the other's shared experience of Aphrodite's grace.

Both girls are thought of as enduring the same separation, but one of them has left the Sapphic circle while the other remains. One has evidently forgotten the full Sapphic lesson, while the other is being taught afresh, and this is why one is imaged as wandering and wailing, the other as surrounded by worshipping friends. The girl at Sardis is beyond the reach of Sappho's voice and teachings, and without these, though there are women about her, she seems to be alone as she is devoured by her desire. Her memories decline from ideal to carnal real,[97] for she has forgotten that all beauty has a single nourishing source. By contrast, the girl on the island is still immersed in the Sapphic life: Sappho herself sings to her, reminds her that love finds beauty, that beloved beauty endures, and that it may be contemplated as a moon. Thus instructed, Atthis may take her place at the centre

---

[94] Pace Liebig (*Puella divina*, 15) who would have stanza eight refer once again directly to the distant girl's comparisons: 'It is easy for her to compare you . . .' Saake produces a true translation of the text as reported by Voigt: 'Zwar ist es für uns nicht leicht, in der gegehrten körperlichen schönheit mit Göttinnen zu wetteifern, du aber hast . . .' (*Kunst*, 165).

[95] For the association of Aphrodite with Selene, see *h.Aphr.* 89 and cf. Plut. *Amat.* 766b.

[96] I am extremely dubious, however, about the further echo between ἔλθην (18) and ἴξο[μ᾽ (36) that is heard by Treu *HzL*, 207 note 5.

[97] However lines 15–17 are read, it is plain that the girl's sensations are described as explicitly visceral – something like those of the singer in φαίνεταί μοι. Note the remarks of Turyn, op.cit., 65, on the erotic quality of ἐπιμνάομαι, and cf. McEvilley, op.cit., 261.

of the rite that offers her, perhaps, a drink from a golden goblet. On the opposite shore, separation produces wailing, but here on Lesbos it is met with music; errant movements on the mainland become dance on this island, and a passion that destroys, over there, is evoked here in the general worship that rejoices all of Aphrodite's devotees.

About the final ritual that makes joy once more an integral part of the here and now, very little can be said.[98] No one knows even how the song ends, but what we do know is that in its last section Atthis is not treated simply as a girl who listens to a teacher and friend. Evidently the singer has never pretended to speak to her privately, as the single Sappho, but has all along meant us to picture the girl as standing among her celebrating peers and listening to a song that comes from them all. The publicity of this imagined occasion is announced in line 21, where the singer praises Atthis with the voice of a group, saying: 'We can't be compared with divinities, but you . . .!' The plurality is undoubted, and more important, the playful self-denigration – so like that of the girls of Alcman's *Partheneion* (or Theocritus' *Helen*) – is a sign that the group here hails Atthis as its leader for some rite or game. She seems to be their representative or proxy,[99] chosen because her goddess-like form is proof that Aphrodite's grace has recently touched her.

Speculation can go no further, since the final stanzas have been reduced to a kind of sacred memorandum ('Aphrodite, Peitho, nectar, goblets, etc.') but this is really all we need to know. It is not a case of identifying an actual rite but of appreciating a poetic one,[100] for this festival is simply the dénouement of Sappho's song. She uses it, within her fiction, to show how the circle greets Atthis' return from the absorption of a particular love, and she uses it again, more ambitiously, to celebrate Atthis' initiation into the mysteries of beauty. The song has drawn raw passion from over the water, tempered it with a Lesbian sense of love as a cosmic fact, and then poured it out in praise of the girl whose present love-fed predominance testifies to Aphrodite's power. Meanwhile, however, Atthis has been led out of desire, taken briefly to a cool realm of memory, and then brought finally to a place that is sacred. She has been instructed and she has been shown the moon's revelation, and so she brings a kind of knowledge with her into the final (imaginary) festivity. This *gnōsis* is one with Sappho's song,

[98] See Page's note, *S&A*, 92, and the references there.

[99] As Agido and Hagesichora are in a sense proxies for the others in the *Partheneion*; see C. Calame, *Les Choeurs de jeunes filles en Grèce archaïque* ii (Rome 1977) 137ff.

[100] McEvilley, op.cit., 269, seems to envisage an actual rite which he supposed to be a sad preparation for marriage. Nevertheless, he also represents this final ritual as a poetic conceit, which seems nearer the truth: 'It is this rite of the pure admiration of beauty (represented in its eternal aspect by the goddess), which Sappho in the "normal" poems puts in place of the wedding rite and which she seems to present as a paradigm of the proper activity of the soul.'

but if it must be reduced to non-magical prose, the lesson is that tangible beauty is to be desired because it is an aspect of a perfect and unattainable beauty that is known only through memory, yet present always in the worship of Aphrodite.

Index of Passages

Page numbers are in bold type; numbers in bold italic indicate major discussions.

Archilochus (West)

Alcaeus (Voigt)

Sappho (Voigt)

General Index

Page numbers in bold type indicate major discussions.